Public Policy and Federalism

Issues in State and Local Politics

Public Policy and Federalism

Issues in State and Local Politics

Jeffrey R. Henig
George Washington University

St. Martin's Press
New York

For Robin, Jessica, and Samantha

Library of Congress Catalog Card Number: 84-51680
Copyright © 1985 by St. Martin's Press, Inc.
All rights reserved.
Manufactured in the United State of America
98765
fedcba
For information, write St. Martin's Press, Inc.,
175 Fifth Avenue, New York, NY 10010

cover design: Ben Santora

ISBN 0-312-65557-6
ISBN 0-312-65560-6 (pbk.)

Library of Congress Cataloging in Publication Data

Henig, Jeffrey R., 1951–
    Public policy and federalism.

    Includes bibliographies and index.
    1. Federal government—United States. 2. Local government—United States. 3. State governments.
I. Title.
JK325.H42 1985   321.02′3′0973   84-51680
ISBN 0-312-65557-6
ISBN 0-312-65560-6 (pbk.)

Preface

States and localities are not dull or insignificant, but they have been made to seem that way. University catalogues and academic journals show a growing interest in the broadly defined field of public policy. All too often, however, the interesting and controversial policy issues are interpreted as coming under the more or less exclusive purview of the national government. During the 1960s and early 1970s, cities, in particular, were seen as the battleground on which exciting issues having to do with race and class conflict were being resolved. Textbooks today, however, give the impression that state and local government involves little more than balancing revenues against expenditures.

A personal experience brought this point home to me not too long ago. One of my favorite bookstores in Washington, D.C., where I teach, focuses its collection on the social sciences. One of the reasons I enjoy the store is that it boasts a special section of books dealing with urban issues. When I first discovered the store, that urban section was located just inside the front door, on two floor-to-ceiling shelves—a prominent display. A few years later, I noticed that the section had been relocated to a table near the rear of the store. Then, more recently, the section was moved to an upstairs loft. Now it was really tucked away out of sight. The loft is small, and the steps to it hidden. Only a hand-lettered sign helped me find the apparently shrinking collection. Last year, the final blow was delivered: a more permanent and visible sign was installed to point customers toward the loft, but the sign said nothing about books on urban issues. The books still were up there, but now they shared the area with a newly added collection, designated COMPUTER BOOKS UPSTAIRS.

Today, state and local officials *are* more preoccupied with financial and management concerns. It is, therefore, probably inevitable that the book buying public—and the average college student—will find such current concerns less intriguing and compelling than those that were faced when rioters were prowling city streets, when angry parents were blocking buses carrying students that would integrate their schools, and welfare mothers were picketing city hall.

It is my belief, though, that some authors of college textbooks have embraced too enthusiastically the notion that times have changed. Discussions of budgets and matters of administration allow one to adopt an air of seriousness and pragmatism. And seriousness and pragmatism are characteristics that are valued quite highly these days. But such discussions can obscure as well as enlighten. Pursued too exclusively, they have the effect of *depoliticizing* the decisions made by state and local government.

State and local officials act in an intergovernmental web in which the national government is the more visible partner. They continue to exercise great influence and discretion over how they utilize their influence. The decisions they make—even those garbed in the language of budgetary adjustment and bureaucratic reorganization—are intensely political in the sense that they reflect conflicting interests among competing groups, and effect the distribution of power and resources among these groups.

In this book, I have tried to rekindle some of the excitement of state and local government in a couple of ways. First, I have attempted to present important policy issues in a truly intergovernmental context. Political scientists have given much lip service to the idea that the United States is an example of "marble-cake" federalism: that most policies reflect the input of decision-makers at all levels of our government. But textbook coverage of intergovernmental relations and federalism has been too preoccupied with the transfer of grants from level to level. I have attempted to clarify the ways in which decision-making at the various levels shapes public policies.

Secondly, I have emphasized the theoretical and ideological underpinnings of the policy issues that officials confront. Since particular programs come and go, the student who diligently strains to memorize the rules for AFDC eligibility or the intricacies of the Section 8 housing program will take from the course a brainful of facts that will soon become obsolete. The premises and analytic approaches that characterize conservative, neoconservative, liberal, and radical approaches to policy will not go out of date. Nor will the broad issues of centralization versus decentralization and privatization versus public responsibility—issues that I give particular attention to throughout the text—disappear.

Public Policy and Federalism can be used as a complement to existing state and local government textbooks, many of which offer only abbreviated, pro forma chapters on policy issues, or it may stand on its own. Chapters 1 and 2 are introductory in nature, and should be read first. The subsequent chapters fall naturally into clusters. Chapters 3 and 4 outline the theoretical and empirical dimensions of the poverty issue and provide a critical analysis of social welfare policies. Chapter 5, on urban and regional decline, should be read along with Chapter 6, "Fighting Decline," and Chapter 7, "Dealing with Growth." Similarly, Chapters 8 and 9, on crime and law enforcement, and Chapters 10 and 11, on schools and education policies, should be treated as units. The order in which these units, or clusters, are taken up is not critical, however. I have chosen to present them in an order that corresponds roughly to the extent to which decision-making responsibility is decentralized, but instructors who shuffle the order so as to ensure compatibility with other texts or with their own theoretical schema will not encounter problems of discontiniuty.

Some friends and colleagues were kind enough to read and comment on portions of the book as it moved toward its final draft. They include: Christopher Deering, George Washington University; Neal Milner, University of Hawaii; Max Neiman, University of California (Riverside); and Howard Sumka, Department of Housing and Urban Development. They, along with the reviewers engaged by St. Martin's Press—Gary Halter, Texas A & M University; Jean McDonald, University of Oklahoma; Timothy O'Rourke, University of Virginia; Donald Ranish, Antelope Valley College; Mavis Mann Reeves, University of Maryland; Mark Schneider, SUNY (Stony Brook); and Alan Wyner, University of California (Santa Barbara) made numerous suggestions that have made this a better book. I would also like to thank Richard Cole, University of Texas (Arlington); Richard C. Rich, Virginia Polytechnic Institute; and Stephen J. Wayne, George Washington University, for suggestions and encouragement for the project when it was in its formative stage. Margaret Holmes, my research assistant, scurried after clippings, articles, and reports with energy and effectivenesss. Michael Weber, my editor at St. Martin's, let me convince him, and myself, that this was a project worth undertaking, and then allowed me the freedom and discretion to carry it out.

Jeffrey R. Henig

Contents

1 State and Local Governments in the Policy Process   1

  The Policy Functions of States and Localities   4
    Basic Service Delivery   5
    Education, Health, and Social Services ✓   5
    Physical Infrastructure   6
    Business and Professional Regulation   7
    Economic Development   8
    Law Enforcement   9
    Land Use Planning   10

  Have the States and Localities Been Elbowed Aside? ✓   10
    A Federal System   10
    What Does the Constitution Say?   12
    Dynamics of Federalism   14
    Backlash Against Centralization   16
    States and Localities Have Not Been Eclipsed   20

  Summary and Conclusions   24
  Suggested Readings   25

2 Privatization and Decentralization: Should Governments Shrink?   26

  Looking to the Private Sector   27
    Varieties of Privatization   28
    Privatization as an Economic Concept   33
    Privatization as a Moral and Political Concept   33

  Centralization Versus Decentralization   34
    Can State and Local Governments Be Trusted?   35
    Decentralizationists Respond   39

  The Reigning Ideologies   42
    Conservatism and Neoconservatism as a Policy Guide   43
    Liberalism as a Policy Guide   46
    Marxism and Radical Analysis as a Policy Guide   48

  Summary and Conclusions   52
  Suggested Readings   53

3 Poverty and Inequality — 54

Explanations of Poverty — 56
  The Individualistic Perspective — 57
  The Cultural Explanations of Poverty — 61
  The Structural Explanations of Poverty — 69

A Look at the Poor — 74
  How Poor Is Poor? — 75
  Who Are the Poor? — 79

Summary and Conclusions — 83

Suggested Readings — 85

4 Social Welfare Policies — 86

Welfare Today — 88
  System or Hodgepodge? — 88
  Myths and Realities — 92
  The Evolution of Welfare in a Federal System — 97
  Three Views of the "Welfare Mess" — 104

Looking Toward the Future — 111
  Localism and Its Limits — 112
  Privatizing Welfare — 115
  Jobs Provision and Economic Development — 120

Summary and Conclusions — 124

Suggested Readings — 126

5 Urban and Regional Decline — 127

Dimensions of Decline — 129
  Violence and Unrest — 129
  Fiscal Strain — 131
  Physical Deterioration — 133
  Housing Abandonment and Neighborhood Decline — 135
  Regional Dimensions — 137

Is There an Urban "Crisis"? — 139
  Crisis? . . . or Inconvenience? — 140
  Urban Revitalization — 141
  Urban Crisis? Or Societal Crisis? — 143

Is Decline Natural? — 145
  The "Logic" of Metropolitan and Regional Change — 146
  Decline as Mismanagement — 149
  Political Dimensions of Decline — 153

Summary and Conclusions — 157

Suggested Readings — 159

6 Fighting Decline — 161

Reassessing the Record — 162
  Public Housing — 162

Urban Renewal	168
Model Cities	175
The Indirect Approach	177
Housing and Community Development Act of 1974	183

Models for the Future? 190
Unleashing the Private Sector	191
Local Self-Help	196
A Bigger Role for the States?	200

Summary and Conclusions 203
Suggested Readings 206

7 Dealing With Growth 207

Varieties of Growth 208
Suburbanization	208
Growing Cities	211
A Rural Renaissance?	213
Challenges to the Market Model of Growth	214

Growth Reconsidered 217
The Pro-growth Coalition	217
Facing the Costs	219

The Struggle over Growth Policy 224
Indirect Growth Controls	224
Direct Limits on Growth	228

A Guise for Exclusion? 230
Discrimination Against Minorities and the Poor	230
Unfortunate Side Effect . . . or Shrewd Hustle?	232

Legal Aspects of the No-growth Controversy 233
Who Can Sue?	234
The "Taking" Issue	235
Discrimination and the Courts	236
"Hands Off" by the Federal Courts	238
Some State Courts Are More Assertive	238

Summary and Conclusions 240
Suggested Readings 243

8 Understanding Crime 244

Theories About Crime 246
Crime as Deviance	246
The Neoconservative Alternative	250
Social Structure and Crime	254

Patterns of Crime 258
Is Crime Exaggerated?	258
The Distribution of Crime	265

Summary and Conclusions 266
Suggested Readings 267

xii Contents

9	**Fighting Crime: The Limits of Intervention**	**268**
	Competing Goals	270
	Rehabilitation	270
	Deterrence	270
	Incapacitation	272
	Punishment	273
	The Limits of Policing	274
	How Crimes Are Solved	276
	Do Police Deter Crime?	278
	The Noncrime Functions of Police	280
	Sentencing and the Courts	283
	The Argument for Tougher Courts	284
	Judicial Discretion	288
	Prison Reform	291
	Overcrowding	291
	Schools for Crime?	293
	Rehabilitation	295
	Deinstitutionalization and Alternative Sentencing	297
	Summary and Conclusions	300
	Suggested Readings	303
10	**Schooling Society**	**304**
	The Roots of Public Disenchantment	305
	The "Empty Nest" Syndrome	306
	Skepticism That Schools Equalize	306
	Skepticism that Schools Educate	307
	Threat to Traditional Values	307
	Loss of Local Control	308
	Education for What: Ideology and the Goals of Schooling	312
	Schools and Meritocracy	312
	Schools as the "Great Equalizer"	313
	Instrument of Social Control	318
	The Limits of Schooling	321
	Parallel Systems: Public Versus Private Education	323
	The Private Alternative	323
	Arguments for a Strong Private Alternative	325
	Criticisms of Private Education	328
	Are Private Schools Better Schools?	330
	Education and Life Chances: Do Schools Make a Difference?	333
	Better Schools . . . Better Skills?	333
	Better Skills . . . Better Jobs?	336
	Summary and Conclusions	337
	Suggested Readings	339

11 Controversies in the Classroom: Policy Issues of the Eighties	**341**
Busing: The Issue That Will Not Die	342
After Brown: *Desegregating Southern Schools*	342
The Court Looks to the North	342
Is Busing Practical?	346
Does Busing Work?	349
Making Busing Work Better	351
Turning Students into Consumers	359
Sources of Resistance	360
Regulated Versus Unregulated Voucher Plans	362
The Track Record	363
High Tech in the Classroom	365
Computers: High Hopes . . .	366
. . . Or High Hype?	368
Summary and Conclusions	370
Suggested Readings	372
References	**374**
Index	**389**

1

State and Local Governments in the Policy Process

A tour of state legislatures and city councils can take one from the ridiculous to the absurd. Consider the Illinois legislature in the summer of 1981, for example. One legislator, calling the presiding officer a "son of a bitch," threw aside his chair and stormed the front, apparently intent upon making his point with a physical flourish. Another legislator slowed him down with a punch. As *Time* magazine reported, "It was the first time that violence had marred the orderly processes of the Illinois legislature since, um. . . ten days earlier, when armed officers were called in to break up a brawl on the floor of the house" (July 13, 1981, p. 12).

Or take the case of Chicago, where the new black mayor and the predominantly white city council risked paralyzing the city government with their shenanigans. Sharing the same political party, though not the same race, the mayor and the majority faction of the council found themselves unwilling even to stay in the same room. When Mayor Harold Washington called a special session of the council for August 2, 1983, only eighteen of the fifty aldermen bothered to show up. Because this number was eight short of the quorum legally required, the meeting had to be adjourned. Alderman Edward Burke, one of the mayor's chief antagonists on the council, said that he figured his colleagues had stayed away "because it's a beautiful day for golf" (Klose, 1983, p. A2).

Textbooks tell us that ours is an intergovernmental system in which responsibility for shaping policies is shared between a national government and nearly 80,000 state and local governments. Yet sometimes it is difficult to take state and local governments seriously. Much of what state and local governments do seems far removed from the weighty issues of justice, racial equality, economic policy, and war and peace that dominate the headlines and seem the particular province of Congress, the president, and the Supreme Court. The student who reads that the fifty states are the "keystones of the American governmental arch" (Elazar, 1984) can find it puzzling to discover that much of what state legislatures do concerns such yawn-provoking issues as "the alignment of irrigation ditches, the speed of motorboats on mountain lakes, the salaries of justices of the peace, and whether or not barbers and beauty parlor attendants should be high school graduates" (Neuberger, 1941, p. 83). The naive teacher who takes a class to a city council meeting as a lesson in civics may find it a bit embarrassing to explain to students why so many minutes are wasted in such activities as recognizing the accomplishments of a local cheerleading squad or reading into the record one councilperson's birthday wishes for an eighty-five year-old widow from his or her ward.

Money and media attention are sometimes taken as measures of power and significance. By those measures, states and localities seem to be slipping into second-class status in the intergovernmental system. In 1929, state and local governments spent just under three times as much of their own funds as did the national government. By 1983, national policymakers were spending nearly two and one-half times as much as state and local governments combined (Advisory Commission on Intergovernmental Relations, 1984). The national news media give us careful analyses of U.S. Supreme Court decisions and feed us intimate details of policy deliberations in the White House. They even may tell us what the president had for dinner and how many times he visited his grandchildren last year. But aside from a few charismatic exceptions, state and local officials generally labor in obscurity. How many governors can *you* name? Do you know the name of even one judge on your own state's highest court?

Some citizens and some scholars have concluded that the national government has effectively elbowed the states and localities aside—leaving them to occupy themselves with carrying out federal policies and allowing them power only in the sphere of the trivial and mundane. This perceived nationalization of significant decision-making functions has contributed to a tendency to underplay the distinct role of states and localities in formulating policies that determine the quality of our lives.

Yet, as Figure 1-1 reveals, most Americans feel that the state and local levels of government give them more for their tax dollars than do their policymakers in Washington, D.C. Thus, the perceived nationalization of policy-making has spurred some deep feelings of resentment from the public and the potential for a major backlash. Some citizens and some important political leaders believe that it is now necessary to scale down the size of government and to give greater power and authority to those

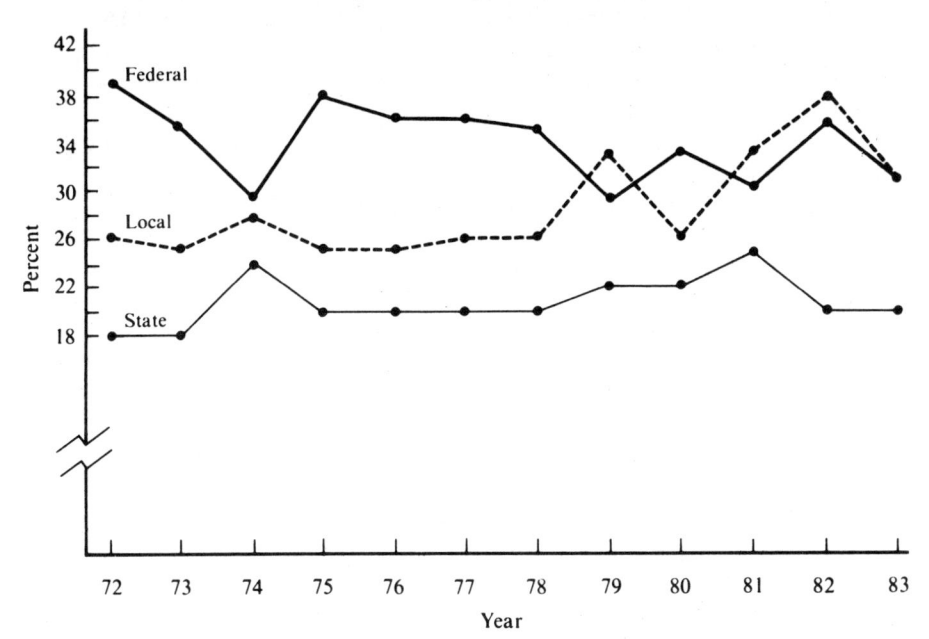

Figure 1-1 From Which Level of Government Do you Feel You Get the Most for Your Money—Federal, State, or Local?

SOURCE: Advisory Commission on Intergovernmental Relations, *Changing Public Attitudes on Governments and Taxes, 1983*. Washington, D.C.: Government Printing Office, 1983, Appendix Table A-1.

levels of government "closer to" the people and more capable of earning the public's loyalty, involvement, and faith.

In this text, we will be considering several important policy areas: decline, growth, poverty and welfare, crime, and education. The national government has become the most visible force dealing with poverty and decline, whereas states and localities retain a much more significant role in dealing with crime, education, and growth. Yet, as we will see, the notion that our system is intergovernmental is more than just empty words. Each level of government is involved in each of these policy areas. Sometimes they work hand in hand, sometimes they battle tooth and claw.

We will explore the nature of the problems and the failures of past efforts by governments at all levels to deal with them successfully. We will consider some specific recommendations for dealing with these problems: Should cities offer greater tax breaks to attract new industry? Will requirements that welfare recipients work significantly reduce the costs of caring for the needy? Are more police and stricter courts the best hope for reducing crime? Should government provide the poor with vouchers so that they, like the wealthy, can afford to send their children to private schools?

While considering such specific policies, however, we will also evaluate some broader questions regarding the role of states and localities in the policy-making process. One of these questions concerns the issue of *decentralization*. Are the states and localities capable of fairly and efficiently shouldering a greater share of responsibility for governing our lives? A second question has to do with the issue of *privatization*. Should responsibility for dealing with the various social problems be left to the public sector at all?

This chapter begins with a discussion of the policy functions of states and localities and an evaluation of the argument that states and localities have been elbowed aside. I will argue that although there have been important changes in the way our federal system operates, states and localities retain a major role in shaping the public policies that bear upon the quality of our lives.

THE POLICY FUNCTIONS OF STATES AND LOCALITIES

Much of what states and localities do is mundane, but *mundane* does not mean unimportant. Policies generated at the state and local levels probably have a greater effect on your day-to-day existence than the more dramatic doings in Washington, D.C. Are your streets and bridges crumbling? Is your garbage uncollected? Does your landlord charge too much rent and provide too little heat? Are there too few police in your neighborhood, or are police surly, slow, and rough? Do you think your doctor is a quack, or that he or she charges exorbitant fees? Are there plans to build a nuclear facility near your home? Do you think there should be computer instruction, bilingual education, or a back-to-basics curriculum in your public schools?

If you are concerned about these types of issues, your first point of attack probably should be your town or city hall, local school board, county government, or state capital—a letter to your congressman is not likely to get you very far at all. There is no simple and clear-cut rule of thumb, however, to help you decide at which level of government a particular function is likely to be handled. As we shall see throughout this book, most policy areas are characterized by a multiple government approach, with local, state, and federal governments involved—sometimes working together, other times working at cross purposes. A decision made by city officials in one part of the country, moreover, may be made by state or county officials in another part of the country. Federal officials may have a great deal to say about some aspects of certain broad policy areas (in the area of education, for instance, they are directly involved in issues of racial and sexual discrimination), and very little to say about other aspects (for example, teacher qualifications and the content of the courses that the students take). States and localities are particularly likely to exercise direct and substantial power in the spheres of service delivery, physical infrastructure, business and professional regulation, economic development, and law enforcement.

Basic Service Delivery

Provision of the most important basic services is normally carried out at the local level—by counties, cities, or towns. Such services include police and fire protection, water and sewage, garbage collection and disposal, street construction and repair, and public transportation. Today, we tend to take many of these services for granted. Earlier in the century, however, their adequate provision was more the exception than the rule. Also, their life-and-death nature was more apparent then. It is pretty easy to recognize that a speedy response by police or fire services can save lives and property. But we tend to be less appreciative of the historic and ongoing role of local governments in gaining control over the epidemics that regularly ravaged the population in earlier years. Programs to drain swamps, install sewers, collect garbage, and regulate food providers have done more to increase the life expectancy of the average American than have the building of hospitals or advancements in surgical techniques.

Basic services also can play an important role as "hidden multipliers of income" (Miller and Roby, 1970, p. 84). Families living in neighborhoods with poor schools may be forced to spend more of their paychecks on private education. Those living in areas with inadequate police and fire protection will have difficulty obtaining, and may have to pay higher rates for, insurance against fire and theft. Streets filled with potholes mean shorter lives for neighborhood residents' cars. Families living in areas with inconvenient or poorly equipped parks may find themselves spending more money on alternative recreational activities. In distributing basic services, therefore, local officials have the capacity either to moderate or to exacerbate existing inequities: to help close the gap in quality of life between poorer and wealthier communities, or to widen that gap by targeting more and better services to those neighborhoods in which incomes are higher and need presumably is not as great.

Education, Health, and Social Services

Less than 10 percent of the nation's expenditures for public elementary and secondary school education comes from the federal government; the remainder is provided by state and local governments in approximately equal shares. Although the federal government's role both in funding and otherwise influencing the education process has increased fairly dramatically over the last twenty years, most of the key educational decisions continue to be made by locally elected school boards, or by the state government. It is at these levels that decisions are made regarding teacher qualifications, teacher salaries, curriculum, acceptable textbooks, competency tests to determine eligibility for graduation, the extent of extracurricular activities, and the opening of new schools and closing of old ones.

The states finance, regulate, or directly provide much of the health care we receive. As of 1977, there were 512 state hospitals and 1,760 locally run public hospitals, which had a total of almost 500,000 beds. A few cities also offer extensive health and hospital services. New York City's is the oldest and the largest local public health care system in the country. Its public hospital system dates back to 1736. By the 1920s almost one-third of the hospital beds in that city were located in city-owned hospitals, with a majority or near majority of the population qualifying for free medical care (Norris, 1980). New York City's commitment to health care provision is unusual. In 1980, the city spent $1,239,300,000 on health and hospitals, over 13 times the amount spent by Chicago, and over 163 times as much as Los Angeles (*U.S. Bureau of the Census,* 1981).

State and local governments are responsible for originating or delivering many social services. They are especially involved in those services aimed at either end of the age spectrum. Your grandparents may be eligible to take part in a "meals on wheels" program that delivers hot food to the immobile elderly, and your younger brothers or sisters may be watched over in a public day-care facility. Whether such services are available, and the quality of the services provided, will depend, at least in part, on what state or county or locality you happen to call home.

Physical Infrastructure

Streets, highways, bridges, tunnels, public buildings, and sewage systems are, quite literally, the foundation on which our cities and towns are built. They are the vital channels of transporation that make commerce possible. State and local governments must plan, build, and maintain them, sometimes with federal financial support. Like basic service delivery, care of the physical infrastructure is generally a thankless, largely invisible task. Yet recent information makes it clear that maintenance and renovation of such facilities must be a high priority if disaster is to be avoided. According to one study, ominously titled *America in Ruins:*

- "One of every five bridges in the United States requires either major rehabilitation or reconstruction."

- "The 756 urban areas with populations of over 50,000 will require between $75 billion and $110 billion to maintain their urban water systems over the next 20 years."
- "Over $40 billion must be invested in New York City alone over the next nine years to repair, service, and rebuild basic public works facilities that include: 1,000 bridges, two aqueducts, one large water tower, several reservoirs, 6,200 miles of paved streets, 6,000 miles of sewers, 6,000 miles of water lines, 6,700 subway cars, 4,500 buses, 25,000 acres of parks, 17 hospitals, 19 city campuses, 950 schools, 200 libraries and hundreds of fire houses and police stations" (Choate and Walter, 1981, p. 2).

The federal government has played an increasing role in financing the initial construction of physical infrastructure, but the authors of this report say that the federal government has been slower in aiding states and localities to properly maintain infrastructure that already exists. If the challenge is to be met, if these crucial facilities are not to succumb to rot and rust, policy responses must evolve at the state and local levels.

Business and Professional Regulation

State and local governments set many of the rules that govern the activities of the public utilities and private businesses. They determine the cost of water and power, the location of facilities such as nuclear generators, and the encouragement, or discouragement, given to those who wish to pursue alternative sources of energy such as solar and wind power. They set rules applying to nursing-home facilities, consumer protection, insurance-company procedures, pollution control, and the lending and interest-charging policies of most banks and savings and loan institutions. It is primarily the states that oversee the medical profession: the states define what a "doctor" is through their rule-setting power over educational, testing, and licensing standards. It is largely the local governments that determine where different kinds of buildings can be built, what materials must be used, and under what conditions landlords can evict tenants or raise their rents.

The most interesting aspects of regulatory policy sometimes have to do with what is not done. States have the power to force corporations to adhere to stricter pollution standards; but the influence that large corporations carry, as major employers and taxpayers, makes this a "potential" power that frequently goes unused. Some of the most biting criticisms of the ways in which state governments handle major social issues—problems such as poverty, racial discrimination, and general urban decline—focus on the failure to act rather than on finding fault with what actually has been done.

Economic Development

State and local governments have always had a stake in the health of their economies. A strong and growing economy means jobs for citizens who want them, taxes to support desirable programs, and a general atmosphere of optimism helpful to elected officials who hope to maintain their positions. It is only recently, however, that state and local governments have self-consciously devoted themselves to the task of pursuing economic development—the use of public taxing, borrowing, and spending powers to attract new businesses and to encourage existing businesses to remain and expand.

Economic development has become something of a fad in recent years. There are, according to some estimates, "about 15,000 organizations in the United States devoted to the promotion of local economic growth, and their number appears to be increasing rapidly" (Levy, 1981, p. 1). Organizations such as the National Association of State Development Agencies (NASDA) and the Council for Urban Economic Development (CUED) have established themselves as important actors in national policy-making, ensuring that the interests and concerns of state and local officials responsible for economic development are communicated to members of Congress and the executive branch.

There are a number of tools that state and local officials may use to encourage business growth within their boundaries. They can reduce or defer taxes for new or expanded businesses. They can provide direct grants or loans to help finance construction. They can offer planning and design assistance. They can target additional public expenditures—increased fire and police protection, construction of new roads, expansion of sewage lines and treatment facilities—to make a site more attractive. They can reduce certain environmental, building, or safety regulations. They can take out advertisements celebrating the many attractions and congenial business climate that might appeal to high-level corporate executives looking for new areas in which to expand.

Not everyone is convinced, however, that such economic development strategies are likely to leave states and localities any better off. Growth, as we shall see in Chapter 7, often carries with it as many problems as it solves. Critics charge, in addition, that economic development programs are easily exploited by private businesses to generate profit "windfalls" for themselves. They cite evidence that economic development incentives play little more than a secondary role in influencing business decisions about whether to move or expand. And they note the lack of empirical support for the expectation that jurisdictions with more aggressive economic development programs enjoy either higher tax revenues or lower unemployment rates (see, for example, Jacobs, 1979; Schmenner, 1980; and Pascarella and Raymond, 1982).

Law Enforcement

Crime and the fear of crime are major concerns to citizens throughout the country. When asked whether they feel safe being out alone at night in their own neighborhoods, over half of the residents of Newark, Detroit, Oakland, and Baltimore replied that they felt "somewhat" or "very" unsafe (Skogan and Maxfield, 1981). In another survey, citizens were asked to rank two or three major problems facing their local community. Forty-five percent of city residents, 23 percent of suburban residents, and 16 percent of those living in small towns or rural areas mentioned law and order or crime as major problems, (U.S. Department of Housing and Urban Development, 1978, p. 96).

The most visible aspect of law enforcement, policing, is also the most localized. As of October 1981, there were approximately 11,700 law-enforcement agencies in the United States employing about 444,000 full-time officers (U.S. Departtment of Justice, Federal Bureau of Investigation, 1981). Not only does nearly every city and town have its own police force, but most communities are patrolled by police from more than one police force. They range in size from that of Ariton, Alabama, with 1 uniformed offer, to that of New York City, with over 21,000. Every state but Hawaii has its own state police force, and nearly every county boasts a sheriff. Large cities may have special transit police to patrol subways, housing police to protect public-housing residents, and park police to guard parks. Your own college or university may have a police force that is deputized by the local police department. Although these various forces often have distinct responsibilities—for example, state police in most states are responsible only for patrolling state highways (Berkley and Fox, 1978)—jurisdictions and functions frequently overlap. Usually this overlap is dealt with on a cooperative basis. Sometimes it is not.

Courts and prisons are predominantly a state responsibility, with a considerable role often delegated to local authorities. Most crimes are violations of state laws, and most trials take place in state courts. "State courts now process over three million cases a year, compared to about 150,000 by the federal courts" (Berkley and Fox, 1978, p. 336). More than fourteen times as many persons were being held in state prisons as were in federal prisons at the end of 1980 (U.S. Bureau of the Census, 1981, p. 189).

Local governments may have their own laws and courts, but these are anchored in each state's legal system and can exist only if compatible with state law. Still, the lower courts, which process most of the nation's cases, often have a great deal of discretion in practice. "In nearly two-thirds of the states, the lower courts are autonomous 'little kingdoms' with scant supervision from the higher tribunals" (Advisory Commission on Intergovernmental Relations, 1976, p. 125).

Land Use Planning

One of the most cherished powers of local governments is the power to affect land use through zoning. Zoning can best be understood by envisioning a large map of a city, any city. Through its zoning power, the city can subdivide that map, specifying what uses are and are not permitted within each of the designated areas.

There are a number of reasons why supporters of zoning believe it to be critical to community well-being. By prohibiting certain types of structures, or limiting construction in areas deemed risky due to flood or unstable ground conditions, zoning might increase safety. Planners feel that zoning can ensure that the city develops in a rational fashion; through zoning, officials can coordinate the growth of an area, making sure that private builders will construct their new homes where officials are placing roads and sewage lines. Perhaps most central to the history of zoning is its role in protecting the value of private property. In a clearly zoned jurisdiction, the new home buyer need not worry about waking, a few months later, to the sound of tractors digging the foundation for a factory in the previously unspoiled woods beyond his or her backyard. One of the most interesting controversies surrounding state and local policy-making, however, involves the charge that many localities are hiding narrower and less attractive motives behind the rhetoric of these goals. Zoning, and other land use powers, may be used to exlude minorities and the poor and to protect the perceived self-interest of some residents by infringing upon the rights of others to live where they choose.

Traditionally, zoning power has been exercised almost exlusively by local governments. Beginning around 1970, however, a few states have become more aggressive in exercising their own authority to control land use. The movement toward a stronger state role in land use planning has been referred to as a "quiet revolution" (Bosselman and Callies, 1971).

HAVE THE STATES AND LOCALITIES BEEN ELBOWED ASIDE?

A Federal System

We live in a federal system, and federalism often is messy. A federal system is one in which power and authority are shared between a central government and one or more levels of subgovernments.

> Federalism in the United States is an arrangement whereby: (1) the same territory and people are governed by two levels of government, both of which derive authority from the people and both of which share some functions and exercise other functions autonomously; (2) the existence of each level is protected from the other; and (3) each may exert leverage on the other (Glendening and Reeves, 1977, p. 11).

Although the United States is generally regarded as the first government established on federal principles (some argue that ancient Greece deserves this label), it is by no means the only one. Most of the world's land area today is governed by federal systems. Examples include India, Brazil, Canada, West Germany, and Australia. These systems, while similar in key respects, nonetheless vary considerably; federal systems may be very centralized or very decentralized, depending upon how power and authority are shared across the levels of government.

Accounts in textbooks and in the popular media often present federalism in the United States as if it were tidy and precisely defined. The powers and functions assigned to the central and subgovernments are listed, as are the limits to these powers. Such neat assignments of responsibility are derived, at least in theory, from the nation's Constitution. They result in a highly compartmentalized image of policy-making: national leaders deal with one set of problems, state leaders with another set of problems, and county and municipal leaders presumably do the same.

Complaints about the growth of the national government—and charges that this growth impinges upon the legitimate powers of the states and localities—sometimes reflect this idea of a compartmentalized federalism. The current distribution of power among the levels of government, it is argued, represent a deviation from that intended by the Founding Fathers, a fall from grace.

Poring over the Constitution, however, will tell you only a part of the story of federalism, and probably not the most important part. Relations among the levels of government have been fluid, not stable, responding throughout the nation's history to changes in judicial philosophy, national needs, and political demands. In order to understand the role of states and localities in addressing problems such as poverty, crime, education, growth, and decline—and in order to take an informed and sophisticated stance in the ongoing debate over whether their role should be expanded—it is important to shed outdated and overly simplified notions of what federalism entails. If it ever made sense to think of federalism in terms of separate levels with distinct and independent responsibilities set by law, it does so no longer.

What *Does* The Constitution Say?

The authors of our nation's Constitution were an unusually thoughtful and intelligent crew. Washington, Madison, Franklin, et al., were not only the elites of their day; time has proved their intellects to have been among the sharpest in our lengthening national history. From this truth, however, a misleading myth has grown. This is the myth of the omniscient Founding Fathers, wise and all-knowing, who peered deep into human nature and far into the future and drafted a definitive document capable of guiding the nation unambiguously through whatever changes and challenges would occur. This myth presents the Constitution as if it were a ready reference guide to the proper etiquette of government and policy-making. Is it proper to serve corn on the cob when hosting your boss at dinner? Ask Amy Vanderbilt. Does the national government have the authority to outlaw a local school board's dress code for junior high school girls? Check the Constitution. But it does not work that way.

What *does* the Constitution tell us about the proper allocation of functions among the levels of government? *About the division of responsibilities between the national and state governments, the Constitution gives us ambiguous and conflicting messages, and about the powers and authority of the cities and other local governments, the Constitution tells us nothing at all.*

One message of the Constitution is that the national government is supreme and has been granted the flexibility to expand its powers as the needs arise. Article I, Section 8, seems to convey this image. Listed there are seventeen powers expressly given to the national Congress, including the power to levy taxes, regulate interstate commerce, coin money, maintain an army and navy, and grant copyrights and patents. These are capped with the famous "necessary and proper" clause, which holds that the national Congress may "make all Laws which shall be neccessary and proper for carrying into Execution the foregoing Powers." This proviso muddies the waters considerably because some have stretched the concept of "necessary and proper" (hence the nickname "the elastic clause") in such a way as to deem permissible a wide range of national activities that the Constitution never mentions and the Founding Fathers probably never had in mind.

Article VI would also seem to suggest that the framers of the Constitution had in mind a strong central government, supreme over its constituent states. The Constitution and the laws made under it, Article VI reads, "shall be the Supreme Law of the Land and the judges in every state shall be bound thereby, anything in the Constitution or laws of any state to the contrary notwithstanding."

But what, then, is one to make of the Tenth Amendment, which states that any powers not delegated to the national government or forbidden to the states "are reserved to the States respectively, or to the people"? The "reserved powers" clause is interpreted by some to imply a fundamental limit to the national government: the central authority extends only to those functions *explicitly* allocated to it by the Constitution; all other powers are reserved to the states or to no government at all. Those who hold this interpretation argue that the "necessary and proper" clause must be read quite narrowly: unless a power can be traced quite directly and immediately to one of the enumerated powers, such a power cannot be assumed to exist at the national level.

The Founding Fathers were not sloppy; the fact of the matter is that they did not all agree. There were those—Alexander Hamilton, for instance—who favored a very strong central government. At one point, Hamilton even went so far as to propose that the nation be headed by a "Governor," elected for life, who would have the power to appoint the governors of each state (Miller, 1968). Yet there were others—Thomas Jefferson, for example—who, although acknowledging that there were shortcomings in the Articles of Confederation that had governed the nation in its early years, were fearful that the new Constitution might give so much power to the national government that the states would be emasculated. The opposing groups are sometimes referred to now as, respectively, the Federalists and the Anti-Federalists.

Ambiguity is sometimes the salve of conflict; if we cannot agree on principles, we can sometimes phrase compromises so vaguely that we can vote for what we choose to see. The Tenth Amendment, in fact, was a last-minute addition, the result of desperate wheeling and dealing to draw enough support for the Constitution so that it would be approved. The compromise allowed the disagreements between the Federalists and Anti-Federalists to be submerged for long enough to get the document approved, but the disagreements would not remain latent for long.

Local governments are a different matter. About counties and cities and villages and towns the Constitution is not contradictory; it simply says nothing at all. We may tend to think of our federal system as if it were a three-layer cake, but in formal legal terms it consists of just two layers. The national and state governments can trace their existence and authority to the Constitution; local governments are legally the creations of the states. What happens if a city or town claims a power or enacts a policy that puts it in conflict with those of the state? Judge Forrest Dillon reasoned in 1911 that municipalities possess only those powers expressly or implicitly granted by the state: "Any fair, reasonable, substantial doubt concerning the existence of a power is resolved by the courts against the [local government], and the power is denied" (Lineberry and Sharkansky, 1978). This has come to be known as "Dillon's Rule," and it has restricted considerably the discretion of local officials, especially in such areas as taxing and borrowing.

In order to give local officials more flexibility, and in order to save state legislators from the need to involve themselves in the day to day management of the local jurisdictions, most states have passed various sorts of *home rule charters,* granting broader areas of discretionary powers to specific cities or to local governments falling into specific categories. But these home rule charters did not result in the clear and dramatic empowerment of cities, as some of the advocates of home rule had hoped. The delegation of authority varies across states, and even across local governments within the same state. State legislatures were not always eager to give up their say-so, and when they did, it was often in broad terms that were themselves sufficiently ambiguous as to allow conflicting interpretations. Here, as in the division of authority between the national government and the states, federalism in practice proves to be a much more fluid and dynamic process than a consideration of law books could possibly convey. Laws and the Constitution *are* important; they fix the broad boundaries within which the ongoing changes take place. But other factors, having to do with judicial philosophies, political power, financial dependencies, tradition, culture, and broad forces of modernization and technological change have determined, for given historical periods, just how much power each of the levels of government can exercise.

Dynamics of Federalism

The ambiguities in the Constitution left the issue of the distribution of authority among the levels of government still contested and still unresolved. The result has been an ongoing battle in which those favoring greater decentralization and those favoring greater centralization have each had their share of victories and defeats.

Round #1 was won by the Federalists. Under the first Supreme Court chief justice, John Marshall, a broad interpretation of the "necessary and proper" clause was defined. Marshall's successor, Roger Taney, held a quite different notion of the relative roles that should be played by the national government and the states.

Dual Federalism. Under Taney, the Supreme Court relied on a conception of dual federalism. "In this conception, the distribution of power between the two levels was seen as fixed and immutable; the states were seen as on an equal basis with the national government; and the Tenth Amendment was viewed as carving out an area of exclusive jurisdiction which the supremacy clause could not touch" (Reagan and Sanzone, 1981, pp. 20–1).

The Court pretty much held to this doctrine for over one hundred years. During the late 1800s and early 1900s, for example, the concept of dual federalism was used to restrain efforts by the national government to institute minimum wage requirements and to establish child labor laws. The turning point did not come until the Court came face to face with Franklin Roosevelt's sweeping efforts to pull the nation out of the Great Depression.

Cooperative Federalism. Roosevelt's New Deal consisted of a battery of emergency programs that moved the national government far deeper into the regulation and control of the private sector than it had ever gone before. It also marked the onset of cooperative federalism, a new style and new philosophy of federalism distinguished by *joint undertakings* between the federal and state governments and the expansion of the use of *federal grants-in-aid* (direct transfers of money from the national to state or local governments).

The logic of dual federalism seemed to preclude direct cooperation between the states and the national government; each level, after all, was expected to concern itself with its distinct sphere of responsibility. Such a chasm between the states and national government was never quite as sharp as the theory of dual federalism implied, however; as Morton Grodzins has pointed out, episodes of cooperation between the levels of government can be found throughout the history of American federalism (Grodzins, 1966). Cooperation, nonetheless, underwent both a quantitative and qualitative change during the New Deal. *In such areas as public housing, highway construction, and aid to poor children and their families the national government instituted large programs that depended, for their implementation, on the financial and administrative cooperation of officials at the state or local level.*

The major vehicle for expanded cooperation was the grant-in-aid. All of the major grants during this period were *categorical,* meaning that they were provided for a narrowly designated purpose such as building a highway, demolishing a slum, providing technical advice to farmers, or aiding the elderly. Nearly all were also *matching* grants, meaning that the state or local government that received the grant had to promise to spend some of its own money on the project as well. Most of these grants were *competitive* in nature; state and local governments submitted applications to federal agencies, which decided who would get a share of the available money and who would not. Grants-in-aid existed prior to the New Deal, but it was in response to the economic trauma of the depression—a period during which hundreds of state and local governments faced bankruptcy—that this mechanism for coordinating national and state and local efforts came into its own.

Creative Federalism. The administration of President Lyndon Johnson, and the declaration of a national War on Poverty, marked a shift in the nature of cooperative federalism toward a more adversarial relationship. During this period of creative federalism, the national government began to wield its control of grants more forcefully, to entice or badger state and local officials into undertaking programs and assuming responsibilities that they would have preferred, in some instances, to avoid. There had often been tensions between the different government levels before this—complaints by federal officials about sloppy administration at the state level, complaints by state officials regarding overly restrictive guidelines and unnecessary paperwork—but during the first three decades of cooperative federalism there had been general agreement on the basic goals and the legitimacy of the projects undertaken jointly. *Now, in areas such as civil rights, job training, welfare, and housing for the poor, federal officials were deliberately using the carrot and the stick of grants-in-aid to redirect state and local efforts in the name of broader national goals.* The assumption, sometimes stated, sometimes not, was that state and local officials in many parts of the country simply could not be trusted to pursue effectively the goals of racial equality and justice to the poor that the civil-rights movement had brought to the fore.

Backlash Against Centralization

By the late 1960s, creative federalism was under attack. Public officials at the state and local levels were among those who were most vocal in expressing the need for reform. They argued that the proliferation of categorical grants had led to an overly complex, fragmented, and burdensome system. By 1968, there were nearly 400 distinct grants available to state or local jurisdictions, 209 of them products of the Johnson years. Expansion of the grant system had been piecemeal, with the result that there was little coordination and much inconsistency. Kevin White, former mayor of Boston, claims that his city had to submit seventy-two applications to nine federal agencies just to get the permits and resources needed to revitalize four acres of downtown property (Hale and Palley, 1981). Matching requirements, local officials argued, forced them to skew their budgets toward programs and expenditures that the national government favored, even at the cost of other programs that were more popular and possibly more appropriate for their own situation. The federal government was too far removed to understand the unique problems that each locality faced, and the centralization of power in distant Washington, D.C., was increasing the dissatisfaction and alienation of average voters, who no longer believed they could exercise control through the political system over the policies that would determine their quality of life.

New Federalism, The Nixon Version. President Nixon responded with a call for a New Federalism, one that he claimed would bring the country closer to the concept of federalism that the Founding Fathers originally had conceived. "The time has now come in America," he declared, "to reverse the flow of power and resources from the States and communities back to Washington and start power and resources flowing back from Washington to the States and communities and, more important, to the people all across America."

The most striking facet of Nixon's New Federalism was the introduction of *general revenue sharing*. Revenue sharing provided funds to states and to local governments, over 39,000 in all. (Later, the states were eliminated; today, revenue-sharing monies are distributed only to local governments.) Unlike competitive grants, revenue sharing is *formula based:* each recipient jurisdiction receives an amount based upon a complex formula that takes into account population, relative income, urbanization, and tax effort. Unlike categorical grants, revenue-sharing money came with very few restrictions. This was the key. With revenue-sharing money, it was argued, state and local officials would be able to use their own discretion in determining how the grant money was spent, and they would be free to address problems that were unique to their areas, with programs specifically tailored to their areas and in a style consonant with the traditions, values, and expressed needs of their own constituents.

President Nixon's New Federalism also included an expanded use of *block grants*. Like categorical grants, block grants are to be used for assigned purposes. But these purposes are defined much more broadly than is the case with categoricals. Rather than there being three separate grant programs for, say, the purchase of police cars, the provision of riot training, and the renovation of prison facilities, a single, much larger grant for law enforcement would be provided. As with revenue sharing, recipient jurisdictions have greatly expanded flexibility in determining how those federal dollars should be used. Nixon's plan was to combine existing categoricals into a few major block grants (he referred to this idea as "special revenue sharing") in such areas as law enforcement, community development, manpower training, and education.

Revenue sharing and block grants have become significant components in the federal aid strategy. But it is fair to say that the hopes and expectations of the advocates of Nixon's brand of New Federalism were largely disappointed. Revenue sharing never accounted for more than about 12 percent of federal grants to state and local governments, and during the decade after its enactment, it was gradually pared back. Today, only about 5.5 percent of federal aid comes in the form of general revenue sharing.

Two major block grants—the Comprehensive Employment and Training Act (CETA) and the Community Development Block Grant (CDBG)—were enacted in 1973 and 1974, but although they, like revenue sharing, proved to be very popular with local officials, they never succeeded in replacing the categorical grants, even in their own functional areas. Early analyses of the uses of revenue sharing and the major block grants suggested that they were not sparking the innovation and greater citizen involvement that had been predicted (Nathan and Adams, 1977; Kettl, 1979). By providing federal money to many more jurisdictions, it was argued, New Federalism was providing fewer resources to those areas with the greatest need. And stories of abuses—the use of revenue-sharing money to build tennis courts, the use of law-enforcement block-grant funds to provide tuition for the children of top police officials in one state, the use of CETA to hire patronage workers and political cronies rather than the hard-core unemployed—put pressure on Congress to reassert its control.

Creeping Categorization and Federal Mandates. Even as Congress was granting greater leeway to states and localities with one hand, by passing revenue-sharing and block-grant legislation, it was limiting discretion with the other. State and local abuses were only one reason that Congress sought to reassert control. Another had to do with concern that state and local officials could not be counted upon to pursue aggressively certain important national goals—such as the pursuit of racial equality, the elimination of discrimination against the handicapped, and the stimulation of citizen participation in public-policy decisions. Nor could members of Congress forget for long that categorical grants were a potent form of political "goodies." By announcing a grant award for a local government in his or her district, a member of Congress can build a reputation as someone who takes care of the folks back home. A shift to revenue sharing and other formula-based grants robs Congress of a potent source of political patronage.

Congressional efforts to reassert control took various forms. Rather than approve additional funding for revenue-sharing and block-grant programs, Congress tended to allow them to be eroded by inflation while launching new categorical grants in related areas. To eliminate abuses, Congress imposed new conditions on revenue-sharing and block-grant monies, undermining, to some extent, the original conception of "stringless" aid. This tendency is sometimes referred to as creeping categorization.

One of the most significant facets of creeping categorization is the "piecemeal, yet persistent proliferation of conditions that applied generally or specifically to all or most of the federal assistance programs" (Walker, 1981, p. 180). These federal mandates, sometimes referred to as crosscutting requirements, are intended to ensure that states and localities do not replace national priorities with their own.

The first important contemporary example of a crosscutting requirement was Title VI of the Civil Rights Act of 1964, which states that: "No persons in the United States shall, on the ground of race, color, or national origin, be excluded from participation in, be denied the benefits of, or be subjected to discrimination under any program receiving federal financial assistance." This provision gave federal officials an important weapon in their efforts to force some recalcitrant states and localities to end racial segregation in the schools. Jurisdictions that were found to discriminate could be threatened with the loss of federal grants that were being used to help finance education programs. Reacting to this apparent success, Congress went on to establish other crosscutting requirements related to such national priorities as protection of the environment, historic preservation, citizen participation, and the elimination of discrimination on the basis of race, color, national origin, age, sex, or handicapped status. Some of the approximately sixty such conditions are worded by Congress so as to apply automatically to all grants-in-aid.

New Federalism Rides Again: The Reagan Version. By 1980, a new president was declaring still another New Federalism, once again calling for a shifting of power from the federal government to the localities and states. Ronald Reagan, in his inaugural address, declared: "it is my intention to curb the size and influence of the Federal establishment and to demand recognition of the distinction between the powers granted to the Federal Government and those reserved to the States or to the people. All of us need to be reminded that the Federal Government did not create the states; the states created the Federal Government."

Ronald Reagan's New Federalism, like Richard Nixon's earlier version, was based in large measure on the goal of giving states and localities greater *flexibility* in their use of federal grants. This was done in at least two ways. First, President Reagan combined existing categorical grant programs into larger and more loosely defined block grants. Second, he encouraged federal agencies to adopt a "hands-off" approach when administering both the new and the preexisting block grants. Reporting requirements for the recipient jurisdictions were loosened, for example, and states and localities were permitted to spend their funds on a broader range of activities without fear of federal complaint.

In addition, Reagan's New Federalism sounded a new theme. Reagan proposed a major *swapping of responsibilities* between the federal government and the states. Existing arrangements were too muddled; citizens, and sometimes even officials, were uncertain as to which level of government was responsible for which functions. The national government, Reagan suggested, could take complete responsibility for providing food and medical care to the poor. The states, in return, would take over the major cash assistance program for poor families with children. By re-sorting responsibilities in this fashion, President Reagan intended to make the federal system clearer and more straightforward. In some senses, it might be said that he wished to return more to the idea of dual federalism, in which states and the national government would operate independently within their own spheres. In spite of his broad legislative successes in other areas, Ronald Reagan was unable to get Congress to give serious attention to this "Big Swap" notion during his first four years in office.

Some of the resistance to Reagan's New Federalism was based on the concern that his professed goals of increasing flexibility and clarity might be less significant than a third objective—*cutting domestic expenditures.* Reagan's proposals to combine categorical programs into block grants were accompanied, in each instance, by plans to reduce the total federal funding by about 20 percent. It was argued that this cut would not really reduce services, because the greater flexibility and decentralization would allow the remaining funds to be applied more efficiently and effectively. But state and local officials, who at first welcomed Reagan's New Federalism, came to suspect that they were being asked to take on greater responsibility at the same time they were being told to expect less financial aid. Some of the more skeptical among his critics questioned whether Reagan's New Federalism might not simply be a shrewd attempt to pass the blame for budget cuts and reduced services away from the White House and toward the statehouses and city halls.

States and Localities Have Not Been Eclipsed

Not everyone, however, agrees with the assertion by Presidents Nixon and Reagan that the national government has usurped the powers of cities and states: "it is easy to exaggerate the role of the national government," Ira Sharkansky has written. "One of the great ironies in Federal-state relations is that both ultraliberal critics of states rights and ultraconservative advocates of states rights argue that Washington has more control over the states than is actually the case" (Sharkansky, 1972, p. 105).

The scope of the national government's influence has, indeed, grown. This is most obviously the case in the arena of fiscal federalism. As Figure 1-2 demonstrates, the expanded use of intergovernmental grants means that more and more of the money that cities and states spend comes from the federal government rather than from the jurisdiction's own sources. Federal grants, which equaled 11.8 percent of the amount of money states and localities raised from their own sources in 1955, had risen to 31.7 percent by 1980. President Reagan's New Federalism and budget-cutting efforts began to reverse that trend in the early 1980s. By the late 1970s, at least 67,000 governments—including school districts, special districts, and public authorities—were receiving federal grants of some kind (Walker, 1983). This fiscal connection has enabled the national government to expand its scope of influence into areas that tradition and the Constitution seemed to reserve for the cities and states. Congress, as Thomas Dye

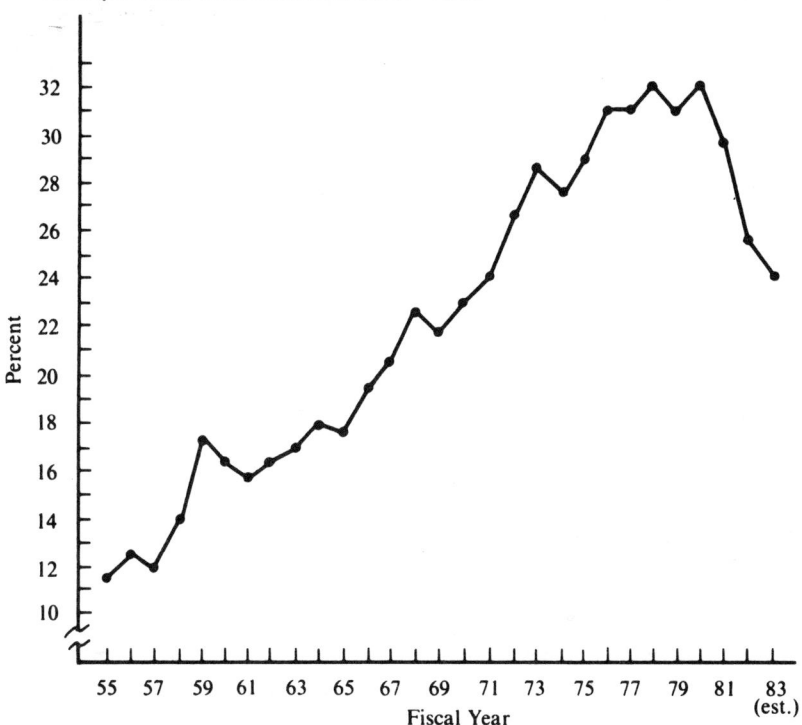

Figure 1-2 Federal Grants-in-Aid in Relation to State/Local Receipts from Own Sources, 1955–1983

Source: Advisory Commission on Intergovernmental Relations, *Significant Features of Fiscal Federalism, 1982–3*. Washington, D.C.: Government Printing Office, 1983, p. 120.

explains, has no Constitutional claim to the power to outlaw billboards along scenic highway routes. But Congress *can* provide highway assistance to states and then threaten to withdraw that aid to those states that fail to regulate billboard placement on their own (Dye, 1981).

State or local officials could, in theory, refuse to accept federal money and thereby retain their freedom of action, and in a few dramatic cases this has been done. But the political and financial realities that face state and local officials make this course highly risky. "If you don't apply for this money," Governor Nelson Rockefeller once noted, "somebody will get up and say, 'why don't you ask for this money? Here is free money in Washington you are not using.'" (Haider, 1974, p. 97).

Although academics and state and local officials have focused much of their attention on fiscal federalism, it is probably the case that the average citizen has come to perceive the expanded scope of the national government more clearly in the judicial arena. Two of the policy areas that have traditionally and fervently been considered to be almost exclu-

Figure 1-3 Federal, State, and Local Spending From Own Funds as a Percent of the Gross National Product, 1929–1983.

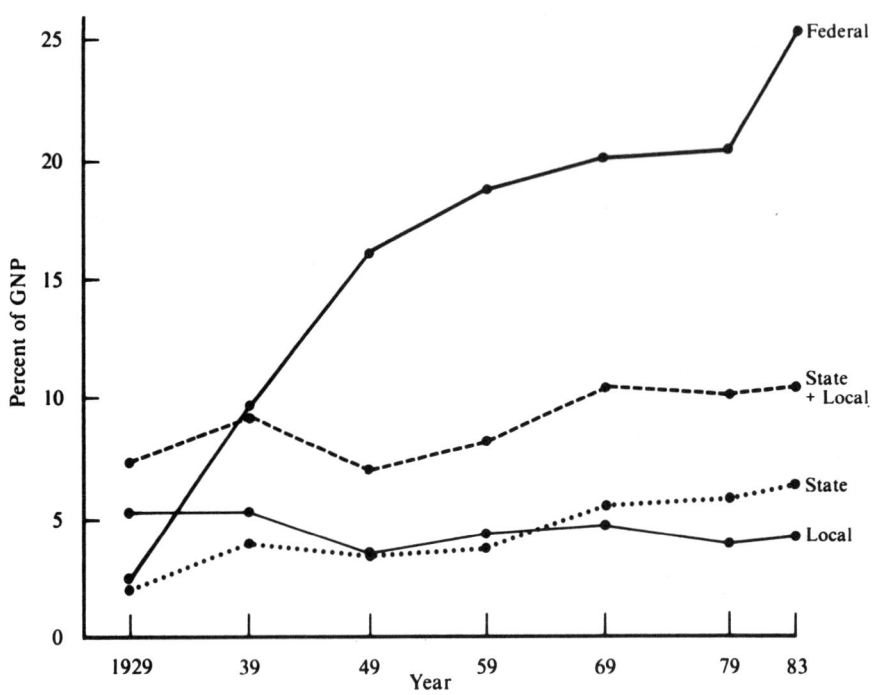

SOURCE: Advisory Commission on Intergovernmental Relations, *Significant Features of Fiscal Federalism, 1982–3*. Washington, D.C.: Government Printing Office, 1983, p. 6.

sively local responsibilities are education and law enforcement. Yet a series of highly controversial Supreme Court decisions have emphatically established that, even in these areas, some of the most dramatic events take place at the national level. Federal courts have forced local school boards to integrate, to bus, to modify dress codes, to provide free education to illegal immigrants, and to risk lawsuits in cases in which controversial books are removed from school libraries. Federal courts have forced local police departments to respect certain specified rights of the accused and to hire minorities, and in several cases federal courts have found state prison systems to be unconstitutional by virtue of overcrowding, poor conditions, or lack of rehabilitation programs.

The increases in size and scope of the national government, however, have not all come at state and local expense. Figure 1.3 shows the expenditures by each of the levels of government expressed as a percentage of the Gross National Product (GNP), which is a measure of the value of all the goods and services produced in the country in a given year. The data reveal that, although the national government was growing most rapidly, most of that growth occurred between 1929 and 1949, the product of the domestic expansion associated with the New Deal and the military expansion due to World War II. Moreover, state and local expenditures were increasing also, at least until the mid 1970s. It is the overall growth of the public sector, at the expense of the private sector, that is the real story here.

The national government has sometimes expanded its scope at the *behest* of the states and cities rather than at their expense. In other cases, state and local officials initially resisted national initiatives, only later to decide that the reassignment of responsibility was in their interest after all. "The governors are generally the most vocal on the utter necessity of decentralization," Grodzins observed. But, in response to attempts by President Eisenhower to return certain powers from the national government to the states, "federal administrators were willing to give the states far more than the governors were willing to accept" (Grodzins, 1966, p. 311). It seems that some powers are such political "hot potatoes" that each level of government does what it can to pass the responsibility somewhere else.

Those who underestimate the current influence of states and local governments tend to overestimate the capacity of the national government to oversee and effectively control the implementation of the programs it launches. *Rather than pushing state and local governments to the side, most of the national initiatives of the last forty years have relied on state or local officials to administer them.* The national legislation has established broad goals and general procedures, but these have generally been vague or ambiguous and difficult to enforce. Pressman and Wildavsky have argued that the complexity of our intergovernmental system makes it inevitable that national programs will be reshaped, refined, or effectively undermined by state, local, and private actors who play a role in their implementation (Pressman and Wildavsky, 1973). "Despite many protestations to the contrary," Daniel Elazar adds, "only in rare situations have federal grant programs served to alter state administrative patterns in ways that did not coincide with already established state policies . . ." (Elazar, 1984, p. 110).

Finally, there is the fact of reciprocal influence. *States and local officials are not limited to maneuvering within whatever parameters the national government sets; individually and collectively, they have the political clout to influence national legislation.* Many mayors and governors are national figures in their own right, influential party leaders, potential senators or congressional representatives, potential presidential candidates. Presidents, members of Congress, and federal grant administrators must court their favor; they will be slow to cut off federal dollars or overly aggressively enforce grant requirements when, as is sometimes the case, the political consequences will be severe.

Since the mid-1960s, moreover, state and local officials have enhanced their personal influence and their influence as party leaders through expanded collective lobbying in Washington, D.C. The National League of Cities, U.S. Conference of Mayors, National Governors Association, Conference of State Legislatures, and National Association of Counties are only a few of the major public-interest groups that represent state and local interests in the nation's capital. Through research, testimony at congressional hearings, and adroit use of the media, the public-interest groups—so-called P.I.G.S.—are able to stimulate national policies and reshape, stall, or defeat proposals that they feel will limit their own resources and power (Haider, 1974).

SUMMARY AND CONCLUSIONS

Federalism is a dynamic system, and it continues to change. Time has broken down some of the walls separating the national government from the localities and states. Once it made some sense to speak of broad arenas of responsibility in which one or another of the levels of government reigned supreme. Localities dealt with police, fire, garbage, land use, and schools. States oversaw highways, courts, and prisons. The national government concerned itself with foreign policy and interstate commerce. Today, public policy is much more likely to be the result of a working partnership that includes officials at all levels. Indeed, a local housing official may interact and identify with state and federal housing officials more than with representatives of the mayor's office or members of the city council.

Through some of the changes, the national government has come to cast a larger shadow. Federal grants have played a role in this. So have Supreme Court decisions. And, so, for that matter, have changing public values and expectations. We are a much more nationalized citizenry than we were in 1776, 1876, or even 1976. Those born in Rhode Island may attend college in Illinois and settle in Florida. A five-year-old in Montana watches the same television programs as a five-year-old in Pennsylvania. Adults get much of their news and analysis of current events from the national media. With this has come a certain homogenization. Parochial values and traditions have become less forceful. As a result, the goals we set are more likely to be national goals. Variations in rights and services are less likely to be tolerated. To ensure uniformity and to enforce national priorities, we have become more willing to entrust national officials with power and authority.

But this does not mean that states and localities have become insignificant actors. They are not simply water boys for the government in Washington, D.C. Broad policy shifts and dramatic pronouncements emanate from the White House, the Congress, and the Supreme Court.

But these often have more to do with policy-in-theory than with policy-as-fact. For although the national government has expanded the range of its involvement, it is as reliant as ever—some would say more so—upon state and local officials to put its programs into effect. And with the power to implement a program often comes the power to reshape that program to better fit local needs or the balance of local political power.

SUGGESTED READINGS

Advisory Commission on Intergovernmental Relations. *Regulatory Federalism: Policy, Process, Impact and Reform.* Washington, D.C.: Government Printing Office, February 1984.

———. *State and Local Roles in the Federal System.* Washington, D.C.: Government Printing Office, April 1982.

Grodzins, Morton. *The American System.* Chicago: Rand McNally, 1966.

Hanus, Jerome, ed. *The Nationalization of State Policies.* Lexington, Mass.: D.C. Heath and Company, 1981.

Reagan, Michael, and John Sanzone. *The New Federalism.* New York: Oxford University Press, 1981.

Wright, Deil S. *Understanding Intergovernmental Relations.* Boston: Duxbury, 1982.

2
Privatization and Decentralization: Should Governments Shrink?

Discussions of public policy must frequently center on "What should we do?" questions. Should we guarantee the poor a minimum income, or should we provide aid only to those who prove themselves to be deserving of a helping hand? Should we target governmental aid in order to rebuild those cities and towns in greatest need, or should we use public dollars to help individuals escape from such depressed areas? Should we hire more police, demand stricter judges, build more prisons, compensate the victims of crime?

But there is another kind of question that probably needs to be answered first. This is the "Who shall decide?" question. Should strategies to care for the needy, deal with urban and rural decline, fight crime, and educate the country's children be determined by each local government or by the states? Or should a national policy be formulated and enforced by federal policymakers in Washington, D.C.? Alternatively, it is possible that these problems should not be considered the province of government at all. Should the primary responsibility for dealing with poverty be met by family and church? Can neighbors, cooperating among themselves, do more to prevent crime than senators, governors, or city council members? The answers to the broad questions of who shall decide will determine, to a significant extent, the answers to the questions of what should we do.

Throughout most of this century, the trends have been to invest greater and greater decision-making responsibility in the public sector, and to centralize that public sector responsibility more and more in the national government. Not everyone, however, is convinced that this trend has been for the best. Today, strong arguments are being offered for the proposition that less government would mean better government.

Proposals to shrink the scope of governmental activity come in two broad forms: calls for decentralization and calls for privatization. The call for decentralizing responsibility by shifting power from the national government to the cities and states was introduced in the previous chapter. This chapter will probe more deeply into the question of whether states and localities can be trusted to handle the responsibilities that advocates of New Federalism propose to grant to them.

Decentralization calls for shrinking the scope of governmental activity by putting decision-making responsibility in the hands of smaller units of government. Privatization goes farther. Advocates of privatization argue that governmental authority should be reduced in the aggregate, not simply shifted among the levels. Some problems might be more effectively and efficiently handled if we do not involve the public sector at all.

LOOKING TO THE PRIVATE SECTOR

Scottsdale, Arizona, has an unusual fire department. You probably could not tell just by watching it in action. In Scottsdale, fire fighters ride fire engines much like those you would observe in other cities. They shoot water through hoses and rely on other fire-fighting techniques that are, for the most part, standard. What is unusual is that the fire fighters in Scottsdale are not public employees, the fire engines not publicly owned. Rather than provide its own fire services, the city of Scottsdale has contracted with a private firm. What makes this particularly interesting is that there is some evidence that this private firm is able to provide fire-fighting services much more cheaply—and with no loss in quality—than would be the case if Scottsdale followed the traditional route. The cost of hiring the private Rural-Metropolitan Fire Protection Company worked out to about $3.78 per resident. One study estimated that it would cost just about twice that amount—$7.10 per resident—if Scottsdale had chosen to provide its own public fire department (Ahlbrandt, Jr., 1973).

Not all problems or opportunities call for a public-policy response. The size of government has increased dramatically over the past fifty years. In 1929, federal, state, and local governments combined spent the equivalent of 9.4 cents for every dollar in goods and services that the economy produced; by 1979, they were spending over 28 cents for each dollar (Advisory Commission on Intergovernmental Relations, 1984). During the same period, the influence of the public sphere was expanding in another sense. Areas previously considered to be personal in nature, issues to be handled and discussed only within the family—issues such as abortion, wife-beating, interracial contacts, and child abuse—were carried into public view and onto the public agenda by media coverage, popular concern, legislative initiatives, and judicial activism. Some observers consider this expansion of the public sector to be unwarranted, overly expensive, or even dangerous. They argue that we have been too quick to turn to government for a public policy "fix" whenever a problem or opportunity has seemed to arise. They favor privatization—an increased reliance on voluntary and market forces as a mechanism for achieving social goals.

Varieties of Privatization

Policymakers, like fashion designers, are influenced greatly by what is in fashion, what is in vogue. Just like the hot new look—a new color, a new cut—suddenly can be found in store windows everywhere, newly popular concepts like privatization tend to be overly used. As a result, the boundaries of the concept—what it means—can easily become blurred. A variety of policy options have been linked to the term *privatization*. Although they are linked by a shared commitment to the notion that the laws of supply and demand can generate more rational outcomes than the tinkerings of public officials and bureaucrats, these options are, in other ways, quite distinct.

To some, privatization simply means that the public sector should *adopt the orientation and management techniques* that seem to make private businesses more efficient and innovative. That government does not exist to make a profit has been an article of faith (Hicks, 1982). But without the pressure to consider the "bottom line," public officials have few incentives to be cost-conscious. Adding new programs, building new roads and bridges, hiring more workers have, in the past, been sure routes to winning votes. At times, such measures have been approved by state legislatures and city councils all too eager to accept the principle that where the happiness and welfare of their constituents is concerned, "money is no object." But today, with growing concern about budget deficits, tax increases, and governmental waste, there is a new readiness among officials to seek ways to streamline operations.

Another mild form of privatization—mild because it does not entail any significant relinquishing of responsibility by the public sector—consists of *public-private partnerships*. The problems that face our states and localities are massive. To rebuild our declining cities and stagnated rural areas will require a huge investment of resources. Government cannot provide so huge an investment on its own; to try to do so risks overtaxing citizens and businesses to such an extreme that the national economy suffers greatly. Accordingly, some argue, government should seek to work with the private sector to achieve public goals. Instead of launching multimillion-dollar programs, paid for entirely by governmental revenues, public officials should seek to "leverage" public dollars: to use public expenditures as a catalyst to stimulate private-sector investment. The Urban Development Action Grant (UDAG) program is an example of this public-private partnership approach. Under that program, the federal government provides grants to help support projects that will bring jobs and housing to the declining inner city—but those grants are made available *only* after commitments have been obtained from private businesses in the area to invest substantial amounts of their own resources in the proposed project.

Contracting out, as Scottsdale does for its fire services, is a more extreme form of privatization, because it involves hiring private firms to provide services normally handled by public-sector employees. Under contracting-out arrangements, public officials are the service arrangers: they decide what needs to be done and solicit bids from private firms that are willing to perform the specified tasks. Officials might specify the desired service very narrowly—collect garbage from the curb in front of every home two days per week and deliver it to the municipal incinerator, for example—and simply award the contract to the firm that proposes to do the service at the lowest cost. Alternatively, officials might define a task broadly—maintain sanitation, provide crime protection, meet health needs—and permit the private firms to devise their own strategies for accomplishing these goals.

The competition to obtain these potentially lucrative contracts, it is reasoned, forces the firms doing the bidding to seek the most cost-efficient procedures and to devise innovative methods for improving the quality of services as well. Should a firm fail to perform adequately, it can be replaced by another private company when the period of the contract has expired.

The Rural-Metropolitan Fire Protection Company spends more on research and development than public fire companies and, as a result, has come up with several unusual techniques for providing good fire protection to Scottsdale residents while keeping the costs low. According to some accounts, for example, Rural-Metro developed a small robot fireman, called a "snail," which can be directed by remote control to travel through a burning building and shoot water from an attached hose. The company also was innovative in the use of lighter hoses and smaller trucks. To save on the costs of equipment, Rural-Metro builds or subcontracts the construction of its own trucks. And, rather than pay fulltime firefighters to sit idly in the station waiting for a call, Rural-Metro has trained city workers in other departments in fire-fighting techniques. These "wranglers" work only when needed, and they are paid only when they work (Ahlbrandt, 1973).

Contracting out already is employed by many local governments. Over 300 municipalities currently contract with private firms to provide their refuse collection and street lighting. One advocate of privatization, E. S. Savas, claims that public-sector refuse collection is 29 to 37 percent more costly than equivalent services provided under contract by private firms. Savas argues that nearly 100 services—including hospitals, street maintenance, sewage disposal, libraries, legal services, crime laboratories, parks, jails, welfare, transportation, and day care—are also being provided by this arrangement (Savas, 1982).

Contracting out leaves a considerable responsibility in the hands of public officials, who retain the authority to specify contracts, select winners, monitor performance, and, where performance is inadequate, replace the provider. *Load-shedding* involves the complete withdrawal of the public sector from responsibility for certain services. Advocates of load-shedding argue that the public sector has simply become too large. In expanding the sphere of its activities, it has squeezed out small entrepreneurs and voluntary organizations that have the capacity to provide the same or better service at a lower cost. Should government discontinue certain operations, small businesses, neighborhood organizations, and various self-help efforts will emerge to take its place.

Transportation provides a good example of the way that privatization through load-shedding is expected to work. Currently, licensing and regulation make it very expensive to run a taxi service. A medallion, required by New York City officials for each cab operating in the city, sells for over $60,000; only 11,787 medallions are available, putting a low ceiling on the number of cabs that can operate legally (Williams, 1983). The small entrepreneur, the hustler who seeks to make a few extra bucks by chauffering his neighbors to the market and back, cannot afford the expensive license fees. Such entrepreneurs currently must operate illegally. In New York City, it is estimated that as many as 15,000 unlicensed "gypsy" cabs operate, providing lower-cost transportation, primarily in minority neighborhoods.

Public regulations have nearly extinguished the network of jitneys—eight-to-twelve-passenger vehicles providing transportation along a regular route—that once flourished. "In 1915 there were nearly 62,000 of them, in every major American city," writes Robert W. Poole, Jr. "So successful were jitneys that they threatened to put the trolley lines out of business. Owners of the latter—generally well connected politically—succeeded in having laws passed in most cities completely outlawing jitneys" (Poole, 1980, p. 113). Illegal jitneys continue to operate in a few cities; in Chattanooga, according to Poole, eighty-five illegal jitneys carry about 20 million riders per year, and in Pittsburgh illegal jitneys outnumber the city's contingent of legal taxicabs.

Advocates of privatization argue that if cities cut back on publicly provided transportation, while deregulating the provision of taxi services, the range of alternatives open to residents actually will increase. Gypsy-cab and jitney services will expand and flourish. Costs will decline. Underserved areas will be better served. Beginning in the late 1970s, a few major cities began to experiment with deregulation, among them Los Angeles, San Diego, Philadelphia, Seattle, and Eugene, Oregon. "In each case," according to Poole, "deregulation is leading to more service and lower fare levels" (Poole, 1980, p. 116).

Load-shedding advocates argue that where private business does not step in, community organizations and self-help efforts can take up the slack.

> Even today the vast majority of American fire departments are manned by volunteers, costing the taxpayer not a penny. Some of the country's best emergency ambulance service is provided by a large volunteer rescue squad in the Bethesda/Chevy Chase area of Maryland adjoining Washington, D.C. Volunteer groups can provide valuable services in schools, recreation, and social services as well. And in many big cities, volunteer block associations are providing security patrol services that take some of the patrol burden from hard-pressed police departments (Poole, 1980, p. 27).

It is claimed that only the heavy hand of government—its licensing and regulatory requirements, its tax provisions, its minimum wage restrictions, and the attitude of dependency it fosters—currently keeps such grass-roots efforts from expanding into a much stronger force.

Finally, many advocates of privatization recommend *voucher systems*. Vouchers are grants that can be used by the recipients to purchase certain clearly specified goods or services. The food-stamp program is the most well-known existing voucher system. In lieu of cash, eligible low-income households receive coupons that are redeemable for groceries. There is growing support for moving toward voucher systems in education and housing.

One of the criticisms of other forms of privatization is that they do not sufficiently address the needs of the poor. The poor need public-sector programs and services, it is argued, precisely because they are not able to compete with other families in the private market. Voucher systems represent an attempt to respond to such criticisms. The answer to the problems of the poor, voucher supporters argue, is to give them the means to compete in the private market. With their incomes supplemented by vouchers, the poor will be free to exercise the kinds of freedoms and choices that other consumers enjoy. Direct provision of governmental programs, to the contrary, may lock the poor family into a state of dependency, eroding its capacity to exercise judgment and initiative on its own.

By giving the poor the capacity to compete in the private sector, it may be possible to kill two birds with a single stone. The chance to

Table 2-1 Major Forms of Privatization

Form	Definition	Example
Contracting Out	Public agency awards service contract to one of competing firms.	*Social Welfare:* Private collection agency hired to find and collect support payments from fathers who abandoned welfare families. *Law enforcement:* Public Housing Authority replaces existing patrol force, consisting of public employees, with private security firm.
Load-shedding	Public agency ceases providing service, with expectation that private entrepreneurs and voluntary organizations will step in.	*Transportation:* City ceases regulating taxi industry; gypsy cabs and informal jitney services fill the gap. *Sanitation:* City ceases trash pickup to large apartment buildings; landlords forced to hire private firms but get lower tax charges in return.
Vouchers	Selected recipients, usually those with low incomes, get certificates that can be used to purchase specified services from private-sector providers.	*Housing:* Poor families are given certificates worth $50 per month to enable them to afford home improvements or higher rents. *Education:* Families with school-age children are given certificates that can be used to pay tuition at public or private schools.

exercise free choice, in competition with other families, might give the poor greater self-confidence and sharpen their economic skills. At the same time, giving the poor the freedom to seek alternatives may exert pressure on both public- and private-sector providers to offer better products to the poor. The poor are exploited in part because they are a captive market. Principals of public schools offering poor instruction and lax discipline, grocers in ghettos offering poor produce and little variety in brands, managers of publicly supported housing projects in which ceilings are cracking and gangs of youths terrorize the halls will have to mend their ways or risk empty classrooms, quiet cash registers, and loss of rental income.

Table 2-1 summarizes some of the major types of privatization and gives some examples of their use. Proposals based on a philosophy of privatization are being seriously considered, today, in each of the policy areas that will be considered in the later chapters of this book.

Privatization as an Economic Concept

Privatization is usually presented as an economic concept. It is argued that the private sector is more efficient and more innovative because of the discipline imposed by competition and the need to make a profit in order to survive. If a business offers flawed merchandise or charges too high a price, the laws of supply and demand will tend to bring about a correction. Alienated customers will look for an alternative product; if none exists, some shrewd entrepreneur is likely to spot the chance to make a quick profit by establishing a competing firm. The corrective pressures brought on by the laws of supply and demand do not work well, however, when the provider of the good in question possesses a monopoly. Customers who are disenchanted by a monopoly's performance have nowhere else to take their business. Monopolies, moreover, can use their dominant economic position to squeeze out most potential competitors before they can establish themselves as viable alternatives.

Government, it is argued, acts as a public monopoly in many spheres. Most of those who are dissatisfied with public schools, the quality of police protection, or dirty and potholed streets cannot readily turn to a competitive product. In some ways, moreover, public monopolies represent potentially greater threats than private monopolies. The customer who is not satisfied by a private monopoly can refuse to deal with that company, although this may mean having to do without the good or service the company provides. But a "customer" who is dissatisfied with the services that governments provide may not have that option. Those who choose to send their children to private school or hire security guards to protect their neighborhoods are required to continue paying, through their taxes, for the services they no longer consume. With an income that is more or less guaranteed, whether or not the customers are satisfied, public-sector service providers can afford to become complacent and lazy, more concerned with expanding their power and their own comfort than with responding to citizens' needs.

Privatization as a Moral and Political Concept

Privatization also draws support as a kind of moral crusade. Some supporters of privatization are drawn less by the promise of a dollar-and-cents payoff than by the expectation that privatization can help to revive such traditional American traits as independence, self-discipline, self-help, and an entrepreneurial spirit. Overreliance on governmental bureaucracies, they suggest, has allowed these desirable traits to whither and atrophy from disuse. By patrolling their own neighborhoods to prevent crime, by cooperating with their neighbors to hire disadvantaged local youths, or by organizing local cleanup campaigns, citizens may gain not only better services but a renewed sense of community, commitment, and self-worth.

Movement toward privatization, however, may benefit some groups and individuals at the expense of others. In this sense, privatization has a political dimension that is sometimes overlooked. Many of the public regulations and services that advocates of privatization criticize evolved in direct response to the needs and demands of previously disadvantaged groups. These groups are wary of privatization: it was the private sector, they feel, that discriminated against them for racial reasons, that exploited them as consumers, that ignored their needs in favor of those whose greater wealth made them a more attractive clientele. Not all of the various public programs launched in the name of the disadvantaged actually have helped the disadvantaged, and fear and suspicion of the private sector may risk cutting off channels of advancement that the disadvantaged can ill afford to lose. But history suggests that the poor have legitimate reasons to be cautious about privatization. The public sector *has* operated fairly consistently as a force for the redistribution of opportunity and wealth. Advocates of privatization claim that its benefits will be shared by all, but it is not unusual for various groups to mask their own narrow self-interest behind reforms made in the name of the general good.

CENTRALIZATION VERSUS DECENTRALIZATION

Even the most ardent champions of privatization concede that government must retain a substantial role in meeting the public's needs. Once it has been decided that a particular problem or opportunity does call for a public-sector response, it is necessary to establish which level(s) of government should have the responsibility, authority, and capacity to act. The U.S. Constitution is one point of reference for those seeking to determine the proper distribution of powers across the governmental levels. But although the Constitution clearly establishes that power is to be divided between the national government and state governments, it does not, as we have seen, unambiguously state *how* those powers are to be divided. The actual shape of federalism, as a result, has shifted and changed over time. For the past ten or fifteen years, the tides of momentum seem to have been running with those who favor a greater decentralization of power, a reallocation of authority from the national government to the states, localities, and even neighborhoods.

Such a shift in power toward smaller units of government, some feel, will make the policy-making process more democratic, more effective, and more efficient—more democratic because citizens have greater interest in and knowledge about local events, which may translate into greater participation in political affairs; more effective because officials will be able to tailor programs to the particular needs of their own communities; more efficient because local governments will be less likely to waste money on programs that their own citizens do not really want, and because an inefficient government will risk losing its taxpayers, who will "vote with their feet" by moving to a jurisdiction where efficiency keeps taxes down.

Can State and Local Governments Be Trusted?

But can the states and local governments be trusted with greater authority? At least one line of reasoning suggests that they cannot. The argument is largely a historical one. "Look at the record," these "pro-nationalists" suggest. The relative growth of the national government, they argue, has been a direct response to proven shortcomings at the state and local levels. Some of the charges leveled against both the states and local governments include the following.

State and local governments lack expertise. Public office at the state and local levels is often a part-time affair, low in salary and low in prestige. As a result, Christopher Jencks has argued, talented and ambitious individuals are likely to look elsewhere—to the private sector or the federal government—when staking out their careers. Candidates for state legislatures "tend to be local hacks sponsored by more sophisticated and powerful men." Once in office, these legislators tend to set salaries too low to attract talented bureaucrats and staff. "A vicious circle is established, in which mediocrity attracts mediocrity"; without quality personnel, government is unable to plan, to use resources efficiently, or to independently assess the validity of claims made upon it by well-financed private-sector interest groups (Jencks, 1964, p. 9). Donald Kettl found such lack of planning in the way in which cities distribute community development block grants (CDBG). The four Connecticut cities he studied: (1) used CDBG money to "buy off" some vociferous neighborhoods with tennis courts, parks, and sidewalks; (2) gave little attention to problems above the neighborhood level; (3) failed to coordinate projects in different parts of the city; and (4) substituted a "nifty-idea-I'm-for-that" approach for serious planning (Kettl, 1979).

State and local officials tend to be narrow-minded and parochial. Because they are concerned with the political and economic health of their own jurisdictions, and because they are responsible to a narrow constituency, state and local officials may favor local interests, values, and traditions at the expense of the broader national interest. This is exacerbated by the background of many state and local elected officials, who are more likely than the average citizen to live, as adults, in the same communities into which they were born. Such parochialism, it has been argued, explains the reluctance of many states to come to grips with the problems of the urban crisis developing within their midst (Martin, 1965, p. 78). It has led, in other cases, to counterproductive competition among neighboring cities and states. During the depression, for example, Rhode Island officials passed a law designed to protect the local dairy industry from out-of-state competitors. The law, later declared invalid by the courts, required that all milk imported from outside the state be colored with pink dye before being put on the counter to be sold (Stedman, 1979).

State and local governments are unable or unwilling to raise enough money to meet demands. This argument has traditionally been based on the supposed *inelasticity* of the types of taxes relied upon by most cities and states. Elasticity refers to the way in which a tax responds to changing economic situations. Taxes with a high elasticity raise more money during a period of inflation. Graduated income taxes have a high elasticity because increases in income due to inflation tend to push people into a higher tax bracket, forcing them to pay more taxes even though their real income may not have increased. Sales taxes have a lower elasticity because people tend, as their income rises, to save more and to spend a smaller share of their income on taxable services and goods (Ecker-Racz, 1970). Because the federal government relies most heavily on the income tax, it has generally found it easier to increase revenues than have states (which rely more heavily on sales taxes) or local governments (which depend primarily on the property taxes).

This economic constraint has been exacerbated, moreover, by increasing political limitations on the ability of states and local governments to introduce new taxes or raise their tax rates. The passage of Proposition 13 in California in 1978 stirred a brushfire of tax-limitation efforts that came to be known as the "tax revolt." Proposition 13 was an amendment to the state constitution that was passed in a popular referendum by a vote of approximately two to one. It limited property taxes throughout the state to 1 percent of the assessed value, limited the rate at which assessed value could increase, and made it more difficult for local and state officials to introduce new taxes. A similar measure, Proposition 2½, passed in Massachusetts in November of 1980, cut back property taxes to a maximum level of 2.5 percent of the market value; experts predicted it would drain $1.3 billion from local governments in the first year alone. (*Newsweek,* 1980). Faced with the threat of mounting deficits, several states have, in more recent years, moved in the other direction by instituting new or larger taxes. But political resistance remains high, and there is little reason to believe that the era of the tax revolt will prove to have been an aberration of the 1970s.

State and local governments are more racist than the national government. Racial discrimination has left an indelible stain on the record of state and local governments. It is increasingly easy to shrug off past episodes of discrimination with the observation that this is ancient history. But your parents and their peers grew up during a time in which blacks and whites, in a large section of the nation, went to separate schools, used separate public rest rooms, drank from separate water fountains, and rode in separate sections of buses and trains. Separation along color lines occurred, moreover, not because of choice or preference or convenience or happenstance, but because it was required by state and local laws. Remembering this, blacks and liberal whites cannot easily shake the notion that a return to state and local power might mean a return to second-class citizenship for minorities in some parts of the United States.

States and local governments are dominated by a conservative business-oriented elite. When Floyd Hunter studied Atlanta in the early 1950s, his conclusions caused quite a stir. The city, he argued, was run by a tight circle of elites whose power emanated not from their ascension to popularly elected office but from their role as a business elite. The result, he suggested, was a conservative government, dedicated to the maintenance of existing distributions of wealth and power, and resistant to efforts to raise new issues, consider new policies, or accommodate the interests of the city's have-nots (Hunter, 1953). Although Hunter's methods were imperfect and his conclusions extreme (see Polsby, 1980), the years since have seen his basic charge reasserted in other studies and other cities (for example, Ewen, 1978; Newfield and DuBruhl, 1977). Case studies at the state level also reveal a number of states in which major business lobbies—Anaconda Copper in Montana, the Farm Bureau in Alabama, insurance in Illinois—exert significant influence on state policies. Such influence may be used by these businesses to lower their own tax burdens; to limit public oversight into the environmental, occupational-health, and consumer-rights consequences of their procedures; and to mute initiatives for social-welfare programs that might increase the size of the public sector, decrease the relative attractiveness of low-wage employment, or stir expectations for social change.

If state and local governments are dominated by a conservative elite, efforts to decentralize authority may simply be exploited by this elite to prop up its own position. Shifting government "closer to the people" might benefit *some* people—those who are already advantaged—at the expense of others. Some studies of the uses of CDBG funds at the local level, for example, indicate that, left to their own devices, local governments tend to direct less money into the poorest neighborhoods. During the first year in which CDBG grants were distributed, 69 percent of all funded projects were located in low-income neighborhoods; two years later the figure had fallen to 61.7 percent, and federal officials feared that only stricter guidelines could ensure that local decision-makers would not dilute to an even greater extent efforts to help the poor (Rosenfeld, 1980).

Localities, and perhaps states, are structurally incapable of engaging in policies that redistribute from the rich to the poor. Cities and states have penetrable boundaries. People and businesses may, for the most part, come and go as they please. According to some analysts, this has important implications that are only beginning to be recognized. The penetrability of their boundaries means that states and localities are vulnerable to the threat that, should their taxes be too high or their services insufficient or targeted at the wrong groups, middle- and upper-income taxpayers as well as job- and revenue-producing businesses might move to another jurisdiction. This threat is greatest the smaller the size of the jurisdiction. Citizens and businesses risk less when they move to a neighboring town than when they relocate over greater distances. A move from a central city to a suburb, for example, allows a family to remain in contact with friends and neighbors and to retain its membership in social organizations; a move to a nearby jurisdiction with a more favorable tax structure may allow a business to keep most of its employees and existing clientele.

Penetrability also means that jurisdictions may be "invaded" by citizens or businesses that find its package of services attractive. Officials worry that if they offer welfare, education, and health benefits that are more attractive to the poor than those offered elsewhere, they will find themselves swarming with new, lower-income residents who will put a drain on the treasury without contributing to tax revenues.

The twin effects of the threats of out-migration by taxpayers and in-migration by service demanders works, according to Paul Peterson, to make redistribution infeasible at the local level (Peterson, 1981). This suggests that failures by officials at the local level to substantially address the needs of the poor are rooted in the nature of local government, and not in the personal stinginess or ideological conservatism of the officials themselves. Although Peterson focuses his attention at the local level only, others have commented upon the fact that state governments too, may find it extremely difficult to pursue policies regarded unfavorably by major business interests that threaten to relocate (Orren, 1974; Greer, 1979).

Even those who are most vehemently resistant to the idea of giving greater authority to local and state governments admit, of course, that there are multiple exceptions: cities and states that, at various times, have been innovative, efficient, and progressive in racial and economic affairs.

But, they argue, the weight of the historic evidence indicates a general failure, and it would be careless or naive to presume that past tendencies suddenly will be reversed.

Decentralizationists Respond

At the same time that advocates of a stronger state/local role acknowledge past shortcomings, they insist that there have been a series of significant and lasting changes. Changes in population, coupled with financial, legal, and political reforms, have transformed the states, and some localities, from unwieldy and anachronistic contraptions to sleek and progressive political machines.

Changes in population have made the states more competent and more sensitive to urban needs. "Every decade," Daniel Elazar argues, "more states reach the critical mass of population necessary to provide the widest range of services demanded of them, in the most sophisticated manner, leaving fewer too small to do so" (Elazar, 1984; p. 256). He also argues that every decade, population changes have made our states more urban in character. This growing urbanism makes it less likely that the states will retain the anti-city bias with which they have been charged in the past (Elazar, 1974).

Changes in tax structure have made states and localities more flexible and progressive raisers of revenue. Both states and localities have diversified their tax systems. In 1957, states received 58.1 percent of their revenue from sales taxes; by 1983, only 48.0 percent came from this source. In 1957, localities relied on property taxes for 86.7 percent of their revenues; by 1983, revenues from this source had declined to 76 percent (Advisory Commission on Intergovernmental Relations, 1984). Diversification makes states and localities somewhat less vulnerable to the ill effects of broad swings in the national economy.

While moving toward diversification, states and localities have added new elements of equity as well. Many states and localities have tried to shift some of their tax burden from the poor to those who are wealthier. One way this has been done is by moving toward the use of a progressive income tax. A total of forty states now offer broad-based personal income taxes and all but five states have corporate income taxes, with the result that the elasticity advantages of the national government's revenue-raising mechanisms are not as distinct as they may once have been (Advisory Commission on Intergovernmental Relations, 1983). In 1957, only 9.5 percent of combined state and local revenues came from income taxes; by 1983, 24 percent. Equity is increased, also, by provisions to exempt certain necessities—such as food and drugs—from sales tax, an option taken by about one-half of the states. Circuit breakers—special property tax relief for poor or elderly households—are another means of making state and local tax systems less regressive. In 1972, only thirteen states had circuit-breaker legislation for homeowners; by 1982, the number had increased to thirty states.

Legal changes, at the federal and state level, have made states and localities more responsive to the interests of minorities and the poor. Many decentralizationists acknowledge that racial discrimination *has* been a problem, but they emphasize that it is a problem most states and local governments have outgrown. Surveys of popular opinion seem to show that support for racial integration has been growing, in the South as well as in the North. Congressional civil-rights and voting-rights legislation, moreover, has made it more difficult for states and localities to discriminate against minorities, even if they should attempt to do so. This legislation presumably would stay in effect, safeguarding the gains that minorities made with the national government as their ally. The reapportionment of legislative districts ordered by the Supreme Court in the mid-1960s reduced the heavy dominance in state legislatures of parochial, rural interests. In recent years, moreover, decentralizationists point out that state courts have become more active in defining and protecting the rights of minorities and the poor. On certain issues—such as school finance reform—some states have taken a more liberal stance than has the U.S. Supreme Court.

Political reform movements have succeeded in bringing about structural changes that are expected to make state and local governments more effective, professional, and responsive to citizens' needs. States, in particular, have made progress in shaking off the constraints that often left them unable to meet the demands put upon them. In the past, many states had legal limitations on the frequency and length of time during which their legislatures could meet. In 1951, only ten states allowed their legislatures to meet annually. By 1979, the number had increased to thirty-seven, and additional states have made it easier to call special sessions of the legislature when necessary (Advisory Commission on Intergovernmental Relations, 1982). The low pay and mediocre staffing at the state and local levels have been major targets for reformers, and the record shows some genuine successes. Staffing for state legislatures, for example, grew by about 130 percent between 1969 and 1974 (Advisory Commission on Intergovernmental Relations, 1983). Other changes intended to improve the performance of states have included strengthening the governor's powers, reorganizing the executive branch, installing new budgetary practices, and expanding civil-service coverage.

One very popular kind of reform involves the passage of "sunset legislation." Sunset legislation is intended to increase the efficiency of government by identifying and weeding out programs and bureaucracies that are not performing well. Under the sunset provisions, some programs or agencies are assigned specific dates on which they will be terminated unless the legislature votes for the renewal. Colorado adopted the first sunset law in 1976. By 1980, it had been joined by thirty-four other states (Advisory Commission on Intergovernmental Relations, 1982).

Those who favor a stronger state and local role in the federal system do not pretend that these various population, financial, legal, and political changes have made states and localities perfect. Many of the structural reforms, for example, may prove to be fairly superficial in their effect. Some of the federal laws are not easily enforced. And although population changes may diminish the disparities, political and racial attitudes continue to vary according to region.

What the decentralizationists argue, rather, is that the sins of the past ought not to confuse our assessment of the current capacity of states and localities to perform their responsibilities effectively and with justice. Not only are state and local governments getting better, they argue, but some of the problems have been due to the lack of authority enjoyed by those governments in the past. The overinflated national government left little room for the development of mature and responsible governments at the lower levels. Reduced to administrative handmaidens for the national decision-makers, state and local governments could not attract vibrant leadership and were unable to obtain experience in setting important priorities or planning for the future. The states and local governments are performing much better than most people imagine, but they can and will do even better if only they are allowed to come out from under the national government's shadow.

That some jurisdictions will be more conservative than others cannot be doubted, of course, but advocates of decentralization see this as an advantage rather than a defect. Decentralization, they insist, allows expression of the diverse values and political traditions that make up the American experience as well as provides citizens with a greater range of choice regarding the type of community in which they would like to live.

Yet broad institutional reform—such as is recommended by those who call for a radical New Federalism—is a risky undertaking; it may take years before problems are recognized, and major reforms, once instituted, are not easily undone. And the decentralizationists have not yet addressed what may be the most problematic aspect of the proposals to grant greater authority to localities and states: Given the penetrability of their boundaries and the mobility of corporate and residential taxpayers and service demanders, are states and localities structurally capable of dealing effectively with the regulation of business and the redistribution of resources from the wealthy to the poor?

The debates over decentralization and privatization are long-lasting precisely because issues such as these are so difficult to resolve. Some of you will find it easier to grapple with these questions when we confront them later in a less abstract form. As we shall see, disputes regarding the proper role of government versus the private sector, and centralized government versus a greater state and local role, reemerge as each substantive policy area—poverty, decline, growth, education, crime—is discussed. Before moving into these substantive arenas, however, some of the relevant political and ideological dimensions need to be introduced.

THE REIGNING IDEOLOGIES

The process by which the state and local political agendas are set seems at times chaotic and undirected. The media and political leaders seem to run from one issue to another. Different issues give rise to different interest groups. Those who seek to impose order and rationality can be overwhelmed by what one observer labels "streetfighting pluralism": "a political free-for-all, a pattern of unstructured, multilateral conflict in which many different combatants fight continuously with one another in a very great number of permutations and combinations" (Yates, 1977).

Beneath the surface turmoil, however, there is a regularity, a relatively stable pattern shaped by theory and ideas. Whereas special-interest and single-issue groups come and go, several cohesive ideological perspectives provide a fairly stable framework within which most political debate occurs. Ideology, in this sense, refers to *a set of premises about the nature of man and society from which are derived expectations about the way the world works and normative standards against which societies can be judged.* At times, ideologies may mislead people about their own interests and those of others and may provide elaborate rationalizations for actions, events, or institutions, making these appear to be "natural" or "inevitable" when they really are not. But ideologies can also serve as necessary tools for understanding, helping us to sort through complexities and idiosyncracies, to recognize underlying regularities in the social system, and to provide insights into how that social system might effectively be reformed.

Three ideological perspectives—neoconservatism, liberalism, and radicalism—are especially important as contemporary influences on public-policy debates. The insights, and prejudices, they bring to bear are integral components of all informed discussions of the advantages and disadvantages of privatization and the arguments for and against greater decentralization. These are not the only ideologies we might consider. Nor are they entirely cohesive and well-defined, as any brief presentation might suggest. Some writers and thinkers who are associated with a given perspective might not accept all of the assumptions and doctrines that are associated with that perspective as laid out below. In grasping the basic elements of each of these ideological perspectives, however, you will find that you are better able to understand why some writers take the position they do, and why different analysts, referring to the same studies and using the same sources of data, seem to arrive at incompatible positions.

Conservatism and Neoconservatism as a Policy Guide

Traditional conservatism comes in at least two varieties (Dolbeare and Dolbeare, 1978). The older form—that identified with the philosopher Edmund Burke—emphasizes the importance of tradition and continuity. Society, according to Burkean conservatives, represents the accumulation of generations of experience and wisdom. In this sense, society has a life and meaning of its own that is independent and even superior to the lives of the individuals who make up society. Individuals are shortsighted, selfish, and impulsive. The principles and rules of behavior that have evolved in the social realm are necessary and must be conserved if we are to hold the destructive tendencies of individuals in check.

The second variety of traditional conservatism puts a much greater emphasis on individualism and freedom. the individual is seen as the source of innovation, progress, and economic growth. This form of conservatism is deeply suspicious of government, which it sees as a threat to personal freedom. The "natural tendency of government is to expand in the direction of absolutism," wrote Barry Goldwater in his 1960 book, *The Conscience of a Conservative* (Goldwater, 1960). Wherever possible, we should rely, instead, on the private market as a means for getting things done. According to Milton Friedman, an economist whom some consider to be the most important contemporary spokesman for this form of individualistic, market-oriented conservatism, the role of government is to step in only in "cases in which voluntary exchange is either exceedingly costly or practically impossible" (Friedman, 1962, p. 27).

Traditional conservatism continues to be an important political and intellectual force. The 1970s, however, saw the full emergence of a new political philosophy of the right. Articulated by respected intellectuals such as Irving Kristol, Daniel Bell, Daniel Patrick Moynihan, Nathan Glazer, James Q. Wilson, and Edward Banfield, neoconservatism combines a commitment to some traditional liberal values with the traditional conservative's skepticism about the perfectability of man and the capacity of government. Neoconservatism has begun to challenge traditional conservatism for the position of being the more influential ideological force on the right side of the political spectrum. The appeal of traditional conservatism is limited by the extreme nature of its rejection of governmental and social reform. Major expansions of governmental power such

Table 2-2 Neoconservatism Compared with Traditional Conservatism

Unlike Traditional Conservatism	Like Traditional Conservatism:
Accepts the essentials of the welfare state	Seeks to limit bureaucratic power and intrusion
Supports equalizing opportunity for racial and other minorities	Opposes affirmative action and efforts to equalize outcomes
Recognizes that an unregulated market leads to abuses	Favors market solutions when feasible
Rejects notion of class and hierarchy as "natural"	Accepts unequal wealth and status as inevitable
Values cultural and religious diversity	Sees values and religion as the key underpinnings of social order
Does not emphasize *moral* constraints on what government ought to do	Points to *practical* limits on what governments can effectively do

as Franklin Roosevelt's New Deal and the civil-rights initiatives of the 1950s and 1960s are accepted by most Americans as legitimate and admirable. Neoconservatism accepts these changes, too, and therefore can draw on a broader range of popular support (see Table 2-2).

Neoconservatism borrows from both forms of traditional conservatism a pessimistic view of human nature and an aversion to governmentally orchestrated change. By their very nature, people are prone to error and misjudgment, and are unequal in capacity, both mental and physical. And they are self-concerned and selfishly motivated. Left to their own devices, then, individuals will create for themselves a harsh, competitive, and unpredictable environment. Some will use their greater ability or strength to further their own interests at the expense of others. This is the existence that philosopher Thomas Hobbes envisioned as the natural, unregulated order: a "life of man, solitary, poor, nasty, brutish, and short."

To the neoconservatives as well as to Hobbes, government is a necessity. Without government there is so little order and security that economic accumulation and investment are infeasible. But government is constrained by the fact that it is the product of human beings. The flaws of people—their lack of knowledge, their desire for personal power, their aspirations that outstrip their abilities—are magnified in the political institutions they create. These institutions accumulate power, and with power comes the power to do harm, even to do harm deliberately. But the neoconservatives focus less on the threat of totalitarianism (at least when they are considering domestic policy) than on the unintentional damage that governments may do. Social problems are complex. Government, in its well-intentioned aspiration to do good, often stirs consequences that are neither anticipated nor desired. The danger is greatest when government attempts to do too much, when its reins are captured by idealists who would use the power of government to remake the world. Ultimately, government is limited by human nature: when it tries to make people equal, when it assumes that they will act out of altruism rather than self-interest, when it presumes too great an understanding of the world and its complexities, government will fail in its undertakings.

The history of liberal policy initiatives—particularly those associated with the War on Poverty instituted by the federal government under Presidents Kennedy and Johnson—is read by neoconservatives as a case in point. The story of this period, they argue, is a chronicle of good intentions gone awry.

The neoconservatives' policy agenda calls, first of all, for a *lowering of expectations*. "What is called 'the revolution of rising expectations' has reached such grotesque dimensions," writes Irving Kristol, "that men take it as an insult when they are asked to be reasonable in their desires and demands" (Kristol, 1972, p. 26). High expectations generate a destructive cycle of hope and despair. Led to believe that poverty and racial inequities could be wiped out rapidly, liberals and the poor during the 1960s pushed for expensive programs that fueled the growth of the governmental bureaucracy, cramped the private market, and stirred conflict and controversy. When poverty did not vanish and black families' incomes continued to lag behind those of whites, bitterness, alienation, and disillusionment set in. Disappointment, in some cases, led to radicalization and was used as justification for violence. The irony, according to the neoconservatives, is that extreme expectations blind the population from recognizing real gains that have been made.

Neoconservatives also call for a *greater reliance on the private sector* to deal with social problems. This emphasis does not rest on the traditional conservative's rose-tinted view of the benefits of an unregulated economy. Many neoconservatives are leery of large corporations. "Corporate power clearly is the predominant power," writes Daniel Bell, "and the problem is how to limit it" (Bell, 1973, p. 270). But in recognizing and accepting the growing strength of the corporate sector, neoconservatives have concluded that solutions to social problems must depend on harnessing that strength rather than working around or overpowering it. Thus neoconservatives have been influential advocates of the notion of a "public-private partnership" and have been among the champions of privatization as a general policy trend.

Although government plays a critical role in maintaining law and order, many neoconservatives emphasize the fact that nongovernmental institutions also play an important role in creating a peaceful, stable, and cooperative environment. Thus the *reestablishment of a sense of community* plays a significant role as a policy goal. Such a sense of community depends upon a system of values and traditions, those traditionally inculcated in churches, family, and community groups. Where this informal nexus is intact, citizens can deal with many social problems on a self-help basis, neighbor helping neighbor, friend helping friend. But the sense of community has been disrupted, in part by the onslaught of change associated with modernization, in part by large-scale governmental actions that seemed to make voluntary and self-help actions unneeded or irrelevant. As the weight of the public sector is lifted, some neoconservatives argue, in its place this informal mechanism for addressing community problems will again blossom.

On the issue of centralization versus decentralization, neoconservative writers generally side with those who seek to *return power to the cities and states.* According to this outlook, decentralization is linked with greater freedom. Like the alert customer in front of the cereal shelf at the supermarket, the alert citizen will be free to select a jurisdiction whose package of taxes and services best meets his or her personal tastes.

Finally, neoconservatism calls for the *deemphasis of race* as a central policy concern. Key to this plea is an emphatic assertion that racial discrimination in this country is largely a thing of the past. "Almost everything said about the problems of the Negro tends to exaggerate the purely racial aspects of the situation," Edward Banfield argues (Banfield, 1974, pp. 79–80). Today, blacks and some other minorities have lower incomes, live in poorer neighborhoods, attend segregated schools, and suffer greater levels of illness and crime not because of their skin color but because of habits, outlooks, and behavior patterns associated with their culture and worldview. Policies premised on the notion that racial discrimination is a major source of social problems are destined to fail, Banfield and others suggest, because they stir intense resistance, because they sap energy and resources, and because they do not address the real problem.

Liberalism as a Policy Guide

The term *liberalism* has had a long and somewhat confusing history. One writer, after reviewing several seemingly contradictory accounts, was tempted to ask, "Will the real Liberalism please stand up?" (Bluhm, 1974, p. 61). There has long been a tension within liberalism between an image of man as selfish and acquisitive and an image of man as sociable and educable. There has been a tension, too, between an image of government as a necessary but potentially dangerous creation and an image of government as the culmination of the best in men and the mechanism through which men can best fulfill their potential for learning and growth. Out of these seemingly abstract tensions come compromises that lead to policy orientations concretely different from those of the neoconservatives.

The skeptical side of liberalism is more evident in the writings of the early, classical liberals than in the arguments of those whom we are likely to label as liberals today. Classical liberalism assumed that men are motivated primarily by self-interest, and that self-interest is defined largely by the desire to accumulate material wealth. This was not considered a bad thing, all in all, because it was the drive for accumulation that led men to work, to invent, and to improve their lot. Although John Locke and John Stuart Mill rejected Hobbes's dismal view of the state of nature, each granted that without government to adjudicate situations in which interests clashed, men's pursuit of their self-interest would drive them to behave in ways that would leave them stunted and insecure. Government was necessary, then, but it was to be a limited government. To Locke, the central role of government was to protect men's property, that which they had created or improved with their own labor. To Mill, government could legitimately constrain or regulate individuals' private actions only if those actions could be shown to cause harm to somebody else. It is not surprising, in light of classical liberalism's wary view of man and government, that some neoconservatives claim that they are the true heirs to the liberal tradition on the contemporary scene.

When we think of liberalism today, we are more likely to think in terms of an optimistic outlook, particularly as regards the potential for an expanding government to improve the quality of our lives. Individuals often may act selfishly, but they are capable of being motivated by more socially oriented and altruistic goals as well. Government, from this perspective, is not only a device to restrain people's destructive impulses; it is the product of their cooperative nature and testimony to the power of ideals, such as justice, equity, and security, to unite individuals in a collective effort to reshape the world. The liberal assumes that the responsibilities of government are not just to keep people from slitting one another's throats. Indeed, through education and example, the government has the capacity and responsibility to *change* people—to help to make them wiser, more considerate, more temperate in their pursuit of personal gain.

In taking this stance, contemporary liberals do not see themselves as breaking away from the doctrine that classical liberals espoused. They argue, instead, that they have adapted the insights provided by the classical theorists in response to very real changes in the world. The balance between the public and private sectors in the preindustrial world of Locke and Mill was heavily tipped in favor of the public sector. Business was small, entrepreneurial, and unorganized. Power, both real and potential, was concentrated in the hands of monarchs or parliaments. Although both private and public actors might abuse power, the danger of public abuse was ever so much greater—not so much because it was more likely but because its impacts would be more severe and of greater scope. Power within the private sector subsequently has become greater and more concentrated. In this light, it is the abuse of power by the larger corporate sector that might carry the greatest threat to liberty today. Expansion of the public sector, contemporary liberals argue, is a necessary counterweight.

To note that liberalism contains an element of optimism is not to suggest that it is naive. Liberals do not consider the public sector to be infallible or the solution to every ill. But the liberal is a "tinkerer." Where the neoconservative sees the failure of government to save cities or eliminate poverty as proof of government's fundamental incapacity, the liberal sees signs of remediable errors, correctable misjudgments, careless implementation, or immature theorizing. Like Mill, the contemporary liberal retains a firm belief in the possibility of learning and the role of trial and error in fueling that learning process. Like the loyal Mets fan, the liberal is quick to announce that "we'll do better next time."

Marxism and Radical Analysis as a Policy Guide

To many Americans, Karl Marx brings to mind revolution, class warfare, and little more. As the radical left in the United States has lost its vitality and visibility, and as the social and political unrest of the 1960s has dissipated and gone underground, the impression has grown that Marxism has become irrelevant, except perhaps as a political force in the Third World. Key aspects of Marx's perspective, however, have not died out or become hopelessly outdated. Some critics of both the neoconservative and liberal perspectives draw on Marxist concepts in constructing their alternative conceptions of the origin of policy problems and the form that the solutions to those problems ought to take. Because some of these critics are quite selective in their utilization of Marx's theories—acknowledging an intellectual debt, yet emphatically declaring themselves to be nonMarxists in other senses—I will use the broad and less-than-ideal label "radicalism" to rope under one convenient term a cluster of thinkers who share key assumptions about man and government.

The radical perspective considers individuals to be active, social, growing beings who are shaped by the world and, in turn, shape the world themselves. The materialism and selfishness that neoconservatism and classical liberalism portray as natural traits are, to the radical, a single dimension of the human personality. This side of people is drawn out and reinforced by the institutions and culture associated with modern capitalist societies. Capitalist societies put a premium on competition, personal advantage, and accumulation. They accord status to those who best succeed at the buying and selling game. But, the radical argues, people have the capacity to alter these institutions in ways that will reflect and build upon their capacity to cooperate with others, to respond to collective goals, and to gain satisfaction from nonmaterial rewards. In order for this to happen, however, there will have to be a fairly distinct and comprehensive overhaul. Some radicals feel that this can be accomplished peacefully and incrementally through a series of directed and digestible changes; others feel that resistance is likely to be so great that only massive, immediate, and forceful action, with a likelihood of violence, can succeed.

The current system, radicals argue, operates to preserve and expand the interests of one class at the expense of all others. This class is defined, according to Marx, by its ownership of capital. Others define this upper class differently: by its domination of authority, for example (Dahrendorf, 1959), or simply by virtue of wealth. The presumption that there must be a conflict between the classes, a cleavage that irretrievably sets the interests of the one group against those of the other, is another key component of radical thought. Those with power and status seek to maintain that power and status, and one way they do is through control of the political and policy-making machinery. Through control of the policy process, the privileged elite can control the flow of information to the poor, structure the process of socialization as carried out by the schools, and manipulate the delivery of services so as to punish the dissident, placate the restless, and reward the passive citizen.

Both the liberal and neoconservative presume a basic tension between the public and private sectors. To the neoconservative, that tension grows out of the tendency of government to expand, absorbing resources, undermining incentive, and imposing burdensome regulations. To the liberal, the tension grows out of the responsibility of government to counter the harshness and injustices of the free market. In contrast, many radicals have concluded that the government, in modern capitalist societies such as ours, is so intertwined with and dependent upon large corporations and the financial community that in the long term its interests and those of the dominant economic class tend to merge. From this perspective, public-sector policies to regulate corporate practices or redistribute wealth through progressive taxation and social welfare are likely to be mild tinkerings, designed to quiet political unrest by covering over dramatic injustices without in any substantial way addressing the genuine needs of the poor. True reform—reform granting the poor access to economic and political power—will be regarded by government as a potential threat to economic stability and will be resisted as long as possible.

Radical policy analysis tends to be critical, to expose the manner in which the true impact of programs ostensibly intended to benefit the poor differs from the publicly stated goals. As a source of positive guidance, the radical perspective has been somewhat less productive. Like the neo-

Table 2-3 Overview of the Neoconservative, Liberal, and Radical Perspectives

	Neoconservative	Liberal	Radical
Human Nature	People are unequal, materialistic, power-seeking	People are flawed but perfectable, self-oriented but capable of valuing others	People are social beings; materialism and self-interest are reinforced by capitalism
Private Market	Efficient, rational; best adapted to human nature; harsh but necessary; preserves freedom	Efficient, rational, but with definite limits; increased size of corporations concentrates too much power	Source of inequality; pursuit of profit means wages must be kept low, people and places made obsolete
Government	Legitimate role in softening the harsh edges of market; good-hearted and naive efforts to improve world usually backfire	Makes mistakes but represents the best elements in human nature: cooperation, justice, progress	Primarily allied with owners of capital; protects private property and private privilege; maintains social order
Severity of Problems	Exaggerated; things are getting better but expectations rise faster	There are many problems, but they are discrete and manageable	Severe and systemic

Privatization and Decentralization: Should Governments Shrink? 51

Source of Problems	Limits of human nature; broad forces of technological change; breakdown of family/community	Lack of know-how; selfish actions of a few "bad apples"	The nature of capitalist, racist society; the interests of a powerful few prevail
Interpretation of recent policies	Failures due to over-governing, over-centralization	Mixture of failures and successes; a learning process	Only true reforms forced by political pressure and disruption; pseudo-reform coopts lower classes
Policy Thrust	Privatization and decentralization	Grab bag of new ideas; national government must oversee	Public control over capital; build political power of poor
Some Specific Proposals	Return major welfare programs to states; lower taxes and reduce regulation to stimulate investment in slums; more certain punishment of criminals; education vouchers	Target existing urban programs more at needy; nationalize welfare; alternative sentencing to reduce prison crowding; more dollars for schools; busing for integration	Impose limits on rights of businesses to leave community; redistribution of wealth; public sector guarantees jobs and housing for all

conservative, the radical is often pessimistic about the likelihood that new programs will bring about significant improvements. Unlike the neoconservative, the radical believes that the limitations are politically imposed upon government and, therefore, that different and successful policies could be put into effect *given* a radically different political and economic environment.

Some radicals who take a pragmatic approach—rejecting the extreme Marxist stance that only revolution can bring positive change—have begun to point out policies that they believe can point the country in the proper direction and not simply prop up the status quo. To some, the proper direction should be toward political decentralization and community control. They reason that because existing institutions at the federal, state, and local levels do not respond to the needs of the lower class, we should give power to the poor directly, in the neighborhoods in which they live. To others, the proper direction should be toward increasing the public control of capital. This might be done through much more restrictive regulation of the investment policies of banks and insurance companies, through limitations on corporations' freedom to close a factory or move to another community, or through increasing public ownership of transportation facilities and utility companies.

SUMMARY AND CONCLUSIONS

The issues of privatization and decentralization cut across nearly every domestic policy debate. Specific proposals and specific programs come and go. But questions about the proper responsibilities of the public sector versus the private sector must be faced continually by governments all over the world. And questions about the allocation of responsibility among the federal, state, and local governments are inevitable and ongoing in a federal system.

These questions, in turn, are rooted in deep and long-lasting ideological differences about the nature of people, markets, and government. Table 2-3 on pages 50–51 summarizes the neoconservative, liberal, and radical perspectives, and illustrates the way that basic theoretical premises about human nature and government evolve into specific proposals for dealing with concrete issues such as hungry children, deteriorated cities, and rising crime.

Contemporary policy debates do not always acknowledge such ideological underpinnings. There are at least three reasons for this. First, we are a highly *specialized society*. Experts on poverty formulate their proposals in isolation from other experts who deal with crime, and neither group consults with those who study urban and regional decline or problems in education. As a result, parallels are overlooked. Second, we are a pragmatic, self-consciously *anti-ideological society*. We want to know what works in the real world, not simply what abstract theories tell us should work. Finally, the *fiscal problems* facing all levels of government have made us increasingly preoccupied with narrow discussions about the dollar cost of various policy options. Although the dollar cost is an important consideration, there are other costs and benefits attached to policy options that are equally significant.

Ignoring the ideological underpinnings of public policy in our federal system, however, does not make them disappear; it simply makes it harder to appreciate why the debates are so intense and the battle lines so firmly drawn. The discussion of specific policy issues in the remainder of this text will reinforce this basic fact.

SUGGESTED READINGS

Bish, Robert L., and Vincent Ostrom. *Understanding Urban Government.* Washington, D.C.: American Enterprise Institute, 1973.

Elazar, Daniel. *American Federalism: A View From the States.* 3d ed. New York: Harper & Row, 1984.

Hale, George E., and Marian Lief Palley. *The Politics of Federal Grants.* Washington, D.C.: Congressional Quarterly, 1981.

Peterson, Paul E. *City Limits.* Chicago: University of Chicago Press, 1981.

Poole, Robert W., Jr. *Cutting Back City Hall.* New York: Universe Books, 1980.

Savas, E. S. *Privatizing the Public Sector.* Chatham, New Jersey: Chatham House, 1982.

Steinfels, Peter. *The Neoconservatives.* New York: Simon and Schuster, 1979.

3

Poverty and Inequality

It must have been a shock as well as a surprise to officials in the state of Michigan. It was 1982, and the state was in the throes of a terrible economic recession. Since 1980, the state had borrowed over $2 billion from the federal government to make payments it owed to the unemployed; interest payments alone were $216,000 each day (Sawyer, 1983). The local economy, based on automobile production, was suffering. The temporarily unemployed, as well as those with the foresight to recognize the perilous nature of their jobs, were moving elsewhere. Newspapers from southwestern cities were selling briskly to those scouting the "Help Wanted" pages.

One of the last things state officials could have expected was a new influx of the needy poor, but that is just what they got. Hundreds of needy Asians, recent refugees from Indochina, were traveling halfway across the country, coming from Seattle and other cities in the Northwest. Jobs there, it seems, were also in short supply. Many of these Asian Americans had lost their jobs; now their unemployment benefits had been depleted. Michigan held out little hope for better employment prospects, but its welfare payments were relatively generous. "We are very fearful" of a major influx, a state official revealed (Mathews, 1982).

Poverty and inequality pose critical problems for decision-makers at all levels of government. Indeed, some would suggest that these are the central problems underlying nearly all the other problems public officials face. It is the poor, for example, whose needs for social services, education, and health care put severe strains on public budgets, contributing to a general climate of fiscal stress. It is poverty that accounts for much of what we refer to as the housing crisis: when residents cannot pay their rents, when they must overcrowd their dwellings, and when landlords cannot charge enough to meet the costs of housing repairs and property taxes, housing and neighborhoods decline. Poverty and inequality, some say, have put a crippling burden on many school systems and fuel the nationwide increases in crime. Do away with poverty, this argument suggests, and people will be able to find their own housing, fix up their own neighborhoods, and support, through taxes, those services the majority desires and needs. Do away with inequality, and the fear and mistrust that infuses interclass and interracial relations will dissipate.

As the Michigan example reveals, however, poverty and inequality pose special dilemmas for the localities and the states. Because of the permeability of their boundaries, states and localities must walk a fine line between taking care of their own poor and attracting new poor, between taxing the wealthy to benefit the needy and driving the wealthy away. It is not surprising, therefore, that much of the responsibility for dealing with poverty and inequality has gravitated, in recent times, toward the national government. The trend toward nationalizing responsibility for the poor can be overstated, however. States and localities, as will be seen in Chapter 5, continue to play a major role. Some feel that role should be expanded even more.

For a while, it looked as though we had the problem of poverty beat. Between 1960 and 1975, the number of people officially labeled poor in this country dropped dramatically. More than a few analysts were ready to declare that the War on Poverty had been won. Even today, there are some who would argue that the number of people who are truly poor is small. Later in this chapter we will consider why policy experts cannot agree even on the definition of poverty. No matter how we define poverty, however, the early 1980s showed that it was a more obstinate and lasting problem than the optimists had hoped. The number of poor people once again begain to rise.

What, if anything, can be done to put an end to poverty once and for all? Does the answer lie in broad federal programs or in decentralized local initiatives? Can government wipe out poverty with a massive and comprehensive attack or does the solution ultimately depend upon the private sector—the health of the economy and the charitable initiatives of voluntary groups?

Before considering policy responses, we will analyze certain theoretical issues concerning the nature of poverty and inequality. We shall see that disagreements about particular strategies for addressing poverty are often rooted in deeper disagreements about who is poor, why they are poor, and whether poverty exists at all. The ambiguity and confusion are due in part to the actual changes in the experience of poverty that national affluence has brought about. The broad distribution of material wealth that our country produces has blurred the edges of the concept of poverty. Mass production of many consumer goods has reduced their relative costs, increasing their availability to the poor and, at the same time, making it easier for the rest of us to pretend that poverty no longer exists. Michael Harrington, commenting on the phenomenon of the "well-dressed" poor, suggests that "it almost seems as if the affluent society had given out costumes to the poor so that they would not offend the rest of society with the sight of their rags" (Harrington, 1963, p. 6).

To understand the bitterness and intransigence with which the opposing positions are offered, we must see how the *study* of poverty is interwoven with the ideological debates sketched in Chapter 2. In considering the nature of poverty, we are drawn, almost irresistibly, into such thorny and emotional issues as (1) society's responsibility for caring for the needy versus the individual's responsibility for caring for him or herself; (2) the tendency of the unregulated capitalist economy to exacerbate inequalities between the rich and the poor; and (3) the hope that governmental intervention will shape a more just society versus the fear that it will offer only marginal benefits at crippling cost. These issues, in turn, bear directly on our understanding of the legitimacy or illegitimacy of the current political and economic system. In this chapter, we will review much of the data that are available concerning the extent of poverty and who is actually poor. Before doing so, however, it will be informative to consider some of the alternative theoretical orientations through which such information is commonly screened.

EXPLANATIONS OF POVERTY

Why are there poor people in the United States? When sociologist Joe R. Feagin asked this question of 1,017 Americans, he found the most frequently cited explanations to be (in order): lack of thrift and proper money management, lack of effort, lack of ability, loose morals and drunkenness, sickness and physical handicaps (Feagin, 1975). These explanations are *individualistic;* that is, they explain the origin and persistence of poverty by referring to characteristics of an individual poor person without considering the nature of the social, political, and economic environment in which that individual lives. Traditional conservativism has often relied upon such individualistic explanations of poverty to bolster its claim that poverty is not due to any substantial flaw in existing institutions.

Mentioned less often by the respondents in the Feagin study were low wages, poor schools, racial discrimination, insufficient jobs, and exploitation by the rich. Radical analysts argue that it is *structural* factors such as these that are the true cause of poverty. Individualistic explanations simply shift the blame to the victim as a means of denying the need for broad social reform.

In the following pages, we will consider these alternatives more fully and contrast them with a third kind of explanation of poverty. This third alternative, based on the idea that there is a *culture of poverty*, contains elements of both an individualistic and a structural perspective. Both neoconservative and liberal thinkers have drawn on the culture-of-poverty notion. Not surprisingly, however, they draw quite different conclusions. To liberals, the cultural perspective provides reason to expect that the cycle of poverty can be broken. To neoconservatives, the lesson is that poverty is deeply rooted and largely impervious to governmental policies.

The Individualistic Perspective

The undercurrent of individualism that marks Americans' image of the poor has roots in three sources of intellectual thought: Calvinism, free market capitalism, and Social Darwinism. Although each has distinctive origins—Calvinism in religion, the ideology of capitalism in economic theory, Social Darwinism in the natural sciences—these intellectual traditions combine to promote the belief that there is an association between material success and moral and social goodness; poverty is the result of sinfulness, ineptitude, sloth.

The Calvinist Ethic. Traditional Christianity presumed no necessary connection between goodness of the soul and the accumulation of wealth on earth. The reward to the pious was to be found in the afterlife. John Calvin, the Swiss religious leader whose thoughts and practices were carried to this country by the Puritans, saw things differently. Calvinism did not disdain material success. Instead, it preached a notion of predestination, holding that the fates of men were written in the book of God even as they were born, and that hard work and practical success were the mark of the chosen—"at once the sign and reward of ethical superiority" (Tawney, 1926, pp. 266–7). By equating material success with moral purity, this outlook can have the effect of placing the blame for poverty on the poor themselves. What is more, it seems to offer a policy prescription as well—a prescription for limited intervention. If poverty is visited upon the sinful by God's own command, mortal and moral men must take care not to interfere.

Classical Economic Theory: Adam Smith's Invisible Hand. Adam Smith's *The Wealth of Nations* was published in 1776, the very year the Declaration of Independence was signed. This was a coincidence, but a symbolic one. Smith's economic theory sought to explain how the conflict among self-interested businesses and businessmen, each narrowly concerned with its own profit, led not to anarchy and fragmentation but to economic progress and growth. His concept of the Invisible Hand came to be woven into the self-image of an increasingly entrepreneurial America. Americans found in Smith's theory a doctrine that seemed to both explain and justify the unfettered market system that was beginning to evolve.

In a competitive market, prices are determined, Smith reasoned, by supply and demand. The farmer who brings to market the only sweet corn in the region will be able to sell it at a high price—as long as there are consumers who want that corn and are willing to bid up the price. By the same token, in a year when tomatoes are in abundance, consumers will be able to insist on lower prices, and farmers, unwilling to have the fruit rot in their stalls, will have to accept a lower profit or even a loss. It is the heat of competition—among rational and self-interested producers, consumers, and laborers—that introduces discipline and efficiency. In order to maximize their profits, producers must accurately assess consumers' desires and seek technologies that allow them to produce the same product as their competitors at a lower cost. In the crucible of competition, some fail, but those who succeed do so because they have been able to produce more efficiently and to more accurately judge and deliver what buyers actually want and need.

Although Smith's interest was not to develop a theory of poverty and inequality, the implications of his doctrine seem reasonably clear. Progress requires competition; competition requires losers as well as winners; it is the chance to accumulate wealth that drives the winners to take risks and invest in new technologies; losers will suffer the harsh economic costs of reading the market wrong.

Like Calvinism, then, classical economic theory accepts inequality as inevitable. Where Calvinism associates poverty with moral failure, Smith's doctrine associated poverty with economic failure: inefficiency, lack of judgment, lack of thrift. As with Calvinism, classical economic theory seemed to carry a broad policy prescription. The message was that of laissez-faire; the government's role should be limited to the basic functions of protecting property and maintaining peace so that the market may function. For government to aggressively intrude, for it to seek to redistribute wealth from the wealthy to the poor, would risk undermining the delicate incentive system that encourages the most skillful and productive individuals to devote their energies to production that, in the end, benefits us all.

Social Darwinism. Whereas Calvinism attributed extremes in poverty and wealth to the laws of God, and Adam Smith to laws of economics, Social Darwinism found the explanation for poverty in an insight into biology translated into a natural law. Charles Darwin's *The Origin of*

Species, published in 1859, had broken new intellectual ground with its theory of evolution through natural selection. Darwin's focus was on change and adaptation among plants and animals; he argued that competition among species for the resources needed for survival led to a situation in which those organisms with traits best suited for survival would tend to survive and reproduce and those less suited would fail. Herbert Spencer, a British philosopher, broadened the scope of Darwin's philosophy by applying it to humans and human institutions.

Spencer was something of an eccentric, hardly the likely choice to become an American folk hero. An insomniac and a hypochondriac, Spencer frequently wore earmuffs, even while inside, in order to shut out the unwanted excitement of conversation (Peel, 1971). Yet for two decades after the Civil War, Spencer became something of an American craze. Oliver Wendell Holmes doubted that "any writer of English except Darwin has done so much to affect our whole way of thinking about the universe" (Hofstadter, 1959, p. 32).

Like Calvinism, Social Darwinism considered inequality in wealth to be inevitable, and like both Calvinism and classical economics, social Darwinism linked material success with a social good. "Society advances," Spencer wrote, "where its fittest members are allowed to assert their fitness with the least hindrance, and where the least fit are not artificially prevented from dying out" (Wiltshire, 1978, p. 197). Nature is a harsh and stingy provider; it usually will not provide enough for all Man's needs, and when it does so, Man responds by surviving longer and reproducing more, creating new population pressures that outstrip available resources. Although all men start with equal opportunity, they do not begin with equal abilties. In the competition that follows, those who are stronger, swifter, shrewder, and wiser become wealthy and pass that wealth on to their heirs.

The poor are viewed harshly. "The whole effort of nature is to get rid of such, to clear the world of them, and make room for the better," Spencer declared (Hofstadter, 1959, p. 41). For people to seek to alter this, to establish policies that aim to support and maintain the poor, would be folly. "The law of survival of the fittest was not made by man and cannot be abrogated by man," wrote William Graham Sumner, the American sociologist who embraced and refined Spencer's social Darwinist ideas; "if we should try by any measure of arbitrary interference to relieve the victims of social pressures from the calamity of their position we should only offer premiums to folly and vice and extend them further" (Sumner, 1963).

Individualism and Welfare Policies. Taken together, these three individualistic perspectives offered a set of clear messages to those who shaped American social-welfare policies in their early years. Among the messages implied:

- *Poverty and Inequality Cannot be Eliminated:* The conditions of the poor may be made more palatable, but poverty and inequality cannot be erased. They are natural and inevitable; part of God's law, economic law, natural law.

- *Poverty and Inequality Should Not Be Eliminated:* To eliminate poverty and inequality, even if it were possible, would be to court disaster. It is fear of poverty that motivates individuals to lead moral lives, economically productive lives. It is destitution that weeds out the weak and allows the strong to thrive and reproduce.

- *It Is Necessary to Distinguish Between the Worthy and Unworthy Poor:* The Calvinist ethic has long recognized a distinction between the "worthy" and the "unworthy" poor. The worthy poor are those whose poverty, although attributable to personal characteristics, seems to be due to factors outside their direct control. Widows, the elderly, the sick and the handicapped, women and children have been regarded as worthy of pity and charity, if not of respect. The Social Darwinists perceived themselves to be *scientists,* and to many this implied a conscious rejection of religion, which deals with unobservables and is cemented by faith rather than verifiable facts. Yet within the writings of the Social Darwinists we find echoes of the Calvinists' distinction between the worthy and unworthy poor, and a moralistic and surprisingly vehement denunciation of the latter group. The physically incapacitated and those unable to earn a living "are an inevitable charge on society," wrote Sumner. "About them no more need be said. But the weak who constantly arouse the pity of humanitarians and philanthropists are the shiftless, the imprudent, the negligent, the impractical, and the inefficient, or they are the idle, the intemperate, the extravagant, and the vicious" (Sumner, 1963).

- *The Unworthy Poor Must Be Treated Harshly:* The belief that sinfulness and sloth were at the root of much poverty led to policies framed in terms of punishment, banishment, moral exhortation, and the sharp distinction between the worthy and unworthy poor. Plans for relief for the poor written for the city of Zurich, Switzerland, by a follower of Calvin in 1524 called for special institutions for the sick and the elderly, but begging was to be forbidden, needy travelers were to be aided only on the condition that they leave the city the next day; "no inhabitant was to be entitled to relief who wore ornaments or luxurious clothes, who failed to attend church or who played cards or was otherwise disreputable" (Tawney, 1926, pp. 114–5). In the 1600s, several New England colonies had laws calling for the flogging or imprisonment of the able-bodied poor; "strangers who appeared to be potential paupers could be requested to leave ('warned out'), then fined or otherwise punished if they refused" (Feagin, 1975, p. 25). To ensure that the stigma of poverty was severe and in the possible hope that the poor person could be embarrassed into mending his or her ways, both New York and Pennsylvania required the poor to wear brightly colored letters on their sleeves, much as Nathaniel Hawthorne's Hester Pryn was made to bear her scarlet letter.

- *With Harsh Treatment Should Come Conversion or Therapy:* The source of poverty is within the individual; therefore, the reduction of poverty calls for individuals to be changed. "Because many reformers saw the causes of poverty in un-Christian character flaws such as immorality and slothfulness, the solutions were thought to lie in conversion of the poor to the Christian way of hard work and sober living" (Feagin, 1975, p.30). During the 1700s and into the 1800s, this often took the form of placing the poor in workhouses, where they were to engage in labors that would help to pay for their support while at the same time being exposed to a harsh discipline and religious instruction that, it was hoped, would help them to see the error of their ways.

Today, ours is a more secular culture, and the individualistic perspective, when it is applied, tends to be offered in less moralistic garb. Even so, the notion that the poor bring poverty on themselves remains quite deeply ingrained. The individualistic perspective offers a sense of comfort to those who are doing well. It suggests that their own successes are a mark of their superior energy, intelligence, prudence, shrewdness, or morality. It also suggests that although one may feel sorry for the poor, there is no reason to feel guilty.

In addition to making the rest of us feel better, the individualistic perspective has an important political function. By placing responsibility for poverty on the poor themselves, the individualistic perspective is useful to those who are advantaged by the status quo. Expensive poverty programs, efforts to redistribute wealth, and other political reforms will not eliminate poverty because they cannot succeed in changing the poor themselves.

The Cultural Explanations of Poverty

Mary Ann Thompson is black, single, a mother, and poor. Although she is a real person (the name is not real), her biography may seem like a stereotype. Mary Anne's father died when she was an infant.

Her mother raised her and her twelve brothers and sisters while on welfare. When she was fourteen, Mary Anne had her first child. By the time she was nineteen, she had had two more. She has never been married, and she no longer sees either of the two men who fathered her children. She dropped out of high school when her mother had another baby—she was needed to baby-sit. Now she is raising her own children on welfare. She is a member of the pool of semipermanent poor that sometimes is referred to as America's underclass (Auletta, 1983).

The apparent tendency of poverty to be passed down from generation to generation makes its impacts more dangerous and its explanations more complex. The existence of an underclass, whose parents were poor and whose children will be poor, may indicate that the cleavages between classes in our society are more fixed than we like to believe. Some social scientists warn that societies that fail to provide for upward mobility between the classes are destined to suffer internal tension and political and racial turmoil.

Individualistic explanations of poverty do not easily account for the existence of such a familial pattern. It is possible, of course, that poverty is linked to a trait that is passed on genetically, like blue eyes or blond hair. A few social scientists have been willing to make such a claim (Jensen, 1972). But the evidence on this point is very weak (Jencks, 1972) and most Americans have tended to reject such a notion as inflammatory, unfounded, and potentially dangerous.

Yet if heredity does not account for the frequently observed pattern of intergenerational poverty, what does? In order to answer this question, some social scientists have turned to the notion of a culture of poverty, a sophisticated conception of the cause and perpetuation of poverty that considers the environment of poverty and the way that environment might shape the personalities of the poor.

Culture as a Cause of Poverty. In our daily conversation, the term *culture* may mean nothing more than refinement or sophistication. As social scientists use it, however, the concept is considerably broader and more complex. According to one definition, culture "consists of the rules which generate and guide behavior. More specifically, the culture of a particular people or other social body is everything that one must learn to behave in ways that are recognizable, predictable, and understandable to those people" (Valentine, 1968, p. 3). Culture determines what is good manners at the dinner table as well as what kinds of food are prohibited or offensive to "good taste." Culture also supplies us with our models of family, government, and career; it is culture that shapes our expectations regarding the extent to which women should be passive or aggressive, the degree to which a leader should instruct by example or direct by means of force. It is because culture is so ingrained and widely shared among those with whom we normally interact that we come to take it for granted—until we are transplanted into a different place in which the rules by which people live are much different from ours.

Anthropologists who lived among and observed non-Western peoples and tribes were the first to appreciate the variation among cultures and the power of culture to alter not only the way people behave but also the way that they *see* the world. Although some of the early anthropologists held a snobbish and superior view of the people they studied—as if their subjects were proved to be simple and gullible by virtue of their strange customs and beliefs—it was only a matter of time before the concept of culture would be turned inward to reveal something about more industrialized nations as well.

Turned on the poor in more industrialized nations, the concept of a culture of poverty seemed to offer a sophisticated explanation for the persistence of poverty within the context of increasing affluence. This explanation depended upon the observed tendency of many of the poor to exhibit behaviors and beliefs that differed from those associated with the middle and upper classes. Oscar Lewis, who studied poor families in Mexico, Puerto Rico, and New York, developed a list of seventy traits that he felt characterized the cultural worldview of the poor. Among the most important are a *short time horizon* that keeps the poor from planning for the future or considering the long-term consequences of their actions, and *feelings of fatalism and dependence* that prevent the poor from aggressively acting to improve their conditions. Other traits supposedly associated with this culture of poverty include: weak ego structure, confusion of sexual identity, lack of impulse control, belief in male superiority, early initiation into sex, high incidence of the abandonment of wives and children, tendencies toward authoritarianism, and a tolerance for psychological pathology (Lewis, 1966).

Although this characterization of the poor is certainly as unflattering as that associated with individualistic interpretations of the unworthy poor, the culture-of-poverty approach differs in at least two key respects. Rather than focus on individuals, the culture-of-poverty perspective focuses on *collectivities:* families, tribes, racial or ethnic groups. This has the effect of diffusing responsibility and preventing any simple assertions of personal blame; poverty is not a life chosen but a life-style into which one is born and from which it is most difficulte to escape. The culture-of-poverty perspective differs also in its recognition of the adaptive nature of some of the poverty traits. Among those born into a harsh and unpredictable environment in which the pressures of poverty make life a day-to-day struggle in which success must be measured in tiny increments, if at all, the person who considers only the short-term consequences of his actions and who expects little may have a competitive advantage over those who set unrealistically high standards for themselves and who constantly stop to weigh the immediate costs and benefits of their actions.

The Culture of Poverty as Self-Perpetuating—The Neoconservative View. Although the culture-of-poverty thesis assumes that the characteristics of the poor can be understood as collective adaptations to their environment, one school of thought holds that the originally functional aspects of that culture have subsequently become dysfunctional. "By the time slum children are six or seven," Lewis hypothesized, "they have usually absorbed the basic values and attitudes of their subculture and are not psychologically geared to take full advantage of changing conditions or increased opportunities which may occur in their lifetime" (Lewis, 1966, p. xlv). This perspective is shared by many contemporary neoconservative analysts.

Although the poor in this country may once have lived under conditions so harsh and hopeless that fatalism and present-orientation were natural and adaptive responses, advocates of the self-perpetuating thesis suggest that this is no longer the case. Dramatic changes in the political and economic environment, symbolized by civil-rights legislation and the evolution of a powerful labor-union movement, have shattered the barriers of racial discrimination and class exploitation that at one time anchored the lower classes to an inescapable life of poverty. Although the doors of opportunity have swung open, however, the poor have failed to step through. Their failure is accounted for by aspects of their culture that the poor have not shed, traits that make them unable or unwilling to compete in the labor market and to improve their financial status.

A quite controversial statement of this perspective is found in Daniel Patrick Moynihan's 1965 report on *The Negro Family,* popularly known as the Moynihan Report. Moynihan argued that the root of poverty among lower-class blacks in this country is in the disorganized family structure in which black youths are raised. "The white family has achieved a high degree of stability and is maintaining that stability," the report indicated. "*By contrast the family structure of lower class Negroes is highly unstable, and in many urban centers is approaching complete breakdown*" (italics in original).

Moynihan cited various statistics to substantiate his premise that the black family was in disarray: nearly one out of four urban marriages among blacks dissolved; nearly one out of four black births was illegitimate; almost one out of four black families was headed by a female. This has direct economic consequences; without the earnings of a male head of household, many black children are forced to spend their childhood dependent upon welfare. It may have sociological consequences as well. "By and large, adult conduct in society is learned as a child," Moynihan suggested. Young black males raised in female-headed households are deprived of the traditional male role model. One result, presumably, is an increased machismo, a need on the part of these youths to prove their manhood through daring and sometimes violent escapades (Moynihan, 1965, p. 5).

The essential components of this self-perpetuating perspective are the assumption that *key personality traits are fixed at a very early age* and the notion that the *conditions that gave rise to the culture of poverty are to be found in the past and not the present.* Banfield lays blame on the mother-child relationship; he argues that lower-class mothers provide their children with a much less rich verbal interaction that may stunt their intellectual growth at an early and critical stage (Banfield, 1974). In a study that seems to give some credence to this perspective, Hess observed 160 black mothers and the manner in which they interacted with their four-year-old children. Poorer mothers, he concluded, tended to *tell* their children what to do, without explaining to them the reasons. Middle-class mothers were less likely to rely on physical feedback, preferred motivating their child, and tended to explain the meaning or purpose of a task (Hess, 1970).

David McClelland, who discovered that blacks scored consistently lower in tests he devised to measure a person's "need for achievement"—an attribute he felt to be critical to personal drive and success—explained his finding by reference to the matriarchal structure of the black family and a reliance on child-raising practices that he believed could be traced back to the period of slavery. "Negro slaves," he suggests, "developed child-rearing practices calculated to produce obedience and responsibility not [need for achievement], and their descendants, while free, should still show the effects" (McClelland, 1961, pp. 376–7). Moynihan also traced the breakdown of the black family to the period of slavery and the forced separation of families that era produced. Opportunities for young blacks are now available, but the legacy of slavery and discrimination has not been easy to shake. "Three centuries of injustice have brought about deep-seated distortions in the life of the Negro American. At this point, the present tangle is capable of perpetuating itself without assistance from the white world" (Moynihan, 1965, p. 47).

By placing the responsibility in the past, the self-perpetuating culture-of-poverty thesis turns the focus away from the need for reform of current institutions and places the burden of change back on the poor themselves. It is not racial discrimination in hiring practices that today impedes the economic advancement of lower-income blacks, this argument goes, but the failure of young blacks to dress appropriately for job interviews, to show up for work on time, to save their wages, to invest in their own education, to respect authority. But others, who nonetheless cling to the broad culture-of-poverty thesis, argue that the role of the social environment is not limited to the past.

The "Adaptive" Culture-of-Poverty Thesis—The Liberal View.
Several decades ago, a social scientist devised an intriguing experiment involving schoolchildren and candy bars. With the permission of school authorities, the experimenter would enter the grade-school classroom with a tempting offer. Students were told that they could choose either of two options: those who wished could have one candy bar right away; those who were willing to wait for a week would be given two. The result revealed a sharp pattern: those who demanded immediate satisfaction were more likely to have come from lower-income families and families in which no father was present. Their time horizon was apparently too short, their need for instant gratification too strong to allow them to take advantage of the opportunity to double their take. This, according to some, was sure proof that a culture of poverty did exist, and that it was this that kept the poor from making the decisions that would lead to upward mobility.

Some years later, however, another group of experimenters gave the original study an interesting twist. Once again the "one today, two if next week" offer was made, and once again class and family status seemed to predict the choice that students made. When the experimenter came back a week later, however, half of those who had chosen to wait for the two candy bars were not given any at all. The stage was set for the true test, which came even later, when the experimenter returned and offered the same deal to the students once again. Some students again chose to wait, and others chose the bird in hand. But this time the characteristics that best differentiated between those who waited and those who did not had changed. No longer were class and family status the best predictors; now, the best predictor was simply the students' own experience in the previous test. Those who had chosen to wait and were rewarded for doing so tended to choose to wait once again. But those who had waited and been disappointed tended this time to insist on taking the single candy bar when it was offered the first time (Miller, Riessman, and Seagull, 1966).

What does this prove? To some, the study suggests that the original interpretation of the first experiment had been wrong. Rather than a deeply ingrained cultural trait, ongoing patterns of experience may have accounted for the behavior of the lower-class children. Living in poverty, competing with brothers, sisters, neighbors, and relatives, these children may have come to see much more quickly that the world was unpredictable, that promises frequently are broken. That wealthier children, based on a single such experience, began to exhibit the same present-oriented behavior suggests that something other than intergenerational socialization is involved; traits such as time horizon, which had been conceived of as deeply held and unresponsive to environmental change, were shown to be more flexible and malleable.

The adaptive-situational perspective views culture as more dynamic and less confining than does the self-perpetuating perspective. It is *this* perspective that animated many of the liberal policies associated with the 1960s War on Poverty. It differs from the self-perpetuating version in the following senses:

- *The behavior and attitudes of the poor are presumed to have their origins in present circumstance, not history.* Some historical analyses indicate that the black family showed remarkable resiliency and tenacity in withstanding the pressures of the slavery experience. It was not until later, under the pressures of urbanization and industrialization, that black families, uprooted by the search for employment and strained by the difficulty of obtaining decent wages, began to show the patterns of dissolution that we recognize today (Gutman, 1976).

- *The poor share the essential values of mainstream Americans.* Those with a culture of poverty, according to Oscar Lewis, "are aware of middle-class values, talk about them and even claim some of them as their own, but on the whole they do not live by them" (Lewis, 1966, p. xlvi). Hyman Rodman offers, instead, the notion of a "lower class value stretch." The poor cherish many of the same things as the middle-class, Rodman argues: material comfort, self-fulfillment, the respect of their peers. But the environment of poverty does not allow those values to be expressed in the same way. As a result, those values are stretched to encompass behaviors that the middle class regards with scorn. The child of the middle class can save his allowance in order to purchase a ten-speed racing bike, achieve status by excelling in tennis or becoming an eagle scout. The lower-class child, with fewer options, may seek material comfort through thievery and status by joining a gang (Rodman, 1963).

- *The culture of poverty provides the life of the poor with its own sources of organization and structure.* Although culture, by definition, is supposed to provide structure and order, "lower-class culture" came to be used by some as indicative only of the disintegration of order, as synonymous with unpredictability, violence, and anarchy. To Banfield, the lower-class individual "is suspicious and hostile. . . . He is unable to maintain a stable relationship with a mate. . . . He feels no attachment to community, neighbors, or friends" (Banfield, 1974, p. 62). Yet Suttles's study of a slum neighborhood in Chicago led him to conclude that, in spite of the high rates of delinquency, unwed mothers, and gang activity, the slum was "intricately organized according to its own standards"; these standards "require discipline and self-restraint in the same ways as do the moral dictates of the wider community" (Suttles, 1968, p. 3).

- *Changes in their environment will bring about changes in the attitudes and behavior of the poor; change may be relatively rapid and certainly need not take generations to occur.* Oscar Lewis, whose writings generally have been used to support the self-perpetuating version of the culture-of-poverty thesis, nonetheless offers an anecdote that suggests, like the second candy bar experiment, that the culture of poverty is not so ingrained as others believe. Lewis visited a slum in Havana before the Cuban revolution. When he returned to the same slum after the revolution, he found that although the residents remained poor, there was much less hopelessness and despair, greater confidence, organization, and a sense of power (Lewis, 1966). Such a rapid change, if genuine, would seem to be incompatible with the notion of a self-perpetuating culture.

The Culture of Poverty and Welfare Policy. If the culture-of-poverty thesis is correct, the implications for policy are rather different from those drawn from the individualistic perspective. The self-perpetuating version leaves open the possibility that poverty can be eliminated, but it cautions that progress will be very slow. The values and behaviors that mire the poor in their poverty—the present-orientation, fatalism, self-interest, and the like—were inculcated through generations of experience and socialization. Even if the conditions under which the poor currently live were to be changed dramatically, those values, and the resulting poverty, would not disappear. "Slums may be demolished," writes Banfield, "but if the housing that replaces them is occupied by the lower class it will shortly be turned into new slums" (Banfield, 1974, p. 234). Operating from this premise, neoconservatives have argued that Americans must scale down their expectations; hopes for the rapid elimination of poverty will simply lead to sharper disillusionment.

Whatever progress can be made will have to come from focusing on children. Because the habits and beliefs of the poor are passed down within the family and the environment, progress will depend upon weaning the poor child away from his or her parents, relatives, neighbors, and other sources of bad influence. Banfield has gone so far as to suggest that the most effective policy for eliminating poverty calls for the removal of poor children from their homes. Placing such children with families holding middle-class values presumably would better prepare the child for advancement and personal success. Banfield does back off from this notion—it would probably be unconstitutional, he concedes, and resistance would be so fierce as to be counterproductive—but he suggests that more modest strategies might be in order. Parents, for example, might be paid to send their preschool children to day care, where the influence of middle-class teachers would counterbalance the cultural messages that the children receive at home.

The adaptive-situational perspective is more optimistic in its policy message. Although cultural traits may be tenacious, they *will* respond to changes in the environment. Policy, therefore, should combine mild social reform with efforts to retrain the poor. Part of the problem for the poor is that avenues for advancement through socially acceptable behavior have been blocked by: racial discrimination, inadequate schooling, and biases in the housing market that locked the poor into ghettos where living conditions are harsh. Open up those opportunities and the poor *will* respond—slowly and hesitantly, perhaps, as they begin to maneuver in unfamiliar territory, but respond nonetheless. Training in job and social skills can ease the transition. Like the self-perpetuating version, the adaptive-situational perspective suggests that such training might be most effective when aimed at the young who are not yet set in their ways. The assumption is, however, that the basic values of the poor are compatible with those of the larger society; teenagers, young adults, even some of the older poor can be given the skills to allow them to earn a decent living—if only society is willing to give them the chance.

The Structural Explanations of Poverty

Radical analysts argue that focusing on the attributes of the poor—whether one considers those attributes as individually or culturally derived—is a mistake. Attitudes, race, family breakdown, and lack of education might help to explain why a particular individual is poor, but only a structural explanation begins to explain why, in a society as wealthy as ours, there must be poverty and inequality at all.

Blame the System, Not the Victim. Among the claims made by structuralists that serve to differentiate them from individualist and culture-of-poverty theorists are the following:

The problem is not that the poor will not work, but that there are not sufficient jobs. Marxism, the most fully elaborated structuralist theory, explains the failure of the capitalist system to provide jobs to all who want them in two ways. Owners of capital, in order to survive in the competitive environment of capitalism, must continually seek to increase profits. Because, according to Marx, it is labor that is the source of value, the capitalist must do this in two ways: by increasing the output of his workers and by limiting the reimbursement provided to the workers for the labor they invest. To increase the output of his workers, the owner of capital is driven to invest in more and more innovative machinery and production techniques. Although this benefits the owner of capital, it works to the disadvantage of those who must sell their labor in order to survive, because it means that the skills they offer are constantly in danger of being made obsolete. In order to keep workers manipulable—to prevent them from effectively demanding a larger share of growing profits or a promise of job security in the context of the modernization of production techniques—the capitalist depends on a pool of the unemployed and underemployed. The existence of such a pool of potential workers, according to Marx, weakens the bargaining position of labor; workers have little leverage with which to make demands when faced with the threat that they easily may be replaced.

Many conventional economists, although rejecting Marx's intepretation and the conclusions he draws, nonetheless accept the notion that to provide enough jobs for those who want them would throw our economic system into disarray. The assumption that full employment is not feasible is seen most explicitly in the concept of *the Phillips curve*. The English economist A. W. Phillips charted the historical relationship between unemployment rates and inflation rates and concluded that as the former declines the latter rises. This seemed to indicate that there is an inherent trade-off between the goals of reducing unemployment and keeping inflation under control. Employed as a policy guide, this has meant that, during periods of inflation, national economic policies have frequently been aimed at increasing unemployment, trading off lower prices for everybody against the suffering and disruption to the fewer numbers who are no longer able to find work. It is partially in response to this understanding of the Phillips curve that mainstream economists have come to take it for granted that unemployment cannot be eliminated. Early editions of Samuelson's classic macroeconomics textbook indicated that a reasonable and feasible "full employment" would entail an unemployment rate of 2.5 to 3 percent. More recent editions suggest that 4 percent or higher may be expected, even if the system is pushed to its greatest capacity (Lekachman, 1976). Ronald Reagan, during his first year in office, suggested that 6 percent might be the most realistic goal. That would mean that, even in the best of situations, over six and a half million persons actively looking for work would be unable to find a job.

Inequality in wealth, incomes, and employability are not due primarily to differences in education, intelligence, or skill. The notion that ours is essentially a meritocratic system, one that rewards and punishes in proportion to the contribution that each individual makes, is tempting and reassuring. It is tempting, in part, because a superficial review of the evidence suggests that this must indeed be the case. The more schooling you have, the less the likelihood that you will be poor or unemployed. This is reassuring because it seems to suggest that we can determine our own fates; by educating ourselves and obtaining the skills that are in demand we can greatly reduce the chance that we will ever be counted among the poor. It is reassuring also because it suggests that the system in which we live is consistent with at least one conception of justice.

Although not denying that education, intelligence, and skills play some role in the determination of income, structuralists argue that the relationship is much more erratic than is generally presumed. The observable correlation between education and income may be due in large part to the phenomenon of *credentialism*. Faced with more job applicants than they can handle, employers may simply use years of education as a convenient winnowing-out device. As the overall educational level of the labor pool increases, employers begin to insist on evidence of higher levels of education; college diplomas may be required for applicants for positions that were capably filled by nongraduates for many years before. Yet as Bradley Schiller points out:

> bestowing a high school diploma, or even a Ph.D., on all the poor will do little to alter the number or kinds of jobs available. A few more vacancies might be filled, but the greatest impact would be to alter the composition of the poor and to raise their educational attainments. By itself, such an effort would do little to reduce the extent of poverty (Schiller, 1980, p. 121).

Nor is it the case that education credentials are necessarily a reliable predictor of performance on the job. Studies of insurance agents, laboratory technicians, and air-traffic controllers suggest that those with fewer years of schooling often are more productive, get higher performance ratings from their superiors, win more awards, and have lower rates of job turnover than their more educated peers (Berg, 1974).

Extremes of wealth, as well as extremes of poverty, may be insufficiently accounted for by differences in intelligence, productivity, or skill. If wealth were a reflection of individual merit—wisdom in investment, entrepreneurial talent, management expertise—the biographies of the very wealthy might be expected to show repeated examples of unusually astute decisions resulting in unusually large material rewards. In reviewing such biographies, however, economist Lester Thurow concluded that "it is impossible to identify anyone whose personal fortune was subject to two or more upward leaps. The typical pattern is for a man to make a great fortune and then settle down and earn the market rate of return on his existing portfolio" (Thurow, 1980, p. 177). Although skill and ability undoubtedly play a role in determining who will suddenly become rich, Thurow argues that blind fortune plays a major role in deciding which of the many persons with such abilities actually will strike it big. According to his "random walk" hypothesis, "the winners are, as in any lottery, lucky rather than smart or meritocratic" (Thurow, 1980, p. 175).

Some individuals and groups benefit from the existence of poverty and inequality, and they use their disproportionate power to make sure that the conditions that give rise to them will not be undermined. Many analysts tend to depoliticize the issue of poverty by assuming that poverty is a technical or administrative quirk in the system that all members of society would love to see wiped out. Structuralists argue that, rather than a quirk, poverty is integrally entwined within the fabric of our system, providing benefits to many who therefore have a political stake in seeing that it is maintained. Herbert Gans, for example, suggests at least five functions that poverty serves. (1) The existence of the poor ensures that someone will be available to do society's *dirty work* to collect garbage, fight wars, administer to the personal needs of the very well-to-do. (2) Poverty *creates jobs,* for social workers, charities, police. (3) The poor provide a *market* for goods and services that others would reject; they buy used clothes, stale bread, and spoiling vegetables and fruit; they purchase the services of incompetent, old, poorly trained doctors, lawyers, teachers, and other professionals who are unable to compete except among those who have no other choice. (4) The poor provide a convenient *scapegoat* on whose shoulders politicians and other national leaders can successfully place the blame for problems they might otherwise be held responsible for. (5) The poor guarantee the *status of the nonpoor,* providing an important psychological buffer for the lower-middle-income family, which can look with satisfaction on a group of individuals who clearly have fared much worse than they (Gans, 1972).

Those who benefit from the existence of the poor have an incentive to maintain their advantage, and they have the financial and political resources to make sure that their interests are taken into account. The elimination or reduction of poverty, therefore, is a political problem as much as it is a problem of economics or management; serious efforts will not be undertaken, the structuralists argue, until the poor themselves can mobilize into a political force that cannot be easily distracted, co-opted, out-muscled, or ignored.

Inequality is not a prerequisite to societal progress and economic growth. Conventional economic theory holds to an unflattering image of human nature. Driven by self-interest, men will invest energies and wealth only in return for the promise of personal, material gain. What is more, it is generally taken for granted that absolute wealth is not in itself a sufficient incentive; men do not fully appreciate their own wealth unless they can compare themselves to others who have less than they have. To narrow the gap between the rich and the poor, according to this reasoning, would be to strip wealth of some of its appeal, and therefore to discourage the near-wealthy from striving to become the wealthy and the very wealthy. Because of the meritocratic assumption—the assumption that those who have accumulated wealth are those who have special skills and talents—this would be tantamount to taking out of circulation the brightest, most innovative, shrewdest, and most efficient women and men.

Marxist analysts tend to agree that people living in capitalist societies behave according to such a model. But they regard this behavior as an artifact of capitalist culture, rather than as a window into the true nature of human beings. They argue that under the right conditions, men can gain direct satisfaction from their labors, rather than simply working for the sake of a paycheck and the capacity to buy more than their neighbors and friends.

Most structuralists do not go as far as to suggest that inequalities in income and wealth can or should be eliminated entirely. They question the assumption, however, that such inequalities need to be anywhere near as large as they are today. In 1982, the 20 percent of all families with the highest incomes earned over nine times as much as the poorest 20 percent (U.S. Bureau of the Census, 1983, p. 438). If this ratio were reduced to 3 to 1 or even 2 to 1, would the motivation to work and invest really disappear? "A priori," Charles Lindblom notes, "that result is no more likely than its opposite: when extra income becomes harder to get, a person may work harder to get it" (Lindblom, 1977, p. 43).

Structuralists and Social-Welfare Policy. Structuralists criticize contemporary policies, which, they argue, fail to challenge the basic structure of the existing institutions: thus leaving the root of the problem intact. Francis Fox Piven and Richard Cloward (1971), for example, argue that welfare policies in this country have been designed to protect rather than restructure the capitalist system: benefits are kept low to provide a spur to the low-wage worker, to make welfare so unappealing that, by comparison, even low-wage, low-status, unhealthy work is preferable; benefits and coverage are expanded only when unemployment and inequality create conditions of political unrest that threaten to coalesce into political movements aimed at bringing about more radical change.

There is a positive agenda as well. One component is the *creation of jobs*. Marxists are skeptical that this can be accomplished within the current economic system, but others contend that, with the government acting as an "employer of last resort," unemployment could be cut at least in half. *Redistribution of income and wealth* is another component of the structuralist policy agenda. This, as noted earlier, is not the same thing as suggesting that income and wealth need to be equalized. The equation of redistribution with absolute equalization of results is, according to William Ryan, a "caricature" of the true structuralist position, one that plays into the hands of those who oppose any effort at all to bring about a more fair system of sharing the nation's wealth (Ryan, 1981).

Government, some argue, needs to exert *stronger influence over decisions currently reserved to the private sector alone.* When a business chooses to adapt a new technology (replacing, for example, assembly-line workers with computer-programmed robots) or relocate its facilities in pursuit of higher profits, such a decision imposes severe costs on many individuals and families, costs that are not figured in on the corporate managers' balance sheets. Where possible, some argue, control over capital should be transferred out of the hands of those corporate managers and into those of workers and community residents. This might take the form of workers banding together to buy their own companies. Such worker-run corporations presumably would show greater loyalty to the community in which they are located and devote more of their own resources toward retraining workers as technologies change. Some argue that low-income neighborhoods can best promote their own interests through the formation of development corporations in which residents would own shares of stock.

The structuralist perspective is at once more optimistic and more pessimistic than the others we have discussed. It is more optimistic because it suggests that poverty and inequality are neither natural nor necessary for economic comfort and growth; it suggests also that most of the poor are willing and able to make a fuller contribution once society has reshaped. It is more pessimistic because, unlike each of the other perspectives, it recognizes that many individuals and groups benefit from poverty and inequality, that these groups are likely to oppose efforts to bring about reform, and that these same groups hold sufficient power to give their desires extraordinary weight. The question is not a technological one, not one of devising a better plan. We have the wealth and know-how to eliminate poverty right now. The true problem is a political one: how can the poor and disadvantaged be given the political clout to force a fairer and more equal system to be brought about?

A LOOK AT THE POOR

But who is right? Do the structuralists provide the most accurate insights into the nature of poverty? Is an emphasis on the culture of poverty more appropriate? Or is the individualistic interpretation that most Americans instinctively favor a better guide correct? Each theory suggests a different policy direction. A clearer understanding of the poor—their numbers, their characteristics—might generate better policies. Such an understanding is made more difficult, however, by the high emotions that cloud some discussions of poverty and by methodological problems that plague efforts to define and identify the poor.

How Poor Is Poor?

Carmen Santana is a welfare mother. She wears a fourteen-karat gold watch as she brushes clusters of cockroaches off her kitchen table. She "has never subscribed to a magazine, owned a car, a rug, or an air conditioner, or bought insurance, but she and her children love clothes and spend about two thousand five hundred dollars a year to dress themselves in the latest styles" (Sheehan, 1976, p. 39). Her children frequently call her long distance, collect, so her phone bill sometimes reaches sixty dollars a month. She has never lived in a place with closets. Each month she runs out of money, and until her next welfare check and food stamp allotment are due, she must buy her food on credit. Her cramped and filthy apartment boasts two televisions and a stereo.

One of the preliminary and vexing questions facing policy-makers today is that of determining who is, in fact, poor. Mrs. Santana is not alone in presenting the confusing juxtaposition of deprivation with material possession. According to some analysts, the broad distribution of material wealth in our country is evidence that poverty has, to all extents and purposes, been eliminated. Such a claim, if accurate, suggests that massive expenditures or untested innovations to reduce poverty are misplaced efforts. Rather than address a true need, the benefits of such efforts may be absorbed by a comfortable welfare bureaucracy or simply serve to salve the collective consciences of a liberal "do-gooder" clique. Those benefits that do reach the less well-off, according to this perspective, foster dependency and reduce the incentive to work.

Can someone who owns a television set, dresses fashionably, or drives a large car legitimately be considered to be poor? Uncertainty about the meaning of poverty in an affluent society has contributed to the sharp, almost incapacitating debate between those such as Michael Harrington, author of *The Other America,* who believe that poverty in America is a critical problem and one that is likely to grow, and those such as Martin Anderson, former domestic-policy adviser to President Reagan, who proclaims that "the war on poverty has been won, except for perhaps a few mopping up operations" (Anderson, 1978, p. 15).

Counting the Poor. There are good reasons to search for a reliable method for counting the poor. An accurate estimate of the number of poor persons gives us a sense of the scope and severity of the problem; this helps us to establish policy priorities. Collected over time, such a measure allows us to make assessments of trends: is poverty declining, or is it getting worse? Collected, in standard form, across different jurisdictions, it can also help us to judge the effectiveness of different antipoverty strategies so that we can make informed judgments about what works.

On the face of it, devising such a measure seems a fairly straightforward, technical task. The recent history of intense debates regarding the "proper" measure of poverty, however, belies this image. Choosing a way to count the poor can be a highly political act, sometimes carrying hidden implications for the standard by which the contemporary political and economic arrangements are to be judged.

Standards for measuring poverty may be broadly classified into those that are *absolute* and those that are *relative*. Absolute standards are based on some fixed assessment of the package of goods and services that are necessary if a person is to enjoy some minimal standard of living. Once this particular mix of food, shelter, clothing, and the like has been determined, a market price can be established and this price then is totaled to reach the poverty cutoff. As prices rise or fall, the absolute standard rises or falls accordingly, but the quality of life presumed to accompany the threshold level of income remains the same. Relative standards of poverty seek to take into account the social and economic context in which the poor person lives. People's idea of a decent life are, according to this perspective, socially defined. We take our cues about what is and is not acceptable and necessary through our observation of what those around us have and expect. When only a few elite households were able to afford their own televisions, those who could not own one may have felt envy but they did not feel poor. An accurate measure of poverty, according to this perspective, must take into account the conditions and expectations of others and must change as those change.

The Official Cutoff. The most widely used measure of poverty was developed by the Social Security Administration in 1964. Because this index is the basis for many census reports, the distribution of some federal grants, and the determination of eligibility for some social programs, we would hope that it would be based on a careful and precise analysis of people's needs. What might one want to take into account? A task force might be established to review various scientific studies of nutritional requirements, differentiating according to gender and age. Another group might be assigned the task of determining a basic shelter allowance sufficient to maintain health and security. Others would need to come up with estimates of minimal needs in such areas as clothing, utilities, medical and dental expenses, transportation, furniture, and the like.

The approach actually taken by the SSA has the advantage of being much simpler, but at the cost of being much less precise. The base of this index is a nutritionally adequate diet designed by the Department of Agriculture for "emergency and temporary use when funds are low." The cost of the food needed to provide this diet was determined and then multiplied by three. Why three? The multiplier is based on a 1955 study that determined that poor families spent about one-third of their income on food. Since 1969, the poverty-level cutoff, thus obtained, has been automatically adjusted each year to take into account changes in the Consumer Price Index (an indicator of the cost of living). Different multipliers are provided for single persons or families of different sizes. Until 1980, farm families were presumed to require only 85 percent of the income required by nonfarm families, who must purchase all of their food. The SSA poverty level for a family of four in 1982 was $9,862. About 34.4 million persons, 15 percent of the total population, fell below the poverty level in that year.

Do Official Statistics Exaggerate the Number of the Poor? How, with almost 35 million poor people—more than one out of every seven Americans—can some analysts claim that poverty has been all but eradicated in the United States today? The answer is that Banfield, Anderson, and many other neoconservatives believe that the government's official estimates, based on the SSA index, significantly overstate the actual number of persons who are poor. Their major criticism centers on the fact that the SSA index, as applied, does not take into account in-kind benefits. If the cash value of food stamps, public housing, subsidized school lunches, and free medical care were considered, they argue, many households currently classified as poor would be boosted over the poverty threshold.

The United States distributed about $107 billion in noncash assistance in 1982. This equaled nearly 30 percent of all transfer payments and over 70 percent of the "means tested" payments—payments associated with programs limited to the poor and near poor. If the cash value of these benefits were taken into account, the official poverty rate would have dropped from 15 percent to only 9.6 percent (Stockman, 1983). Counting the "hidden income" of poor households—unreported income derived from part-time labor, gambling, the sale of drugs, or other illegal activities—would, some argue, result in an additional significant decline in the number found to be truly living below the poverty line.

The argument is convincing. Certainly a family with less than $9,000 in reported cash income, that lives in public housing, receives food stamps, is eligible for Medicaid, and collects another $1,000 per year that it fails to acknowledge or report may be much better off than a family with no in-kind benefits that earns just enough to be boosted over the poverty line. There are some technical problems. Hidden income is not counted precisely *because* it is hidden. And estimating the cash value of in-kind benefits is not as simple and straightforward as it initially seems. Is $50 worth of food stamps the equivalent of $50 in cash? Some argue that the restrictions put on in-kind benefits make them less valuable than money, which can be spent on whatever the poor family itself feels are its most important needs. Indeed, evidence suggests that food-stamp recipients sometimes are willing to sell their coupons at less than face value. Is this "market value" a better indicator of what the stamps are worth? Even more problematic is the treatment of in-kind medical care. Should a seriously ill Medicaid recipient, with a cash income of $4,500, be classified as not poor simply because she and her children received over $5,000 worth of treatment and hospital costs? We will need to rethink just what we mean by "poor" before we will be able to come up with a fully satisfying methodology to account for in-kind income in estimating the extent of poverty.

Whereas neoconservative analysts such as Banfield and Anderson charge that the official statistics overestimate poverty, radicals such as Harrell Rodgers argue that there are *more* poor people than the government's surveys recognize. Rodgers argues, first of all, that the food budget on which the SSA index is based is simply too low. Originally intended for emergency use only, the thrifty food budget was adopted as a permanent standard because more adequate budgets resulted in estimates of poverty that were, for political reasons, considered too high (Wilcox, 1969). Secondly, Rodgers argues that the practice of multiplying the food budget by three is based on assumptions that are out-of-date. "Most recent studies indicate that poor people spend about 28 percent of their income on food. Thus, the food budget should be multiplied by a factor closer to 3.4 rather than 3" (Rodgers, Jr., 1979, p. 26).

Using a more realistic food budget, based on a "low cost" rather than "thrifty" plan, coupled with the 3.4 multiplier would have raised the estimates of the number of poor in 1974 from 24.3 million to 55.4 million. This, Rodgers argues, is more than enough to counterbalance the decrease in poverty that results from the adjustments the neoconservatives suggest. "Thus, a much improved measure that considered in-kind benefits, taxes paid, unreporting of income, and raised the food budget and multiplication factor would probably show anywhere from five to twenty million additional poor" (Rodgers, Jr., 1979, p. 30).

Relative Measures of Poverty. Relative measures of poverty seek to reflect the fact that poverty may be socially defined. Whether you are poor may depend on more than whether you earn enough to fill your belly, cover your body with clothes, and cover your head with a roof. Absolute definitions of poverty are usually anchored upon a notion of minimum physiological needs that are basic to men and women no matter where and when they have lived. Relative definitions try to take into account the norms and customs of the society in which the person lives.

Measures of the distribution of income give some insight into relative poverty. As Table 3-1 shows, the poorest 20 percent of the nation's families received less than 5 percent of the nation's income in 1982. The wealthiest fifth, by comparison, received 42.7 percent. The wealthiest 5

Table 3-1 Share of the Nation's Income of Families Held By Each Fifth and the Highest 5 Percent: 1950–1982

Year	Lowest Fifth	Second Fifth	Third Fifth	Fourth Fifth	Highest Fifth	Highest 5%
1950	4.5	11.9	17.4	23.6	42.7	17.3
1960	4.8	12.2	17.8	24.0	41.3	15.9
1970	5.4	12.2	17.6	23.8	40.9	15.6
1982	4.7	11.2	17.1	24.3	42.7	16.0

SOURCE: U.S. Bureau of the Census, *Current Population Reports*. Washington, D.C.: Government Printing Office, 1950, 1960, 1970, 1982, series P–60, Nos. 129 and 140.

percent earned 16 percent of the nation's income, more than three times as much as the poorest 20 percent. This unequal sharing of the nation's income has changed very little, moreover, through time.

Is Poverty Fading Away? Assessments that we had "licked" the problem of poverty seemed more reasonable in the early 1970s. By 1973, there were about 16.5 million fewer people officially classified as poor than there had been in 1959. The poverty rate had been cut in half, from 22.4 percent to 11.1 percent of the total population. As Figure 3-1 makes clear, however, projections that poverty would continue to fade have proven to be unrealistic. The poverty rate remained relatively stable through most of the 1970s, and in the early 1980s it once again began to rise.

A more encouraging picture would emerge if various noncash forms of support could be considered. If food stamps and other forms of in-kind assistance are treated as income, the number of those living below the poverty level continued to drop through the 1970s. The recent increases in poverty, however, exist even when such unofficial estimates are employed. In 1981, the poverty rate, adjusted for noncash assistance, was about 8.5 percent; in 1982, it was 9.6 percent (Stockman, 1983). In addition, as our discussion of relative definitions of poverty suggested, the poor are failing to gain ground on the rest of Americans either in terms of their share of the nation's income or their status when compared to the median family.

Who Are the Poor?

The Location of Poverty. Poverty is frequently thought of as a big-city problem, concentrated, regionally, in the Northeast and upper Midwest. Yet as Table 3-2 indicates, only about 37 percent of all poor persons live in central cities, and there are nearly as many poor in the South as in the Northeast and North Central states combined. Still, it is true that poverty is increasingly becoming more of an urban than a rural

Figure 3-1 Poverty Rate, 1959–1982

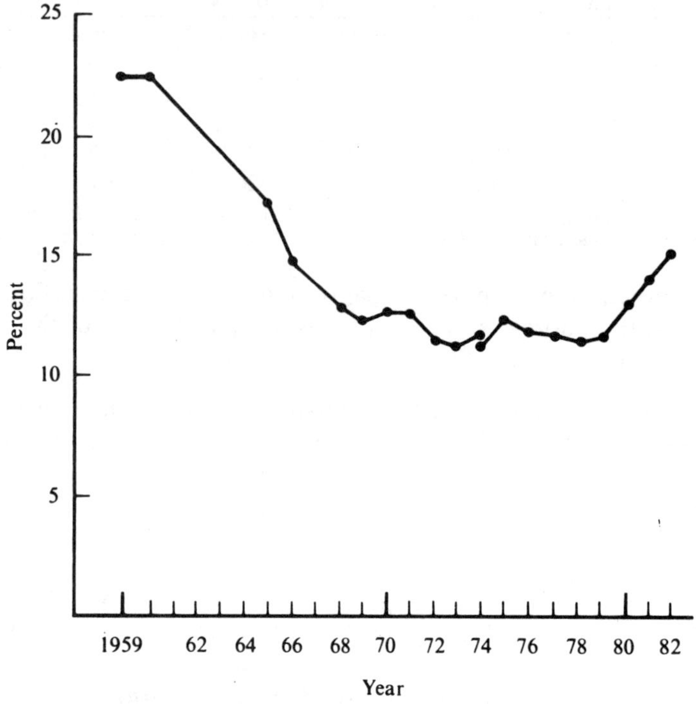

*Procedure revised in 1974.
SOURCE: United States Bureau of the Census, *Current Population Reports*. Washington, D.C.: Government Printing Office, 1959–82, series P–60.

problem. A 1934 study found poverty to be most severe in America's rural areas. That study, which established a poverty cutoff of $2,000 per year, found that over half of all farm families—about 17 million people—were earning less than half that amount (Patterson, 1981). Today, over 60 percent of the nation's poor reside outside the rural areas.

The Feminization of Poverty. It seems likely that many of the Americans who blame poverty on laziness and other individualistic characteristics assume that the typical poor person is a healthy but unworking male. Increasingly, however, poverty in the United States is becoming the province of women. Female-headed households, where no husband is present, are more than 4.5 times as likely to be poor as the married-couple familes. Only about 15 percent of all United States families are female-headed, but female-headed familes account for over 45 percent of the poor.

Poverty, Family, and Race. Over two-thirds of the poor are white (see Table 3-3). If you are Hispanic or black, however, you are two

Table 3-2 Where the Poor Lived in 1982

	Number Below Poverty (1,000s)	Percent of All Poor
Type of Residence		
Total	34,398	100.0
Inside Metropolitan Areas	21,247	61.8
Inside Central Cities	12,696	36.9
Outside Central Cities	8,551	24.9
Outside Metropolitan Areas	13,152	38.2
Region		
Northeast	6,364	18.5
North Central	7,772	22.6
South	13,967	40.6
West	6,296	18.3

SOURCE: U.S. Bureau of the Census, "Money Income and Poverty Status of Families and Persons in the United States: 1982," *Current Population Reports*. Washington, D.C.: Government Printing Office, 1982, series P–60, No. 140.

and a half to three times more likely to be poor than if you are white. The median income for black families in 1982 was $13,599; for families of Spanish origin, $16,228; for white families, $24,603.

One reason that poverty rates are so much higher among some minorities is that they are much more likely to live in female-headed families. "In 1979, 55 percent of all black children in the United States were born out of wedlock and into female-headed homes, compared to an estimated 15 percent in 1940," Ken Auletta reported in his book *The Underclass*. The figure for Mexican Americans is less than half that high, but Puerto Rican families also are likely to be headed by a woman. "The Census Bureau reports that 50 percent of all Puerto Rican children under eighteen live in female-headed homes" (Auletta, 1983, p. 39).

According to some analysts, the breakup among black and Hispanic families—and the resultant cultural deficits—goes far to explain the high rate of poverty among minorities. This point sometimes is linked by Edward Banfield, among others, to a claim that racial discrimination is largely a thing of the past. The reasoning goes something like this: if

Table 3-3 Poverty, By Race and Spanish Origin, 1982

Characteristic	Number Below Poverty (in thousands)	Percent of All Poor	Poverty Rate
White	23,517	68.3	12.0
Black	9,697	28.2	35.6
Spanish origin	4,301	12.5	29.9

SOURCE: U.S. Bureau of the Census, "Money Income and Poverty Status of Familes and Persons in the United States: 1982," *Current Population Reports*. Washington, D.C.: Government Printing Office, 1982, series P–60, No. 140.

Table 3-4 Poverty Rate By Family Status, Race, and Spanish Origin, 1982

Family Status	All Families	White Families	Black Families	Spanish Origin
All	12.2	9.6	33.0	27.2
Married Couple	7.6	6.9	15.6	19.0
Male Head/No Wife	14.4	12.2	25.6	17.0
Female Head	36.3	27.9	56.2	55.4

SOURCE: U.S. Bureau of the Census, "Money Income and Poverty Status of Families and Persons in the United States: 1982," *Current Population Reports*. Washington, D.C.: Government Printing Office, 1982, series P–60, No. 140.

poverty among minorities can be shown to result from something other than their race (such as their family status), then race, and racial discrimination, can be shown to be insignificant forces in and of themselves. Family status is indeed a potent predictor of poverty. But family status cannot be the sole explanation for high rates of poverty among blacks and Hispanics. As Table 3-4 reveals, the poverty rate among black married-couple families is more than twice as high as that for married-couple families that are white.

Poverty and Age. Children and the elderly are the two age groups most likely to be poor. One out of every three poor persons is a child under the age of 15; nearly half the poor are either children or people over sixty. Increases in Social Security benefits and coverage, however, have been dramatically successful in reducing the poverty rate among the elderly. In 1959, 35.2 percent of those over sixty-five were poor; in 1982, only 14.6 percent were poor—a poverty rate below that for the population at large.

Poverty and Education. Americans have long believed that the schoolroom is the alternative to the breadline, and it is true that those with higher levels of education are less likely to be poor. One half of those twenty-five years old and over who have no schooling are poor, whereas only 17.3 percent of those with at least some college are poor. Yet, as Table 3-5 shows, education is by no means a sure ticket out of poverty. Almost half of the adult poor (47.6 percent) are high-school graduates. The payoffs of education are particularly limited for blacks. Over one-half of adult blacks who have completed four years of high school remain poor; over one-third of those with at least one year of college are poor.

Work Experience of the Poor. Common advice to the poor is that they should "get a job." If some of the poor look back with an expression of puzzlement, we should not be surprised. For the fact of the matter is that many of the poor who *can* work, do. Of the 34,398,000 poor in 1982,

Table 3-5 Poverty Rate and Education, by Race and Spanish Origin, 1982

Educational Attainment	All Families	Whites	Blacks	Spanish Origin
No Years Completed	50.6*	44.2*	71.4*	60.5*
Elementary:				
Less than 8 years	48.0	43.8	56.9	66.7
8 years	38.7	31.5	57.3	64.2*
High School:				
1 to 3 years	50.2	41.5	63.5	65.5
4 years	29.5	21.4	51.3	35.3
College:				
1 year or more	17.3	12.5	34.3	19.5

*Base less than 75,000

SOURCE: U.S. Bureau of the Census, "Money Income and Poverty Status of Families and Persons in the United States: 1982," *Current Population Reports*. Washington, D.C.: Government Printing Office, 1982, series P–60, No. 140.

22,812,000 (66.3 percent) were fifteen years old or older. Four out of every ten of these individuals worked during 1982. Two million worked full time, all year long, and yet remained poor. Of those who did not work at all, two-thirds were either ill or disabled, going to school, unable to work, or retired. Generally, poor whites were somewhat more likely to have worked (43.1 percent) than either poor blacks (31.6 percent) or Hispanics (39.8 percent). As for the reasons the poor gave for not working, blacks had higher reports of illness or disability and were more than twice as likely to indicate an inability to find a job.

SUMMARY AND CONCLUSIONS

When I was a boy spending my first summer at a sleep-away camp, our counselors suggested that we go on a hunt for snipes. Armed only with the information that snipes were "sort of like pheasants," we set out eagerly, armed with flashlights and burlap sacks.

Policy-makers, anxious about poverty and inequality, are sometimes a bit like campers on a snipe hunt. They select their weapons, plot their strategies, and set to work without even agreeing on the nature of their prey. After many, many studies, there is still sharp disagreement about how much poverty there is, what are the principal causes of poverty, and why poverty lingers even as our aggregate wealth as a nation continues to grow.

The reason for this disagreement is not that policy-makers are naive or incompetent. Nor is it simply that they have relied on different defini-

Table 3-6 Ideological Perspective on Poverty

	Neoconservative	Liberal	Radical
Extent of Problem	Poverty is exaggerated; virtually wiped out by economic growth and existing programs	An important problem; policies during Sixties showed we can have effect, but we've got a long way to go	Existing estimates grossly understate true extent
Preferred Standard	An absolute measure; near subsistence	An absolute measure based on a decent quality of life	A relative measure; goal is equality, not just raising floor
Cause of Poverty	Self-perpetuating culture, family breakup	Adaptive culture of poverty, blocked opportunities	Racism and the nature of capitalism

tions or chosen different tools for measuring. To explain the sharp debates over the nature and causes of poverty in these ways would be to trivialize disagreements that are actually quite sharp and quite meaningful.

The disagreements, in fact, hinge on the deeper political and ideological conflicts that separate neoconservatives, liberals, and radicals (see Table 3-6). They are potent and divisive because they carry with them quite distinct messages about the adequacy and fairness of our basic institutions. Liberals focus attention on sticky points in our economic system—points at which opportunities for minorities and the poor are unnecessarily limited. Radicals rely on structural explanations that pin the blame for poverty and inequality on aspects of our system that are so central they must be replaced rather than reformed. Individualistic and self-perpetuating culture-of-poverty explanations, favored by conservative and neoconservative analysts, suggest that the fault lies elsewhere, in the poor themselves or in the culture and beliefs they nurture.

Looking at statistics about the poor can help us weed out blatant stereotypes and fundamental misinformation, but it cannot resolve conclusively the kind of disagreements that we find ourselves faced with here. The disagreements about the nature and cause of poverty translate into disagreements about policies, and these, ultimately, are resolved through political conflict and compromise, not by poring over census tables. As we shall see in the next chapter, political conflict and compromise have left us with a social-welfare system that is not neatly compatible with any of the theoretical perspectives we have considered. Instead, ours is a fragmented and ideologically schizophrenic collection of programs that is understood by few and supported by even fewer.

SUGGESTED READINGS

Auletta, Ken. *The Underclass.* New York: Vintage Books, 1983.
Banfield, Edward. *The Unheavenly City Revisited.* Boston: Little Brown, 1974.
Harrington, Michael. *The Other America.* New York: Macmillan, 1962.
Rodgers, Harrell R., Jr. *Poverty Amid Plenty.* Reading, Massachusetts: Addison-Wesley, 1979.
Ryan, William. *Blaming the Victim.* New York: Vintage, 1971.
Valentine, Charles A. *Culture and Poverty.* Chicago: University of Chicago Press, 1968.
Waxman, Chaim I. *The Stigma of Poverty.* New York: Pergamon, 1983.

4
Social Welfare Policies

"I have called for a national war on poverty," President Lyndon B. Johnson declared in a message to Congress in March 1964. "Our objective: total victory." Twenty years later, it is clear that the elimination of poverty has not come about. This is true whether we measure poverty by an absolute standard or by a relative standard; it is true whether we consider only cash income or we include in-kind programs.

The War on Poverty is history, but it is a history that continues to live with us. It lives with us through its influence on the way that contemporary policy-makers think about poverty and the role that government can or cannot play in reducing poverty and inequality. Neoconservatives argue that the War on Poverty was an experiment that failed dismally. Also discredited in that experiment were both a theory of poverty and a set of assumptions about the proper and feasible role of the national government in addressing domestic policy problems.

Behind the War on Poverty was a belief that the roots of poverty are more structural than individual. Poverty, according to this perspective, is not natural, not somehow rooted in Man's moral flaws. Rather, it was assumed, poverty is sustained through a cycle in which experiences at home, in the streets, in the schools, with police, and in the political sphere reinforce attitudes and behaviors that destine the poor child to remain mired in the underclass. Responsibility lies in the environment and institutions. It is these, rather than the poor themselves, that must be changed. Changing these, moreover, can break the cycle of poverty rapidly and permanently. Some neoconservatives argue that the failure of the resulting programs to eliminate poverty proves the inadequacy of the theoretical foundation on which they were built; the poor carry the causes of their poverty within themselves, they suggest.

The War on Poverty also was characterized, some of its critics argue, by mistrust of the private sector, naive faith in the public sector, and a misguided attempt to impose a single, national program upon a heterogeneous assortment of states and localities. This reading of our not-too-distant history has helped to fuel the current calls for a more decentralized and more privatized social-welfare approach. Rather than a single, centralized national welfare system, President Reagan and others called for greater decentralization—a shifting of much of the responsibility for welfare back to the localities and states. Recent calls for reform also include a new emphasis on the private sector. Government, it is argued, has proved itself unable to deal effectively with poverty and inequality. Corporations, community organizations, and charity offer an alternative that might be more efficient, more innovative, and more effective.

Have we come to rely too much on the national government in our efforts to deal with poverty? Can states and localities provide a more flexible, innovative, and responsive approach? In addition, have we come to rely too much on government at all levels? By defining poverty as a public-sector problem, have we underestimated the potential of charity and stifled the self-help impulses that seemed to deal effectively with poverty in earlier years?

There is little question but that past governmental policies have failed to live up to the promises with which they were launched. We have learned that we cannot eliminate poverty by creating a new program blessed with a healthy price tag. But a careful look at history will suggest that the lessons are more subtle and complex than this alone. Governmental policies, including federal policies, can boast of successes as well as failures. And the records of the states, localities, and private sector in dealing with the needs of the poor are spotty enough to show us that neither decentralization nor privatization offers a sure-fire cure.

In this chapter, we will review the major programs that constitute our national welfare policy. As we shall see, ours is not a cohesive, integrated, consistent system animated by a clear conception of what poverty is, what can be done, or who should do it. The poor in our cities and states encounter a somewhat bewildering and ad hoc array of programs, the product of conflicting theories, shifts in political tides, historical accretion, and unplanned consequences. The result is a pseudosystem that leaves no one satisfied and has drawn critical fire from both the political right and the political left. Nonetheless, we shall see that the system is not the complete and utter failure that it is sometimes portrayed as being.

WELFARE TODAY

System or Hodgepodge?

The poor in the United States have many possible routes for support. The most important social-welfare programs available include:

- *Old Age Survivors and Dependent Insurance* (Social Security). Provides a monthly payment to eligible retired or disabled workers and their spouses and survivors.
- *Medicare.* Provides payment for some of the health and hospital costs for the elderly.
- *Supplemental Security Income* (SSI). Offers a monthly payment to blind or permanently handicapped persons, or elderly persons whose Social Security payments and other income still leaves them poor.
- *Aid to Families with Dependent Children* (AFDC). Gives aid to poor families with children who are lacking one parent or, in some states, whose parents are unemployed.
- *Medicaid.* Provides medical relief to AFDC families, recipients of SSI, and some other "medically needy" segments of the population whose health expenses are great but whose income may be too high to qualify for AFDC or SSI.
- *Unemployment Compensation.* Those who have lost their jobs may be eligible to collect benefits for from twenty-six to thirty-nine weeks.
- *General Assistance* is available in some states to provide monthly payments to some of the poor who do not qualify for AFDC—for example, single persons or couples without children.
- *Food Stamps* help about one out of every ten American families in paying for their food costs.
- *Public Housing.* About one out of ten renting households lives in housing owned and managed by local governments; another one out of every eight receives rent subsidies of some kind.

Other programs—school lunch support, special benefits for veterans, workman's compensation, benefits to victims of black lung disease, pensions for retired railroad workers—are also available to some of the poor with special needs or special qualifications.

If you are confused, you are not alone. So are many of the poor. Not only must they deal with the large number of programs, they also must confront the fact that eligibility standards and average payment levels vary widely, depending not only on the program but, for some of these programs, on the state in which a person lives. Confusion and lack of accurate information are two of the reasons why many of the poor never collect the benefits to which they are legally entitled.

Even the administrators of the welfare system find the array of programs bewildering and, at times, incomprehensible. Joseph Califano, former secretary of the Department of Health, Education, and Welfare, considered it an "administrative nightmare." Responsibility for directing, implementing, and overseeing the existing programs, he pointed out, must be shared among 9 federal executive departments, 21 congressional committees, 54 state-level welfare agencies, and over 3,000 local welfare agencies. Rigid and complicated eligibility requirements result in burdensome paperwork. If one laid the pages of the welfare form used in Los Angeles end to end on the floor, it would make a path seventy feet long. In Atlanta, there are 229 separate forms used for applicants to AFDC (Advisory Commission on Intergovernmental Relations, 1980). By considering how the various programs differ in terms of type of benefits, form of funding, level of government, and extent of targeting on the poor, we can begin to get a better understanding of the structure of this system and the reasons it has evolved in this way.

Type of Benefit—Cash Versus In-Kind. Most social-welfare programs provide the recipient with cash. A cash grant provides flexibility—the extra money can be spent for food, if that is needed; heat, if the winter is too cold; rent, if the landlord is getting impatient. Providing flexibility makes sense, if you assume that the poor family is the best judge of its members' own needs and how they can be most effectively met. But as Table 4–1 indicates, there has been a growing tendency by Congress to turn to in-kind benefits. In-kind programs provide poor people with goods or services that they are presumed to need. The food stamp program, for instance, provides poor families and individuals with vouchers that may be traded in at supermarkets for eligible products. Medicare and Medicaid reimburse doctors and hospitals for part of the health-care costs of the elderly and poor, respectively. Public housing and various rent and mortgage programs (about which we will have more to say in Chapter 6) pay a portion of the housing costs of the eligible low-income household.

In-kind programs have a special appeal to politicians and voters who hold to more individualistic perceptions of poverty and therefore doubt the capacity of the poor to utilize cash grants wisely. In-kind benefits cannot readily be squandered on drugs, entertainment, wine, women, or

Table 4-1 The Growing Reliance on In-Kind Benefits Federal Outlays, 1970 to 1980

	1970	1975	1976	1977	1978	1979	1980
Cash benefits							
millions of $	48,567	109,585	128,736	138,299	147,909	161,732	200,307
percent	80.7	78.5	78.2	77.0	75.7	75.1	73.9
In-kind benefits							
millions of $	11,641	30,053	35,875	41,357	47,467	53,721	70,909
percent	19.3	21.5	21.8	23.0	24.3	24.9	26.1

SOURCE: U.S. Bureau of the Census, *Statistical Abstract of the United States, 1981*. Washington, D.C.: Government Printing Office, 1981, Table No. 522, p. 322.

song. Food stamps, for example, are, by law, restricted to use in the purchase of food and food products; they may not be used to buy tobacco or alcohol.

In-kind programs also appeal to those organized interests that produce the goods and services the government is helping the poor to buy: farmers, doctors, hospitals, nursing homes, housing developers, and the like. To these groups, in-kind programs may provide more business; and these groups are not shy about using their political clout to obtain provisions especially favorable to their own well-being, even if those provisions limit the freedom and benefit to the intended recipients. Thus food-stamp recipients, for example, find themselves prohibited from using their stamps to buy imported packaged food, imported meats, or imported meat products—restrictions that make little sense if the goal is to meet nutritional needs and encourage efficient consumer shopping by the poor, but that are certainly understandable to domestic farmers and food producers.

Form of Funding—Insurance Versus Assistance. Life can be harsh and unpredictable. A sudden illness or the death of a spouse can wrench a middle-class family out of its stable and comforting environment and toss it permanently into the struggle for survival that haunts the poor. Insurance is designed to shelter a family from such harsh and uncontrollable shocks. Left to their own devices, however, many people are unable or unwilling to set aside the money or purchase sufficient private insurance to meet all the disruptions that life can bring. It is often these persons who later must throw themselves on the public mercy for charity or other types of assistance.

Social insurance as a public policy seeks to address this problem by forcing individuals to prepare for harsh futures by setting aside money while they are healthy, young, and employed. Social Security and unemployment compensation were established by Congress in 1935. Both require employers to make regular contributions to funds from which benefits could be paid to their workers if and when they retired or lost their jobs. In the case of Social Security, the tax is shared equally between the employer and the employee. Medicare, enacted in 1965, is also an insurance program, funded out of the same pool as Social Security benefits.

One of the appealing features of such insurance programs is that they lack the stigma often associated with "being on the dole." Because eligibility and benefit levels are linked to what you put into the system, recipients feel that they are simply collecting something they deserve.

This is not the case with public-assistance programs like food stamps, Medicaid, and AFDC. These programs are "means tested"; eligibility is determined not by past contributions but by a demonstrated level of need. Public-assistance programs are funded from general tax revenues rather than from payroll deduction; recipients may or may not have contributed themselves. Voters, therefore, are quicker to perceive those assistance programs as unfair burdens on taxpayers.

Targeting. Not all of the benefits of the various programs broadly characterized as social welfare go to the poor or even the near poor. For some of the programs, eligibility is closely linked to actual need. This is the case, for instance, with AFDC. Federal law requires that each state develop a statewide standard of need, which is to be used in determining eligibility and the amount of the assistance payment. States are free to choose their own method of deriving such a need standard, however, "with the result that many States define need in vague general terms" (U.S. Department of Health and Human Services, 1982).

Food stamps also are targeted almost exclusively at the poor and near poor. To qualify for food stamps, a household must have less than $1,500 in disposable wealth ($3,000 in a two- or more person household in which one member is at least sixty years of age) and income that, after certain deductions, meets poverty guidelines (U.S. Department of Health and Human Services, 1980). The actual value of the coupons provided depends on income and household size. As of January 1, 1981, an eligible, four-person household with no income could receive up to $233 worth of coupons per month. One-person households just meeting the income cutoff might receive as little as $10 per month.

For programs like Social Security and Medicare, need has very little relationship to eligibility. Those programs were instituted in response to the high levels of poverty that were found among the elderly. In 1959, for example, 35.2 percent of those people sixty-five and over lived in poverty, compared to 22.4 percent among the population at large. Largely because of Social Security and Medicare benefits, recent census statistics reveal that the per capita income among the elderly now may actually be higher than that for the population at large.

Because they are insurance programs, Social Security and Medicare provide benefits to those who contributed to the system, regardless of how wealthy they may be. *Of families headed by an elderly person, about 92 percent of those receiving Social Security payments are not poor* (U.S. Department of Health and Human Services, 1980). Those who earned the highest salaries prior to retirement—those who, therefore, made the largest contributions to the Social Security fund—are those who receive the greatest monthly payments. Unemployment, similarly, is often associated with poverty, but most of the unemployed who are eligible for payments have savings and own possessions normally not associated with poverty status. Many recipients have spouses; their household income may boost them well above official poverty levels.

Does it make sense for the federal government to send a $500 check to a retired millionaire whose private investments bring in twenty times that amount? If the goal is the efficient use of limited resources in caring for the poor, the answer would seem to be no. It is the breadth of the recipient population, however, that has given Social Security and Medicare the sizable and influential political constituency that has enabled the program to grow, even in the face of widespread budget cuts in other areas. In addition, because the programs are so large, Social Security and Medicare provide more money to poor people than any other program. Without governmental aid of any kind, 55.1 percent of the elderly in this country would be poor. Social-insurance programs reduce this figure by about 85 percent, to a poverty rate of 7.9 percent. The impact of means-tested cash-assistance programs is much smaller; their effect is to reduce the poverty rate a little further, to only 5.6 percent (Stockman, 1983).

Myths and Realities

Who Gets Welfare? Martin Anderson points out a paradox in Americans' attitudes toward poverty and welfare. Most Americans favor providing help to the poor. Yet most Americans also harbor deep resentments toward our current welfare system. One national survey asked how serious a loss it would be if welfare expenditures were cut by one-third; fully 58 percent answered that it would be "hardly a loss at all" or only a "moderate loss" (Anderson, 1978).

Resentment toward welfare often is based not on information but on stereotype and anecdote. The welfare family is envisioned, almost exclusively, as a racial or ethnic minority living in the inner city. Welfare families also are perceived as unusually large families; some critics even charge that lower-class women may deliberately have additional children just to increase their benefits. It is presumed, quite often, that welfare recipients are able to work but choose not to do so. Many, it is claimed, are not even poor. This image, although politically potent, is only partially based on fact.

The realities about welfare include:

- *Most recipients are white:* In 1979, there were about 3.4 million families receiving Aid to Families with Dependent Children. Just over half (51.7 percent) were white; 43.9 percent were black, and 4.4 percent were American Indians or members of another racial minority. Recipients of Supplemental Insurance Income aid are even more likely to be white. Of the approximately 4.1 million SSI recipients in 1980, 63.6 percent were white and 27.5 percent were black. It is true that blacks are overrepresented among recipients; in 1980, blacks made up 11.7 percent of the total population in the United States.
- *Most recipients are unable to work:* The most obvious reason is that most are children. Of the 11.1 million individuals receiving AFDC, 7.6 million (68.5 percent) are children; over two-thirds of these are under age eleven. Almost nine out of every ten of the children receiving AFDC have no father living at home; in another 5.3 percent of the cases, the father is incapacitated. About 1.8 million (43.7 percent) SSI recipients are aged; 78,000 (1.9 percent) are blind; 2.3 million (54.5 percent) are disabled.
- *Welfare families are not unusually large:* About 42.5 percent of all AFDC families have only one child; another 28 percent have only two children.
- *Many who are eligible for welfare programs do not enroll:* According to one study, the participation rate among families legally eligible for food stamps is only about 40 percent. That same study estimates that only 55 percent of those eligible for SSI are enrolled in the program (Hill, et al., 1981). Lack of knowledge about the programs is the most frequently cited reason. Especially likely to be unaware are the elderly, employed, childless, and those not receiving any other form of aid.

The Dynamics of Welfare. One issue that is of concern to analysts at all points on the ideological spectrum is the possibility that existing welfare policies may have the effect of creating and maintaining a permanent welfare class. Although welfare certainly does not accommodate a comfortable life-style, it may, in some states, compare favorably with the minimum wage and part-time jobs that are available to the relatively unskilled. Given the low wages, insecurity, unpleasant working conditions, lack of opportunity for advancement, taxes, and commuting costs associated with holding a job, it would not be surprising to find that some recipients might "settle in" to welfare life. Children raised in such families, it is feared, may develop habits of dependency at an early age. They may carry the tradition of welfare into their own life and pass it on to subsequent generations. The threat that such a permanent welfare class is in the making is of concern to those primarily on the political right, who resent the need to impose the burden of supporting this dependent underclass on the productive middle class. It also is of concern to those primarily on the political left, who see a link between personal dependency and political impotence; conditions of dependence may generate fear, fatalism, and insecurities that undermine the potential for the political mobilization of the poor.

There is growing evidence, however, that the core of long-term recipients is matched in size by a rotating pool of individuals and families who are pushed onto welfare by short-term forces, then pull themselves off again as soon as possible. *Welfare, for most who use it, is a way station, not a permanent trap.* For many recipients—long-term as well as short-term—welfare and food stamps are supplements to earned income; dependency is not complete. A national sample of about 12,500 persons was followed and resurveyed each year between 1969 and 1978. That study found that approximately one-fifth of all households received welfare (AFDC, SSI, Social Security, food stamps, or general assistance) at some time during the ten-year period but that less than 10 percent received more than one-half of their income from welfare. "Long term welfare receipt," the study concluded, "is the exception rather than the rule." Of all the welfare recipients over the ten years, one-third received aid during only a single year, and only about one-fourth received aid during six or more of those years (Coe, 1981, p. 160).

Living on Welfare. One of the semi-hits of the spring of 1970 was a country and western single called "Welfare Cadillac." Recorded by Guy Drake, the song chronicled, through the eyes of a working man, the rich and unfettered life supposedly enjoyed by welfare recipients. The song and its popularity reflected the widely shared belief that for many welfare and food-stamp recipients the living is easy. Is welfare too generous? In our well-meaning efforts to rescue the poor from abject and dehumanizing poverty, have we gone too far; have we created for the poor a sheltered and comfortable existence underwritten by the sweat and labors of an overburdened middle class?

When one considers the size of the grants involved, it is hard to make a case that any one of the programs constituting our welfare system is overly generous. Consider AFDC. In 1980, the average monthly payment per family was $280. On a yearly basis, this would provide $3,360, or about one-third the poverty level for a family of four. In some states, welfare recipients do a lot better. In California, the average monthly payment was $399; in Hawaii, it was $386; in Michigan, it was $379 (U.S. Bureau of the Census, 1981, p. 345). An AFDC family in Mississippi, however, could expect to receive only $88 per month, South Carolinians received $107, and Texans received $109.

Secretary of Agriculture John R. Block decided, during the summer of 1983, to see for himself whether the allotments under his department's food-stamp program were adequate. The millionaire farmer, his wife, his teenage daughter, and her friend spent one week adhering to the "thrifty meal plan" designed for low-income families. They pledged to spend no more than fifty-eight dollars, the maximum allowed for a family of four with no other income. Sue Block, according to the *Washington Post* report, "was sobered by the amount of time and restraint required to adhere to the stringent budget." Secretary Block "said he 'missed most' his weekly ice cream sundae, and would have liked to have had a beer or soft drink during the sticky Washington evenings during the last week." But Block found the diet "quite adequate"; no one even lost weight (Fishman, 1983).

The thrifty food plan was developed in 1975 to replace the "economy food plan," which had been used to determine food-stamp allotments in prior years. The economy plan has been criticized for being severely inadequate; the Department of Agriculture itself considered the diet appropriate only for short-term use.

The fifty-eight-dollar allowance provides less than seventy cents per person per meal. It assumes that poor families can shop extremely carefully, obtain bulk-rate prices, and prepare all of their meals at home. It does not take sales tax into account.

Nobody doubts the fact that a healthy, normally well-fed family such as Secretary Block's can live on such a diet for a week with no harmful effects beyond inconvenience. But extended reliance on this diet by a family that may not have a car to drive to the stores with the lowest prices, or a family with growing children younger than the two nineteen-year-olds in the Block household, could be infeasible. Poor diets are blamed by some nutritionists for physical and mental impairments among the children and newborn infants of the poor. Doctors at the Boston City Hospital studied 400 children who were under the age of five; they found that, because of poor nutrition, three times as many as expected were at the bottom of the growth charts for children their age.

AFDC and food stamps are insufficient, in and of themselves, to provide more than a very meager life-style. But consideration of these programs in isolation may present a more dismal picture than is warranted. "[M]ost poor people receiving welfare," according to Martin Anderson, "have numerous other sources of income" (Anderson, 1978, p. 32). Many work. About one-half of the cash income received by poor families comes from earnings. Because this estimate is based on reported earnings—and does not include that obtained through illegal activities, or occasional baby-sitting, handyman, domestic, or day-labor activities that might not be reported—it probably overestimates the extent to which many poor families are dependent upon the public assistance they receive.

Others may be able to *pyramid* the aid they are provided by taking part in more than one program. Anderson cites the admittedly "atypical case" of one welfare mother who was highlighted in a story by the *Boston Globe*. The cash value of the various benefits provided to this mother was estimated to be $16,028. Because the aid is not taxable, this would be equivalent to about what a working family earning $20,000 before taxes could anticipate having for its own needs.

Yet the extent to which pyramiding significantly improves the quality of life among poor families is easily exaggerated. Most pyramiding is done by elderly households, which collect both Social Security and Medicare. Nearly 18 million households collected Social Security along with at least one in-kind benefit during 1979; but most of these households were not poor. Of the approximately 11 million poor households, only 3.8 million (35 percent) received welfare plus at least one noncash benefit; only 1.8 million (16 percent) received public cash assistance along with three or more in-kind programs (U.S. Bureau of the Census, 1981, p. 323). "Cashing out" the equivalent of in-kind expenditures, moreover, can be a misleading indicator of their impact on the lives of the poor. Of the $16,000 in benefits that Anderson reports as going to the Boston welfare mother, $6,000 consisted of subsidized tuition for her older children, $1,000 came in the form of day care for her youngest child, and $1,750 consisted of estimated health-care costs that would be covered under Medicaid. This leaves only $7,250 to cover all other necessary expenditures, including food, rent, transportation, clothing, utilities, and the rest. A family with particularly severe health-care needs, or a family that fully exploits all subsidized educational and training opportunities, might receive aid with a substantial cash equivalency—but one could hardly argue that such families are, by virtue of this, living high off the hog.

When it comes to describing life on welfare, the simple stereotypes just do not apply. Stories of high living on welfare are built on a shaky foundation—a small proportion of recipients engaging in wholesale fraud; a failure to understand that many recipients earn most of their own money and are as free as others to spend it as they please; misinterpretation of the sight of a food-stamp family, with a bulging supermarket cart, buying in bulk to get lower prices, spending a month's worth of stamps at once rather than risk their theft.

Just as inaccurate, in many cases, may be the tales of the destitute recipient managing a bare subsistence as dictated by the welfare budget alone. Many welfare families *can and do* manage to provide themselves with a decent and dignified life-style. They do so by taking advantage of the programs offered, by working when possible, by spending wisely, and by cheating in small ways. Even for these families, however, the existence is a perilous and distressing one. Because several programs have strict limits on the assets a recipient may own, saving is not feasible, even for those who might be able to squirrel away a few dollars here and there. Only the strictest of budgeting makes a decent life-style possible. The few "treats" that make living worthwhile—taking the family to a movie once a month, the purchase of a winter coat that is not third- or fourth-hand, buying a wedding present for a close friend or relative, a cool beer on a sweltering night—come at a heavy cost. An unanticipated event—a sudden illness, loss of a part-time baby-sitting job, a welfare check that is late—can upset the precarious balance. For those who *are* getting by on welfare, there is little or no margin of error; it is a hard and tension-ridden existence. That it can nonetheless provide for basic needs, a chance for advancement, and an element of personal discretion is a mark that the system is moving in the right direction.

The Evolution of Welfare in a Federal System

Our welfare system today bears the clear stamp of the national government. It is to the national Social Security Act of 1935 that we can trace Social Security, unemployment compensation, AFDC, and the separate aid programs for the aged, blind, and permanently disabled that were merged, in 1974, to form SSI. More recent innovations—food stamps (1961), Medicare (1965), and Medicaid (1965)—were also born in Washington, D.C.

But caring for the poor has not always been considered a national government responsibility in the United States. Throughout early American history, welfare was marked by local efforts. Friends and neighbors provided aid to widows and orphans—the "worthy poor." During the nineteenth century, the states became gradually more active. It was not until the 1930s, in the aftermath of the Great Depression, that the national government moved onto center stage.

This section reviews the history of the shift toward a more centralized social-welfare system. It is important for a couple of reasons. Some recent proposals for the reform of our welfare system have called for a return to the tradition of localism that guided the provision of aid to the poor in this country from colonial times. Understanding the shift toward more central control may help in evaluating the calls to reverse that shift.

In addition, understanding the history of our welfare system can help us to make sense of the complexity that otherwise is bewildering and seemingly irrational. Although it is common to assume that welfare policy somehow "belongs" to the national realm, welfare is a perfect example of "marble cake federalism"—the *sharing* of responsibility across the levels of government. States and localities have not been relegated to the sidelines in the task of caring for the poor. Most states have their own general assistance programs, the specifics of which vary markedly from place to place, that provide cash payments to some of the poor who are not eligible for the various federal programs. Many public education and health programs that provide significant benefits to the poor are funded and directed at the state and local levels as well.

The states, and some localities, are integrally involved in the funding and administration of many of the nominally national programs. Unemployment compensation, AFDC, and Medicaid are examples of programs funded jointly by the federal and state/local levels, and in which the states have considerable discretion in determining who can receive aid and how much aid they may receive. States determine, for example, whether families headed by unemployed fathers are eligible for AFDC (in twenty-nine states, including Alaska, Idaho, Indiana, Iowa, Maine, New Hampshire, Oregon, Washington, and nearly all of the South and Southwest, they are not), and whether Medicaid benefits will cover such optional expenditures as dental services, physical therapy, prescribed drugs, dentures, eyeglasses, and certain kinds of mental and psychiatric care. States determine welfare-benefit levels and whether poor residents other than those eligible for AFDC and SSI can be covered by Medicaid.

This sharing is one major reason why the system is so complex; indeed, it is fair to say that we have many systems, each with its own regulations, biases, priorities, and styles. Although it is based in part on theoretical considerations concerning the proper distribution of power among the levels of government, the particular shape of our intergovernmental approach to welfare owes more to the process of compromise and incrementalism that marks its political history. When new elements were added, old elements were not always replaced. The growth of the state role did not eliminate local involvement; the onset of national involvement did not spell the end of a significant state role.

From Localities to the States: Centralization in the Nineteenth and Twentieth Centuries. Localism, as a welfare strategy, is best suited for a society made up of relatively small, stable, and cohesive communities in which people have a desire and capacity to "take care of our own." Early America resembled such a society. It is in such a context that individuals are least threatened by the poor and most able to identify with the poor as persons who are similar to them—they may be relatives or acquaintances—but who have simply come upon hard times. It is in such a context that private and voluntary impulses to charity are most likely to be forthcoming and public efforts less burdensome and intrusive.

As the nation developed and industrialized, some of the conditions that made localism workable began to change. Communities became larger, more heterogeneous, more anonymous. Populations became more mobile; families and individuals moved across the country looking for jobs or a better way of life. The nature of the poverty problem also changed. In an agricultural society, able-bodied men were able to provide for themselves as long as they could gain access to land to farm. With industrialization came swings in the business cycle that sometimes left large numbers of males unemployed.

With these changes came pressures that local institutions were not fully able to meet. Population mobility posed a problem to local governments in the form of growing numbers of *wandering poor.* And business cycles exposed *fiscal limitations,* as localities found they simply could not afford to meet the welfare needs of those who looked to them for aid. The states, sometimes reluctantly, found themselves stepping into the breach.

Even in the largely stable, rural environment of the seventeenth, eighteenth, and nineteenth centuries there existed the phenomenon of the wandering or unsettled poor, individuals with no clearly established residences who fell, therefore, outside the bounds of communal sentiment. The early colonies dealt with the unfamiliar poor by limiting assistance to those who met strict residency requirements and by dealing harshly with strangers who did not have readily identifiable means of self-support.

> ... New England officials scrutinized the economic status of strangers; shipmasters were required to post bond to cover the possible dependency of passengers. Poor migrants to an area usually endured a waiting period before they could become official residents. Those strangers who appeared to be potential paupers could be requested to leave ("warned out"), then fined or otherwise punished if they refused (Feagin, 1975, p. 25).

It was the need to provide some protection for the unsettled poor that first drew the states into playing a direct welfare role. Rather than displacing the local welfare function, the states moved in to fill a gap. They did so, moreover, in a gingerly and hesitant fashion; wherever possible, responsibility was to remain at the lower level. For example, in 1795 Connecticut accepted responsibility for "any noninhabitant who needs relief for the duration of three months, after which expenses are to be paid by the town" (Advisory Commission on Intergovernmental Relations, 1980, p. 7). Even as the states began to take on greater responsibilities for welfare, the tradition of limiting aid to "our own" remained: many states continued to exercise strict residency requirements until the Supreme Court ruled them unconstitutional in 1969.

Inability of local jurisdictions to meet extreme welfare burdens due to unusual occurrences was a second prod to the expansion of the states' role. By the end of the nineteenth century, states were showing increasing willingness to supplement local welfare efforts in the area of disaster relief. "In the Midwest and Plains states, particularly, disaster relief was extended to unfortunate farmers and settlers visited upon by 'Acts of God' " (Advisory Commission on Intergovernmental Relations, 1980, p. 8). Inefficiency and corruption at the local level made a bad situation worse. Lynn writes that "deplorable conditions and abuses in the local welfare programs contributed to the impetus behind the reform-oriented movement to establish state-run asylums in the decades preceding the Civil War" (Lynn, 1980).

The Civil War created additional unusual welfare needs in many localities, which were suddenly faced with an expansion of their needy populations in the form of wounded civilians and veterans, farmers and businessmen whose properties were destroyed, and emancipated blacks who were freed from slavery only, in many cases, to face greater economic hardship than ever before. By this time, moreover, even "normal" times were presenting local governments with tremendous welfare demands: "the needs generated by the Civil War were compounded in the decades following by continued migration and immigration, the accelerated pace of industrialization, and the effects of recurring depressions, all of which created near crisis conditions in the larger cities by the turn of the century" (Lynn, 1980, p. 20).

Philosophies of welfare also were changing in ways that encouraged a stronger state role. It was in the 1870s and 1880s that some reformers successfully pushed for a greater reliance on "indoor relief," the institutionalization of the needy in almshouses, where their physical support could be more directly linked to their moral reform. Although some reformers hoped that indoor relief recipients could be forced to work in order to pay for their own care, the costs of indoor relief proved to be high, again necessitating the financial support of the states. State aid to mothers with dependent children was first provided by Illinois, in 1911. By 1926, all but eight states offered some version of "mothers' aid." Twenty-five states established social welfare or public welfare agencies between 1917 and 1929 (Patterson, 1981).

By the time of the Great Depression, then, states were beginning to establish themselves more clearly as partners of the local governments in the function of providing for the poor. But even then the state role was spotty, and many states were proving less than enthusiastic about accepting this additional and costly responsibility. Only 93,260 of the 3.8 million female-headed families in the United States were receiving mothers' assistance from the states in 1931. The average grant in Arkansas was only $4.33 per month. In addition, most states remained anxious to bar the door to the mobile poor; in 1929, eighteen states refused aid to those living in the state for less than two years" (Patterson, 1981, p. 29).

The Great Depression burst upon this relatively fragile support network with the force of a tidal wave. In 1933, unemployment reached about 15 million, and an estimated 18 million were receiving some sort of relief. Unable to pay their bills, many local governments defaulted. Philadelphia had developed a municipal relief program considered to be among the most effective in the nation. The city was spending an unprecedented $1 million per month by 1931, "yet so many people turned out for help that needy families could get but $1.50 to $2 per person per week in grocery orders" (Patterson, 1981, pp. 55–7). By June of 1932, both the city and the local private charities had exhausted all of their funds.

Suddenly, states were forced to take a more aggressive role than they had been willing to take in calmer times. In September 1931, New York State passed legislation providing for the state to reimburse local governments for 40 percent of their unemployment relief expenditures; by January 1932, twenty-four states had appointed administrators to provide relief on a statewide basis (Advisory Commission on Intergovernmental Relations, 1980).

The Federal Government Steps In. As even the state treasuries began to be overwhelmed, pressure grew for a national response. President Herbert Hoover, loyal to the traditions of localism, was loath to see the national government take a major role—charity and local efforts could, he insisted, support the added load. With the election of Franklin Roosevelt, that hesitancy in the White House disappeared. The Federal Emergency Relief Act of 1933 put the federal government into the business of providing grants to states for the provision of welfare services and gave federal officials completely unprecedented powers to oversee, and in extreme cases assume control over, the administration of relief by the states. The stage was set for the passage of the Social Security Act of 1935, which moved the federal role from one of temporary and emergency relief to one of stable and major responsibility.

Although dramatic, the movement of the federal government into the social-welfare business did not replace the fragmented and decentralized welfare hodgepodge with a comprehensive, centralized welfare system. Even in the atmosphere of crisis, the tradition of localism remained strong. And the ties of tradition were backed by the continued political clout of interests anxious to resist additional threats to the general concept of states' rights. The bill to establish Aid to Dependent Children (later to become Aid to Families with Dependent Children) initially required states to provide a "reasonable subsistence compatible with decency and health." Opposition by southern conservatives—framed in the name of states' rights—led Congress to diminish that requirement. As finally passed, the key clause merely asked states to fund the programs "as far as practicable under the conditions in such states" (Patterson, 1981, p. 68).

Also working against comprehensive reform was the fact that many of the antipoverty actions taken by the national government during this period were perceived, at the time, as a temporary response to a crisis situation. Programs such as Aid to Dependent Children were expected to "wither away" as the economy strengthened and as Social Security took care of the needs of the elderly poor (Steiner, 1966).

But the demand for a federal welfare role did not disappear. Even as the economy improved, a growing class of female-headed welfare-dependent households was beginning to develop into a more permanent dependent group. This group was not in a position to benefit markedly from an improving economy.

One War . . . Or Localized Skirmishes? As the nation recovered from the Great Depression, many Americans found it easy to convince themselves that poverty, as a large-scale policy problem, was a thing of the past. It was not until the publication of Michael Harrington's *The Other America,* in 1962, that the nation came to grips with the fact that general prosperity could mask a poverty that was genuine and widespread.

That poverty had proven more obstinate than expected seemed to provide proof that a more comprehensive and intensive attack was needed. Unlike the situation in the 1930s, moreover, the idea that the national government had a legitimate role to play was already accepted. The stage was set for a further expansion of central control.

The result was the War on Poverty. Because the supposed failure of this federal effort plays so important a role in shaping current proposals for decentralizing and privatizing the welfare function, it is particularly important to separate policy as declared from policy as carried out. The rhetoric with which the War on Poverty was launched suggested a more comprehensive, theoretically unified, centrally directed onslaught than was, in fact, delivered.

Poverty, President Johnson reasoned, "cannot be driven from the land by a single attack on a single front." Accordingly, the War on Poverty was designed as a multitactic assault. But multiplicity of tactics ought not necessarily to be confused with breadth and depth of commitment. According to one estimate, the War on Poverty legislation provided only about a half billion dollars in new program commitments (Lowi, 1979, p. 211)—small potatoes when compared to the more than $2 billion being spent on the *real* war being waged in Vietnam by 1968 (*U.S. News and World Report,* 1968).

Nor should multiple tactics be assumed to represent a theoretically cohesive approach. Some neoconservative accounts seem to suggest that the War on Poverty programs were designed by radical structuralists and unified by the theme that poverty cannot be eliminated unless the capitalist system is fundamentally reformed. It is more accurate to label the programs "a mixed bag" (Lynn, 1977, p. 66). In order to broaden support for what might have been a controversial piece of legislation, efforts were made to ensure that something was included for nearly every relevant and potentially powerful interest. This unavoidably came at the cost of coherence and theoretical consistency.

Rather than seeking to restructure society, most of the programs sought primarily to reshape the poor, to provide them with the education and job skills that would enable them to compete more successfully. Most of these programs, in keeping with a culture-of-poverty perspective, were focused primarily on the young. *Head Start* was to provide pre-kindergarten schooling to educationally deprived children so that they would be better prepared by the time their formal schooling began. *Upward Bound* was to find bright but underachieving high-school students from low-income families and prepare and orient them to pursue higher education, usually by sending them to summer sessions on college campuses. *Neighborhood Youth Corps* provided federal assistance to state and local programs that hired low-income teenagers for part-time and summer community projects, the idea being to provide work experience and needed income while reducing the pressures on such youths to drop out of high school in search of a full-time job. *Job Corps* arranged for high-school students to be given two years of job training and education in basic-skills centers located away from the distractions and potentially corrupting influences of their homes and neighborhoods.

Only two major programs seemed "more concerned with restructuring the social institutions by which the poor gained access to jobs and goods and services, and less concerned with the personal traits of the poor" (Haveman, 1977, p. 5). The *Legal Services* program was intended to ensure that the poor were not denied rights to which they were entitled due to prohibitive legal costs. The *Community Action Program,* the most controversial of all the elements of the poverty war, provided a decision-making role for the poor by requiring the establishment of local Community Action Agencies that included representatives of the poor. These CAAs would, in theory, coordinate the delivery of services in their neighborhoods, make decisions regarding the specific mix and style of the programs undertaken, and provide the poor with a greater sense of involvement and commitment.

Other programs that are associated with the War on Poverty include Medicare and Medicaid; Title I of the Elementary and Secondary Education Act of 1965, which provided federal aid to the states for compensatory education for disadvantaged children; VISTA, which sent volunteer workers into poor communities as a domestic counterpart to the Peace Corps; and expanded food-stamp and school-lunch programs.

Although some of these programs were attacked at the time as radical public-sector intrusions into the functioning of the free market economy, *the emphasis was on equalizing opportunity so that the poor could compete, like others, in the private sphere.* There was no presumption that the economic system was faulty or unjust by its nature; emphasis was on changing the poor to fit the system, not restructuring the system to benefit the poor. Nearly all of the job-training programs were premised, in fact, on the assumption that the private sector would be ready and willing to hire the poor, black, and disadvantaged once they were provided with skills—an assumption that experience did not always bear out. In a few cities, the CAAs did emerge as direct and radical political challenges to the existing political order. It was the example and rhetoric of these cases that gave credibility to the charge that the Economic Opportunity Act's call for the "maximum feasible participation" of the poor was, in fact, a blueprint for a basic restructuring of the political system. In a few cities, Legal Services became party to class-action suits that challenged state and local authorities, claiming, and sometimes winning, vast expansions in the rights of the poor to services and privacy. But CAAs and Legal Services most often posed no such unsettling threat. In most cities, they engaged primarily or exclusively in conventional service delivery and noncontroversial legal action. That these programs could vary so notably from jurisdiction to jurisdiction, however, brings us to another significant point.

Although the War on Poverty was characterized as representing an overly centralized federal intrusion into state and local affairs, *the major mechanisms for implementing the programs were highly decentralized.* The states were given substantial discretion in determining the precise uses of federal dollars in such programs as Title I and Medicaid. Localities and school districts could choose among various strategies in deciding how to implement Head Start and other educational and training programs. Much of the criticism made by state and local officials about federal intrusion was based on a concern that the programs were *too decentralized,* putting some decision-making authority at the level of the low-income community and bypassing state and local officials entirely.

In one sense, then, it is possible to say that there was no War on Poverty; instead, there were many localized skirmishes. Many of the so-called federal programs were federal in name and funding source; style, strategy, and substance varied, often considerably, from place to place. Blame for the failure to eliminate poverty, then, must be dispersed as well. It will not do to attribute all the shortcomings of the social-welfare policies of the 1960s to a monolithic national government seeking to impose its own pet theories on the cities and states.

Three Views of the "Welfare Mess"

Complexity makes it likely that differing groups, with differing ideologies and political interests, will find something in the present welfare system to like. But, clearly, this kind of complexity makes it even more likely that many people from differing perspectives will find something that they consider terribly wrong. Politicians of all political stripes and at all levels of government have found they can strike a responsive chord by making a target of the "welfare mess." Yet reformers on the right and on the left have quite different changes in mind, including quite different notions of what the proper role for state and local governments should be. There is, moreover, a middle-ground position, one that acknowledges the awkwardness and inconsistencies of the current system yet concludes that the system is functioning more effectively than is generally recognized.

View From the Right. The most vocal and insistent criticisms of the existing social-welfare arrangements in this country have come from conservative and neoconservative spokespersons from the political right. Their criticisms have focused on the issues of rising costs, fraud and abuse, disincentives to work, threats to the family, and the political clout of the welfare bureaucracy.

During the 1960s, the cost of providing for the poor increased dramatically. This was partially due to the institution of new programs, such as food stamps, Medicare, and Medicaid. But just as dramatic—and politically more controversial—was a sharp increase in the cost of a program born three decades before: Aid to Families with Dependent Children. During the 1950s, AFDC rolls had risen by about 17 percent; over the next ten years, they more than doubled. In the five largest urban counties—those including New York City, Philadelphia, Chicago, Detroit, and Los Angeles—the number of welfare cases more than tripled (Piven and Cloward, 1971).

Several factors accounted for this increase. The most apparent cause, at the time, was the *increased generosity of the benefits and the liberalizing of eligibility requirements* in some states. Between 1960 and 1970, the average monthly payment to an AFDC family rose nearly 75 percent, from $105.75 to $183.13 (U.S. Department of Health and Human Services, 1980, p. 232). Increased benefits drew a firestorm of criticism from conservatives, who charged that middle-class taxpayers were being forced to subsidize the whims and luxuries of the unproductive.

Probably more troublesome to conservatives than the absolute cost of social welfare has been the perception that much of this cost is unnecessary; conservative critics of welfare charge that much of the *money is going to persons who are ineligible, because their incomes are too high, or to able-bodied persons who should and could be working instead.* There is no question but that fraud and abuse do occur. Consider, for example, the case of Dorothy Mae Palmer, California's "welfare queen." State welfare officials charged her with having bilked the state out of more than $350,000 in AFDC, food stamp, and medical benefits. Investigators suggested that she had used nine aliases to file claims for herself and thirty-eight nonexistent children. Police, arriving to arrest her at her $250,000 home, discovered that she owned six late-model luxury cars, including a Cadillac, Lincoln, and Mercedes-Benz (O'Brien, 1981).

Such examples are undoubtedly extreme, but there is reason enough to expect that the incomes of many other welfare recipients are higher than they admit. Illegal income, derived from traffic in drugs, gambling, prostitution, or theft, along with legally obtained, but undeclared, income such as tips earned by waiters and waitresses and hire-for-cash services by handymen, day laborers, and the like, constitute a massive "underground economy" that rarely shows itself on welfare applications or income-tax forms. Estimates of the size of the underground economy are notoriously unreliable. The Internal Revenue Service estimates that unreported income increased from $29 billion in 1973 to $87 billion in 1979. Most of this underground economy involves those who most definitely are *not* poor—doctors, lawyers, businessmen, salespeople, and the like (Cowan, 1982).

Although the possibility that some welfare recipients are exploiting the programs is disturbing, conservative critics raise what may be an even more distressing specter with their consideration of the role of welfare in promoting dependency. Welfare, they charge, is not simply supporting the poor; it may be *helping to create poverty and to maintain poverty by undermining the incentive for the poor to seek jobs.* At its most emotional level, this concern with dependency is manifested in popular complaints about welfare recipients as "chiselers" and "parasites." But there is a deeper concern as well. If some neoconservative critics of the welfare system are correct, the problem lies not only in the personal values or lack of ambition of the poor but in the structure of the system itself—a system that may make it *irrational* for the welfare family to seek work.

As earnings rise—because the recipient finds a better job or because an older child or the spouse finds work—benefits are reduced. At the same time, taxes, especially Social Security taxes, rise. A family that is unlucky enough to have its new earnings push its income above the threshold that determines eligibility for Medicaid might even find that its added income has left its members worse off than they were before. Anderson cites the example of a mother of three receiving benefits from AFDC, Medicaid, food stamps, and public housing. For each dollar of the first $700 per month that she would earn, if she could find a full-time job, she would stand to lose about 80¢ in benefits.

> Why should someone work forty hours a week, fifty weeks a year for, say, $8,000, when it would be possible not to work at all for, say, $6,000? People on welfare may be poor, but they are not fools. Any rational calculation of the net returns from working by someone on welfare would discourage any but the most doggedly determined (Anderson, 1978, p. 47).

The result, concludes Anderson, is a " 'poverty wall' that destroys the financial incentive to work for millions of Americans. Free from basic wants, but heavily dependent on the State, with little hope of breaking free, they are a new caste, the 'Dependent Americans' " (Anderson, 1978, p. 43).

Another criticism of welfare, associated with but not limited to the political right, centers on concerns that the current welfare system may *encourage the breakup of families.* "Often a male head of household may absent himself from his wife and children in order to maintain [their] eligibility for welfare. This situation arises because male heads of households are presumed to work and therefore not eligible for welfare" (Dobelstein, 1980, p. 134).

A major policy experiment conducted in Seattle and Denver indicates that some forms of cash assistance are associated with higher rates of family breakup. Families that were guaranteed a minimum income as part of the experiment tended to show higher rates of breakup than the "control" groups, which had no such guarantee. The relationship was relatively weak, however, and decreased with the amount of the promised assistance; some other studies have found no relationship between assistance and family dissolution at all. "Thus," as one review of the evidence concludes, "while there is some support for high AFDC payment levels being a marriage destabilizer, there is very little support for its being a powerful destabilizer" (Bishop, 1981, p. 389).

Finally, there is concern among neoconservatives and others on the political right about a political implication of welfare. Along with the expansion of social-welfare legislation has come an *expansion of the bureaucracy* that administers the programs at each level of government. This bureaucracy is somewhat insulated from popular control and may have goals of its own, goals that do not coincide with those of the electorate or with the interests of the nation as a whole. Some critics of the existing welfare system argue, in fact, that it has been the needs and interests of this bureaucratic class, rather than those of the lower-income constituency it claims to serve, that has shaped our welfare system. They argue that this bureaucratic class has masked its own interest with its claim to be helping others, and that much of the resources devoted to public welfare are absorbed by the bureaucracy, never reaching the poor families who were the intended targets.

View from the Left. Liberal and radical analysts of the American welfare system also are generally critical, although not for the same reasons. They challenge, for example, the conservatives' argument that increased benefits and liberalized policies account for the escalating cost of welfare. They suggest that more significant than the increase in benefit levels—which, after all, remained quite low—were two changes of a more fundamental and long-lasting character. The first had to do with demographic changes in the American public. The population of the country was slowly changing, and it was changing in ways that were leading to a greater need for the kind of support that AFDC offered. Most notable of these demographic changes was the sharp increase in the number and proportion of single-parent, especially female-headed, families. In 1960, 4,194,000 families—about 9.3 percent of all families—were headed by a female with no spouse present. The number of female-headed families increased by 1.4 million (33.3 percent) between 1960 and 1970, and by an *additional* 2.9 million (52 percent) between 1970 and 1980 (U.S. Bureau of the Census, 1981, p. 48).

To note that greater numbers of households needed and were eligible for AFDC is not, in itself, enough to explain the growing cost of the program. Since the program had begun, many more families were eligible than had ever actually applied for and received benefits. It was political change, not just demographic change, that forced welfare programs to expand. The political activism of the 1960s led to greater organization among the poor, as well as to a redefinition of what poverty meant. Organizations such as the National Welfare Rights Organization preached that the poor should not be ashamed of their poverty, that aid was a right to which they were entitled, not a handout that stigmatized them as failures. This message broke down some of the psychological barriers that had led many poor families to suffer in silence. Lobbying and legal efforts by representatives of the poor broke down some of the administrative barriers that state and local officials had further erected.

Since the early 1970s, moreover, growth in social-welfare expenditures has been due primarily to cost-of-living adjustments in Social Security payments and escalating medical costs under the Medicare and Medicaid programs, *not* to increasingly or overly generous benefits. Benefits from AFDC, in most states, have not even kept pace with inflation. In Texas, in 1973, the maximum cash payment for a family of four on AFDC was $140 per month. By 1981—with the cost of living having risen over 100 percent—the maximum benefit was $141 (Rich, 1982). Nationally, the purchasing power of AFDC benefits declined more than 30 percent between 1970 and 1983 (Rubin, 1983).

Liberal critics, although acknowledging the importance of ferreting out welfare abuse, have focused their attention on *insufficiency and inconsistency of benefits to legitimate recipients*. The average monthly payment per person on AFDC in 1980 was $100 (U.S. Bureau of the Census, 1981, p. 343); the average monthly food-stamp allotment was $34.34 (U.S. Department of Health and Human Services, 1980, p. 82). Liberals question whether this is sufficient to provide a decent and dignified existence.

Whereas food-stamp benefits are set by the national government, and are consistent throughout the country, AFDC and Medicaid benefits very considerably depending upon where one lives. In 1980, the average AFDC payment to a family in California was $399; in Mississippi, the same family would collect only $88 (U.S. Bureau of the Census 1981, p. 345). In Arkansas, in 1970, there were 10 Medicaid recipients for every 100 poor people, while in California—where many nonpoor qualify for benefits—there were 174. Even for those covered by Medicaid, there are wide differences in benefit levels from state to state. In 1974, the average Medicaid recipient from Minnesota received payments more than four times as high as those in Missouri. "For dependent children, payments ranged from a low of $62 in Wyoming to $326 in New York" (Davis and Schoen, 1978, p. 69). "Is it fair," some liberals query, "for a poor family's fate to vary so greatly based simply on where they happen to live?"

Radicals are more critical. Whereas liberals see the problems with welfare as remediable flaws, many radical leftists feel that the system is fundamentally flawed. Liberals see the goal of the system as being the provision of a decent existence even to the poor. Radicals see the goal as a broad redistribution of wealth from the privileged to the needy. Liberals tend to believe that welfare *is* making life better for the poor, though not so efficiently or effectively as they would prefer. Many radicals feel the current social-welfare system actually works against the interest of the poor.

Frances Fox Piven and Richard Cloward, analyzing the history of social welfare in England and the United States, conclude that in capitalist societies, *welfare's primary function is to manipulate the poor and defuse unrest* when it threatens to erupt in political violence or organized dissent. Welfare, they claim, has been expanded not when the needs of the poor are greatest, but when, as during the depression and the middle 1960s, the potential for violence and disruption have been most severe. Once turmoil has been muted, eligibility criteria have been tightened and benefit levels cut back (Piven and Cloward, 1971). Moreover, there is little reason to expect this to change. Rooting their argument in Marxist theory, Piven and Cloward argue that such a pattern of manipulation of welfare is to be expected in capitalist societies because of the need to maintain a pliant and low-cost work force. Marx argued that capitalists must make profits; mainstream economists are unlikely to disagree. In order to make these profits, Marx further argued, capitalists must pay their workers less than the true value of the labor that they provide. Piven and Cloward carry these points to what seems to them the logical conclusion. Only if unemployment is made painful and welfare humiliating and inadequate will workers remain sufficiently intimidated to allow their exploitation by the capitalist class to continue.

A Middle Ground: Welfare as "Messy" but Functioning. Not all analysts offer such a gloomy view of the country's welfare system. "The charges that AFDC has been a colossal failure must be recognized for what they are," write Levitan and Taggart, "simplistic political sloganeering" (Levitan and Taggart, 1976, p. 62). Those who challenge the bleak portraits of the welfare "mess" are not simply apologists for the existing system; they see much in it that is wrong. But they reject the claim by the political right that welfare is a wasteful subsidization of an undeserving poor and a critical threat to family and the work ethic. And they also reject the claim by the left that welfare is a political tool through which the wealthy seek to purchase social peace without addressing genuine human needs.

Three major points characterize this perspective. First, the major social-welfare programs introduced in the mid-1930s and mid-1960s, and subsequent refinements of those programs, have led to a *substantial improvement in the quality of life of the nation's lower-income residents.* Since poverty statistics began to be collected in 1959, the number of persons living in poverty has declined by nearly 15 million. Food stamps, Medicaid, and other in-kind programs make life much more tolerable, even for those whose money income leaves them poor or nearly poor.

Secondly, the chaos and inconsistencies of the welfare hodgepodge may not be as alarming as they initially seem. *Such a fragmented system may be the only practical and feasible response to the political environment in which social-welfare policies in this country must be formed.* It is a fact that many Americans perceive a sharp distinction between the "worthy" and the "unworthy" poor. It is a fact that many see insurance programs, such as Social Security and Medicare, as conferring well-deserved rights, whereas other assistance programs are considered as grudging handouts. It is also a fact that states and localities differ in their orientations toward the poor; some regard the poor as a public responsibility, others as a persistent nuisance.

In this context, what kind of universal, comprehensive social-welfare program could be passed and effectively implemented? In order to gain the needed political support for such a program, its architects might be forced to aim for a lowest common denominator. The relatively generous benefits and automatic cost-of-living adjustments attached to the politically popular Social Security would not be politically acceptable if expanded to a program whose recipients would include large numbers of minority households and the persistently unemployed. The fairly livable AFDC and Medicaid benefits provided in the wealthier and more liberal states, such as California and New York, could not easily be politically or fiscally grafted onto the cultural and economic environments in Mississippi or Arkansas.

The result is that some groups would *do worse* in a uniform system than they currently do now. Significantly, those groups most likely to find their benefits shaved down to meet a uniform standard would be the elderly and the urban poor of the wealthier states—the very groups that make up the most politically astute and mobilized subsets of the general social-welfare coalition.

Finally, *with fragmentation comes a certain element of flexibility.* For those households that are sufficiently informed and aggressive, our current hodgepodge offers a wide range of types of aid from which to pick and choose. "Each program examined in isolation, has important shortcomings and inequities," write Cochran, et al., "but taken together they balance out to some extent and provide for many of the poor a basic minimum standard of living" (Cochran, et al., 1982; p. 224). At the same time that fragmentation makes it possible for some families to pull together the most appropriate "package" of benefits, given their particular needs, it may also serve to protect the welfare system against sudden and unanticipated shocks. Fiscal and political pressures occasionally lead a particular state, or the federal government, to drastically tighten its welfare standards and reduce the benefits available.

The very fragmentation that at one time may leave recipients confused and bewildered can, under such circumstances, provide them with alternative sources of aid. Thus, for example, the harshness of Mississippi's welfare standard is moderated somewhat by federal food-stamp policies that provide greater allotments to those whose income (including assistance payments) is low. Thus, some states and cities also have been able to expand their existing assistance programs in the face of recent cutbacks at the federal level.

LOOKING TOWARD THE FUTURE

Dissatisfaction with the current welfare system is widespread; each new administration issues a call for comprehensive welfare reform. President Nixon proposed a Family Assistance Plan (FAP), which would have provided a federally funded income floor to all Americans, reducing the complexities and inequities caused by state-to-state variations and extending coverage to many childless households and the working poor who fell between the cracks of the existing programs. Under President Ford, the Department of Health, Education, and Welfare proposed an Income Supplement Program, which would have replaced AFDC, SSI, and food stamps with a single cash payment. In September 1977, President Carter submitted to Congress his administration's plan for Better Jobs and Income, which combined proposals for the creation of public-service jobs, tax credits for low-income workers, and a cash grant—replacing AFDC, SSI, and food stamps—guaranteeing a minimum income of $4,200 for a family of four.

Each of these comprehensive reform proposals sought to replace a fragmented system with a centralized and uniform federal system of support.

Each relied on the basic concept of a negative income tax, which establishes some guaranteed minimum level of support, with the size of the income supplement diminishing on a much less than one-to-one basis with each additional dollar the family might earn. Each proved politically infeasible.

The trend today appears to be quite different. Many officials, and much of the American public, have come to regard recent history as evidence that governmental efforts, particularly dramatic federal efforts like the War on Poverty, are destined to be destructive failures. Rather than seeking uniformity and comprehensiveness by moving toward a single, national welfare system, they believe we should grant even greater responsibility and discretion to localities and the states. President Reagan's call for the states to take over the AFDC program reflects this call for decentralization. A decentralized welfare system, it is argued, would be *more efficient,* because it would eliminate one entire level of bureaucracy; it would be *more effective,* because it would allow officials to shape programs to fit the particular needs of the local poor and the particular strengths and weaknesses of the local economy; and it would be *more democratic,* because it would reflect local culture and local ideas about the nature of poverty and the proper role of government in addressing the needs of the poor.

They favor privatization, as well as decentralization, of the welfare function. Two rather different, though complementary forms of privatization are suggested. One emphasizes the role of charity and voluntary efforts. It is argued that such efforts sufficed to deal with the problems throughout most of the country's history. As the government expanded its involvement, however, these grass-roots efforts were pushed aside. Why should we sacrifice to help our friends and neighbors if the government is willing to do the dirty work? The second form of privatization involves economic development as a means of providing jobs. Policies designed to expand the economy can ensure that those who want to work will be able to do so. Under such circumstances, those who refuse to work can be forced to, or face the loss of their benefits.

The last section of this chapter considers the prospects for welfare policy if the call for decentralization and privatization is heeded. Although states, localities, voluntary efforts, and economic development have much to offer, they are not a panacea. Each has its own limits. These limits are substantial enough that policy-makers should be wary about dismantling the existing national welfare system. A step in the direction of decentralization and privatization might prove to be a step backwards.

Localism and its Limits

The nation's shift from a localized to a more centralized welfare system was not an accident of history. Nor can it simply be attributed, as some suggest, to bureaucratic and governmental imperialism that leads public officials always to seek to expand their powers and big government always to seek to become bigger. As our economy became more industrialized and national, and as our population became more mobile and less able to support itself through farming or crafts, the limitations of the traditional welfare system were exposed. Two manifestations of these limitations, we suggested earlier, were the inability to handle the wandering poor and the inability to handle the financial drain imposed by economic or natural disasters. There is no reason to expect these limitations have become less meaningful or less troublesome in recent years.

The Wandering Poor. The wandering poor pose a problem for a decentralized welfare system because each jurisdiction has a financial incentive to pass on the responsibility of caring for the poor to another city or state. States that might otherwise wish to improve their coverage or expand benefits are faced with a painful dilemma: any attempt to provide better protection for their own residents may spur an influx of poor from other parts of the country, putting an insupportable fiscal burden upon their treasury.

There is some reason to fear, moreover, that this dilemma posed by the mobility of the poor is more serious today than it was in earlier times. The Supreme Court ruled, in 1969, that states may not rely on strict residency requirements to limit access to their welfare programs. This deprived states of a tool that allowed them to raise benefits for "their own" poor without risking an influx of outsiders. In addition, the poor themselves are probably more mobile today. They have better access to information about the comparison in welfare benefits and job opportunities across the states, and due to improvements in transportation, they are better able to move in response.

The image of the scheming poor who constantly scan newspapers and public documents in search of the jurisdiction in which they can gain the best welfare coverage is undoubtedly exaggerated. The poor, at least as much as other Americans, are slow to pick up stakes and resettle, due to tradition, family ties, habit, cost, and fear of the unknown. But this is not to say that such strategic relocation does not sometimes take place. As we noted earlier, when unemployment benefits were suddenly cut for Indochinese refugees, officials noted a sudden migration from the economically depressed states of Oregon and Washington to Michigan and California, where welfare benefits were higher.

Terry Nichols Clark and Lorna Crowly Ferguson studied migration trends to determine whether minorities are more likely to move into jurisdictions with relatively generous welfare benefits. They found that "nonwhite net migration was indeed higher in counties with higher welfare benefits" (Clark and Ferguson, 1983, p. 214). Though statistically significant, the effect was small. A 10 percent increase in welfare benefits raised nonwhite net migration by just under 1 percent. This does not necessarily indicate that minorities are systematically moving to areas with benefits. It may simply reflect that they are less likely to leave such areas. The fiscal impact on those jurisdictions is nonetheless the same.

The result can be an unproductive and seemingly irrational competition among jurisdictions to "pan off the poor." When large numbers of unemployed auto workers from the Detroit area began to move to the Southwest in order to look for jobs, officials in Texas were moved to initiate an advertising campaign warning potential inmigrants that jobs were scarce, welfare benefits skimpy, and that they would be wise to stay away. Ohio used some of its federal employment and job-training money to pay its unemployed to seek work in other states (Balz, 1982). It is in recognition of the fruitlessness of such competition that some advocates of welfare reform, including many state officials, have called for a uniform *national* welfare system rather than further decentralization.

Fiscal Limitations. Under normal circumstances, the proportion of needy persons in any given locality is likely to be small enough that more fortunate residents can support them relatively easily, though with the expected grumbling. Abnormal circumstances, such as natural disasters and economic depressions, however, can increase the need for public welfare support while at the same time greatly impeding the jurisdiction's capacity to pay for such programs. The inability of local jurisdictions to meet welfare needs was a major prod to the expansion, during the mid- to late 1800s, of the states' role in welfare; and the inability of the states to cope with the welfare burdens imposed by the Great Depression sparked the national government's assumption of greater welfare responsibility in the mid-1930s.

The national economy has been spared shocks of the magnitude of the Great Depression for over fifty years. But swings between inflation and recession continue. In bad times, of course, all levels of government suffer. But the effects of economic swings are not felt equally by all localities and states. The evidence indicates that older urban areas are hit the hardest by recessions and gain the least in recovery. During the national recession in the early 1980s, although six states were finishing 1982 with budgetary deficits, the energy-rich states were reporting sizable surpluses (Bahl, 1984). A nationalized welfare system forces those in more fortunate areas to carry some of the burden of helping those in localized areas of need.

Political and Structural Limitations. Even when states and localities have the money to afford their own welfare programs, there is no guarantee that the political willingness to enact and fund such programs will exist. Although a few states and localities have been innovative and imaginative in the area of social-welfare policy, the record clearly shows that many others have dragged their feet. Liberal and radical analysts explain this by reference to the efforts of localized political elites. These elites may seek to surpress the welfare issue in order to keep the poor politically weak, more concerned with day-to-day survival than in forging a collective challange to the status quo. They also want to keep welfare benefits low in order to minimize the state and local taxes that they will have to pay. These liberal and radical analysts predict that unless the poor are able to build stronger political organizations in the states and localities, decentralization will leave us with a harsh and inadequate welfare system.

Paul Peterson more recently has argued that the inability of local governments to provide much in the way of welfare is inherent in the structure of local government (Peterson, 1981). Local governments, he suggests, must base their policies on their anticipated effect on the average taxpayer. If the average taxpayer feels that the ratio of taxes paid to benefits received is too high, he or she will choose to relocate. Redistributive policies such as welfare—which take from the average taxpayer in order to support those with lower incomes—necessarily work against the interests of the local jurisdiction by driving out these residents and businesses that contribute the most to the jurisdiction's financial and social health. Because it is relatively easy for a household or business to move from locality to locality, local jurisdictions are less able to redistribute than are states or the federal government. This structural limitation, Peterson suggests, applies whether or not local politics are dominated by a conservative elite. If he is correct, decentralization of welfare might lead to stingier benefits, even if local officials are personally and ideologically inclined to be more generous.

Privatizing Welfare: The Limits of Charity

Critics of the national government's welfare bureaucracy do not necessarily expect states and cities to pick up the entire burden if federal poverty programs are scaled down. Indeed, the basic objective for many is not to bounce responsibility for the poor among the levels of government but to shift a substantial share of the responsibility out of the public sector entirely. President Reagan said as much in September 1981: "The truth is that we've let government take away many things that we once considered were really ours to do voluntarily . . ." (Salamon and Abramson, 1982, p. 219).

Arguments for Privatization. Advocates of the privatization of welfare argue that private giving, because it is voluntary, reinforces the spirit of community and eliminates the burden of a tax-hungry bureaucracy.

This private sector, they argue, has been displaced and squeezed aside in recent decades by public-sector welfare activities that stifle the impulse of generosity, turning the joy of helping into the disgruntlement of the overtaxed. The private sector, they suggest, can also be more flexible and can better target its attention on those individuals who can best be helped and are most likely to respond.

The public sector, in contrast, is constrained by political and legal pressures. As a result, government must take a more universalistic approach, with the result that eligibility may be spread so broadly that available funds are spread too thinly to do much good. In addition, the public sector is presumed to be more wasteful: "government bureaucrats, secure in the belief that they have the seemingly limitless resources of the States behind them, may be more careless than the administrator of a voluntary agency" (Kennett, 1980, p. 338).

There is no doubt that the private sector can and must play a significant role in the task of helping the poor. It *has* done so for many years: in 1878 the city of Philadelphia boasted over 800 mutual-aid societies and private charities that functioned to protect its citizens from the vagaries of economic cycles and personal tragedies (Lynn, 1980). It continues to do so today. In 1974, more than one out of every five Americans devoted some time to unpaid labor for religious, educational, hospital, civic, community, or social-welfare groups. In 1980, individuals gave 39.9 billion dollars to charity, over five times as much as they had given twenty years before (U.S. Bureau of the Census, 1981).

Corporations have played a relatively minor role in private philanthropy: in 1980, they provided only 2.6 billion dollars. Much attention has been focused recently, however, on a few corporations that have sought to address the needs of the poor in particularly innovative ways. In Minneapolis, for example, General Mills, Honeywell, and Dayton Hudson, three locally based corporations, have worked closely with community groups to spur redevelopment in declining neighborhoods. Several financial institutions lent money and expertise to the efforts by Inqilinois Boricuas en Accion, a Hispanic organization in south Boston, to build over 800 units of housing for low-income families (Bratt, Byrd, and Hollister, 1983). In Washington, D.C., several large corporations have agreed to cooperate with the school system in devising career-oriented education programs in the overwhelmingly black public school system.

Cutting Public Support: Will the Private Sector Take Up the Slack? To note the vitality and importance of private-sector giving, however, is not to prove that privatization of existing public welfare activities is desirable or even feasible. The premise that the expansion of public-sector welfare has displaced private activity must itself be regarded with caution. As Table 4-2 indicates, the past thirty years have seen only

Table 4-2 Percent of Expenditures for Social Welfare Provided by the Public Sector: 1950 to 1978

	Income Maintenance	Health	Education	Welfare and Other Services	Total
1950	91.0	25.5	85.3	65.8	65.8
1960	88.1	24.7	82.8	59.1	65.3
1965	86.0	24.5	82.5	68.0	64.4
1970	83.9	36.7	84.0	79.6	68.4
1973	85.2	38.4	84.2	84.5	70.2
1975	86.3	41.6	85.3	87.8	72.4
1978 (prel)	85.2	40.8	84.3	89.3	70.4

SOURCE: U.S. Bureau of the Census, *Statistical Abstract of the United States, 1981*. Washington, D.C.: Government Printing Office, Table No. 519, p. 319.

a modest increase in the share of social-welfare expenditures accounted for by the public sector; over the last ten years, there has been virtually no change at all (U.S. Bureau of the Census, 1981). If it is not the case that the public sector has squeezed out private-sector welfare activity, there is little reason to be confident that a cutback in governmental activity will open a floodgate through which compensatory private resources and energies will automatically appear.

Moreover, and just as important, private-sector and voluntary efforts to handle social-welfare needs are fundamentally limited in a number of ways. These limits will not miraculously vanish if the federal, state, and local governments are taken out of the picture. Indeed, it was the fact of these limits that, in some instances, was originally responsible for drawing the public sector into the welfare arena. Volunteer labor, for instance, is not as reliable a foundation as simple charting of the number of volunteers might suggest. Although 36,812 persons over fourteen years of age donated some labor in 1974, Table 4-3 indicates that for most, the commitment was very small indeed. Over 70 percent of the volunteers indicated that they had donated less than 100 hours of labor, less than 17 minutes per day (U.S. Bureau of the Census, 1981, p. 350).

Vulnerabilities of the Private Sector. The private sector, moreover, may be least reliable at the very times that the need is greatest. The vulnerability of private charities to the same economic forces that affect individuals and families was vividly demonstrated during the Great Depression. "When the depression hit, the bulk of poor relief was still handled by private and local charities. As the number of poor rose dramatically, the abilities and resources of these institutions declined just as dramatically" (Advisory Commission on Intergovernmental Relations, 1980, p. 9). A similar phenomenon seems to be at work today.

The effort by parishioners from St. Paul's Episcopal Church in Wash-

Table 4-3 Frequency and Amount of Volunteer Work, 1974[a]

	Number (1,000)	Percent
Total volunteers	36,812	100.0
Volunteer work[b]		
Once a week	13,125	35.7
Once every 2 weeks	3,714	10.1
Once a month	5,230	14.2
Only a few times	7,979	21.7
Once only	2,758	7.5
Other	3,884	10.6
Hours per year		
Less than 25	13,638	37.0
25–99	12,578	34.2
100–299	7,700	20.9
300 or more	2,737	7.4

[a]Volunteer work refers to unpaid activities for religious, educational, hospital, civic and community, social, and welfare groups.
[b]Excludes not reported.
SOURCE: U.S. Bureau of the Census, *Statistical Abstract of the United States, 1981.* Washington, D.C.: Government Printing Office, Table No. 575, p. 350.

ington, D.C., to feed growing numbers of the hungry illustrates the limitation on the potential for charity to carry the burden of dealing with the poor when poverty and unemployment are high. St. Paul's program began with small and manageable objectives in the winter of 1981. Two homeless men had frozen to death, and members of the church hoped that by carrying sandwiches and soup to such homeless persons, further deaths might be avoided. As the program continued, it became clearer that the need outstripped the small-scale effort that had originally been planned. Rather than turn their backs, the parishioners expanded their efforts, yet each time they did so, demands seemed to expand as well. The church opened a sandwich line on March 26. After one month, about thirty people were being served each night. By August, this number had quadrupled. Finally, the parishioners gave up. Not, according to one of the parishioners, because the program was too costly. "It closed because we had become victims of our own success." The program grew to the point where it simply put too many demands on the volunteers and on the church facilities.

Potential Biases. One of the claimed advantages of private-sector social-welfare effort—greater flexibility—may also represent a potential flaw. Because they can be selective, charities, corporations, and foundations can target their aid so as to have the greatest possible impact. But although such targeting may be efficient, it may also be unfair. Those who will benefit the most from aid are not necessarily those in the greatest need. To the contrary, it is the temporarily hard-up person, the well-educated individual facing short-term unemployment or temporary disability, who will be most likely to prove to be a charity "success story"; the long-term poor are more likely to remain mired in their poverty in spite of any aid that social welfare (public or private) can provide.

Private-sector givers, moreover, have been known to employ criteria grounded in neither effectiveness nor need. Charities often focus their efforts on particular subgroups, as defined by religion, race, sex, place of residence, and the like. They may be motivated to do this because they define their mission as that of helping "their own kind," or because some groups of the needy are more popular and attractive to potential donors than are others. Corporations, seeking to allocate their limited charitable contributions, may consider drama and publicity as essential as hardship and need. The anticipated result of relying on the private sector, then, is that support will be erratic, with substantial gaps in the coverage provided, gaps through which many of the least fortunate might be destined to fall. Government, through its power to tax, can force citizens to provide aid even to those—the illiterate, illegitimate, immigrant—whose plight earns only limited sympathy.

Private-Sector Inefficiencies. Nor should the inefficiencies of public bureaucracies obscure the fact that private social-welfare institutions suffer inefficiencies of their own. Much of the money that private charities and foundations raise must be channeled back into the fund-raising effort and general overhead expenditures. During 1982, for example, the Muscular Dystrophy Association channeled 22 percent of the money it raised back into its fund-raising activities; the American Cancer Society, 16 percent; the March of Dimes, 21 percent (Tivnan, 1983). For all the scorn heaped on governmental bureaucracies, moreover, there are times when they can operate more efficiently than the private sector can. This seems to be the case, for example, when the public Social Security system is compared to private insurance operations. "For every two dollars of private insurance benefits paid in 1973," Levitan and Taggart note, "the companies took a dollar in dividends, taxes, administrative, advertising and sales costs. In comparison, total administrative costs of the OASDI system, in 1972, were only 1.8 percent of benefits paid" (Levitan and Taggart, 1976, p. 41).

Welfare as Charity Versus Welfare as Right. Finally, it must be recognized that there is a fundamental difference between aid that is provided as a charitable gesture and aid that is provided as a legal right. The former is conditional; it may be summarily and arbitrarily withdrawn.

This provides the giver with a point of leverage, a threat that can be exploited in order to encourage the recipient to change his or her behavior in ways consistent with those that the giver of aid believes to be desirable. It was this potential for inducing the poor person to "change his ways" that provided much of the early impetus to the private charity movement in this country. In some cities in the late eighteenth century, this took the forms of "reclamation societies," which "tried to lure the idle or vicious poor back onto the path of industry and virtue," and "uplift organizations," which "aimed to keep the potentially poor from falling into poverty" (Alexander, 1980, p. 133). But such leverage can just as easily be used to punish the unconforming, the unattractive, and the unsubmissive. By reinforcing dependency, this aspect of private welfare may isolate the poor even more than they would be otherwise, reaffirming their status as second-class citizens and impeding, in that way, their integration into the mainstream of social, political, and economic life.

Finally, the notion that policy-makers face a *choice* between public versus private approaches to social welfare must be regarded skeptically. Some advocates of privatization argue that an increased private role must be preceded by a decreased public-sector role. Yet as Salamon and Abramson point out, "far from displacing nonprofit organizations, the federal government has come to rely on them extensively to carry out the functions the public has called on it to perform" (Salamon and Abramson, 1982, p. 234). Many federal, state, and local education, training, and social-service programs work by providing grants to nonprofit organizations. It is the latter that ultimately deliver the goods to those in need. These nonprofit organizations, for their part, have relied on such public contracts in order to expand their size and capacity. "As a result, the same policies that reduce the role of government [such as lower taxes and lower social-welfare expenditures]—and, hence, increase the need for nonprofit organizations—also reduce the ability of these organizations to meet this need" (Salamon and Abramson, 1982, p. 220).

Jobs Provision and Economic Development: An Alternative Approach?

For all their disagreements, neoconservatives, liberals, and radicals might agree on at least one point: it is generally preferable to provide the poor with the opportunity to earn a satisfactory income than to offer a bare subsistence stipend through welfare or charity. Jobs for the poor—if they provide decent, healthy working conditions, if they offer an above-poverty wage, if they do not destabilize a family by forcing a parent to leave his or her children unattended or in an unsatisfactory day-care arrangement—can provide the poor person with a sense of self-worth, free the family from dependency, provide a role model for the children, and improve the nation's overall productivity. Today, there are many who argue that we have not given jobs the emphasis they deserve as an alternative to social welfare. Various proposals are being touted. Are programs to get the poor working the answer to the poverty that many of our states and localities find within their boundaries?

Work Incentives. Efforts to replace or supplement welfare with a jobs-oriented strategy come in several types. One approach has focused on work incentives. Because eligibility and benefit levels are affected by earnings, welfare recipients risk losing some or all of their payments if they take new or better-paying jobs. Conservative critics of the system, we saw earlier, have been particularly concerned about the possibility that this may create incentives for the poor *not* to work. Recognizing this, Congress in 1967 passed the Work Incentive (WIN) program. WIN was designed to make work more attractive to welfare recipients in several ways. Congress made money available to the states to establish job training, placement services, and day-care assistance. Also included was the "thirty plus one-third" provision: in calculating recipients' income, in order to determine the proper level of benefits, officials would exempt the first thirty dollars earned each month and one-third of the remainder, along with legitimate work-related expenses. This provision meant that the poor would be allowed to keep their earnings without suffering the one-to-one loss in benefits that some feared created an incentive for recipients *not* to take jobs.

Work Requirements. The widely shared premise that many of the poor choose not to work out of laziness or greed has led, at various times, to a work-requirement strategy. Along with the "carrot" offered by the WIN program, Congress offered a few shakes of a "stick." In a series of provisions, sometimes referred to disparagingly as the "Slave Labor Amendments," Congress required the states to deny AFDC aid to any parent (including mothers) or teenage child considered able to work unless that person registered for WIN and accepted employment or training when offered (Advisory Commission on Intergovernmental Relations, 1980).

The result of work-incentive and work-requirement provisions has been disappointing. "In its entire history only 138,000 individuals are claimed to have entered employment as a result of WIN, and this figure might be inflated by as high as 40 percent" (Dobelstein, 1980, pp. 127–8). Those who were placed through the program tended to be those with the most education and job experience, those who were most likely to have been able to find employment even without the program (Levin, 1977).

Job Training. One reason for the poor showing by these approaches is the lack of basic skills that makes some of the poor unattractive to potential employers. Job-training programs are designed to address this problem. Job Corps, one of the controversial War on Poverty programs, provided disadvantaged high-school youth with two years of intensive training and education in training centers located outside the metropolitan areas. Job Opportunities in the Business Sector (JOBS) was to offer on-the-job training through the private sector. In this program, initiated in 1968, a governmental subsidy was provided to business that hired and trained the hard-core unemployed. The Manpower Development and Training Act (1962) was aimed at those who had become unemployed due to economic or technological change; in the late 1960s, this program was refocused in order to encourage greater participation by the hard-core unemployed who may never have held meaningful jobs.

Public-Sector Jobs Provision. In 1974, most existing federal grants for job training were incorporated into the Comprehensive Employment and Training Act (CETA). CETA provided money to "prime sponsors," usually state or local governments, which were free to choose among a fairly wide range of training, employment, placement, and counseling strategies in devising an approach appropriate for the particular needs of that community. CETA initially was conceived of as a private-sector-oriented program. Yet CETA sponsors found, as had earlier job-training programs, that private employers were not anxious to hire inner-city minority youths and mothers, even when wages were subsidized or training provided. Partially in response, some of the emphasis shifted to public-sector jobs provision. State and local governments, using CETA funds, hired the unemployed to receive on-the-job training while working in public schools, hospitals, and governmental offices. This shift toward public-sector jobs provision was compatible with the belief held by some liberals that government should be the "employer of last resort," stepping in to provide meaningful work opportunities whenever, and to whatever degree, the private sector fails to produce enough jobs for those willing and able to work.

In one sense, the public employment facet of CETA worked too well. States and localities saw CETA as a mechanism to ease their fiscal strain. In some places, CETA workers were hired to perform tasks that otherwise would have been handled by workers entirely on the local payroll. The cost of the program skyrocketed. The public sector, it seemed, was better able, or more willing, than the private sector to accommodate the numbers of persons looking for work. The original intent of the program—to provide a short-term, on-the-job experience so that individuals would become employable in the private sector and without the need of a continuing public subsidy—was not being met. In 1982, CETA died, a victim of its high cost, occasional scandals, and a general impression that it was not working well. But the job-training approach did not die. High unemployment and political pressure led President Reagan to sign, in October 1982, a new job-training bill. A central element in this plan was the establishment of Private Industry Councils to guide job-training efforts at the local level. These councils, consisting of representatives from the local business communities, were expected to inject insights into the "real world" of the job market as well as apply valuable management techniques.

Economic Growth. A final approach returns to the notion of jobs provision but firmly anchors that notion in the private sector. The problem, some conservatives argue, is that all these past efforts have sought in some way to interfere with or replace the normal workings of the private market. *If* the economy were growing, they argue, there would be no need for the government to create jobs or to "bribe" the private sector to hire the unemployed. Efforts should be reoriented toward the general goal of encouraging economic growth. If the economy expands, businesses will need to hire more workers. If businesses need to hire more workers, they will be willing to pay more for skilled labor. As the need for skilled labor grows relative to its supply, business also will have an incentive to provide their own training to those who do not yet have the requisite skills.

One strategy for expanding economic growth is to *subsidize* expansion. State and local governments, for example, can provide businesses with low-cost loans, donate publicly owned land, build or expand roads and sewers, or provide free services for new businesses or businesses that expand. Another strategy is to *unleash* the private sector. By cutting taxes and reducing regulations, some argue, all levels of government can create an environment in which new business find it easier to survive and to grow.

In later chapters, we will have more to say about some specific strategies to encourage economic growth. For now, it is enough to note a limitation shared by each of the approaches considered above. Job training and jobs provision are integral to any effort to lessen the burdens of poverty and reduce the size of the dependent welfare class. Work requirements and jobs provision, however, are not a panacea. Politicians who trumpet jobs as an *alternative* to welfare are misleading the public and themselves. Many Americans on welfare will continue to need support. This would be true even if unemployment rates were to be brought down to the seemingly unreachable level of or 3 or 4 percent. They will need support because they are blind or disabled or too old to work, or they will need help because they are children or mothers with young children who should not or cannot be left alone.

Past efforts to reduce the welfare load through work incentives, work requirements, job-training, public-sector jobs provision, and economic growth have been disappointing largely because they overlook the fact that only a small portion of those currently receiving welfare are in a position to respond. Jobs provision is criticially important to pursue, but it is important for reasons other than its likely impact on the size of the welfare load. More jobs would mean better opportunities and higher wages for the near poor, a stronger fiscal base allowing governments to provide more and better services to all residents, a reduction in the kinds of tensions and insecurities that foment violence and mental distress, and the kind of atmosphere of hopefulness about the future that tends to nurture investment, innovation, and generosity. But more jobs will not make the need for welfare wither away.

SUMMARY AND CONCLUSIONS

Our welfare system is complex. It is made complex by the number of distinct programs, the various criteria for eligibility, and the confusing sharing of responsibility across the different levels of government. What accounts for this complexity that leaves recipients and administrators frustrated and often confused?

The welfare system is complex in part because of the various and somewhat contradictory theoretical premises that animate its various components. As far as the theoretical approaches discussed in Chapter 3 go, our welfare system is an ideological mutt.

The sharp distinctions among different categories of the poor are rooted in an individualist orientation. The "worthy" poor—the elderly, the worker's widow, the disabled, the worker who is temporarily unemployed due to circumstances beyond his or her control—are eligible for programs with relatively fewer bureaucratic impositions and relatively higher benefit levels. Some "unworthy" groups—young healthy males who have never worked, the long-term unemployed, unmarried women without children—are sometimes allowed to fall between the cracks; depending on the state, they may not qualify for Medicaid or cash assistance of any kind. Shades of an individualistic orientation also can be seen in various provisions to force recipients to work, the provision of in-kind benefits rather than cash, and the punitive orientation with which benefits often are provided or withheld.

A culture-of-poverty orientation, however, seems to account for the emphasis on resocializing youth and moderating the impact of their family environments, as in the Head Start and Job Corps programs. And a mild structural emphasis is evidenced in the call for "maximum feasible participation" by the poor that accompanied the War on Poverty programs introduced in the 1960s.

The coexistence of these differing orientations is partly due to our inability to make up our minds about what poverty is really all about. Two other factors—decentralization and incrementalism—are also important. Our perceptions about the nature of poverty and the legitimate role of the public sector in addressing inequality and the needs of the poor are rooted in the political culture into which we are born and socialized. Political scientists have found that there are distinct political subcultures within the nation, and that different subcultures tend to dominate in different regions and different states. The decentralization of responsibility for our welfare policies ensures that programs will vary substantially in generosity and theoretical orientation from place to place.

Incrementalism refers to the way in which political change tends to occur in the United States. The division of power among the branches of our government and between the levels of our governments tends to put limits on the possibilities for radical change. New ideas and political reforms usually are grafted onto preexisting structures. Even the most popular and reform-minded presidents cannot draw their new programs on a slate that has been wiped clean.

Our welfare system has evolved through accumulation and small changes. During the depression, officials and the public were less likely than in the past to subscribe to individualistic perspectives of poverty. This provided a political environment in which major new initiatives could be launched, but there was no clean break with the past. More conservative legislators put limits on these programs, and more conservative states administered those programs in which they retained a role in a manner still consistent with a view that the poor were to blame for their own poverty. The civil-rights movement and the Kennedy/Johnson War on Poverty again offered a more structural analysis of the issues of poverty and inequality, but these programs also had to accommodate themselves to other political forces.

This suggests one final conclusion, one that has to do with the shape social-welfare policy is likely to take in our federal system in the years to come. Although abstract theories may seek to deduce the "proper" level of governmental responsibility for the poor, the ultimate distribution of decision-making responsibility will depend as much upon changes in the balance of power among political forces as upon the power of ideas. Given our diversity, we can expect that welfare will remain an *intergovernmental* responsibility.

Recent efforts to privatize welfare decision-making will not change the fact that caring for the poor will continue to be regarded as a public responsibility. And efforts to decentralize, even if partially successful, will not alter the fact that the national government will continue to play a major role in setting standards for acceptable treatment of the poor. Just as the New Deal and the War on Poverty failed to do away with all remnants of our earlier localized welfare system, the more conservative political outlook that subsequently gained political dominance has failed to result in the gutting of either the New Deal or Great Society programs. Tighter restrictions have been imposed, work requirements stiffened, and benefit levels in some cases reduced, but the core programs remain essentially unchanged.

SUGGESTED READINGS

Advisory Commission on Intergovernmental Relations. *Public Assistance: The Growth of a Federal Function.* Washington, D.C.: Government Printing Office, 1980.

Anderson, Martin. *Welfare.* Stanford, Connecticut: Hoover Institute, 1978.

Haveman, Robert H., ed. *A Decade of Federal Antipoverty Programs.* New York: Academic Press, 1977.

Levitan, Sar. *Programs in Aid of the Poor for the 1980s.* Baltimore: Johns Hopkins University Press, 1980.

Patterson, James T. *America's Struggle Against Poverty, 1900–1980.* Cambridge, Massachusetts: Harvard University Press, 1981.

Piven, Frances Fox, and Richard Cloward. *Regulating the Poor.* New York: Vintage, 1971.

Thurow, Lester C. *The Zero-Sum Society.* New York: Basic Books, 1980.

5
Urban and Regional Decline

Back in the 1930s, the joke was on Philadelphia. "I just won a contest," says Joe to his buddy. "First prize was a week in Philadephia." "Oh yeah?" says his buddy. "What was second prize?" "Two weeks."

Today, the joke is more likely to be aimed elsewhere: at Detroit, perhaps, or St. Louis, or Newark. Arthur Lewis, in 1975, compiled twenty-four measures that he believed were relevant to determining a city's quality of life. Included were measures of pollution, crime rates, unemployment, parks, and characteristics of the residents. He then combined the measures into a single index. Seattle, this crude scale suggested, was the best of fifty large cities in which to live. Tulsa, San Diego, San Jose, and Honolulu were not far behind. Lewis's article was entitled "The Worst American City." Newark was the winner of that dubious prize (Lewis, 1975).

Since the mid-1960s, much concern has been expressed about the decline of American cities. One urban scholar, George Sternlieb, wrote in 1971 that many cities were no longer capable of performing the productive functions they had once served. Instead, the city was becoming a "sandbox": a holding ground for the poor and the unproductive; a place where those who lacked the skills to compete in, and contribute to, the dynamic sectors of the economy might be allowed to play like children entertained by public programs designed to isolate them and keep them preoccupied while the rest of the country goes about more serious business.

By the late 1970s, this concern had begun to take on a broader geographic scope. Some of the very same forces that had been threatening to drain certain central cities of people, jobs, and wealth were found to be operating on a larger scale. The Northeast and North Central regions of the country—the so-called Snowbelt—had begun to lose population to the South and West, much as the central cities had begun to lose population to their suburbs in earlier years.

You may not live in a large city with readily visible signs of decline. Most Americans do not. In fact, most Americans live in suburbs (44.8 percent) or nonmetropolitan (25.2 percent) areas, and not in central cities at all. Of those living in large cities, many live in growing and vibrant cities. Even those who live in cities that are losing population and jobs may live in neighborhoods that are stable, sheltered, even affluent.

But don't get smug or complacent. The problems of Newark, Detroit, and St. Louis may *seem* far away and unlikely to touch your life in any immediate sense, but the general problem of decline is not limited to a handful of cities. Decline spreads into the inner ring of suburbs in many metropolitan areas and takes place even in "pockets of poverty" in the middle of booming Sunbelt cities like Houston. For many rural and southern areas, decline in the 1980s is simply a continuation of a trend that is over fifty years old.

None of us—not even the wealthy—can shield ourselves completely from the social and economic fallout that follows in the path of decline. Affluent suburbanites pay taxes to the state and federal governments to support programs and services in declining areas. The frustration, bitterness, and resentment that sometimes are fueled by decline poison the atmosphere for all of us, heightening tension and brewing fear of crime and social unrest.

In this chapter, we will consider the broad phenomenon of urban and regional decline. Decline has many faces. It may look like a welfare mother facing cuts in already skimpy AFDC benefits, or it may look like unrepaired potholes in major city streets. It may be measured in the number of homeless "bag ladies" patrolling the sidewalks, in a count of addicts succumbing to overdoses, or in the red ink on ledger books in state and local budget offices. These various components of decline are interrelated but nonetheless distinct. Policies aimed at correcting one type of problem may not address the others. Indeed, in some cases, the solution to one aspect of decline may mean that the others are accelerated or made more painful.

After considering some of the various dimensions of decline, we will consider two questions that are central to the policy debate about what—if anything—ought to be done about urban and regional decline. The first question concerns the seriousness of the problem. The second question involves the causes of decline.

Neoconservative analysts charge that rhetoric about a "crisis" in the cities and Snowbelt region exaggerates the severity of the problem. They worry that such exaggeration will create a demand for governmental action, in spite of the fact that there may be little the government can do that does not make the situation even worse. Neoconservatives argue that government and public policies are unlikely to help matters because the roots of decline lie in broad market forces—driven by demographic, technological, and economic change—that move with a logic and certainty that overwhelms anything that tries to stand in their path.

Liberals and radicals tend to agree with each other that action is called for because the problems are real. They disagree, however, about the nature of the problem and the kinds of actions that are called for if real improvements are to be brought about. To most liberal analysts, the answer to urban and regional decline lies in devising more sensitive and more finely tuned policies. Radical critics agree with the neoconservatives that this perspective underestimates the tenacity of the problems we currently face. Where the neoconservative sees broad and insurmountable forces at work, the radical sees the imprint of a particular economic system under which some individuals and groups prosper, while others do not. Decline, the radical argues, flows inevitably from an economic system in which corporations and investors may move their resources around freely in pursuit of their own profit, even when that private profit conflicts with the public good. Small adjustments to existing policies will fail to work because they fail to challenge the market system. But true reforms will not be forthcoming unless they are accompanied by a realignment of political power. Those who benefit from the existing system will not willingly relinquish their privileged position without a fight.

DIMENSIONS OF DECLINE

Violence and Unrest

On July 16, 1964, James Powell and some of his friends were walking down a Harlem street on their way to summer school. Along the way, they became involved in an argument with a building superintendent, who was white. The superintendent, witnesses testified later, had sprayed water on the boys while he was washing down the sidewalk. Police lieutenant Thomas Gilligan was off duty, but he intervened. Powell, he says, attacked him with a knife. Some witnesses say there was no knife. Gilligan shot and killed the boy. A crowd of protesting teenagers screamed at police, and at least one patrolman was hit in the head by a soda can (Jones, 1964). Two days later, violence broke out on a wider scale. A demonstration to protest the boy's killing turned into a march on the police station. The crowd clashed with police. Another person was killed. Twelve police and nineteen citizens were injured. It was just a beginning.

Over the next few days, police and rioters battled in parts of Harlem and the Bedford-Stuyvesant neighborhood in Brooklyn. A week later, there were riots in Rochester, New York. Then, during the first two weeks of August, there were disorders in Jersey City, Elizabeth, and Paterson—all in New Jersey. Over the next five years, there were to be many more riots. Major riots occurred in Newark, Detroit, Washington, D.C., and Watts, a section of Los Angeles. One study concluded that between 1964 and the end of 1968, there were 329 important riots involving thousands of rioters in 257 cities (Downes, 1970). In 1967 alone, there were over seventy riots: over 525,000 were arrested, over 8,300 injured, and approximately 220 killed (Lenberg Center for the Study of Violence, 1968).

It was violence and rioting that catapulted urban problems into the public eye and onto the nation's policy agenda. The National Advisory Commission on Civil Disorders, appointed by President Lyndon Johnson in 1967, concluded that the source of the riots and the conditions of our cities were closely intertwined. The nation, the commission concluded, "is rapidly moving toward two increasingly separate Americas . . . a white society principally located in the suburbs, in smaller central cities, and in the peripheral parts of large central cities; and a Negro society largely concentrated within large central cities" (National Advisory Commission on Civil Disorders, 1968, p. 407).

Since 1968, however, incidents of collective violence seem to have declined. This, of course, is not to say that riots are a thing of the distant past. In July 1977, a power failure left the lights out in much of New York City. Thousands took the opportunity to plunder and loot. An estimated 2,000 businesses were targeted, and property losses were gauged at as high as $1 billion. Hundreds were hospitalized or treated for injuries in emergency rooms. Over 400 police were injured by bottles and bricks thrown at them while they arrested over 3,700 rioters. Forty-four firemen were injured while battling the thousand fires that had been set (*Newsweek*, 1977). When four policemen were acquitted of charges that they had beaten a black businessman to death, three days of violence were sparked in the Liberty City area of Miami; eighteen were left dead. About two and a half years later, in December 1982, about 200 protesters looted and set fires in the same neighborhood, after a Hispanic police officer shot and killed a black youth in a video-game arcade (*Newsweek*, 1983). Further violence followed, in March of 1984, when an all-white jury found the police officer not guilty of any crime.

The threat of renewed violence still seems to hang over each new long, hot summer. But for the moment, the threat has lost some of its bite. Americans still think and talk about an urban crisis, but today they are likely to have something rather different in mind.

Fiscal Strain

In 1975, New York City collected just under $11 billion in revenue. But in 1975, New York City virtually went broke. As tales of the Big Apple's money problems hit front pages, Americans' image of the urban crisis began to shift from broken windows and looted stores to ledger books and bankers.

The city, simply, was spending more than it was taking in, about $2 billion more in that year alone. Operating in the red was itself nothing new. The city owed a total of $4.3 billion in 1961, and it had never erased that debt. Instead, the debt had continued to grow, growing more rapidly in the recent years. Between 1961 and 1975, the city's debt had nearly tripled, reaching a total of about $12.3 billion. Each year, New York City paid $1.8 billion in interest alone.

At the time, it seemed easy for some observers to write off New York City's problems as an oddity, the problems of one extremely atypical city that had spent itself into a tight spot. Analyzing federal officials' deliberations over whether to come to the city's aid, the *New York Times* observed that "the clear consensus is that if New York City is not the root of all evil, it is at least the handmaiden of sin . . . obviously undeserving of aid, which it would only abuse." As one United States senator put it, commenting on the attitudes of his colleagues, "Cities are viewed as the seed of corruption and duplicity . . . and New York is the biggest city."

But New York City's fiscal crisis was a window through which a much broader and deeper problem eventually was to be seen. State and federal relief helped keep New York from formally going bankrupt. This left to Cleveland the honor of becoming the first United States city to default since the Great Depression, a feat that it accomplished in 1978 (Jones, 1983). The next year Wayne County, Michigan, and the Chicago School District both failed to meet their payrolls.

States and localities have been hit, in recent years, by a triple whammy: a recessionary national economy has depressed economic activity, leading to increased unemployment and decreased tax revenues; a fervent tax revolt, kicked off by California's Proposition 13 in 1978, has imposed political and legal constraints on state and local officials' ability to raise taxes in response; and all this has happened at a time when the national government, under the twin banners of budget austerity and New Federalism, has shed certain programs and scaled down its spending, while encouraging the expectation that state and local governments might be willing to pick up the slack.

Attempts to assess state and urban fiscal distress show that more than a handful of governments are in financial hot water. Not all of these states and localities are Snowbelt governments with which we associated

Table 5-1 City Decline Index: Cities Ranked from the Worst Decline Rating (−4) to Least Decline Rating (+4)[a]

−4	Canton, Ohio	Grand Rapids, Mich.	Glendale, Calif.
Boston, Mass.	Elizabeth, N.J.	Hollywood, Fla.	Honolulu, Hawaii
Cambridge, Mass.	Flint, Mich.	Milwaukee, Wis.	Huntington Beach, Calif.
Cleveland, Ohio	Garden Grove, Calif.	New Haven, Conn.	Kansas City, Mo.
Dayton, Ohio	Indianapolis, Ind.	Peoria, Ill.	Knoxville, Tenn.
Hartford, Conn.	Long Beach, Calif.	Pittsburgh, Pa.	Lansing, Mich.
Jersey City, N.J.	New Bedford, Mass.	Portland, Oreg.	Little Rock, Ark.
Las Vegas, Nev.	Oakland, Calif.	St. Petersburg, Fla.	Los Angeles, Calif.
Paterson, N.J.	Oklahoma City, Okla.	Santa Ana, Calif.	Memphis, Tenn.
Trenton, N.J.	Rockford, Ill.	Syracuse, N.Y.	Miami, Fla.
−3	San Bernardino, Calif.	Tampa, Fla.	Minneapolis, Minn.
Atlanta, Ga.	Stamford, Conn.	Warren, Mich.	Norfolk, Va.
Detroit, Mich.	Toledo, Ohio	Youngstown, Ohio	Pasadena, Calif.
Gary, Ind.	Tucson, Ariz.		Providence, R.I.
Newark, N.J.	Waterbury, Conn.	0	Sacramento, Calif.
New York, N.Y.	Yonkers, N.Y.	Allentown, Pa.	St. Louis, Mo.
Philadelphia, Pa.		Birmingham, Ala.	St. Paul, Minn.
Riverside, Calif.	−1	Ceder Rapids, Iowa	San Diego, Calif.
Rochester, N.Y.	Albuquerque, N.M.	Colorado Springs, Colo.	Savannah, Ga.
Springfield, Mass.	Berkeley, Calif.	Columbus, Ga.	Seattle, Wash.
Worcester, Mass.	Buffalo, N.Y.	El Paso, Tex.	Spokane, Wash.
−2	Cincinnati, Ohio	Ft. Lauderdale, Fla.	Winston-Salem. N.C.
Akron, Ohio	Evansville, Ill.		
Anaheim, Calif.			
Bridgeport, Conn.			
Camden, N.J.			

trends of general economic decline. One measure of "fiscal blood pressure," based on the ratio between state and local tax burden and personal incomes, found New York State to be in potentially the most vulnerable position. Other states with a tax burden that was both high and rising included Massachusetts and California. Virginia's pressure was not particularly high, but it was rising rapidly, suggesting that a problem might be coming on fast (Advisory Commision on Intergovernmental Relations 1977).

Table 5-1 ranks over 150 cities according to an index of city decline that is based on trends in unemployment, violent crime, debt burden, and per capita income (Bradbury, et al., 1982). That Boston, Cleveland, Detroit, and Newark fared badly on this index should not be surprising. Most of the other cities in the two least favorable categories are smaller, industrial cities in the Northeast and upper Midwest, so their scores might

Table 5-1 (continued)

+1	Jackson, Miss.	Fremont, Calif.	+3
Albany, N.Y.	Jacksonville, Fla.	Greensboro, N.C.	Austin, Tex.
Baltimore, Md.	Kansas City,	Independence,	Corpus Christi,
Baton Rouge, La.	Kans.	Mo.	Tex.
Charlotte, N.C.	Louisville, Ky.	Lincoln, Neb.	Hampton, Va.
Chattanooga,	Mobile, Ala.	Livonia, Mich.	Houston, Tex.
Tenn.	Parma, Ohio	Macon, Ga.	Lexington, Ky.
Chicago, Ill.	Phoenix, Ariz.	Madison, Wis.	Nashville, Tenn.
Columbia, S.C.	San Francisco,	Newport News,	New Orleans, La.
Columbus, Ohio	Calif.	Va.	Omaha, Neb.
Dallas, Tex.	Scranton, Pa.	Portsmouth, Va.	San Antonio,
Dearborn, Mich.	South Bend, Ind.	Richmond, Va.	Tex.
Denver, Colo.	Springfield, Mo.	Salt Lake City,	Virginia Beach,
Des Moines,	Washington, D.C.	Utah	Va.
Iowa		San Jose, Calif.	
Fort Wayne, Ind.	+2	Shreveport, La.	+4
Fort Worth, Tex.	Alexandria, Va.	Stockton, Calif.	Lubbock, Tex.
Fresno, Calif.	Amarillo, Tex.	Tacoma, Wash.	Montgomery, Ala.
Hammond, Ind.	Beaumont, Tex.	Topeka, Kans.	Raleigh, N.C.
Hialeah, Fla.	Duluth, Minn.	Torrance, Calif.	Wichita, Kans.
Huntsville, Ala.	Erie, Pa.	Tulsa, Okla.	

[a]Listed alphabetically within each rating group.
SOURCE: Katharine L. Bradbury, Anthony Downs, and Kenneth A. Small, *Urban Decline and the Future of American Cities*, Washington, D.C.: The Brookings Institution, 1982.

have been predicted as well. But the low scores of Las Vegas, Atlanta, Riverside, Anaheim, Oklahoma City, and Tucson prove that a warm climate does not guarantee social and economic well-being. In addition, the positive scores for cities such as Albany, Baltimore, Dearborn, and Fort Wayne show that some cities sidestep decline even in the chilly regions that are presumably on the skids.

Physical Deterioration: The City Crumbles

Beginning in the late 1800s, the major United States cities embarked on a prolonged period of physical growth. In order to accommodate their growing populations, and in order to function effectively in their roles as manufacturing and marketing centers, cities needed to lay down an extensive physical infrastructure. This infrastructure consisted of streets, sewers, bridges, water systems, harbors, bridges, public buildings, and utility lines. It was the capacity and foresight with which cities responded to the need to provide this infrastructure that would dictate, at least in part, which would flourish and continue to grow and which would stagnate and decline.

Today, that physical infrastructure is beginning to show its age. The Brooklyn Bridge in New York City is over 100 years old. On a June evening in 1981, two steel cables on the bridge suddenly snapped. Akira Armi, who had been walking across the bridge, was struck and killed. Pieces of concrete regularly fall from the Queensboro Bridge that connects Queens to Manhattan. The problem is so great that a Little League baseball diamond under the bridge had to be closed lest some player be beaned by something other than a pitched or batted ball. In July of 1983, 100 feet of a highway bridge in Greenwich, Connecticut, fell away, dropping two cars and two tractor trailers into the river 70 feet below (*Time*, 1983). There are about 557,600 bridges in the United States: in 1982, about 126,000 were deemed by federal authorities to be "structurally deficient"; about 122,000 more were judged to be "functionally obsolete" (Feaver, 1982).

It's not just bridges that are falling down. On December 10, 1973, a truck fell through a hole in the West Side Highway, an elevated road that runs down the side of Manhattan, and plunged to the ground below. Investigators found the condition of the supporting beams so precarious that they could not feasibly be repaired. A large section of the road had to be closed, and much of it was simply torn down and carted away. Nationwide, the 42,500-mile Interstate Highway System is deteriorating at a pace of approximately 2,000 miles per year. Rates of repair and reconstruction have not kept up, and today, over 8,000 miles need to be rebuilt (Choate and Walter, 1981). In many older cities, the underground water and sewage systems are ancient and crumbling. Leaks in Boston's water mains cause the loss of about one-half of the water the system carries each day. New Orleans needs to replace most of its sewer system; some of its sewers were bought, secondhand, from Philadelphia in 1896 (Morris, 1982).

The problem is not just the age of the infrastructure, although that is an important part of the problem. With regular upkeep and properly staged reconstruction, the physical infrastructure can be adequately maintained. As the infrastructure is aging, however, public investment in public works is declining. From 1965 through 1977, national investment in public works (new construction and rehabilitation) declined by 21 percent, when inflation is taken into account (Choate and Walter, 1981).

Pressed by demands for social services and squeezed by declining revenues, many public officials accept the short-term solution of deferring maintenance. In doing so, they buy themselves some breathing space and, perhaps, an additional lease on their political careers. The bill, eventually, will come due, but by then a different group of officials will have to absorb the economic and political costs.

Housing Abandonment and Neighborhood Decline

On Charlotte Street in the South Bronx, fifty-one apartment buildings once provided housing for about 3,000 people. President Carter went to visit Charlotte Street in 1977; by then, only nine buildings were still standing, eight of them abandoned and sealed shut or else charred and emptied by fire. From 1970 to 1975, the South Bronx lost 16 percent of its housing, 43,000 apartments; over 80,000 apartments were abandoned over a twelve-year period (Auletta, 1979). It was, the president noted, "a very sobering trip" (Dembart, 1977).

Boarded-up and abandoned housing is another manifestation of urban and regional decline. In some ways, it is the most dramatic. A trip along New York City's Cross-Bronx Expressway is startling. Here is a city in which as many as 36,000 are estimated to be homeless; families have been found living in underground tunnels and during cold winters, it is not uncommon for people to be found frozen to death on the streets (Hombs and Snyder, 1982). Yet driving along the expressway, one can see rows upon rows of empty shells of buildings, buildings that, if rehabilitated, would be considered attractive, even beautiful.

The urban reformers of the early twentieth century saw poor housing as the breeding place for all sorts of disorders. They had been impressed by the recent success of medical scientists in proving that diseases such as typhoid, cholera, yellow fever, and tuberculosis were related to the squalid conditions found in the slums. Some carried the disease model further: Lawrence Veiller, a major housing reformer, argued that poverty itself was "a germ disease, contagious even at times" (Veiller, 1910, p. 5). Providing cleaner and brighter living conditions would be the first step toward eliminating illness, violence, and even the poverty disease.

It is partially due to this tradition that housing and urban conditions today are perceived to be so closely linked—a link symbolized by the formation in 1965 of a new cabinet-level agency, the Department of Housing and Urban Development. Until recently, however, poor housing has been more a rural than an urban problem in the United States. Housing outside of metropolitan areas still is more likely to contain some structural problems than is city or suburban housing. Rural families, for example, are still about four times as likely as central city or suburban residents to live in housing that lacks some or all indoor plumbing facilities.

Over the past forty years, the structural condition of housing has improved dramatically (see Table 5-2.) But improvements in these basic indicators mask some very real housing problems that remain. The Annual Housing Survey, begun in 1973, collects a broader range of information about housing structure than does the more widely utilized ten-year

Table 5-2 The Condition of Housing, 1940–1981

	1940	1950	1960	1970	1975	1981
% Lacking Some or All Plumbing	45.2	35.4	16.8	6.5	3.3	2.7
% Dilapidated or Needing Major Repair	17.8	9.8	6.9	4.6	NA	NA
% Overcrowded (1.51 or more per room)	9.0	6.2	3.6	2.0	.9	1.1
Doubling Up (subfamilies in unit)	6.8	5.6	2.4	1.4	1.5	1.5

SOURCES: Carol B. Meeks, *Housing,* Englewood Cliffs, N.J.: Prentice-Hall, 1980, p. 54; U.S. Bureau of the Census and U.S. Department of Housing and Urban Development, *Annual Housing Survey, General Housing Characteristics, 1981,* Washington, D.C.: Government Printing Office, 1983.

census. The AHS statistics show that many households continue to live in structures plagued by peeling paint, falling ceilings, leaking pipes, unlit halls, and scurrying rodents (see Table 5-3).

Policy-makers, moreover, have recently come to realize that it is important to consider each housing unit as part of a broader physical and

Table 5-3 Defects in Housing, 1980

	Total Housing Units	% In Central Cities	% In Suburbs	% Outside Metropolitan Areas
No complete kitchen or shared kitchen	1,265,000	28.5	21.8	49.7
Signs of rats or mice	9,075,000	33.5	26.3	40.2
Exposed wiring	2,356,000	33.2	28.3	38.5
Lacking working outlets in some or all rooms	2,790,000	27.3	24.2	48.1
Leaking roof	5,169,000	31.1	30.5	38.4
Open cracks or holes in walls	4,459,000	41.3	27.4	31.3
Broken plaster	2,818,000	45.7	25.9	28.3
Peeling paint	3,381,000	47.3	24.9	27.8
Holes in floor	1,564,000	41.6	21.1	37.3
No lights or some lights not working in public hallways	1,360,000	61.1	30.5	8.2
Unit uncomfortably cold, 24 hours or more	758,000	20.1	22.2	57.8
Household rates units fair or poor	13,813,000	38.6	28.2	33.2

SOURCE: U.S. Bureau of the Census and U.S. Department of Housing and Urban Development, *Annual Housing Survey, 1980,* Part B, Indicators of Housing and Neighborhood Quality, Washington, D.C.: Government Printing Office, September 1982, Table A-1.

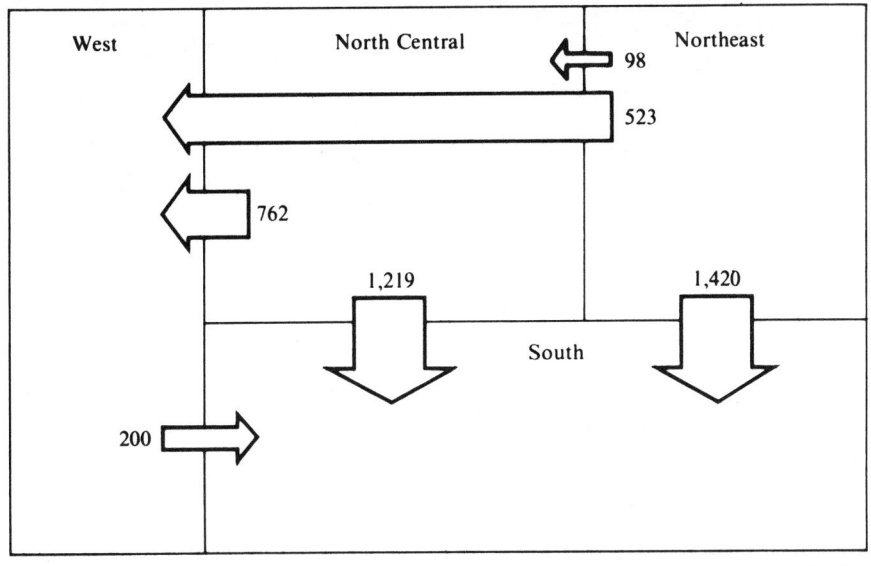

Figure 5-1 Net Interregional Migration, 1970–1978 (in thousands)

```
West          North Central         Northeast
                             ⇐ 98
         ⇐═══════════════ 523
    ⇐ 762
              1,219              1,420
               ⇓                  ⇓
                     South
  200 ⇒
```

SOURCE: Adapted from John Kasarda, "The Implications of Contemporary Redistribution Trends for National Urban Policy," *Social Science Quarterly*, vol. 61 Nos. 3 and 4, December 1980, p. 375.

social environment. When you buy or rent a place to live, you receive a "package" that includes not only your own house or apartment but surrounding structures, neighbors, access to stores, public services, and the like. Discontent with housing today may be based more on a perceived decline in this neighborhood environment than on actual deterioration of the living unit itself.

Regional Dimensions: The Decline of the Snowbelt States

Between 1970 and 1978, the Northeast and North Central regions lost nearly 4 million people due to their migration to other parts of the country. As Figure 5-1 reveals, most of these out-migrants—about 2.6 million—ended up in the South.

Businesses, jobs, and wealth are shifting southward as well. Between 1970 and 1980, the Northeast and North Central states lost over 701,000 manufacturing jobs; during the same period, the South gained 926,000 (Bureau of Labor Statistics, 1980). Some of that loss is due to out-migration by large businesses: Kirkpatrick Sale, one of the more vivid chroniclers of this trend, points to "the flight of thousands of businesses and hundreds of major corporations out of the big cities of the Northeast into the aggressive new cities of the Southern Rim, draining the Northeast of at least forty of *Fortune*'s top-ranked industrial firms in just the last ten

Table 5-4 Change in Per Capita Income, By Region, 1974–1979

Region	1974	1979	% change
Middle Atlantic[1]	5,924	9,110	53.8
New England[2]	5,635	8,916	58.2
Plains[3]	5,270	8,487	61.0
Rocky Mountain[4]	5,157	8,319	61.3
Great Lakes[5]	5,649	9,126	61.6
Southeast[6]	4,692	7,621	62.4
Far West[7]	5,911	9,884	67.2
Southwest[8]	4,968	8,600	73.1

[1]Delaware, District of Columbia, Maryland, New Jersey, New York, Pennsylvania.
[2]Connecticut, Maine, Massachusetts, New Hampshire, Rhode Island, Vermont.
[3]Iowa, Kansas, Minnesota, Missouri, Nebraska, N. Dakota, S. Dakota.
[4]Colorado, Idaho, Montana, Wyoming, Utah.
[5]Illinois, Indiana, Michigan, Ohio, Wisconsin.
[6]Alabama, Arkansas, Florida, Georgia, Kentucky, Louisiana, Mississippi, North Carolina, South Carolina, Tennessee, Virginia, West Virginia.
[7]Alaska, California, Hawaii, Nevada, Oregon, Washington.
[8]Arizona, Oklahoma, New Mexico, Texas.

years" (Sale, 1975, p. 7). But most of the shift is attributable to the location of new businesses and jobs, rather than the relocation of existing firms. As old businesses go out of business—which they do in *all* regions of the country—they are being replaced at a much slower rate in the Snowbelt than in the sunny South.

As a result of the shifts in population and business, per capita income rose more slowly in the Northeast than in any other area during the second half of the 1970s. During that same period, income rose most rapidly in the Southwest, and, for the first time, the Far West leapt into the lead as the wealthiest part of the country (see Table 5-4).

The apparent decline of the Snowbelt region is the source of continuing controversy and distress. Politicians and analysts differ sharply on the question of whether this is a serious problem calling for prompt and substantial action or simply the darker side of a generally benign process through which market forces are redistributing the nation's resources so as to maximize efficiency and economic growth. In the excitement, however, two important points are sometimes overlooked. First, *not all sections of the Snowbelt region are trapped in a downward spiral of decline.* The rise of the Sunbelt has been associated with the shift from a manufacturing to an information-processing, computer-oriented economy. But the Snowbelt region has not uniformly resisted the implications of such a change. The state of Massachusetts, for example, is credited, along with California's Silicon Valley, with being the "high-tech capital" of the United States. Four of the nation's leading companies involved in producing minicomputers are based in the state, and employment in high-technology industries rose by over 20 percent from 1976 to 1978 (Harrison, 1984).

Table 5-5 The 25 Poorest Metropolitan Areas, 1979

Metropolitan Area	Per capita income
Monroe, Louisiana	$6,945
Albany, Georgia	6,943
Killeen, Texas	6,935
Johnson City, Tennessee	6,878
Pensacola, Florida	6,859
Bryan, Texas	6,817
Fort Smith, Arkansas	6,810
Tuscaloosa, Alabama	6,767
Columbus, Georgia	6,758
Clarksville, Tennessee	6,678
St. Cloud, Minnesota	6,620
Bloomington, Indiana	6,571
Panama City, Florida	6,487
Fayetteville, North Carolina	6,448
Biloxi, Mississippi	6,436
Pascagoula, Mississippi	6,343
Anniston, Alabama	6,251
Alexandria, Louisiana	6,236
El Paso, Texas	6,207
Las Cruces, New Mexico	6,091
Lawton, Oklahoma	6,089
Brownsville, Texas	5,731
Provo, Utah	5,721
Laredo, Texas	5,106
McAllen, Texas	5,024

SOURCE: Andrew Hacker, ed. *U/S: A Statistical Portrait of the American People.* New York: Penguin, 1983, p. 158.

Just as frequently overlooked is the fact that *poverty, stagnation, and decline continue to characterize much of the Sunbelt region.* Table 5-5 lists the twenty-five poorest metroplitan areas, based on per capita income in 1979. All but two (St. Cloud, Minnesota, and Bloomington, Indiana) are located in southern or southwestern states.

IS THERE AN URBAN "CRISIS"?

Problems are simply problems, but a "crisis" implies something much more. In medicine, a crisis is a turning point in the course of a malady, a crucial stage at which it becomes clear whether the patient will live or die. If the trends of urban and regional decline constitute a genuine crisis, a distinct policy message is communicated. And that message is to "do something," and to "do it soon." There is no time, in a true crisis, to ponder and plan. Rapid, even innovative and risky, responses may be deemed legitimate. If a condition is mislabeled a crisis, however—if a chronic or nonlife-threatening problem is mistakenly judged to be of crisis proportions—the result can be disastrous. Unnecessary risks may be taken, expensive resources wasted, decisions too hastily made.

Sometime during the late 1960s, a consensus that there was indeed an urban crisis seemed to emerge. President Nixon spoke to Congress, after his election, about the "crisis in the cities." The League of Women Voters published a report on "Crisis: The Condition of the American Cities." The president of the University of California at Los Angeles speculated about "What We Must Do: Universities and the Urban Crisis." And the U.S. Catholic Conference of Bishops released a statement on "The Church's Response to the Urban Crisis." Even *Glamour* magazine got into the act, with a cover story plaintively asking, "The Urban Crisis: What Can One Girl Do?".

Academics and journalists also seemed to agree that a crisis was truly at hand. Books with titles such as *Sick Cities, The Exploding Cities, Our Cities Burn,* and *Cities in a Race with Time* drove home a message of imminent disaster. So did articles, some by noted social scientists, with titles such as "The City as Sandbox," "The City as Reservation," and "The Last Days of New York."

But not everyone agrees that there is an urban crisis, or even that there ever was one. The disagreement rests in part on ideological differences. Neoconservative analysts argue that liberals and radicals measure the world against an unattainable ideal, tending, as a result, to exaggerate current problems and underplay successes. Nor do liberals and radicals see eye to eye. Radical theorists argue that there *is* a crisis, but they generally insist that the crisis is broader than liberals assume—rooted in social structures and institutions that are national, not simply urban or regional, in scope.

Crisis? . . . or Inconvenience?

Edward Banfield argues that the conditions of American cities have more to do with convenience than crisis. The "overwhelming majority" of city residents, he writes, are living better, fuller, and more comfortable lives than ever before. Not only are things better than ever, but urbanites in the United States are living better than *any* large group has in any other time or any other place. Housing is better, schools are better, transportation is better. And, suggests Banfield, things are continuing to improve at an accelerating rate (Banfield, 1974).

What, then, is all the complaining about? According to neoconservatives such as Banfield, Americans' successes have gone to their heads; we have allowed ourselves to believe that all things are possible, and when we find that we cannot have all things, we are disappointed. Life in the real world implies trade-offs. At a personal level, these trade-offs may be between family and job, between income production and the time to enjoy one's leisure, between academic success and personal expression or breadth of experience. At the collective level, these trade-offs take other forms. Americans love cars and prefer them to public transportation as a means of getting to work or getting the shopping done. The cost of our reliance on cars—the cost of the privacy and comfort they provide—is greater pollution and congestion. Americans also like massive suburban shopping centers, with convenient parking, controlled climates, and patrolled corridors. The cost of indulging these preferences, however, is loss of patronage to the central business districts and loss of tax revenues to the central cities.

Pollution, congestion, and central city decline are unfortunate; they are inconvenient. According to Banfield, however, they cannot be considered crises or even major problems. Rather, they are the price we pay for personal freedom, privacy, the ability to live and shop where we choose. They are not crises because they do not threaten our life or our fundamental well-being. They are not crises because those who *are* inconvenienced are primarily a white middle class and business elite. And they are not crises because we already *know* how to eliminate them. It is simply the case that the cost of eliminating these inconveniences—restrictions on the use of automobiles, constraints on suburban development, taxing suburban residents and businesses to pay for the cities' needs—are greater than the benefits foreseen. "That we have not yet been willing to pay the price of solving, or alleviating, such 'problems' . . . suggests that they are not really critical" (Banfield, 1974, p. 8).

Urban Revitalization: The Crisis Leaves Town?

Something may have happened while nobody was looking. That, at least, is what T. D. Allman suggested in a controversial article in late 1978 (Allman, 1978). For decades, Allman suggested, the federal government had been desperately concerned about the fate of central cities, especially those in the Northeast and industrialized Midwest. For many years, that concern showed itself more in rhetoric than in concrete and effective policies; symbolic "wars" on urban problems were declared, but the resources to back up those wars were insufficient, and when the unintended spillovers of these programs were considered, it is possible that they did the cities more harm than good. In the late 1970s, finally, federal aid to the cities—especially, although not exclusively, to declining Snowbelt cities—accelerated rapidly. Ironically, but predictably, according to Allman, this acceleration in aid came precisely at the time that urban problems had begun to fade. There *was* an urban crisis, he suggests, but policy-makers have failed to recognize that it has become a thing of the past.

Allman has not been alone in declaring that a central city revival is under way. "The inner cities of America are poised for a stunning comeback," columnist Neal R. Peirce wrote in June of 1977, "a turnabout in their fortunes that could be one of the most significant developments [in] our history." "America Falls in Love With Its Cities . . . Again," a *Saturday Review* article proclaimed in 1978. *The New York Times Magazine* agreed: its January 14, 1979, cover story announced "The New Elite and an Urban Renaissance."

Indeed, there are signs that some older central cities and parts of the Snowbelt may be reviving. One measure of this is the boom in new office construction. Between 1979 and 1982, thirty high-rise buildings, holding over fourteen million square feet of office space, were completed or under construction in midtown Manhattan alone (Goldberger, 1982). The old downtown area of Washington, D.C., once a bleak and somewhat depressing counterpoint to the gleaming monuments and bustling tourism along the Mall, has sprouted new hotels, offices, galleries, shopping malls, and construction cranes.

Commercial resurgence is another sign of revival: in Boston's Quincy Market, for example, or in Baltimore's Harbor Place, which in 1982 attracted more visitors than did Disneyworld. Along with office and commercial activity has come evidence that young, wealthier households are moving into previously deteriorating neighborhoods in a number of cities. This phenomenon, sometimes referred to as *gentrification*, has been documented in such areas as Queen's Village in Philadelphia, Inman Park in Atlanta, Hayes Valley in San Francisco, Summit-University in Saint Paul, and Capitol Hill and Adams Morgan in Washington, D.C. (for overviews, see Gale, 1984; Schill and Nathan, 1983).

Some neoconsèrvatives point to these signs of revitalization as a double-barreled confirmation of their faith in the greater reliability of private- over public-sector solutions. Years of governmental aid failed to reverse the spiral of decline. Now—partially as a result of years of decline—land and property in the cities have become relatively less expensive, while the suburbs have become more congested and commutes have become lengthier. That wealthier households and businesses are showing renewed signs of interest in the cities is evidence, from this perspective, that free choice within a market structure eventually resolves most social problems.

The implication that urban and regional decline was simply a historical episode—dramatic but brief—meets with skepticism in some quarters. Some liberals fear, for instance, that slight signs of resurgence in a handful of inner-city neighborhoods may be used as an excuse to scale back or terminate urban-aid programs that are still genuinely needed. They point to census figures showing that, although the outflow of people from the cities to the suburbs may have slowed, the trend of relative decline has not been reversed. What is more, surveys of the American public fail to show any sign of a deeply held desire to return to urban life. To the contrary, fewer than one out of every four Americans consider a large or medium-sized city to be "the best place to live." Latent desire to live in the city is even weaker among suburbanites (11 percent) and those living in nonmetropolitan areas (10 percent).

Nor should the activity in the office and commercial sectors necessarily be interpreted as signs of a broad based resurgence. Although professional employment and new construction have boomed in Manhattan, for example, other parts of New York City have not done nearly as well (Savitch, 1983). Detroit's Renaissance Center, a massive commercial, hotel, and office complex that opened to optimistic forecasts in 1977, was flirting with bankruptcy by 1982.

Urban Crisis? Or Societal Crisis?

Radical analysts of urban problems, particularly those drawing on the theories of Marx, also take issue with the notion of an urban crisis. Their complaint is not with the idea that there is a crisis but with the implication that the crisis is somehow particular to the cities or to the Snowbelt at large.

Marx argued that capitalism is marked by internal inconsistencies. These inconsistencies, or contradictions, become more apparent as capitalism develops. Ultimately, these contradictions, which he believed to be inherent, become the rock upon which capitalism founders. What the public, the media, and more conventional urbanists perceive as an urban crisis is, according to Marxist interpretation, a broader and more deeply rooted phenomenon. The crisis is one of the social and economic structure of Western capitalism itself. The contradictions that plague the broader system simply "bubble up" to the surface more quickly and visibly in the dense, heterogeneous, manufacturing-oriented cities of the Northeast.

The outlines of this broader societal crisis are sketched particularly clearly by James O'Connor in his book *The Fiscal Crisis of the State*. (O'Connor, 1973). When O'Connor refers to "the State," he means the public sector broadly conceived; his "state" comprises all levels of government and not the fifty intermediate units with which Americans more commonly associate the term. The crisis, according to O'Connor, is rooted in the relationship between government and the large-scale industries, which he refers to as the "monopoly sector."

Marxists, as we noted in Chapter 2, posit a mutually reinforcing, or symbiotic, relationship between government and the private sector. The private sector produces the wealth upon which the public sector relies. In return, the public sector. serves two functions. First, it uses its power to *maintain conditions favorable to private-sector profitability*. It does this by providing or subsidizing the costs of *physical capital* (roads, highways, airports, sewer lines, urban renewal, etc.) and *human capital* (schools and training to provide a skilled, educated laboring and administrative work force). These types of public expenditures increase the productivity of labor, and therefore increase the profitability of business, which otherwise would have had to bear the cost of providing these things themselves. The public sector also increases profitability by lowering the cost of labor. It does this by maintaining or subsidizing programs such as Social Security, unemployment compensation, and Medicare. If the public sector did not bear the costs of these protections, wokers would demand them from their employers, with the result that profits would be eroded by higher pension, salary, and health-benefit expenditures.

The second broad function that government serves, according to O'Connor, is to *maintain and legitimize the capitalist system*. Unrestrained, the capitalist system generates harsh conditions. These harsh conditions come about due to several tendencies that Marxists believe to be inherent. First, there is the tendency of capitalism to create and maintain an "industrial reserve army": a large pool of the unemployed and underemployed whose presence keeps workers from effectively demanding higher wages. Second, there is the tendency to create "technological obsolescence." In order to increase profits, businesses must continually invest in new technologies to increase worker productivity. But each technological innovation makes the skills and experience of existing workers outdated; many of these, considered too old to profitably retrain, are dumped unceremoniously into the army of the unemployed. Third, capitalism brings about the "proletarianization" of the population. Proletarians are those who must sell their labor in order to survive. In precapitalist economies, and in the early stages of capitalism, many people could support themselves without working for others. They could do so by farming or by selling crafts, or working as skilled artisans. As capitalism develops, these options dissipate—farmland and retail outlets are controlled by large corporations, self-employed artisans are regulated by big government and overseen by large unions, traditional skills of survival are forgotten and lost. Finally, capitalism disrupts traditional networks of mutual self-help. Ethnic, tribal, and family ties are weakened in a capitalist society by the inculcation of an ideology that stresses individualism and modernism.

By forcing many out of work and by crippling channels for self-help and mutual aid, capitalism, according to Marxist interpretations, creates the seeds of its eventual downfall. It is among the proletariat—those who have nothing to lose—that the call for the overthrow of the system will eventually take hold. But government can soften the harsh edges of capitalism and defer that overthrow for some (unspecified) time. It does so by making things a little more tolerable for the poor: by providing welfare, by using taxes to mildly redistribute from the rich to the poor. And it does so by creating an *appearance* that the system is responsive to the needs and interests of the masses: by offering dramatic rituals of democracy; by creating the impression that government regulates businesses aggressively; by hiding its subsidization of business in unseen tax loopholes or packaging it as if it were intended to help the poor.

These functions of the public sector—to maintain profitability and social peace—cannot sustain capitalism forever. Ultimately, these functions come into conflict with each other and with tendencies within the private sector. It is this conflict that is at the root of the fiscal crisis of O'Connor's state. The subsidization of the private sector and the maintenance of harmony and legitimacy are *costly,* increasingly so as capitalism matures. But while the public sector socializes the costs of maintaining capitalism, the private sector continues to claim the lion's share of the profits.

The result is an ever-tightening fiscal noose. The public sector may respond by cutting back on investment in roads, highways, and so forth. To do so, however, is ultimately to decrease the profitability of business, and this, ultimately, is to choke off the government's source of tax dollars. Alternatively, the public sector may cut back on social-welfare expenditures, but to do this is to risk the mobilization of the poor as a disruptive, potentially revolutionary force.

The crisis, then, is one of the system, not of the cities. It is evident in the cities earlier, and more dramatically, because of the central role that cities play in the capitalist system. Cities are particularly vulnerable because they come to house a disproportionate number of the poor and unemployed. Cities play this role in part because it is easier to exert social control over the lower class when its members are concentrated in a fixed place. The physical and social structures of cities, moreover, are built around their role as a source of production and accumulation in the capitalist economy. As technology brings changes to capitalism, the city—like its workers—becomes out of date. Although capitalism needs cities, it needs no particular city. Newark, St. Louis, and Detroit served capitalism well in an industrial age. It is in the nature of capitalism to innovate, however, and it is in the nature of capitalism to shift resources across products and across places in order to maximize their productivity. There is little room for loyalty or "old times' sake." Cities—indeed, entire regions—that do not suit capitalism in the modern, postindustrial era can expect to be left behind.

IS DECLINE NATURAL?

Liberals are, for the most part, tinkerers. They believe that many social problems are caused by technical flaws in government or governmental programs. They are optimistic reformers. By adjusting and altering the structure and processes of government, they believe that we can have an immediate and perceptible effect, that we can make steady progress toward a more perfect world. Marxists, and many other radicals, are more skeptical. Because they see the root of our problems to be seated deep within the economic structure, they have no confidence in the notion that tinkering will have more than a superficial effect. Also, because they believe that the government, in capitalist nations, is wedded to the goal of preserving the economic system, they expect that publicly declared policy "reforms" will be motivated by a desire to quell dissent, rather than by a sincere wish to eliminate the problems themselves. In the final analysis, however, radicals and liberals are alike in at least one key respect. They both tend toward a belief in a perfectible world; where they see problems, they begin to look for solutions.

This notion that all problems have solutions is considered naive by many neoconservatives. Some hardships and inequities are rooted in the nature of Man, the nature of society, and the nature of change. This argument is made about urban and regional decline, which some neoconservatives argue must be considered to be "natural" and inevitable. The notion that decline is natural usually can be traced to a theory about why people and businesses move in response to market forces.

The "Logic" of Metropolitan and Regional Change

The Greeks believed in fate. In their myths, it took the form of three sisters: Clotho, who spins the thread of human life, Lachesis, who determines its length; and Atropos, who cuts the thread. By their actions, these three goddesses were believed to control human destiny; they had the power to determine the outcome of human lives and events before they took place. Social scientists scoff at the idea of fate. Yet by exaggerating the power and predictability of broad social, economic, and technological forces, they sometimes re-create a fatalistic worldview under a different name.

Much of what we consider to be urban decline is attributable, according to Edward Banfield, to three "imperatives" (Banfield, 1974, p. 25). These imperatives are demographic, technological, and economic. By "imperatives," Banfield means to emphasize the "inexorable, constraining character" of the three forces. The demographic imperative refers to population growth: as its population grows, due to in-migration or natural increase, a city must expand either up, or down, or outward. The technological imperative has to do with changes, primarily in transportation, communications, and manufacturing techniques. As it became cheaper and more feasible to transport people and information across distances, it was inevitable that growth would be accommodated by outward expansion (suburbanization) in greater measure than denser, upward construction. Changes in manufacturing techniques, such as the introduction of assembly-line production, made older, central-city facilities outmoded; modern factories would be long, single-story structures, requiring large plots of land that could be found, at reasonable cost, only toward the periphery of the metropolitan area. The economic imperative, finally, determined who was to live near the periphery and who near the inner core. As long as wealth is distributed unequally, Banfield suggests, it is the wealthy—those who can afford the cost of new housing and the time and energy of a commute—who will wind up residing in the more desirable suburban fringe.

What makes this "logic" of metropolitan change so clear and convincing are its parallels to a familiar model of market exchange. The process of urban decline, it would seem, is explainable in much the same way that we would explain a drop in the price of our favorite breakfast cereal or the closing down of the local movie theater after months of dwindling crowds. Like the market model, this theory of urban decline begins with the decisions of tens of thousands of individual actors: families, job seekers, private firms. These actors are presumed to be rational; they seek, in other words, to maximize their personal satisfaction and material wealth. They exercise their rationality by assessing the costs and benefits of various forms of behavior and making their decision—to buy "Fruity Flakes," to watch films on home video machines, to move out of the city—according to the dictates of that calculation. An increase in the cost of living in the city—due to rising rents, fear of crime, private-school tuition, noise, or congestion—makes out-migration more rational. So does a decline in the cost of suburban life, due, for instance, to lower interest rates for new home purchases or the construction of a new highway that shortens commuting times.

Other neoconservative analysts suggest that a similar market-driven process accounts for decline on a regional scale. Popular opinion explains the shift as an inevitable response to the appeal of warmer climates. On blustery Chicago mornings, such an explanation undoubtedly holds intuitive appeal. But climate is not the whole story. The Sunbelt, after all, has *always* been warmer. From 1900 until 1970, the major metropolitan areas in the Snowbelt were all growing in spite of the chill. The more recent signs of decline may indicate that the Snowbelt is becoming economically obsolete.

Aging factories, deteriorating infrastructure, high prices for land and labor, and burdensome taxes make the costs of doing business in the northern urban areas uncompetitive. At the same time, changes in technology, transportation, and communications have made feasible a general trend toward dispersal, or deconcentration, of the American population.

> The advantages of agglomeration and central location have been eroded by technological innovations and new production technologies that have given locational freedom to an ever wider array of industries. Transportation and

communication technologies have reinforced this dispersal because proximity has been eclipsed by electronic proximity. . . . *Increasingly, firms and people have moved away not because they must, but because they can* (emphasis added) (Hicks, 1982, p. 24).

While this has been occurring, other changes in the South itself are making the Sunbelt a more attractive place to live and do business than ever before. We will discuss some of those changes more fully in Chapter 7 when we look at growth in the Sunbelt, the flip side of regional decline.

The power of this market model of metropolitan and regional change is magnified by the strong policy message that it seems to carry. That message, essentially, is that the public sector ought not to interfere. Why? First, because the *dynamic of decline rests on fundamental values, such as personal freedom and economic efficiency.* To stop people and businesses from leaving large cities and the Snowbelt region would mean using the government's power to limit their freedom to choose where they would like to live and work. It would mean, in addition, forcing them to be inefficient: forcing families to suffer higher heating costs or to neglect better job opportunities; forcing businesses to pay more for land and rent. As a nation, presumably, we would experience waste: resources in some areas would be overloaded, while in other areas, clean air, space, water, and energy would be abundant but underutilized.

A second reason to minimize any governmental response is that, given the nature and essential rationality of the market, *public-sector intervention would be likely to backfire.* This was the conclusion of a presidential commission established in 1979. Efforts "to retard or reverse suburban growth may court serious consequences," the commission noted.

> For instance, any effort to slow the construction of new homes, which are most often in the suburbs, would severely depress the housing construction industry (among the nation's largest) and its allied industries. It would reduce the range of housing types and locations available to an increasing diversity of households and would probably drive up land prices, rents and property taxes in central locations (Hicks, 1982, pp. 35-6).

A third and final argument against governmental role is that, left to its own devices, *the market carries its own solutions.* As the central city empties out, as the Snowbelt region continues to lose people and jobs, the seeds for their eventual revival simultaneously are planted. Unused factories and deteriorating housing decline in cost. Unemployed workers become more anxious for jobs, even at low wages. At the same time, competition for land, housing, and labor in the suburbs and booming Sunbelt regions means that prices there will escalate. Astute home-seekers, investors, and businessmen will not take long to spot the opportunity for bargains and profits in the declining areas. Over time, in theory, the free flow of capital will balance out the inequities between city and suburb, north and south. The notion that the trends we now regard as evidence of decline may, in fact, be a self-limiting process of equalization is sometimes referred to as "convergence theory" (Watkins and Perry, 1978, p. 19).

Decline as Mismanagement

In a 1975 article entitled "Going Broke the New York City Way," *Fortune* magazine gave voice to a widely shared belief that part of the city's fiscal crisis was due to the fact that its mayor, John Lindsay, was a "pushover" for the city's public employee unions (Robertson, 1975). Although Lindsay talked tough about unions—denouncing leaders of the transit workers union as "power brokers"—the settlements he finally achieved often seemed to push the city treasury beyond the bounds of sound fiscal policy, or even good taste. According to William Simon, U.S. secretary of the treasury at the time of the city's near bankruptcy, New York City brought many of its problems on itself by spending three times as much, per capita, as other large cities. Simon ruefully noted that a subway change giver earned $212 per week, whereas a bank teller in the private sector typically earned only $150 (Simon, 1978).

By laying responsibility at the doorstep of "pushover politicians" and "bumbling bureaucrats," this perspective suggests that decline is not simply the inevitable side effect of various broad forces of demographic, technological, and economic change. The large central cities and the Snowbelt region would have been much better off, it is argued, if they had simply had better managers at the helm. New York City is frequently used as a case in point.

Spending More For Less. Between 1961 and 1977, New York City added about 2,000 police officers, but the entire police force in 1977 worked 1 million *fewer* hours than did the smaller force sixteen years before. Between 1968 and 1977, ridership on the city's public transportation system declined by 22 percent; the city *added* 384 employees, over the same period, to handle the lighter load. If New York City employees worked a forty-hour week, as most federal and private-sector workers do, about 20 million extra hours of service—the equivalent of over 10,000 new employees—might be saved (Auletta, 1979).

During the Sixties and early Seventies, many state and local governments found themselves spending more but seemingly accomplishing less. Only a relatively small part of this apparent inefficiency was due to increasing salaries for public officials. More important were changes in fringe benefits and pensions. Sanitation workers in New York, for example, received four hours' extra pay as an "out of town" allowance simply for working outside their normally assigned districts. Some employees received up to $265 each year as a "uniform allowance," even though their jobs did not require them to wear uniforms. Transit workers were entitled to special "birthday pay." Police and fire workers were awarded a full day off for donating a pint of blood (Newfield and DuBruhl, 1977).

Public officials have a particular incentive to encourage public employees to trade off salary and fringe-benefit demands for more generous pension benefits. The media often assume that pension deals are too dull and technical to warrant much discussion, and the fiscal effects are not felt until the workers covered by the new contract begin to retire. Politicians sometimes calculate that they can "get away" with pension concession; public inattention limits the political cost, and a new administration is likely to be in office before the fiscal impact is fully felt.

Would Better Management Make a Big Difference? It seems clear that public officials in several large cities made a number of unwise, possibly irresponsible, decisions. Some worsened the situation, too, by adopting a series of questionable budgetary "gimmicks" to mask the true extent of indebtedness that was being incurred. But did these decisions play more than an incremental role in the development of the city's fiscal crisis? Would better managers have avoided all these problems, or would a tightly run ship only float a little longer before beginning to sink?

It is difficult to answer questions such as these with any confidence. We are not free to rerun the film of New York City's fiscal history with different mayors and budgetary officials in charge. There are some good reasons, however, to regard the "bad managagement" thesis skeptically, especially when it is offered as if it identifies the major villain in the scenario of urban decline.

If Mayor John Lindsay's mismanagement was a factor in New York City's decline, it certainly was not due to his lack of respect or understanding of the importance of good management techniques. Lindsay is remembered today primarily as a social reformer; but he made an equal commitment—in rhetoric and in practice—to the goals of planning, efficiency, and scientific management. Bright young outsiders, with fresh degrees from Harvard and other prestigious institutions, were brought in by Lindsay to implement this more rational planning scheme. Highly trained consultants were hired to apply quantitative techniques to devising more efficient means of delivering urban services. These efforts to impose greater rationality were resisted by the entrenched bureaucracy.

In attempting to force these major changes rapidly, and from the top down, the Lindsay administration may indeed have been guilty of a lack of management sensitivity as well as political naiveté. Lindsay found out that the agencies and public employees had ideas of their own—and the political clout to successfully resist many of his reforms. Although Lindsay may have attempted too much, too fast, he *was* attempting to do just what management and public administration schools were saying should be done.

The tradition of higher spending is found deeper into the city's past, and much of that tradition has little to do with techniques of management. New York City spends more in part because the state of New York forces it to. The state requires New York City to shoulder a bigger share of AFDC and Medicaid costs than any other large city in other states is forced to meet. It is not easy to explain why this is so, but it *is* easy to explain why it is not easily changed. For New York State to lift the burden of those payments off the shoulders of the city would require more than a budgetary shuffle or an accountant's sleight of hand. Such a change would shift the burden of caring for the poor onto taxpayers in the suburbs and upstate areas. Residents of those areas do not want that burden, and their representatives in the state legislature are well aware of that fact. In this sense, at least, it can be said that the fiscal problems of New York City are rooted in political conflict rather than in managerial technique.

New York also spends more because it offers more: a clinic and hospital network and a city college system, for example, which most other cities cannot even begin to match. This, too, is best understood in political rather than administrative terms. Minorities, ethnic neighborhoods, and public employees have combined, at various times in the city's history, to represent a potent political coalition whose demands could be met by an expansion of the public sector and the benefits it provides (Shefter, 1977).

In every city, county, and state there are some individuals and groups that are likely to benefit from an expanded public sector and other individuals and groups that believe their own interests are better served by limiting what the government can do. The relative strength of these two groups is affected by many factors, including the local political history, the availability of strong leadership, and the broad tenor of the times. In defending their interests, those seeking an expansion of governmental responsibility have had greater success in New York City than have their counterparts in many other places. But the nature of the conflict, in New York, is not radically different from that in other jurisdictions. Pleas for better management, if they ignore this conflict, are not likely to have much effect. Some radical analysts would go so far as to charge that such pleas are little more than an effort to promote the interests of the better off in the name of the public good. They, along with others, suggest that the bad management thesis may be grounded in a misunderstanding based on too heavy a reliance on the analogy between officials in state and local government and the corporate officers of large businesses.

Are Cities and States Like a Business? The idea that state and local government should be managed like a business is not new. During the early twentieth century, the Progressive Reformers made a similar claim. "The professional politician must be ousted and in his place capable businessmen chosen to conduct the affairs of the city," urged one (Hays, 1964).

But cities and states are not like a business in some very important ways. *Business managers have the advantage of a single, clear goal—profit-making.* Public-sector managers must pursue many goals—safe streets, better housing, better services, helping the needy, protecting citizens' rights, maintaining the physical infrastructure, limiting tax burdens, providing jobs. Often, these goals are ambiguously defined: Should all the needy be helped, or only the "deserving" poor? Does good service provision mean sending the same number of garbage trucks into each neighborhood, or does it mean targeting resources to those neighborhoods in the greatest need? Often, too, the goals may be in tension with each other—more aggressive policing and the use of preventive detention might be needed to achieve safe streets, but this would risk stepping on some of the legal rights of criminal suspects; providing the poor with better housing might encourage them to stay in the city, but if the tax base of the city is to be revitalized, it may be necessary to replace the poor with luxury housing and office and commercial development; greater reliance on nuclear power by state-regulated utilities might reduce energy costs, but the location of new facilities will spark intense concern and instability. A major and difficult task of the mayor, or governor, or any other public-sector executive, is to sort through these goals, to accurately assess what the public wishes and (not necessarily the same thing) what the public needs.

Managers in the private sector also have greater authority than the typical executive in state or local government. Mayors must operate under a series of formal and informal constraints upon their power. Taking office, a new mayor confronts a budget over which he or she has little control. Some expenditures are dictated by federal or state requirements. State law, at the same time, usually prohibits certain forms of taxation and may rule out other strategies for raising revenues. Governors often have a little more latitude, but they, too, are often limited by constitutional provisions earmarking funds for specific purposes and setting strict conditions under which new funds can be raised.

A corporate executive almost always has the power to hire and fire subordinates, but mayors and governors often may not. They may be forced to work with administrators who have their own goals, their own political constituencies, and, often, formal protection from being removed from office. Also public-sector executives, unlike their private-sector counterparts, operate within two- to four-year terms; the pressure to produce the quick and dramatic results is often in conflict with the demands of careful planning, or anything more than superficial reform.

Political Dimensions of Decline

Most discussions of urban and regional decline focus on the losers—the renters whose buildings and neighborhoods deteriorate around them, the taxpayers who must pay more at the same time that services are cut back, the public- and private-sector workers suddenly left without jobs. But there can be winners as well. These may be property speculators, who use the specter of decline to convince others to sell to them at very low prices. Or they may be suburban residents, who benefit not from the fact of decline itself but from the fact that the problems associated with decline are confined within the central city, cordoned off from their insulated communities. Or they may be businesses that, in pursuit of cheaper labor or lower taxes, pick up and head for the Sunbelt, leaving unemployment and other problems behind for others to confront.

Are these winners simply lucky beneficiaries of a process over which they have no control? This is what the neoconservative emphasis on broad and uncontrollable factors would seem to suggest. But some liberal and radical analysts argue that a focus on disembodied market forces or the errors of administrators overlooks the ways in which some groups actively influence events so as to increase their benefits at the cities' expense.

Suburban Exclusion and Exploitation. It seems that most Americans prefer to live in areas consisting of others who are like them in terms of race, religion, and social class. Some believe this preference for homogeneity is natural and ingrained—a throwback, perhaps, to an animalistic herd instinct. Others argue that it is learned, a cultural artifact passed on through observation and reinforced by parental and peer pressures. In either case, it is possible for a society to structure its institutions in ways to moderate *or* to accentuate the impact of such pressures. Because we have so many local governments and because we grant them a significant amount of power to control the land within their boundaries, the drive for homogeneity is given greater expression than it might otherwise enjoy.

The decentralization of land use powers has made it more feasible for wealthy property owners to keep minorities and the poor outside of their communities. This is accomplished through local governments' zoning authority and their power to enforce building codes. *Zoning authority* refers to the power of governments to establish legal guidelines regarding what can and cannot be done in defined areas. *Building code authority* refers to the power to regulate the materials, design, and techniques of construction. The U.S. Constitution has been interpreted as reserving these powers to the states. But tradition and political pressures have led nearly every state to delegate these powers to its local jurisdictions.

Zoning and code enforcement powers can be used to make low-cost housing infeasible—a strategy we will discuss in greater detail in Chapter 7. These powers were designed originally to protect property owners from undesirable land uses—to ensure, for instance, that a noisy factory could not be built in the middle of a residential neighborhood. But these same powers also are easily used to keep out "undesirable" people.

At the same time that they are locking the poor into the central cities, wealthier suburbanites may be continuing to exploit the cities—using their facilities and relying upon them for their own jobs. Suburban residents and their elected officials at times use their political clout at the state and national levels in order to fend off efforts to make them bear a larger share of the metropolitan tax burden or to open their borders to larger numbers of minorities and the poor. Some states, for instance, prohibit their cities from implementing a "commuter tax," an income tax on suburbanites who work within the central city. The ability of the suburbs to protect their self-interests has grown along with their populations; since the mid-1960s, states have been required to redraw the boundaries of their legislative districts to ensure that growing areas receive greater political representation. In addition, the higher level of voter participation among wealthier suburbanites makes their influence even greater than numbers alone would predict.

Radical analysts liken the relationship between the central cities and the suburbs to that between certain developing countries and the colonial powers. The colonial suburbs, this analogy suggests, draw much of their wealth and resources from the city while using their political and economic power to keep the cities in a state of dependency. "Suburbs derive their value from the very city whose problems they seek to close off. Posh suburban Bronxville, located in Westchester County, does in reality possess slums—they can be found in the Bronx" (Savitch, 1979, p. 286).

One must be careful, however, not to overestimate the extent to which unified suburban interests have created the urban crisis by their exclusionary practices. The suburbs do not speak with one political voice. Deteriorating inner suburbs may find that their interests are aligned with the central cities on many political issues. Newer, wealthier suburbs—peopled by an upper-class, educated, and cosmopolitan population—may find that stylistic and cultural differences make it difficult for them to ally themselves with more parochial rural interests in a long-term coalition against state and national policies to help the urban core.

What *can* be said is this: the broad demographic, technological, and economic forces that Banfield and others rely upon to explain patterns of central city and regional decline tell only part of the story. These "natural" forces play on a field on which different racial and class-based groups are using whatever political power they can muster to segment and channel change. Wealthier residents have used their power to create a filter around the central cities, a filter that allows others like them to move out of cities while locking out many who are too poor. The result is that those with the greatest need for public services and the least wealth with which to pay for them are left in the cities, concentrating social problems and exacerbating the fiscal squeeze.

Corporate Mobility and Corporate Power. "When the old corporate tax bite eats away profits, CUT OUT FOR TEXAS." This ad, which appeared in the *New York Times,* was an example of a recent and significant trend. States and localities, anxious to attract jobs and potential tax dollars, have launched aggressive efforts to entice corporations to pick up and move. What the ads are offering is more than a hearty welcome. In the heat of competition, each government feels it must offer lower taxes, fewer regulations, better services, and, most of all, a chance to make more money. "If you think you'd like the Sun Belt," another ad proclaimed, "you'll love THE MONEY BELT" (Sterba, 1978).

The flow of businesses from the Snowbelt and older cities may be the most dramatic aspect of the urban and regional crisis. But the movement of businesses is not simply an outgrowth of broad and uncontrollable market forces. Businesses respond to many factors when making decisions about where and whether to invest. These include changes in the tastes of the buying public, the cost of raw materials, the quality and costs of labor, transportation and public services, and taxes. All of these, with the possible exception of the first, can be altered through political action. Taxes on energy and minerals, or limitations on strip mining, alter the cost of raw materials. Regulations regarding minimum wages, unemployment compensation, compensation for workers' injuries, and the conditions under which unions operate affect the cost of labor. State and local education policies can determine the quality of the work force that is available. Accessibility to highways and other transit systems alters the cost of transporting raw materials, goods, and services. Good public services reduce the private costs of doing business and make an area more attractive, as a place to live, for technological and administrative personnel. Taxes directly affect profits at the bottom line.

Although businesses *respond* to such costs and benefits, they can also seek to *shape* them. Businesses, especially large businesses, have considerable political power in the state and local arena. Their power grows out of their access to traditional political resources, such as money for political candidates, status to help in persuading others, information, and expertise. It also grows out of the implicit or explicit threat of mobility. By fostering an impression that they will relocate elsewhere if denied their requests, business leaders may be able to obtain concessions from political leaders fearful of the consequences of any further loss of tax revenues or jobs. Thus, businesses can demand lower taxes or the provision of low-cost expansion loans. Or they may convince local officials to use public authority and public monies to obtain land for corporate expansion or push for a new highway access spur.

The state of Pennsylvania, in order to entice the Volkswagen Corporation to build a massive new plant within its borders, offered the company an incredible array of incentives. Among the commitments made by the state: a promise to spend $40 million to buy and refurbish an existing plant, then lease it to Volkswagen; $25 million in state bonds would be issued to raise money for special rail and highway connections for the plant; and local governments would forgive 95 percent of the company's tax bill for the first two years of its operation and 50 percent for the next three years (Chernow, 1978).

Although such a "bidding for business" approach to economic development may generate long-term potential for jobs and higher tax revenues, the immediate cost to state and local governments can be high. Moreover, as more and more jurisdictions have gotten into the competition, the bargaining power of each has decreased. Shrewd businesses can play one city against another, and one state against another state, to extract more and more favorable terms. According to consumer activist Ralph Nader, moreover, such incentives play only a minor role in affecting a business's decision whether or not to move. "States are bidding against each other for the right to enrich these big businesses," he insists. "It's a war of all against all and nobody wins except the companies" (Kramer, 1979).

Radical analysts, and some liberals, argue that rather than squeezing all possible concessions from desperate cities and states, the nation's large corporations have a moral responsibility for seeking to aid in the rehabilitation of declining areas. The cities we see today, after all, are in large measure the artifact of the corporate needs of yesterday. When major employers needed them, local governments have built new roads to facilitate the movement of supplies and products in and out of the city. When corporations constructed buildings too large for existing fire-fighting equipment to handle, cities have provided their fire departments with expensive equipment. When large factories created sewage or waste too plentiful or toxic for existing systems, cities have updated these. When businesses needed workers willing to labor at low wages, cities helped to provide housing for those workers and school programs to provide them with the requisite work-related skills. As businesses find their needs changing—due to new market conditions or changes in production techniques—the cities they helped to structure may no longer serve their current needs. Their transportation networks, service capacities, and pool of potential laborers may suddenly become obsolete.

Whether or not the business sector should be free to flee without any restrictions or legal responsibilities to the declining areas is a difficult and controversial question. It is a question we cannot possibly hope to answer satisfactorily here. We can, however, say this: the answer is not predetermined by disembodied market forces or written mysteriously in the cards of technological change. The extent to which capital is free to move within any society is in large measure a political decision, influenced and alterable by the balance of power among competing groups.

SUMMARY AND CONCLUSIONS

Decline does not leave its paw print only on large cities, nor are its impacts limited to a particular region. The fact that an area shows one kind of distress, moreover, does not mean that deterioration is broad-based. A city with high employment, if it refuses to raise taxes in response to public needs, may find itself in a genuine fiscal bind. A city that keeps its budget balanced by cutting police and social services may find itself suffering from social disorder and escalating violence.

Although no city or region is fated to an irrevocable decline, broad economic shifts leave some areas handicapped in their capacity to maintain and attract the resources needed in order to provide a healthy quality of life. Two of the most important of these shifts—the national transition from a manufacturing to a service-providing and information-processing society, and the trend toward deconcentration made possible by changes in communications and transportation technologies—tend to weigh more heavily on the older, northeastern, and upper midwestern cities. Those cities originally thrived precisely because of their manufacturing base and because of their location on harbors and railroad lines, and the economic advantages that density offered when distance carried a heavy cost.

No reasonable person thinks that urban and regional decline is a good thing in and of itself. But analysts working within different ideological traditions differ considerably in their estimate of the severity of the problem and the possibility for launching an effective public-sector response (see Table 5-6). Neoconservative analysts, however, tend to see deterioration as a normal and inevitable part of adaptation and change. Shifting forces of supply and demand alter the attraction of living and doing business in certain areas. It does no good to have government seek to overpower these market forces. It may, indeed, do harm. Locking businesses into regions in which their costs are unnecessarily high will leave them unable to compete with more mobile producers from other

Table 5-6 Ideological Perspectives on Urban and Regional Decline

	Neoconservative	Liberal	Radical
Nature of Decline	Natural expression of market forces; central cities and Snowbelt suffer from aging infrastructure, poor "business climate"	Results from imperfections in market and unanticipated consequences of public policies	Uneven development is inevitable in an economic system that allows free flow of capital in pursuit of maximum profits. Businesses benefit through increased leverage over workers and revenue-hungry local jurisdictions.
Severity of Problem	Creates short-term problems for declining areas and their citizens; in long run promotes efficient use of national resources; tends to be self-correcting (e.g., gentrification)	Disruptive and harmful; can be handled by existing institutions	Reflects fundamental flaws that may ultimately generate severe conflict
Role of Government	Efforts to block or retard change will be counter-productive; past programs anchored poor in declining area instead of helping them to move or retrain to meet needs of changing market	Based on past experience, can devise policies that can moderate ill effects; federal regulation needed to ensure that privileged do not use local zoning and regulatory powers to close doors of opportunity	Genuine reform calls for public control over capital; e.g., regulation of plant closures; such reform unlikely unless forced by mobilized working class

countries. Holding the poor and needy in declining areas, by providing them with benefits and services, only perpetuates their dependency by dissuading them from picking up and moving to other areas where the chances of economic success are greater.

Both liberal and radical analysts reject the deterministic tinge to this perspective. They argue that governmental actions, such as the construction of an interstate highway system or the funding of water development projects in the dry Southwest, have much to do with the trends of metropolitan and regional change. Many liberals believe that new policies will be able to correct the harmful side effects of those past actions. Radicals are more skeptical. Urban and regional decline, in their estimation, result from free flow of capital in the pursuit of the highest return to those private interests that control capital. Decline, in other words, is inevitable *unless* there is fundamental reform of the economic system; such reform will be resisted by those currently in power.

The way we understand urban and regional change, then, directly can shape our orientation toward public policy—whether we think governmental action is desirable and whether we think it is likely to succeed. But our position need not be based on abstract theories alone. In the next chapter, we will review the history of major policies intended to fight decline. As we shall see, conflicting interpretations about what those policies consisted of, and disagreements as to whether they succeeded or failed, ensure that there will be no consensus as to the lessons we should draw. Nonetheless, understanding that history is vital if we are to avoid repeating errors *and* if we are to recognize those aspects of past efforts that are worthy of carrying with us into the future.

SUGGESTED READINGS

Alcaly, Roger E., and David Mermelstein, eds. *The Fiscal Crisis of American Cities.* New York: Vintage, 1977.

Auletta, Ken. *The Streets Were Paved with Gold: The Decline of New York.* New York: Random House, 1979.

Bahl, Roy. *Financing State and Local Government in the 1980s.* New York: Oxford University Press, 1984.

Bluestone, Barry, and Bennett Harrison. *The Deindustrialization of America.* New York: Basic Books, 1982.

Clark, Terry Nichols, and Lorna Crowley Ferguson. *City Money Political Processes, Fiscal Strain and Retrenchment.* New York: Columbia University Press, 1983.

Hicks, Donald A. *Urban America in the Eighties.* New Brunswick, N.J.: Transaction Books, 1982.

Morris, Charles R. *The Cost of Good Intentions: New York City and the Liberal Experiment.* New York: W. W. Norton, 1980.

Sawyers, Larry, and William K. Tabb, ed. *Sunbelt/Snowbelt.* New York: Oxford University Press, 1984.

Soloman, Arthur P., ed. *The Prospective City.* Cambridge, Massachusetts: MIT Press, 1980.

6

Fighting Decline

The story of Pruitt-Igoe was dramatic from beginning to end. Built in St. Louis in the early 1950s, Pruitt-Igoe was public housing—planned, built, and managed by a local public-housing authority whose members were appointed by the local government. It was a project conceived on a grand scale: thirty-three eleven-story buildings holding over 2,700 apartment units. So massive a project, its advocates argued, would stand as a city within the city. It would not be overwhelmed, physically or socially, by the deteriorating areas surrounding it. Skidmore Owings and Merrill, an internationally known architectural firm, designed the project. The design won an award from the American Institute of Architects. (Mayer, 1978, p. 198).

Only twenty years after it was first occupied, television cameras whirred as a charge of explosives sent several of the structures crumbling to the ground. Conditions at Pruitt-Igoe had become so poor that officials were forced to order its demolition. To those who already suspected as much, Pruitt-Igoe became a symbol of the failure of government to stem or reverse the process of inner-city decline. No wonder that sociologist Nathan Glazer was moved to label the public-housing program a "graveyard of good intentions" (Glazer, 1967, p. 35).

The neoconservative message that urban and regional decline is inevitable rests on both a theoretical and an empirical base. The theoretical base lies in commonly understood laws of the market: as tastes and technologies change, neighborhoods, cities, and perhaps even regions may become inefficient and unfashionable. As the demand to live and do business in those areas plummets, the value of properties there falls as well. A spiral of decline is set into motion.

Augmenting this abstract argument is a more concrete interpretation of our recent history. This interpretation holds that the past fifty years have witnessed a series of governmental programs intended to reverse the tide of decline. Most of these efforts, according to neoconservative critics, sought to replace the logic of the market with good intentions and the power of government. Most, they argue, were launched in Washington, D.C., and imposed upon local environments with little sensitivity to their unique mix of problems and opportunities. Many were disappointing. Some, like Pruitt-Igoe, failed dramatically.

The lesson would seem to be one of shaving down our expectations. The forces that lead to change and decline are natural; we should work with them rather than against them. Housing and development policies should seek to accommodate, rather than challenge, the direction set by private corporations and investors. Decision-making should be decentralized. The problems facing a Youngstown, Ohio—which saw its economy decimated by the closing of a steel plant that had employed 4,100 workers—differ from those of an Atlanta, Georgia—in which pockets of poverty coexist with vital and dynamic areas of commercial and office growth. Strategies for revival need to be tailored to respond to the difference between a Youngstown and, for example, a Lowell, Massachusetts—which in spite of severe economic problems combines a downtown of historic interest with ready access to major universities and other sources of technological expertise.

In this chapter, we will review the recent history of housing and urban development policies. In the process, we will see that the lessons of the past are more ambiguous than this simple interpretation suggests. Many of the programs that are characterized as highly centralized, national government efforts actually were quite intergovernmental in structure. Many of the programs criticized for seeking to overpower market signals actually were designed to give the private sector a considerable role. Many of these efforts also can boast of successes, in addition to the failures that were more broadly publicized.

REASSESSING THE RECORD

Public Housing

Pruitt-Igoe does not tell the whole story of public housing. Consider the ninety-six buildings that make up the Queensbridge project in New York City. Opened in 1940, the project was designed to meet a broad range of its residents' needs. Included were a day-care center, a community center, a health clinic, a library, and stores. Later, a psychiatric center, volunteer ambulance corps, and senior-citizens center were added. About half of the buildings are organized into a "tenant patrol," which, in addition to providing more security, "functions as a sort of social service agency—they give out clothes, help people move, keep house for people just back from the hospital, provide lunch for senior citizens and an escort service, take complaints, operate both a summer lunch program and a day camp for kids, provide a monthly forum whereby tenants and management can communicate, stress self-help and beautification (they have flowers and vegetables on the grounds) and in general do whatever is needed" (New York Urban Coalition, 1983, p. 21).

Or juxtapose the image of Pruitt-Igoe being reduced to rubble with the praise that residents offer Stapleton Houses, another New York City project. Florence Ciardiello has lived in the project since 1967. "It is really a nice community here. We all feel like family," she says. Another, more recently arrived tenant claims "this is paradise. . . . We have trees, flowers, sunshine and children playing. . . . It is like being on a vacation here" (New York Urban Coalition, 1983, p. 17). Clearly, the story of public housing is more complicated than it sometimes is made to seem.

Origin and Design. It took the Great Depression to draw the federal government into the housing business. The idea of the public sector owning and operating housing is sharply at odds with the American tradition of free enterprise. Conditions during the depression, however, were severe. Shantytowns, derisively labeled "Hoovervilles" after the then president, were cropping up on the outskirts of many cities. Homeless families—many of them former members of a proud middle class—huddled in makeshift shacks and lean-tos or created temporary housing out of abandoned sewer pipes.

The U.S. Housing Act of 1937 launched the public-housing program "to provide financial assistance to the states and political subdivisions thereof for the elimination of unsafe and unsanitary housing conditions, for the eradication of slums, for the provision of decent, safe, and sanitary dwellings for families of low income, and for the reduction of unemployment and the stimulation of business activity. . . ." Three points about the program that Congress designed to achieve these goals are particularly important to keep in mind:

- *Although national in origin, the public-housing program was intergovernmental in implementation.* Responsibility for designing, developing, and managing each project would lie with an independent local government agency whose officers would be appointed by the mayor or city council. States had to pass specific legislation to enable local governments to participate in the program, and some states used this opportunity to impose restrictions of their own design. The costs of building the public housing were shouldered by the federal government, however, which paid back the bonds the local authorities issued in order to raise the funds needed for construction costs. In the 1960s, the federal government also began to provide special subsidies for each elderly, disabled, and low-income family that the local authority housed.

- *The program, as originally conceived, was not targeted at the very poor.* "Obviously," said Senator Robert F. Wagner, a supporter of the 1937 legislation, "this bill cannot provide housing for those who cannot pay the rent" (Mayer, 1978, p. 189). The intended beneficiaries were the working poor: stable, previously middle-class families facing temporary hardship due to the national economic collapse. Local authorities were required, by the federal legislation, to charge rents sufficiently high to cover the day-to-day costs of operating the projects. Because policy-makers were thinking in terms of the *temporarily* poor, however, they did not stop to consider the strains on the program that serving a permanently dependent underclass might produce.

- *Providing "decent, safe, and sanitary dwellings" was only one of several competing goals.* The original legislation was equally motivated by the desire to give the construction industry an economic boost. Eliminating slums was another target. A requirement that local authorities tear down at least one slum dwelling unit for every unit of new public housing that they built "testifies eloquently to the fact that the original objectives of public housing were as much to tear down ugly slums as to improve housing opportunities for poor people" (Wolman, 1971, p. 30).

- *Public officials sometimes found themselves faced with choices in which the needs of potential residents and the desires of builders and real-estate interests did not coincide.* Builders and real-estate interests were already more organized and politically influential than the somewhat amorphous group of "potential tenants"; the goal of stirring an economic revival gave business interests a greater legitimacy and allowed officials to defer to their desires in the name of the "national interest."

Resistance to Public Housing. Public housing has always led a stormy existence. Over the years, however, the structure of opposition to the program has changed. Early resistance was led by organizations representing private-sector organizations that saw the government as a potential competitive threat. Groups such as the National Association of Real Estate Boards (NAREB) and the National Association of Home Builders (NAHB) attacked public housing as "socialistic and communistic" when it was first proposed (Wolman, p. 62). NAHB later came to realize that a governmental role in housing usually could be counted on to generate *more* business for its members. Although private business opposition moderated, however, resistance from neighborhoods in which public housing was to be built was on the rise.

Popular resistance to public housing grew as the program came to be perceived as a mechanism for racial and economic integration. This resistance was oriented less against the concept of public housing in general than against the locations proposed for specific projects. The racial and economic composition of public-housing tenants changed over time, becoming increasingly dominated by minorities and the dependent poor. A 1976 survey of public-housing tenants in twenty large cities found that 73 percent were black, 49 percent were female-headed families, and 43 percent relied on AFDC or SSI as their primary income source (Struyk, 1980, p. 48).

Long-standing racial antagonism was joined with fears regarding the impact nearby projects might have on property values and already overcrowded schools. When New York City officials proposed building 840 units in the predominantly white and middle-class neighborhood of Forest Hills during the 1960s, the resultant conflict was so heated that some observers believe that the incident dealt Mayor John Lindsay a political blow from which he never recovered. The project, in this case, did proceed, but only after being scaled down to nearly half the proposed size. In other communities, opposition was intense enough to kill proposed projects and to convince many local officials that *public housing* was a term best left unspoken by those who wished reelection for additional terms.

Critics of public housing sometimes suggest that such grass-roots resistance was a natural result of an arrogant effort by the national government to aggressively impose its own conception of integrated living with little or no tolerance for local traditions and cultural mores. But national officials often showed a great deal of sensitivity, frequently condoning local officials' placement of projects in a manner intended to *maintain* ghettos rather than challenge the resistance of the white middle class. It was the federal Department of Interior that, in the early years of the program, developed the "neighborhood composition rule," which indicated that housing projects should not be allowed to alter the racial character of the area into which they were placed (Meyerson and Banfield, 1955, p. 121).

Several factors contributed to the increasing class and racial polarization that fueled the atmosphere of conflict. We have already mentioned the fact that the composition of public housing was changing, becoming increasingly black, female-headed, and dependent on welfare programs. This was, in part, a gradual process that mirrored changes in the broad composition of America's poor. But in 1969, this gradual change was accelerated by the passage of the "Brooke Amendment." This amendment to federal housing legislation prohibited local housing authorities from charging tenants more than 25 percent of their income for rent. The federal government promised to make up the difference between this amount and the normal rent the authority would charge. Previously, the need for local authorities to charge enough to cover operating costs had priced the very poor out of the projects; that barrier had now been broken down.

Sociologists and planners, meanwhile, had begun to insist that a strategy of bunching public housing in existing ghettos destined those projects to fail. Projects built in severely deteriorated neighborhoods would be unattractive to potential residents, apartments would lie vacant, and only the most desperate of families, and those burdened with the greatest emotional and personal disorders, would be willing to stay. This perspective generated support within some circles for a "scattered site" approach—dispersing small clusters of public housing units within stable middle-class neighborhoods.

In 1974, the Supreme Court gave the scattered site approach some legal momentum. A group of blacks, either living in or having applied to public housing, had filed suit against the Chicago Housing Authority (CHA), charging that CHA had selected public housing sites so as to avoid placing black families in white neighborhoods. The Supreme Court agreed with a lower court finding that unconstitutional discrimination had occurred, and it upheld the remedy the lower court had ordered. That remedy called for CHA to build its next 700 units in predominantly white neighborhoods in Chicago. What is more, 75 percent of all future units would have to be located in white areas in Chicago *or* in its suburbs. But the Court did not provide CHA, or other local housing authorities, with the power to *force* such areas to accept public housing.

By the time of this decision in the *Gautreaux* case, moreover, the public-housing program had all but shut down. Charging that too many public-housing projects were "monstrous, depressing places—run down, overcrowded, crime-ridden, falling apart" (Nixon, 1973), President Nixon moved to prevent any new public-housing units from being authorized. Although his action was critcized by some, protest was somewhat constrained. Years of controversy and the specter of Pruitt-Igoe had left few spokespersons willing to champion the public-housing cause.

The Other Side of the Story. Today public housing still lacks a strong, vocal constituency. Although over 3 million Americans continue to live in public housing, only a smattering of units—and those almost exclusively for the elderly—have been built in the past ten years. The trend today is in the opposite direction. As some of the early projects age, local authorities, confronting the high costs of renovation, are fighting a losing battle to maintain even the units now in existence. Some are giving up on the battle. In Alexandria, Virginia, for example, civic and business leaders have proposed selling "The Berg," four square blocks of public housing, to a private developer, who would demolish the units and put luxury townhouses in their place.

But the record suggests that the public-housing story is somewhat more complex than those who label it a dismal failure are ready to admit:

- *Along with its Pruitt-Igoes, the public-housing program can point to some genuine successes.* Many of the most dismal tales are associated with the massive projects, like Pruitt-Igoe and Chicago's 4,415-unit Robert Taylor Homes. One study found, for instance, that one of the best predictors of the rate of crime in any public-housing project was the number of floors (Newman, 1972). Yet not all large cities relied on massive, high-rise projects. Cleveland, Los Angeles, and Pittsburgh, for example, stayed completely away from elevator housing in projects designed for families (Struyk, 1980, p. 28). Even some of the older, larger complexes were relatively well built, offering better housing, certainly, than was available to low-income families on the private-housing market. The surest indicator of that is the painfully long waiting lists to get into public housing in some cities. In Washington, D.C., for example, which has a total of about 11,200 public-housing units, the waiting list is habitually over 7,000 families long. In New York City, there are about half a million on the waiting list (New York Urban Coalition, 1983, p. 9).

- *Some of the failures attributed to the program were imposed by political constraints rather than an inherent flaw in the program design.* Critics often point to the ugliness of public-housing projects as an indication of the lack of creativity and imagination that inevitably comes with governmental control, and the rapid deterioration of projects like Pruitt-Igoe is blamed on tenant abuse. But these factors were due, at least in part, to political compromises that government officials were forced to make. Realtors and builders feared that public housing would compete with their private-sector products. Middle-class and moderate-income families were resentful of the notion that others might pay so little for housing similar to their own. To placate these powerful interests, the federal Public Housing Administration insisted that projects offer only the barest of features. "Anything is extravagance," a federal manual instructed, "which is not necessary to decency, safety, sanitation, or adequate standards of family life . . ." (cited in Meyerson and Banfield, 1955, p. 94). Doors on closets and seat covers on toilets were among the extravagances sacrificed. The result was a harsh and unattractive environment unlikely to earn the loyalty of its tenants or the acceptance of neighbors. To placate neighborhood interests, local authorities often sought to place projects wherever resistance would be minimized. Frequently, this meant locating public housing in desolate, industrial areas with little access to shopping or public transportation.

- *Public housing had been improving.* As is often the case, designers and implementors of public programs were able to learn from their earlier mistakes. By the later years of the program, smaller, less obtrusive projects were the norm. In addition, local authorities were experimenting with various "turnkey" programs that involved private businesses as builders and managers of the housing projects. These were intended to take advantage of the efficiencies and greater expertise that the private sector presumably had to offer. The Turnkey III program gave tenants a direct stake in the health of the project by setting aside part of their rental payments toward the purchase of their own unit. Anecdotal accounts suggest that such innovations held great promise (see, for example, Mayer, 1978, pp. 173–79). But the Pruitt-Igoes cast the longer and deeper shadows; the verdict on public housing already had been shaped.

Urban Renewal

Origin and Design. For a short while, World War II distracted public attention from problems that were developing back home. With the war's end came renewed awareness of domestic issues and a sharpening concern about the conditions that some major cities were experiencing. The real suburban boom of the 1950s was still a few years off, but it was already clear that some central cities were in decline. Then, as now, some attributed this decline to the fact that older central cities simply were becoming obsolete. Structures, designs, street layouts, public facilities, and patterns of land use that made sense in an earlier period were now outmoded.

Part of the problem may have been due to the values and fashions of the time. The late 1940s and 1950s was a time for the celebration of all that was new. Developers and realtors, both responding to and helping to shape these preferences, recognized that the "action" was in the suburbs:

that was where status and prestige could be found. Cities, the mood seemed to have concluded, were weary and unattractive, not sites for smart money to commit itself to.

There was, however, a more structural obstacle to new investment in the cities. New developments, to be economically feasible, had to be big developments. New office, commercial, and residential construction would require large plots of land. What was available for sale, however, were small scattered parcels, held by many different owners. To pull together a developable piece of property meant a series of independent negotiations. This was a time-consuming and expensive prospect, made all the more forbidding by the potential obstacle of the holdout. Any single property owner, sensing plans to develop his or her block, had an incentive to sit back while the sales of the surrounding parcels were arranged. By being the last to settle, the holdout was in position to demand an exorbitant price.

Urban renewal was given birth in Title I of the Housing Act of 1949. Like public housing, urban renewal was a response to a perceived failure of the private market. Whereas public housing involved the government directly as a substitute for private-sector providers, the urban renewal program sketched a less substantial, catalytic, or helping role. The public sector would do the dirty work. Using its power of eminent domain—the authority to compel property owners to sell their property so that it may be put to a use in the public interest—the government would purchase land in deteriorating sections of the city, relocate existing residents and businesses, demolish the outmoded structures, and offer the property to private developers at affordable costs.

Although the private sector would build and manage and realize the profits of whatever development took place, the government could exercise some control by selecting the one proposal, from those submitted by competing developers, that best met the program's stated goals. These goals initially emphasized the elimination of slums and the construction of new residential development. As with public housing, however, the goals of the program were multiple and somewhat ambiguous. Among the other goals that came to be attached to the program were the provision of decent housing to the poor, the revitalization of central business districts (CBDs), the addition of new tax revenues, and the maintenance and attraction of a middle-class population.

Urban renewal, like public housing, was intergovernmental in design. Local urban renewal authorities, structured much like the Public Housing Authorities, were responsible for selecting sites, carrying out land acquisition and clearance, and choosing among developers and their proposals. The federal government agreed to pay two-thirds of the cost of the write-down, the difference between what the local authority paid to accquire and prepare the land and the price it was able to recover through its sale to the private developer. In return, the federal government retained the right to veto plans and to oversee various stages of the project's implementation. Beginning in 1954, the federal government also required that all local authorities file a "workable program," which had to include such things as a strategy for providing citizen participation, a program for the relocation of displaced families, minimal housing-code standards, and a code-enforcement program.

Off the Drawing Board and Into the Fire. Urban renewal started as a plan; it ended up as a controversy. Over the next two decades, the urban renewal program developed a reputation as a destroyer rather than a rebuilder. The criticisms were many:

- *More housing was destroyed than was built.* Between 1948 and 1969, approximately 425,000 units of housing, almost all of it occupied by the poor, were demolished. During the same period, only 125,000 new units were contructed, most of them luxury units intended for the middle and upper class (Mayer, 1978, p. 120).

- *Decent neighborhoods were destroyed.* Deteriorating neighborhoods are not the same as dying neighborhoods. In a number of cases, the neighborhoods targeted for renewal were marked by strong social networks and ethnic ties. Seedy exteriors often hid neat, clean, and affordable apartments. Gans noted, for instance, that "all of Boston was convinced that the West End was a slum which ought to be torn down not only for the sake of the city but also for the good of its own residents" (Gans, 1962, p. 287). Between 1958 and 1960, the neighborhood was leveled. Yet, after living there for half a year, Gans had concluded that the West End, though "a run down area of people struggling with the problems of low income, poor education, and related difficulties," was "by and large a good place to live" (Gans, p. 16).

- *Racial and ethnic minorities bore most of the costs.* Of the families displaced by urban renewal in its first twenty years, a grossly disproportionate number were black. Between 1950 and the middle of 1971, 88.6 percent of the families displaced in Atlanta were nonwhite; in Philadelphia, the proportion was 79.9 percent; in Baltimore, 83.0 percent; in San Francisco, 79.5 percent; in Chicago, 78.7 percent (Sanders, 1980, p. 120). It was on this basis that the program earned, in some circles, the disparaging label "Negro Removal."

- *Rather than solve problems, urban renewal simply shifted them around.* "By reducing the supply of low rent housing, urban renewal probably raised the rents of all poor people in the cities in which it occurred. Where dislocations were heavy, it became profitable for landlords in aging but still sound sections of the city to cut up existing units and put them in the market for slum-dwellers, spreading the slums as well as the dwellers" (Mayer, 1978, p. 121).

- *Those forced to move ended up little better or even worse than than before.* In the case of those relocated from Boston's West End in the late 1950s, relatively minor improvements in living conditions were accompanied by a 73 percent increase in median rents (Hartman, 1967, p. 323). Small businesses that were displaced also suffered. A study of ninety small businesses on a New York City renewal site in 1958 found that 45.4 percent failed, unable to afford to move or unable to maintain a viable operation in their new location (Schorr, 1975, p. 103).

- *The new was not always preferable to the old.* In some cases, local authorities purchased land, displaced residents, and demolished buildings only to discover that there was little interest from developers. The result? Often nothing more than a parking lot or vacant field would stand, for years, in place of a neighborhood that, though dingy, had provided people with a place to live and the city with tax revenues. In other cases, the results were massive, sterile complexes with large, empty plazas on which few people saw a reason to walk. "But look what we have built with the first several billions," lamented Jane Jacobs, one of the most colorful critics of the program's results.

> Low income projects that become worse centers of delinquency, vandalism and general social helplessness than the slums they were supposed to replace. Middle-income housing projects which are truly marvels of dullness and regimentation, sealed against any buoyancy or vitality of city life. Luxury housing projects that mitigate their inanity, or try to, with vapid vulgarity. Cultural centers that are unable to support a good bookstore. Civic centers that are avoided by everyone but bums, who have fewer choices of loitering places than others. Commercial centers that are lackluster imitations of standardized suburban chain-store shopping. . . . This is not the rebuilding of cities. This is the sacking of cities (Jacobs, 1961, p. 41).

Part of the problem stemmed from policy-makers' overestimation of the hidden private-sector demand for central city properties. Advocates of urban renewal had envisioned active bidding among eager developers for the right to acquire the renewal sites. Response, however, often was tentative and slow. Local urban renewal authorities found themselves in a difficult and embarrassing situation. Local money had been spent. Tax revenues from the demolished properties were lost. Surrounding neighborhoods were beginning to deteriorate due to overflow from the relocatees and uncertainty on the part of investors and property owners as to what the future of the area would hold. The pressure was great for the local authorities to get something, *anything,* onto the site fast. This meant, in some cities, a readiness to allow developers to do whatever they wanted. "Find a redeveloper first, and then see what interests him," became the effective criterion in Newark (Kaplan, 1963, p. 24).

Thus, the goals of the program were subtly shifted. In some cities, profitability to the private sector took the front seat. Sacrificed were some of the original goals that the program had set. For what developers deemed profitable was *not* low-income housing; they preferred to build middle- or upper-income residences or commercial and office space. Nor were they anxious to build at all in the middle of slumlike areas. To attract developers, local authorities had to shift their attention from those neighborhoods with the worst conditions to those in "marketable" locations: those adjoining the central business district, near universities or other prestigious institutions, bordering rivers or parks, or offering some other amenity likely to appeal to business interests or the middle class.

Confusion regarding the "true" goals of the program also created problems. Many supporters of urban renewal conceived of it primarily as a program to rehouse the poor. Yet, as we have mentioned, the program as implemented did little to further such a goal. The ambiguity that characterized the legislation's statement of goals was not, however, due to carelessness or confusion on Congress's part. Rather, it represented a legislative victory by private-sector interest groups that wished to see urban renewal used in ways more profitable to themselves. The National Association of Real Estate Boards and other organizations lobbied to have the renewal program separated from the Housing Act altogether. Although they failed in this, they did succeed in keeping the program administratively separate from the Public Housing Administration (presumed to be more sympathetic to the goal of building housing for the poor); the officials who *were* given control over the program at the federal level had a tradition of working closely with realtors, builders, and the financial community (Weiss, 1980, p. 66). As one business spokesman told the U.S. Chamber of Commerce in September 1964, "It is time that the American businessman recognized that the federal urban renewal program is, above all, a program for him" (Vieser, 1964).

The federal government's failure to state the goals and priorities of the program carefully meant that the key choices would effectively be delegated to the local level. Probably inevitably, this resulted in the program varying markedly from place to place. Local urban renewal authorities in some cities were staffed by professionals, skilled in planning theory and techniques and motivated by a desire to improve the city for all its residents. In other cities, this was not the case. In some cases, decision-making authority was imposed on local institutions steeped in the traditions of patronage and machine-style politics; in others, on institutions politically dominated by a downtown business elite. The result, in some instances, was corruption. In Boston, for example, the city purchased a property for $7.40 per square foot, revalued it at $1.40 per square foot, then rented it to a supporter of the mayor at extremely favorable rates (Goodman, 1971, p. 64).

Even in the absence of corruption, the need to entice business involvement led, as in Newark, to a program increasingly geared to the interests of developers rather than those of the poor. As one developer put it: "Where else can I get to build and own $1 million worth of real estate with as little as $30,000 of my own cash?" (Quoted in Berman, 1969, p. 6). In other cases, the result was the redefinition of the program in terms of other private interests: universities, hospitals, and commercial areas were aided in their expansion at the cost of residential neighborhoods housing minorities and the poor.

Was the Book Closed Too Soon? The many failures of the urban renewal program have provided ammunition to those who argue that public-sector attempts to reduce urban and regional decline are unlikely to succeed—especially attempts designed and overseen by a distant federal government. By 1974, urban renewal as a distinct federal policy was a thing of the past. Money previously targeted for urban renewal was instead incorporated into community development block grants that local jurisdictions can utilize according to their own needs and desires (we will further discuss this later in the chapter). Local governments can use this money to shape their own programs modeled on urban renewal if they care to, but many other options are open to them as well.

The passage of time can change perceptions. With time can come a dulling of painful memories; the turmoil, disruption, and racial antagonisms spurred by the urban renewal program are only dimly held recollections now. Any legitimate reevaluation of the program must avoid falling into the trap of dismissing the wounds inflicted by urban renewal simply because the scars have healed. But time can also bring perspective. As with public housing, it seems possible that the failures of urban renewal have been overstated and misinterpreted.

The charge that urban renewal destroyed so many more units of housing than it replaced was, in some senses at least, premature. The basic logic of the program, which called for plots of land to be purchased and cleared before new private construction would take place, dictated that it could be no other way. It is true that new construction came more slowly than anticipated. But, as Sanders points out, by the mid-1970s the gap between housing demolished and housing constructed had begun to close. New housing—not commercial or industrial construction—was the single largest new use of cleared urban renewal land. Almost 55 percent of this new housing was designed for low and moderate income families (Sanders, 1980, p. 106). By the mid to late 1970s, moreover, it was clear that some urban renewal projects were beginning to bear fruit. San Francisco's Embarcadero Center, Pittsburgh's Golden Triangle, Denver's Mile High Center, the Saarinen Arch in St. Louis, and Lincoln Center in New York are attracting tourists and producing revenues in areas that, before urban renewal, most local residents took pains to avoid.

Urban renewal, like public housing, changed over time. Some of those changes were due to shifts in the political strength of the various groups affected by the program. The civil-rights movement and a generally higher level of political mobilization among the urban poor helped to create pressure to strengthen citizen participation requirements and expand relocation benefits to those who were forced to move. Other changes are attributable simply to a learning process. Public officials gradually realized that bigger was not always better. Projects planned on a grand scale were more traumatic and entailed much greater risk. As in surgery, the smaller, more precise incision is generally preferable to the aggressive, "hacksaw" approach.

It is possible to draw a lesson from these changes that is quite nearly the opposite of what is commonly proposed. Sanders suggests that those who blame an overly intrusive federal government for the failures of the program are missing the mark. He argues, to the contrary, that it was the clarification of federal goals and the strengthening of federal enforcement procedures that account for many of the improvements that did take place. Prior to 1967, urban renewal "was marked by an ever-increasing freedom for local choice in project selection with little federal dictation" (Sanders, p. 112). The absence of strong federal direction gave local governments free reign to shape the program according to local values and political currents. Where influential political forces believed that their interests were best served by replacing housing with commercial development or disrupting and dispersing growing minority communities, urban renewal proved to be a convenient tool.

The substance of the program, as carried out, varied considerably across cities and regions in those early years. In Atlanta, for example, the charge that urban renewal equaled black removal was rather accurate prior to 1968. Of the families displaced in Atlanta, fully 88.6 percent were nonwhite. In cities such as Boston, Minneapolis, Denver, and Portland, fewer than half of those displaced were nonwhite. In Atlanta, too, the charge that urban renewal destroyed more housing than it helped build is more accurate than in some other jurisdictions. Sixty-seven percent of the land in Atlanta's pre-1968 renewal sites had been residential; after renewal, only 24 percent remained residential. In San Francisco, by way of contrast, only 33 percent of the sites chosen for renewal were residential in character, and after renewal, 38 percent of that land was devoted to housing.

After 1968, and until 1974, federal officials effectively clarifed goals and reduced local discretion. As this occurred, variation in the program across cities decreased. "The result," Sanders concludes, "was a national shift in the benefits of the renewal program, from an era before 1967 when the average project provided 47% of its new housing to lower-income persons to an era in which low- and moderate-income families occupied over 65% of the new units" (Sanders, p. 124).

In allocating decision-making authority to the state or local level, we shift decision-making power to a political environment in which some interests are less well represented than others. Programs such as urban renewal can end up looking quite different in cities with a strong developer/downtown business coalition than in those in which low-income and minority neighborhoods are effectively organized. Sanders's analysis suggests, however, that as long as federal policy-makers provide a clear sense of direction and an authoritative enforcement procedure, decentralizing implementation does not have to mean that national goals are left behind.

Model Cities

Origins and Goals. Urban renewal reflected a long-standing tendency of American policy-makers to think of urban revitalization primarily in physical terms. This "bricks and mortar" approach reflected, in part, the political influence of those interests—developers, downtown businesses, construction unions—that stood to benefit from an emphasis on demolition and new construction. It also reflected the tenacity of the beliefs of the early planners and urban reformers, who were convinced that physical reconstruction would lead to social mending.

By the 1960s, this physical approach was operating side by side with the social welfare thrust incorporated in the programs of the War on Poverty. But although the two approaches were being applied side by side, they were not working hand in hand. The more people-oriented programs of the War on Poverty were administered primarily through the Department of Health, Education, and Welfare. Congress, in 1965, established the Department of Housing and Urban Development, (HUD) which inherited many of the programs designed to enhance the physical environment. Bureaucratic jealousies and turf consciousness being what they are, there was likely to be little communication and even less coordination between the agencies, though both would be concerned on a day-to-day basis with the phenomenon of urban decline.

The Model Cities program, as proposed by a special task force appointed by President Johnson, sought to improve upon past efforts by addressing three themes. These were the need for *coordination, focusing* of resources, and *flexibility*. Coordination among the various physical and social programs would occur at the local level, primarily through the mayor's office. The emphasis on the local elected executives was significant. Most of the earlier housing and development programs had relied on specially designed local decision-making organs—Public Housing Authorities, Local Renewal Agencies, Community Action Agencies—deliberately shielded from the mayor's direct control. This had contributed to the fragmentation of local decision-making and set local groups competing among one another for control of the resources and power that the federal programs represented.

Model Cities called for local officials to designate a portion of their city as a target area. Efforts in the past had been too diffused. By aiming the full weight of federal efforts at one area, it was hoped that visible and swift progress could be achieved. The framers of the Model Cities concept were sensitive to the thorniness of the problems confronting cities and to the fact that public-sector resources were limited. Their idea was to use this program as a demonstration, to counter the fatalism that was infecting decision-makers in the public and private sectors, and to prove that, with an intense enough effort, deterioration and decline could be reversed.

Targeting of efforts was to be achieved at two levels: by focusing efforts on a single needy area within the participating cities and by limiting participation, initially, to only a handful of cities. The task force, in fact, originally proposed that only three cities be chosen. This would keep federal funds from being spread so thinly that their impact would be reduced. In addition, by forcing cities to compete, HUD could make sure that those cities selected were prepared to take innovative actions with a good chance of success.

Flexibility was to be achieved by adopting what was essentially a block grant approach. The participating cities would be allowed much greater discretion over the uses of federal moneys than was the norm under the existing categorical grants. HUD Secretary Robert Weaver explained at the time that: "this is a local program; it will be planned, developed and carried out by local people. The character and content of the program will be based on local judgments as to cities' needs" (Frieden and Kaplan, 1975, p. 127). Model Cities, sometimes considered a quintessential liberal and Democratic program, was in this sense a forerunner of the New Federalism strategy later advocated by conservative Republican Presidents Nixon and Reagan.

The Politics of Model Cities. Congress showed little sympathy for the targeting aspects of the Model Cities proposal. The problem did not lie in any inability on the part of senators and representatives to grasp the logic of the argument that focusing resources on a few cities would increase the likelihood and speed of success. But the structure of Congress encourages a spreading of benefits so that as many states and districts as possible receive some tangible result. In order to build a political coalition sizable enough to ensure the passage of the program, administration and congressional sponsors had to "buy" the support of key members through the explicit or implicit promise that they would be able to show their constituents that the program had direct benefits for them.

> By the time the Johnson Administration left office, 150 model cities had been chosen. They were located in all regions of the country, in 46 states, the District of Columbia, and Puerto Rico. Five counties and an Indian reservation were among the participants. All but three of the nation's cities with population over 500,000 and almost 90 percent of all cities over 250,000 were included. The goal of resource concentration at the national level was impossible to sustain. . . (Frieden and Kaplan, p. 217).

Mayors also were under pressure from various local interests to "spread the goodies." Some cities proposed selecting huge areas of their downtowns, incorporating more than one out of five of their residents, as model city neighborhoods. A couple sought to declare the entire city eligible.

The Legacy of Model Cities. What was intended as a massive, cohesive, and targeted attack on central city decline ended up as an uncoordinated and halfhearted attempt. One response might have been to renew the federal commitment, to build a bigger, better, more directed national urban policy. Such a response, however, would have depended upon there being strong political support for the cities, enough support to overcome the political and administrative obstacles on which Model Cities had foundered. Such support did not exist. Political winds were blowing in a different direction. Richard Nixon's victory marked a more conservative sentiment in the country. With this conservatism came a skepticism of the notion that bigger would be better. Model Cities, in this atmosphere, was interpreted as the last gasp of liberalism, the final proof that solutions to the urban problem depend upon granting an even broader role to states, localities, and private-market mechanisms.

The Indirect Approach: Mortgage Guarantees, Subsidies, and Tax Deductions

Programs such as public housing, urban renewal, and model cities expanded the concepts of public-sector responsibility and public-sector authority. As a consequence, they frequently were resisted by private-sector interests, which feared that their own spheres of operation would be shaved down, their freedom of action and opportunities for profit constrained. These groups responded by launching campaigns to mount public opposition. Dramatic charges of socialism and fearsome images of big government gone wild were brought to bear. As developers, realtors, and bankers came to realize that these programs could provide opportunities for *greater* profits, their opposition mellowed. But the rhetorical excesses of the earlier period left their mark. In the minds of many citizens, politicians, and future politicians, the perception of government (particularly the federal government) on the warpath against the private market had taken a tenacious hold.

In truth, public policies for urban and regional development in this country have never strayed far from a primary allegiance to a market system of allocation and growth. Public-sector involvement has been to supplement or stimulate private activity, not to replace it on any significant scale. The orientation toward using public authority to facilitate private investment and production is seen best in the series of initiatives designed to increase housing production through mortgage guarantees, subsidies to developers and lower-income homebuyers, and mortgage interest deductions in the federal income tax code. These programs tend to be less place-oriented than people-oriented, less focused on the needs of the very poor. Because they are also less direct and less controversial, these programs sometimes have been overlooked or given fleeting and superficial attention. Yet these programs, for the most part, have absorbed more resources and shown greater staying power than those that have wilted under the hot lights of open and public debate. In that sense, they may characterize, more accurately than their better known counterparts, the essential thrust of national urban and regional redevelopment policies to date.

Protecting Mortgage Lenders. In order to understand the indirect policy approach, one must grasp the fundamentals of the private development process. The key here, as in so many cases, is money: where it comes from, when it is forthcoming, and where it goes. Few home purchasers have the capacity to buy a home by plunking down a full payment in cash. In 1979, the median sales price of a new single-family home was nearly $63,000 (U.S. Bureau of the Census, 1981, p. 770). The median household income that year was $16,553. Nor do most builders and developers who are responsible for housing construction finance their land, material, and labor costs from their own pockets. Both purchasers and builders usually must borrow. They can borrow from a number of sources, but primarily do so from savings and loan institutions (buyers) and commercial banks (builders). These financial institutions, then, are the spigot that controls the flow of resources.

When the spigot is opened—when money is readily available at an affordable interest rate—bulldozers will be busy and rates of construction high. When the spigot is closed, potential buyers will be priced out of the housing market, builders will lay off workers, and the nation's housing stock will age.

During the first third of this century, mortgage money (loans for home purchases in which the home is pledged as security) was difficult and expensive to obtain. Lenders required large down payments and offered primarily "balloon" mortgages, which left a large sum that had to be repaid or refinanced after only a few years. Today, in contrast, the typical mortgage calls for a down payment of about 20 percent, with payments scheduled in equal monthly installments over thirty years. No lump sum payment is required at the end. Lenders' earlier wariness toward mortgage lending was heightened by their experience during the Great Depression. Many families, out of work and with savings depleted, defaulted on their mortgage loans. Lenders were unable to collect the money owed them. Some went bankrupt themselves. Those that did not were willing to lend more money only on the strictest of terms. As a result, housing production slowed to a virtual standstill. Before the depression, new housing was being constructed at a rate of about 900,000 units per year; by 1934, production had slipped to only 90,000 units. In Chicago, only 131 housing units were built in 1933. Nationwide, over 60 percent of housing construction workers were unemployed. It was in this context of a foundering private housing system that the federal government stepped in.

In response to the depression, the federal government instituted a number of steps intended to save the housing finance system from collapse. One of the most important—Section 203 of the National Housing Act of 1934—authorized the newly formed Federal Housing Administration (FHA) to insure lenders against most of the loss they would suffer on approved loans on which the borrowers defaulted. After World War II, the Veterans Administration was empowered to issue similar guarantees for mortgages provided to veterans. Lenders, assured that the government would share the burden of defaults, were encouraged to lend more money on easier terms.

The FHA and VA mortgage guarantee programs offer an effective rebuttal of the notion that federal government programs always are destined to fail. Over 6 million new home mortgages were started under the Section 203 program between 1935 and 1979. During the height of the program, from 1950 to 1960, over 15% of all privately started housing units were financed under the 203 program alone (U.S. Department of Housing and Urban Development, 1980, p. 63). These programs are at least partially responsible for the vast expansion in housing production that, over the past three decades, has led to a sharp improvement in the physical quality of the country's housing stock. What is more, for many years FHA accomplished this without losing money (Mayer, 1978, p. 371).

What the mortgage guarantee programs did *not* do was provide measurable benefits to the poor and minorities. FHA was intended to be run like a profit-making enterprise; it was not expected to make risky or speculative loans. In the early 1960s, as a consequence, nearly nine out of every ten recipients of an FHA guaranteed loan could be classified as middle income to well-to-do. FHA's own "Underwriting Manual" for many years instructed its officials to avoid integrating neighborhoods by introducing "inharmonious racial groups." "Although direct references to race were dropped in the late 1940s, FHA failed to abandon its racial practices for almost two more decades" (Danielson, 1976, p. 204). Between 1946 and 1959, less than 2 percent of the homes financed by federal mortgage insurance were purchased by black households (Grier and Grier, 1968, p. 128).

Nor did the FHA and VA programs help the declining central cities. To the contrary. The overwhelming proportion of the new homes purchased with FHA and VA guarantees were in the booming suburbs. Most contemporary analysts believe that one outcome of the mortgage guarantee programs was the hastening of the process of central city decline.

The successes and the shortcomings of the mortgage guarantee programs stem from the same source. These programs were designed to reinforce—not challenge or reshape—the private market system of distributing investment capital. The key decisions concerning who was to receive loans, where loans would be made, and what activities were creditworthy remained almost exclusively the province of private decisionmakers. FHA officials, in seeking to run their own operation on businesslike principles, replicated the private lenders' behavior. Loans to the poor, to minorities, to central city properties may have been justified in the name of a broader public interest, but they were weighed against the agency's balance sheet of profit and loss; and on that narrower scale, it was decided they were too "risky" to be justified.

Housing Subsidies. Private-sector construction, even when buoyed by governmental mortgage guarantees, simply has not translated into new housing for the poor or moderate-income family. Recognition of this fact led federal policymakers in the 1960s to consider new initiatives more directly targeted at those in need. Housing subsidies, as represented most dramatically by Sections 235 and 236 of the Housing Act of 1968, sought to strike a middle ground between the untargeted nature of the private-sector-oriented mortgage guarantee program and the politically poisonous public housing approach.

Section 235 was intended to encourage builders to construct *owner-*

occupied housing units for low- to moderate-income familes. Section 236 was aimed at producing *rental* units. The key to each was an interest payment subsidy. For low- to moderate-income purchasers of new or rehabilitated housing approved for the 235 program, HUD would pay to the mortgage lender the difference between the standard mortgage interest charge (about 8.5 percent in 1970) and the monthly payment that a 1 percent mortgage would entail. This significantly reduced the monthly payment that the purchaser would be responsible for, in the process making ownership economically feasible to many families who otherwise would have been forced to rent. The purchaser need put up only $200 as a down payment. The pride of ownership, it was hoped, would lead these lower-income families to take better care of their housing, take more interest in their community, and provide a more stable environment in which to raise a healthy family. To encourage banks and savings and loans to lend to such high-risk borrowers, FHA also insured the 235 program mortgages, protecting the lenders in the case of default.

In the 236 program, HUD's subsidy went to the mortgage loan taken out by the private developer. The subsidy was sufficient to "write down" the developer's interest payment to a 1 percent rate. In return for this reduction in his or her own costs, the developer would offer lower rents, generally to a level at which eligible households need pay only about 25 percent of their incomes for rent.

Both programs aimed for a population somewhat higher in income than those occupying public housing. Although the subsidies lowered costs, they did not eliminate them; families without regular incomes that enabled them to meet their monthly payments were not to be allowed to participate. Section 236 also offered tax breaks to developers as a further incentive for these private-sector actors to become involved.

The package of incentives offered were attractive. Developers could launch projects without having to put very much money up front. The federal government promised that there would be renters to rent the apartments and buyers to purchase the homes once they were completed. This had the desired effect of generating private-sector interest in the program, but it may have contributed to the program's undoing in the end. By reducing the developers' risks, the federal incentives also may have lessened the economic pressures on them to do a competent job.

As producers of housing, these two programs were dramatic successes. Between 1970 and 1972, over 300,000 mortgages for new housing were insured under the 235 program; and almost 270,000 mortgages for new multifamily rental units were insured under 236 (U.S. Department of Housing and Urban Development, 1980, pp. 69, 75). But the controversies they stirred were even more dramatic. The programs worked well for some builders and investors. One broker in southeast Washington, D.C., bought a home for $9,600; three months later, having made only minimal improvements, he resold the house under the 235 program for $17,500, an 82 percent increase. A house in Spokane, Washington, purchased for $3,375 was sold under the same program for $11,250, an increase of 233 percent (McFarland, 1978, p. 142).

Stories of unscrupulous developers and unfortunate victims were common. In Detroit, some speculators used "ghost" buyers to make a profit without even bothering to find a real purchaser for their 235 properties. Having bought a house for, say, $3,000, the speculator would forge a mortgage application, obtain financing in the name of this nonperson, and sell the property for, say, $12,000. When subsequently no one made payments on the empty house, the mortgage lender would move to foreclose; HUD wound up with an abandoned building and a debt to repay (Boyer, 1973, pp. 144–5).

Several factors contributed to the environment in which such shenanigans could take place. Some mortgage lenders, particularly small mortgage companies, were willing to lend money without investigating the creditworthiness of the borrower; after all, even if the borrower defaulted, the federal government would pick up the tab. At the same time, FHA was under political pressure to have the programs succeed in producing large numbers of units. This, along with insufficient staff, made it unlikely that FHA would function effectively in regulating the program and eliminating abuse. Moreover, FHA appraisers in some cities were bribed in return for deliberately overassessing the true worth of the properties, increasing by thousands of dollars the profits that the builder or rehabber could make.

Many reputable builders provided decent housing through these programs, and most FHA appraisers were honest, though often seriously overworked. Where abuse occurred, however, it was dramatic and damaging. In Detroit, scores of abandoned, boarded-up buildings, foreclosed after Section 235 families found they were unable to meet monthly payments while dealing with unanticipated maintenance and repair costs, led local officials to refer to the program as "Hurricane HUD."

Some analysts argue that many of these problems could have been ironed out, that better enforcement and better training of FHA officials could have turned the faltering program into a success (Levitan and Taggart, 1976). But President Nixon did not give the 235 and 236 programs that chance. Prompted by the spreading scandal, and no doubt influenced also by the spiraling costs of the subsidy programs, President Nixon declared a moratorium on these programs in 1973. Section 235 was later reactivated but as a much smaller program, revised to serve a higher income population. The idea of improving the living conditions of low-income families by subsidizing private developers was temporarily discredited.

Income Tax Deductions. A less visible—but nonetheless very important—form of indirect stimulus to housing and development takes the form of a tax subsidy to homeowners. The federal government allows homeowners to deduct mortgage interest payments and local property tax payments in calculating the income taxes that they owe. The rationale for this policy is that it opens up to a greater proportion of the public the opportunity to realize the "American dream," a dream that traditionally has been presumed to rest upon the ownership of a single-family, detached house. By increasing the effective demand for housing, the tax subsidy also serves the interest of the construction and real estate industries.

One reason that a tax subsidy such as this tends to be politically popular is that it does not seem to involve the government spending money. The cost to the government comes in the form of foregone revenues—moneys that would otherwise have been collected if this set of deductions had not been allowed. Some people seem to consider this a cost-free program, because the government never actually possessed the dollars involved. As far as the need to keep the government's budget in balance, however, the cost of this program is quite extreme. It is estimated that the combined cost of the mortgage interest and property tax deductions may reach nearly $60 billion in 1985 (Verdier and Smith, 1982).

Because the wealthy are more likely to own their own homes, and because the value of the tax deduction is greater for those with higher incomes, this is a policy whose direct beneficiaries are primarily the well-to-do. Liberal and radical critics have charged that this represents little more than "welfare for the rich." More conservative analysts, concerned about the impact on the federal government's debt, have also proposed that this deduction be eliminated or trimmed. Although more traditional housing and urban development programs were cut substantially during the first Reagan administration, even a mild attempt to limit interest deductions to the primary residence of the taxpayer proved politically infeasible.

Housing and Community Development Act of 1974

The notion that local governments should play a substantial part in the shaping and implementation of public redevelopment strategies has played a central role in federal policy, stretching back to the local authorities established as part of the public housing and urban renewal programs. In spite of this tradition, the dominant perception in the early 1970s was that the concept of decentralization had not been carried far enough. President Nixon's call for a New Federalism was a call for a general expansion of the authority of localities and states. The Housing and Community Development Act of 1974 was a response to this call; central to it was the reshaping of redevelopment programs into the form of a block grant.

Community Development Block Grants. The establishment of the community development block grants (CDBGs) marked the end of urban renewal and model cities as distinct national programs. Moneys previously allocated to those two categorical grants—along with moneys previously budgeted for grants programs for housing rehabilitation, neighborhood development, open spaces, water and sewer projects, and public facilities loans—were consolidated into a single block grant. Rather than compete for these funds, as they had in the past, urban counties and cities of more than 50,000 people receive their total allotment automatically, based on a distribution formula. Local governments are still required to apply for their money, and the Department of Housing and Urban Development can and does ask that certain priorities be considered and certain priorities met, but the intention and the effect of CDBGs was to give local officials considerable freedom to decide how their funds would be spent. CDBG funds are used for such varied activities as building a senior citizens center, repaving streets, installing traffic lights, providing daycare services, attracting commercial development, continuing urban renewal projects, providing health care, building an industrial park, helping tenants rehabilitate and purchase their buildings, and building parks and recreation facilities.

Although the legislation calls for recipient jurisdictions to certify that "maximum feasible priority" is given to projects benefiting low- and moderate-income families, most evidence suggests that in practice, CDBGs are less targeted than the programs they replaced. Several studies indicate that, at least in the early years of the program, local jurisdictions tended to shift resources to neighborhoods less seriously distressed than those that had been the primary beneficiaries of the earlier categorical grants (Rosenfeld, 1980).

There are a couple of reasons why this deemphasis on targeting has tended to take place. Some jurisdictions may have decided that a strategy to direct funds into transitional neighborhoods, rather than those in the worst condition, would be more likely to achieve the desired results. Officials in Raleigh, North Carolina, for example, adopted a strategy of focusing on more easily salvageable neighborhoods as part of a plan to keep middle-class black families in the city (Dommel, et al., 1978, p. 245). Possibly more important may be the political pressures that local officials found themselves subjected to by moderate- and middle-income neighborhoods anxious for their own piece of the CDBG action. Such neighborhoods, generally more organized and politically active than lower-income areas, are not easy for local officials to ignore. Table 6-1,

Table 6-1 Targetting to Low and Moderate Income Tracts, 1975–79

Year	Number of Low/Mod Tracts Funded	Number of non-Low/Mod Tracts Funded	% Low/Mod of Total Tracts Funded
1975	842	755	53
1976	1,076	1,125	49
1977	1,082	1,160	48
1978	1,084	1,161	48
1979	1,095	1,144	49

SOURCE: U.S. Department of Housing and Urban Development, Office of Community Planning and Development, Fifth Annual Community Development Block Grant Project. Washington, D.C.: Government Printing Office (April 1980), pp. 111–13.

based on a study of 137 cities, reveals a tendency by local officials to respond to such pressures by spreading the "goodies" around. Between 1975 and 1979, the number of low- and moderate-income census tracts (roughly neighborhood-sized areas used in census compilations) receiving CDBG funds increased by 30 percent; the number of wealthier tracts receiving benefits increased by over 50 percent. In an effort to compel local governments to target CDBG moneys more directly to those in greatest need, HUD, under President Carter, announced new regulations that called for at least 75 percent of the benefits to be spent on projects primarily benefiting low- and moderate-income persons. Political pressure forced HUD to soften this standard in practice (Rosenfeld, 1980), but there is some evidence that it did slow the spreading tendency somewhat. Under President Reagan, however, HUD announced an intention to do away with the limitation entirely.

The switch to CDBGs deflected aid from some of the areas with greatest need in another sense as well. Many suburbs, towns, and small cities had not competed for the urban renewal, model cities, or other narrower and competitive grants that preceded the block grant legislation. Under the formula used to distribute the CDBG moneys, these areas automatically became eligible for aid. But with the pie divided into so many more slices, large central cities, and older jurisdictions in the Snowbelt, found they had less for themselves. In 1977, the CDBG formula was altered in order to give a higher priority to places with an older housing stock. But the fact remains that the formula approach sacrifices some element of targeting to the goal of broadening the pool of recipients.

Some of the support for the block grant format of the CDBGs was based on the belief that decentralization would stimulate greater citizen participation and a more democratic process through which development policies would be shaped. In keeping with the concept of local discretion, neither Congress nor HUD mandated that a particular formal structure for citizen participation be put into effect. Although federal guidelines do require that information about planned CDBG expenditures be disseminated to the public, and that public hearings be held, there is no requirement that minorities and the poor be given formal roles in the decision process, and the citizens are given no guarantees that their proposals and suggestions will be genuinely taken into account.

For those who had high hopes, the citizen participation component of CDBGs has been disappointing. Citizen interest and involvement in some cities was high. In Minneapolis, a citizens advisory committee, partly elected and partly appointed by the mayor and city council, was given a formal and substantial role in determining CDBG allocations. In Rochester, New York, officials sponsored a television production in the effort to draw the attention and interest of residents. After the first blush of excitement, however, there are some indications that participation has leveled off. Kettl, in his study of four Connecticut cities, indicated that long-term commitments made in the first couple of years left little discretionary money for citizens to battle over (Kettl, 1979). The mayor and council in Minneapolis, responding to general fiscal pressures and traditional political desires for sources of patronage, moved, in the third year, to reassert their control by limiting the power of the advisory board (Dommel, et al, 1978, p. 133). In most cities, moreover, citizens' involvement and influence remained just as low as they had been before. In Auburn, Maine, even the members of the citizens advisory committee could mount little sustained interest. On two occasions, "only two of the eleven members showed up. After each of these meetings public hearings were held—but the public was virtually nonexistent" (Dommel, et al, p. 148). Harris County, Texas, established an elaborate citizen participation task force, but officials felt free to veto or ignore citizens' proposals on the key decisions that had to be made (Dommel, et al., p. 148).

Did the flexibility and discretion of the block grant approach lead to greater local innovation as some had hoped? Not really. Bureaucracies and interest groups spawned by earlier programs did not go away, and local officials did not always have the time or professional capacity to generate new ideas. Although the block grants provided an opportunity to adapt programs to local conditions and demands, they "did not produce a wave of local strategic innovations." One study of five jurisdictions found "a strong tendency for communities to borrow heavily from federally inspired models for neighborhood revitalization" (Dommel, et al., 1982, pp. 233–4).

CDBGs did provide local officials with greater discretion. In doing so it earned the loyalty of these officials, who, through organizations such as the U.S. Conference of Mayors and the National League of Cities, have lobbied hard to keep the program from being scaled back drastically in recent years. Their efforts have not been entirely successful, but it seems clear that without those efforts the program would have been whittled away to an even greater extent.

Under President Reagan, steps were taken to decentralize the program even further. Before 1981, a special Small Cities component of the CDBG program had been administered by HUD, which provided aid to small jurisdictions on a competitive basis. The Reagan administration offered states the opportunity to take over the operation of this Small Cities program for themselves. Most states have done so, and there is some discussion now of *requiring* all states to take over their Small Cities programs in the near future.

Whether CDBGs actually improved urban and regional development in this country is another question. In considering targeting, citizen participation, and innovation, a unifying theme or lesson seems to emerge. *The effect of CDBGs was to move development policy-making to the local level; what happens there depends on a number of factors.* Professional competence is one such factor. The balance of local political forces is another. This may be the inevitable consequence of the broad strategy that the CDBG program represents: "when decentralized decision-making is implemented to maximize local discretion and minimize federal control, the outcome takes on the character of a crap game—you roll the dice and take your chance in the arena of local politics" (Dommel, et al., 1982, p. 242).

Section 8. The provision of housing traditionally has been closely linked to the goal of urban development. The Housing and Community Development Act of 1974 did not sever this link; it offered a new national housing program to complement the block grant approach. This program, known as Section 8, has been the dominant housing program throughout the last decade.

Section 8 originally consisted of two major components. "Both left ownership and management up to private landlords and investors; both required assisted households to contribute between 15 and 25 percent of their incomes toward rent, with the poorest households contributing the least; and both obligated the federal government to make up the difference between tenant contributions and a reasonable market rent" (Struyk, et al., 1983, p. 14). One component—the Existing Housing Program—was designed to subsidize low- to moderate-income households so that they could afford to find their own apartments within the existing rental housing stock. Through the second component—the New Construction and Substantial Rehabilitation Program—the government sought to encourage developers to provide new units. The carrot that the government offered to developers was a contract in which the government made a twenty to thirty year commitment to subsidize tenants in the new units—effectively protecting the developer from the risk that those units might not be filled. Because the Existing Housing Program was the more innovative, and because it became the more sizable, most of the rest of our discussion of the Section 8 program focuses on that component.

Section 8, like Section 236, centers around a rent subsidy. In Section 236, however, the subsidy went to the developer and was "attached" to a specific unit. Tenants who were unhappy with their subsidized unit, the neighborhood, or the maintenance that the landlord was providing were caught in a bit of a trap: they *could* move out, but if they did, they were forced to leave their subsidies behind. The Section 8 program provides its subsidy directly to the low- to moderate-income family in the form of a certificate. The family is then free to use that certificate to search for acceptable housing in the conventional rental market. The landlord, if he or she agrees to participate, signs a lease with the local housing authority (which implements the Section 8 program) as well as with the new tenant. By doing so, the landlord agrees to make any repairs necessary to bring the unit up to HUD and the local authority's standards. The tenant agrees to pay a set percentage of his or her income toward the rent (originally, this was to be no more than 25 percent; under the Reagan administration, changes were instituted to raise this figure to 30 percent). The local housing authority, using the federally provided Section 8 funds, agrees to pay the landlord the difference between the tenant's contribution and the rent that the landlord requests, as long as the rent requested does not exceed a "fair market rent" for the area as determined by HUD.

The Section 8 approach offers several advantages over those that had gone before. Low-income participants are given greater freedom to choose where they want to live. Like the unsubsidized, middle- or upper-income family, they can search throughout the area for the package of housing, neighborhood, convenience, and public services that best suits their taste. They are not limited to the often unappealing public or subsidized projects that already exist. The middle-class family is constrained by its own budget; the Section 8 family is constrained by the need to stay within the fair market rent and the need to find a willing landlord.

By attaching the subsidy to the unit rather than the tenant, the Section 236 program limited the ability of the tenant to demand that the landlord provide adequate services at a reasonable cost. By enabling the tenant to leave—taking the subsidy along—the Section 8 program hoped to give tenants the bargaining power they needed to deal effectively with their landlords. This, it was expected, would improve maintenance and housing quality generally, reduce the need for bureaucratic oversight, and reduce rents (and the cost of the program) at the same time.

The Section 8 Existing Housing Program usually is administered by the local public housing authority. Although the program is federally financed, these local authorities have substantial authority, including responsibility for inspecting dwellings to ensure that they meet HUD standards, qualifying and selecting tenants, approving leases, and overseeing all aspects of the program.

There are approximately 11 million households eligible to receive

Section 8 certificates (Drury, et al., 1978, p. 7). Because this is many more than there is funding available to accommodate, the local authority's role in selecting tenants is an important one. Under the original legislation, a family was eligible if its income was less than 80 percent of the median income in that area. At least 30 percent of the recipients had to be "very low income," defined as those earning less than 50 percent of the median. In 1981, Congress passed legislation requiring greater targeting on the very low income group. For the most part, however, local authorities already had been awarding Section 8 certification to a genuinely needy clientele. A national survey of Section 8 recipients found that 80 percent were "very low income"; 70 percent were receiving income solely from welfare or other benefit programs; about one-half were elderly or disabled; and 37 percent were minorities (Drury, et al.).

Compared to other housing programs, Section 8 has proved to be relatively popular. There seems to be little question that the program has helped thousands of families improve their living conditions. By the end of 1980 there were about 1.2 million families living in Section 8 housing, with several hundred thousand more units still under development in the New Construction and Substantial Rehabilitation programs. Nationwide, about 60 percent of those who had moved to a new neighborhood indicated that they felt their new location was better than their previous neighborhood (Drury, et al., p. 83).

Criticisms have come from two directions. Critics on the left have charged Section 8 with being insufficient and overly oriented toward landlords' needs. The Section 8 Existing Housing Program does little to increase the overall availability of housing for the poor, and funding levels are far from sufficient to meet apparent needs. Although the New Construction and Substantial Rehabilitation component has added units, critics charge that many of these units would have been built or refurbished even in the absence of the program's incentives. They charge that, by increasing the effective demand for housing (by giving more families the ability to pay higher rents) while making only limited changes in the supply, the program has the effect of escalating housing costs. Although landlords are constrained by the fair market rent ceiling, there is some evidence that Section 8 may be exploited by some landlords to get higher rents than they otherwise would charge. One survey found that Section 8 tenants who, upon receiving certification, chose to use their subsidy on the unit in which they were living already received substantial rent increases; even those in units that received no repairs had increases averaging over 25 percent (Drury, et al. p. 65). It is possible that some of these increases are desirable, simply allowing struggling small landlords to charge what they need and deserve. In some cases, however, these increases may represent hidden and unnecessary subsidies to the landlords. The costs of this would be absorbed by the government and, more tragi-

Table 6-2 Assistance Commitments Made Under the Existing Housing and New Construction/Substantial Rehabilitation Components of Section 8, FY 1976–FY 1982

	1976[a]	1977	1978	1979	1980	1981	1982
Total commitments made (in thousands)	517	388	326	325	206	178	112
% New construction/ Substantial Rehab.	39	52	55	61	63	43	12
% Existing Housing	61	48	45	39	37	57	88

SOURCE: Raymond J. Struyk, et al., *Federal Housing Policy at President Reagan's Midterm.* Washington, D.C.: The Urban Institute Press, 1983, p. 15.
[a]Includes a three-month transition quarter between the July-to-July and October-to-October fiscal years.

cally, by low-income households without Section 8 certificates who may face higher rents as a result.

Critics on the right, although appreciative of the program's theoretical allegiance to the market model, have focused their attacks on the program's expense. These complaints have centered mostly on the New Construction and Substantial Rehabilitation component, which costs at least twice as much as the existing program for each unit of housing involved. The Reagan administration, citing data such as these, moved to cut back Section 8 severely. These cutbacks were focused on, but not limited to, the New Construction and Substantial Rehabilitation segments of the program (see Table 6–2). Even Section 8, with its heavy emphasis on individual choice and its reliance on private market dynamics, involves a public-sector role that is more prominent than some conservative and neoconservative analysts believe desirable.

MODELS FOR THE FUTURE?

Sometime during the 1970s, we entered an age of budget consciousness and austerity. Emphasis, since then, has been on sparing programs rather than launching new ones. Do cutbacks in the cost of government mean we must shave down our goals and aspirations as well? Or is it possible to do more with less?

The trends in housing and redevelopment policies, as in other policy areas, point in the direction of greater privatization and greater decentralization. These represent, in part, a repudiation of the programs that went before. Some critics of these past efforts feel that a simple dismantling of the bureaucratic apparatus those programs generated is all that is needed to spark an era of recovery. Their strong allegiance to the notion that the market is the most effective and efficient force for change leads them to conclude that the best hope for the future is to concentrate on undoing the market-distorting programs launched by the federal government. Others, who also believe that non-federal actors must play a greater role if future redevelopment policies are to succeed, feel that lifting the weight of the federal government will not be enough. If the age of austerity is not to be an age of regression and decline, it may be necessary to discover new policies that can better stimulate and support the private and local sectors and the resources they represent. Some of the ideas discussed in this section have been tried on a small scale, others are untested.

Unleashing the Private Sector

Proposals for housing vouchers and enterprise zones represent two rather distinct manifestations of the privatization trend. Both are based on the notion that housing and redevelopment policies of the past have not relied enough on the wisdom and dynamism of the private market. But they seek to remedy that past failing in rather different ways. The housing vouchers idea rests on the notion that the market has worked very well for all but the poor. The vouchers would add to the disposable income of the poor, enabling them to compete in the market with everyone else. Enterprise zones are intended to revitalize declining neighborhoods by reducing the weight and presence of government.

Housing vouchers. Proposals to replace all existing federal housing programs with a system of housing vouchers, or housing allowances, have been heard increasingly in recent years. The housing vouchers idea takes the logic of Section 8 one step further. Section 8 empowered the recipient to act like the unsubsidized consumer in choosing among available rental units. Housing vouchers, as they currently are being discussed, also would allow the eligible recipient to choose between spending his or her allowance on housing or other needs.

Recipients would receive a cash grant, the size of which would be determined by their income. Owners as well as renters could be eligible. The only requirement imposed upon the recipients would be that they live in housing that meets certain specified standards. Recipients could use their grants to move into better neighborhoods if they choose. If they live in substandard housing but wish to remain where they are, recipients could use their grant to pay higher rents in return for landlord repairs or, if they are homeowners, to fix up their property themselves.

Under some voucher proposals, recipients would be required to spend at least some specified portion of the grant on housing-related expenses. But nearly all proposals leave the recipient at least some freedom to spend the money on nonhousing needs. There is an important reason for this. Under the Section 8 program, recipients have little incentive to look for a housing bargain, because the money they save would be the government's rather than their own. Under the voucher system, the subsidy is not reduced if the recipient finds a bargain. The knowledge that they are free to use the money they save to buy food, go to the movies, meet special health-care needs, and so on, will, in theory, make recipients work as the government's partners in the battle to cut program costs.

Interest in the concept led HUD, in the early 1970s, to launch a series of major experiments to see whether the idea would work. The Experimental Housing Allowance Program (EHAP) included three distinct experiments at several sites. The "demand side" experiment, in the Pittsburgh and Phoenix metropolitan areas, was intended to determine who would be likely to volunteer to participate in such a program and whether they would use their allowances to move, to fix up, or to meet nonhousing needs. The "supply side" experiment, in the Green Bay, Wisconsin, and South Bend, Indiana, metropolitan areas, was designed to determine the likely effects on the housing market: Would it lead to increases in rents? Would it stimulate an increase in housing supply? A third "administrative" experiment, involving a number of sites, aimed at identifying problems in implementation that might occur.

EHAP led to a number of interesting findings. Some suggested problems that a national allowance program might entail: (1) Rates of nonparticipation were higher than generally expected, and those least likely to participate were those whose income and current housing conditions showed them to be in greatest need. (2) Most of the money—about three-quarters—did not go to housing at all. (3) Where improvements in housing *did* occur, they were generally quite small, averaging less than sixty dollars per unit (Bradbury and Downs, eds., 1981). There were, nonetheless, some encouraging findings as well: (1) Many families did use the money to improve their living conditions. (2) These improvements came at a relatively low cost. EHAP cost about one-half as much, per household, as the subsidized housing programs that sought to place the poor in newly constructed units. This lower cost gives the housing allowance considerable appeal.

Housing vouchers generally are considered to be a conservative or neoconservative approach to meeting housing needs. If implemented on a broad scale, they would take government completely out of the role of building or managing housing. But vouchers have some support in the liberal policy community as well. Liberals hope that by reducing the need for oversight, vouchers would reduce the percent of program costs that are absorbed by the bureaucracy and increase the amount of aid that actually reaches the target population. Some liberals hope that by giving recipients discretion as to how to spend their aid, vouchers will prove to be less patronizing and manipulative and more responsive to each poor family's needs. Finally, to some liberals, vouchers represent a back-door approach to a guaranteed minimum income program. Because most housing vouchers proposals would provide aid to all who fall below a certain income level, and because recipients would have the discretion to spend that aid on nonhousing goods and services, some of the goals of a guaranteed income program would be realized. But housing vouchers also may be more politically acceptable, for a couple of reasons. First, the general public is more likely to accept the notion that all people have a right to decent housing than they are to affirm the right of all to a specified income. Secondly, because some of the benefits of a voucher program would be enjoyed by landlords and builders, a voucher program presumably would attract a broader political constituency.

A small voucher demonstration was enacted as part of the Housing Act of 1983. The fiscal year 1985 budget proposed by the Department of Housing and Urban Development included recommendations that Congress fund vouchers for 116,000 poor families. At the time this book was written, it was the stated goal of the Reagan administration eventually to have vouchers replace all other existing federal housing programs.

Enterprise Zones. Along with a new decade, 1980 ushered in a "hot" new idea in urban policy. Enterprise zones were first discussed in Great Britain in 1978 and first instituted there in 1981. The concept took the United States by storm. In 1980, two enterprise zones bills were introduced in Congress; 1981 brought six more. On March 23, 1982, President Reagan announced his own proposal for an enterprise zones experiment (U.S. General Accounting Office, 1982, p. 1).

Unlike past revitalization efforts, which have relied on positive governmental action in providing services, funding, and subsidies, enterprise zones are based on the premise that the best way to stimulate revitalization is to provide relief from the taxes and regulations that governments impose. Although the many enterprise zones proposals differ in key respects, all share these basic components:

- *A relatively small distressed area is targeted.* Congressmen Jack Kemp and Robert Garcia, who introduced the best known of the enterprise zones proposals, envisioned that cities would be allowed to designate zones of about ten to fifteen blocks in neighborhoods marked by high unemployment and poverty. Although initially thought of as an "urban" program, the major proposals have expanded the concept to include distressed rural areas as well. President Reagan indicated that over 2,000 localities would be eligible to apply for designation under his enterprise zones plan.

- *Businesses and employees within the zone boundaries would qualify for some combination of federal, state, and local tax relief.* These could include reduced capital gains taxes, investment tax credits, reductions in Social Security taxes for employers and employees, reductions in income taxes, and lower property taxes.

- *Some relief from governmental regulations would also be provided.* Proposals have varied widely on this component. Some extreme proposals have suggested the elimination or sharp weakening of the minimum wage requirement, and environmental and occupational health and safety standards. Those standing a greater chance of being adopted include moderation of building code and licensing regulations and commitments to reduce paperwork requirements.

- *Provisions to target zone benefits to the poor.* Most proposals make some effort to ensure that new jobs and opportunities will be made available to the disadvantaged. Both the Kemp-Garcia and Reagan plans, for example, would offer special tax credits for zone businesses that hire and train disadvantaged workers.

Advocates of enterprise zones argue that this approach will stimulate the establishment and expansion of small businesses. Stuart Butler (1981), for example, predicts the proliferation of "basement businesses"—bakeries, laundries, tailors, and the like. This economic activity, it is hoped, would generate substantial spin-offs: more jobs for zone residents would lead to greater family stability; more disposable local income would allow other local businesses to thrive; crime, vagrancy, and drug traffic in the newly bustling streets would decline; greater community pride and hopefulness will stimulate political involvement and self-help efforts by neighborhood organizations. *Resting beneath these predictions is the premise that it has been the undue weight of government that has stifled entrepreneurial innovativeness and the voluntary spirit upon which revitalization must be based.*

Criticisms of the enterprise zones come in two major types. Some argue that the idea simply will not work. They cite evidence that taxes are only one of a number of factors that businesses weigh in considering where to locate. Others factors, such as access to raw materials, the availability of skilled labor, proximity to customers, adequate roads, schools, and public services, seem to play a more influential role in business location decisions than differentials in taxes alone. The appeal of lower taxes may have been weakened, moreover, by the general tax-cutting policies instituted by the Reagan administration; these lowered the effective taxes on corporate income so much that the added advantage of an enterprise zone location may be too small to warrant the costs of relocating or doing business in a deteriorating neighborhood (U.S. General Accounting Office, 1982).

Others argue that even if enterprise zones succeed in attracting businesses, the benefits will be lower, and the costs higher, than anticipated. Rather than lead to a net increase in business activity, enterprise zones might simply shift existing businesses around. If non-zone businesses migrate into the zones, without expanding their operations, the result would be a loss in tax revenues without any obvious corresponding benefits. It is also possible that the wrong types of businesses will be attracted. Critics have charged that the tax incentives associated with most zones proposals have relatively little appeal for newer and smaller businesses, which typically earn too little to accumulate any significant tax liability. The unattractiveness and perceived crime risk in targeted neighborhoods may deter desirable service and retail businesses, leaving the zone's advantages to be exploited by warehousing and similar activities that are less dependent on the immediate environment but also less likely to stimulate the positive spin-off advantages that the program's advocates foresee.

The zone's successes in attracting businesses and investment, moreover, may carry a heavy cost. If businesses are attracted from surrounding areas, the zone's revitalization might be accompanied by deterioration in those other neighborhoods. If the zone proves to be a strong magnet for investment, long-term residents may find themselves displaced by newer residents and investors who bid up the cost of housing beyond their reach. The dollar cost in tax revenues foregone may make the program more expensive, finally, than any of its promoters has been willing to admit. Estimating the costs of such a program is expremely difficult. Unlike more conventional revitalization efforts, in which a specific budget can be legislated, the cost of the enterprise zones could vary tremendously, depending on such things as the size of the zones and their effectiveness in generating new business activity. The Department of Treasury estimated that the cost associated with the Reagan proposal would be from $9.3 million to $12.4 million per zone. This covered only federal tax losses and was based only on estimates for the first year. If zones proved to be larger than assumed, or if they proved to generate more sales activity than assumed, the costs could easily turn out to be five or ten times as great (U.S. General Accounting Office, pp. 34–5).

As with housing vouchers, the ideological lines of debate over enterprise zones sometimes seem a bit blurred. The emphasis on taking government out of the picture clearly appeals to the neoconservative point of view. Consistent with this is the fact that a neoconservative congressman, Jack Kemp, and a neoconservative think tank, the Heritage Foundation, have been among the most vigorous exponents of the enterprise zones concept in the United States. The cosponsor of Kemp's enterprise zones legislation, however, is Robert Garcia, a liberal congressman, whose district includes the South Bronx. Enterprise zones appeal to some liberals, who see them as a rejection of the notion that broad market forces dictate that areas like the South Bronx are destined to decline. Some liberal interest groups support enterprise zones because they figure they are likely to be better than nothing, and because, in the current political environment, they seem to be the only targeted urban program that is not being sacrificed in the name of reducing the federal deficit.

Radical critics, however, reject the presumption that enterprise zones are unlikely to do any harm. They see enterprise zones as simply the latest in a series of programs launched in the name of the inner-city poor but actually likely to provide benefits primarily to a business elite. They argue that by forcing states and localities to compete in their promises to cut taxes and regulations, enterprise zones threaten to rob these jurisdictions of the tools they ultimately are dependent upon if they are to reverse the process of decline. "Significant new economic development, in inner-city neighborhoods or elsewhere, is going to require major *public* investment in physical infrastructure (roads, street lights, bridges and sewers) and services (police, fire, job training, and maintenance of all that infrastructure," Bluestone and Harrison suggest (Bluestone and Harrison, 1982, p. 228). Declining Snowbelt cities need tax revenues to refurbish, and growing Sunbelt cities need taxes and regulations if new development is not to overwhelm them and erode their quality of life. Bluestone and Harrison charge that enterprise zones offer a seductive, but destructive, trade. Jurisdictions give up the opportunity to raise additional revenues in the hope that this will eventually lead to a healthier local economy. In return, however, they may attract little more than a handful of employers offering low pay, poor working conditions, and little job security.

The uncertainties surrounding the likely impact of enterprise zones have put a damper on enthusiasm at the national level. But while Congress has hesitated, some states and localities have decided to move forward on their own. At least eighteen states have passed legislation authorizing enterprise zones. Connecticut's legislation, for example, went into operation in July 1982. City officials in Norwalk, Connecticut, already credit their enterprise zone with keeping more than a dozen businesses from leaving town (Kurtz, 1983).

Local Self-Help

Along with the greater emphasis on the private market in stemming decline has come a greater emphasis on localized self-help strategies. Homesteading and Neighborhood Housing Services are essentially local policies, although the federal government, in each case, has played a role of encouragement and support. Each seeks to stimulate a declining community's own resources for rejuvenation.

Homesteading. The federal government, in the middle 1800s, found itself the owner of huge tracts of western land—land that was essentially barren and unproductive. In an innovative and exciting move, Congress passed the Rural Homestead Act of 1862. American citizens were invited to stake out tracts of up to 160 acres on the federal land. They were required to build a structure, cultivate the land, and live on the property for at least five years. In return for this, and a twenty-six-dollar fee, title for the land would be handed over to them. The result: thousands of families would be given the chance to become property owners and potentially valuable farmland would no longer go to waste.

One hundred years later the logic behind the Rural Homestead Act began to be applied to declining urban neighborhoods. Some observers were struck by the irony that abandoned buildings in declining neighborhoods were owned by the local government (due to the owners' failure to pay property taxes that were owed), while at the same time many lower-income families wished desperately to be able to own their homes, to get a true stake in their neighborhoods and the sense of permanence and stability that low-income renters rarely can enjoy. "Why not simply give the housing away?" some of these families and a few local officials asked. That, essentially, is what the homesteading program entails.

The homesteading approach is based on a series of beliefs: (1) That there is a strong demand for inner-city housing by families who cannot afford to meet the down payments and high monthly costs that purchasing such housing would entail. (2) That deteriorating neighborhoods can be saved by the residents, if those residents are committed to bringing about a positive change. (3) That homeowners are generally more committed than renters. (4) That individuals are willing to contribute their own time and labor in order to rehabilitate deteriorating properties if they are given the opportunity to own their unit and to finance their repairs.

Baltimore, Philadelphia, and Wilmington, Delaware, were the leaders among a handful of cities that began experimenting with homesteading in the early 1970s. City-owned houses were awarded to low- to moderate-income families in return for nominal prices, sometimes as low as one dollar. The family, in return, pledged to fix up the property and to live in it for at least some specified period of time. It was hoped that these homesteaders would spark a broader wave of investment in the declining neighborhoods. As others saw signs of rehabilitation and a reversal of the trends of decline, they too would be tempted to move into the neighborhood or devote more resources to the repair and maintenance of the properties they already owned.

The program was a dramatic popular success. The demand for homesteading properties far exceeded the supply of the units that the local governments were able to offer. Several cities established lotteries to select the lucky families. About 1,400 families applied for one lottery in the District of Columbia in which only twenty-seven houses were available.

Recognizing the excitement and potential of homesteading, Congress authorized HUD to set up a national program in 1974. Through that program, HUD offered federally owned housing to local governments in order to carry out demonstration homesteading programs. Initially, twenty-three cities were selected. By May of 1980, there were eighty-three (U.S. Department of Housing and Urban Development, 1981, p. 4). During the first four years, almost 50,000 families applied for the approximately 2,100 homestead properties made available under the program. The typical participating household consisted of 3.2 persons headed by a thirty-six-year-old male member of a minority. The average cost of rehabilitation over the first couple of years of the program was $12,400, about 38 percent of which was estimated to be the value of the self-help labor that the families themselves put into their new homes (U.S. Department of Housing and Urban Development, 1979).

The homesteading program has much to offer. Nobody likes to see homes lying empty and abandoned. Such properties impose a psychological trauma on the surrounding area, symbolically announcing that this is a neighborhood in decline. By helping a few eager families earn title to those buildings, local governments have the chance to help them as well as the surrounding neighborhoods, and, by putting the property back on the tax rolls, to give the city a fiscal boost at the same time.

But the appeal of the program ought not be allowed to mask its limitations as an effective answer to the broad problems of housing and urban decline. In spite of the great enthusiasm, the program has remained very small. There is an inherent limit to the number of houses that can be made available in this way. Even more important, it has become clear that homesteading will not work if lower-income families are simply tossed into declining neighborhoods with a new home and the admonition to "sink or swim." Ongoing financial assistance, advice, and a local governmental commitment to improve neighborhood services are also necessary. There is a trade-off, moreover, between helping those who are most needy and those who are most likely to succeed. Homesteading, as it has evolved, is not a program for the very poor. By the third year of the federal demonstration program, average rehabilitation costs had reached $17,141; in order to meet the financial demands associated with the program, participating families had to have regular and fairly substantial incomes. Nor may it be a program for the most deteriorated neighborhoods. HUD's review found that local governments were applying increasingly strict standards in selecting properties, rejecting those that would be too expensive to repair as well as those in neighborhoods that would be unlikely to attract families with enough income to carry out the needed rehabilitation. Some liberal and radical critics, concerned that the program may be helping the middle class at the expense of the poor, have charged that homesteading is saving some neighborhoods at the cost of displacing existing renters who are unable to meet rising housing costs as the area turns around. HUD's efforts to assess the displacement effect, however, have not turned up evidence that this is the case.

Neighborhood Housing Services. Another program born in the 1970s that might serve as a model for the 1980s is Neighborhood Housing Services (NHS). NHS receives some federal support, but it, like homesteading, is a program with a local orientation. NHS seeks to prevent deterioration, rather than reverse it once it has become firmly entrenched. Like the homesteading program, NHS incorporates an element of self-help. The boards that oversee local NHS operations consist of community residents as well as bankers and local officials.

NHS focuses on the relationship between private lenders and property owners in aging neighborhoods. Deterioration, it is reasoned, occurs when property owners fail to reinvest in their properties at the critical point when they begin to decline. Sometimes that failure may be due to the residents themselves, who are unaware of the availability of rehabilitation loans or too uninformed, too intimidated, or too pessimistic to actively pursue them. Sometimes that failure may be due to the lending institutions, which, based on vague impressions, decide that a particular neighborhood is "going downhill" and slowly choke off the availability of affordable loans. The local government, too, can contribute to decline by cutting back on its service provision, allowing schools to deteriorate, targeting capital expenditures in other, more dynamic, parts of town. By drawing the community residents, financial community, and city officials together on the board, NHS seeks to facilitate communication and coordination among them, with the result of stimulating reinvestment by property owners in the targeted neighborhoods.

Neighborhood Housing Services are established in a single neighborhood; they depend on local knowledge and intimacy and therefore are not appropriate for dealing with citywide or regional decline. They work, in those neighborhoods, by advising property owners how to obtain loans and qualify for rehabilitation programs. While helping residents, NHS also serves a screening and counseling function that aids lending institutions by encouraging qualified borrowers and helping them arrange their budgets so as to be able to meet the payments they incur.

Most NHS operations maintain a high-risk loan fund of their own from which they can lend to families too poor to qualify for conventional loans. Loans from this fund can be structured so that repayment schedules are tailored to the family's ability to pay. The NHS in Oakland, California, for example, lent one elderly homeowner $10,000 for needed home repairs—the loan had to be paid back at a rate of only $10 a month. In Cleveland, the NHS lent a sixty-seven-year-old woman $14,000 to help her repair the twenty major code violations that city officials found in her home. The loan was at an interest rate of 2 percent with forty-four years to pay it off. Her monthly payments were only $40. Other services some NHS operations provide include maintaining a file on reliable contractors so that residents are not overcharged or treated to shoddy work, and counseling renters in the neighborhood to encourage them to purchase their own homes. City officials usually promise to support NHS operations by ensuring that police, sanitation, and other services will be improved or maintained, and by coordinating code enforcement activities so as to keep them compatible with NHS strategies.

Like homesteading, NHS has proven to be quite popular. By the spring of 1984, there were NHS programs active in 195 neighborhoods in 136 cities. These include some large cities, like Baltimore, Chicago, Minneapolis, Newark, and Philadelphia. But many smaller cities are involved as well, such as Beaumont, Texas; Chelsea, Massachusetts, Great Falls, Montana; and Mabton, Washington.

Yet, like homesteading, there is a danger that the potential of NHS may be oversold. NHS has been most successful when it has concentrated on neighborhoods with large numbers of homeowners, median incomes about 80 percent of the median for the city, and already established formal or informal networks of community interaction. NHS does not address—or try to address—the needs of the broad urban underclass. Nor does it—or can it—address the forces of economic and technological change that seem to be draining whole regions of vitality and resources for growth. As the national recession in the early 1980s began to pinch, some local governments and financial institutions found it increasingly difficult to put additional dollars into the Neighborhood Housing Services. As a result, dependence on federal aid grew (Struyk, et al., 1983, p. 113. nn.14). Whether NHS can be more than a holding action, buying just a few more years for neighborhoods that are already more healthy than many others, remains to be seen.

A Bigger Role for the States?

Those concerned about urban and regional decline have often pointed their accusing fingers at state governments. At their best, they say, the states have been "reluctant partners" in the effort to meet the needs of large cities and the urban poor; at their worst, they have been downright hostile. For many years, many state governments were dominated by rural legislators who had little sympathy with big city life, which they saw to be immoral, irresponsible, and a direct affront to the values that they held dear. A series of Supreme Court decisions in the mid-1960s forced states to redraw their legislative boundaries in proportion to population, thus undoing some of the formal underrepresentation that had limited the cities' political clout. But reapportionment did not lead to the radical realignment in states' priorities that some had anticipated. Although there is less talk today about antiurban state policies, the sentiment remains strong—especially among local officials—that states have failed to act innovatively or aggressively to come to their aid.

The Advisory Commission on Intergovernmental Relations (ACIR) identifies five broad areas, or strategies, in which some states have provided targeted aid to meet the needs of their distressed communities (Advisory Committee on Intergovernmental Relations, 1981). These are:

- *Housing:* States may establish housing finance agencies to provide low-interest loans to stimulate the construction of single- or multifamily housing in distressed areas. Some states encourage rehabilitation by offering grants or rehabilitation tax incentives.

- *Economic Development:* States can seek to encourage commercial or industrial development in declining areas by providing site development assistance, commercial and industrial loans and grants, job training, small business support, or by issuing tax-exempt bonds on behalf of private industry.

- *Community Development:* Some states target grants, loans, and interest subsidies in order to stimulate the construction or maintenance of sewer and water facilities, streets, transit and recreational facilities, and public buildings in deteriorating areas. About fourteen states have neighborhood improvement programs intended to encourage or support neighborhood-based economic development activities.

- *Fiscal and Financial Management Assistance:* Most states have established revenue-sharing arrangements in which they give to localities money that they can spend pretty much as they please. In distributing that money, about one-half of these states use formulas that are designed to provide more aid to areas in the greatest need. Other state programs that can provide financial relief include education finance reforms to help areas with a poorer property tax base, state assumption of a larger proportion of the welfare cost, reimbursement to localities for the cost of local services mandated by the state, and state assistance to localities in obtaining low-cost loans.

- *Enhancing Self-Help Capabilities:* By expanding the authority of local governments to utilize certain tax strategies, states can give

Table 6-3 Differences in State Programs to Aid Distressed Communities, by Region, and Over Time. (Figures Represent the Percentage of ACIR Indicators in Which States Are Active)

	Northeast	North Central	South	West
Housing	68.2	47.9	27.9	45.5
Econ. Dev.	38.2	30.0	16.3	10.9
Community Dev.	50.0	33.3	18.8	31.8
Fiscal Reform	49.1	46.7	43.8	47.3
Enhancing Local Capabilities	45.4	72.2	47.9	48.4
All 19 Indicators				
1982	50.2	45.6	31.6	35.9
1980	45.5	43.0	35.5	38.8

SOURCE: Calculated from ACIR, *The States and Distressed Communities*. Washington, D.C.: Government Printing Office, 1980 and 1983.

distressed communities a greater capacity to meet the fiscal pressures that confront them.

After reviewing states' activities in these areas in 1980, ACIR concluded that although many states were expanding their efforts, much room for improvement remained. "Few states," the study indicated, "have made extensive use of the full range of powers and tools at their disposal." By 1982, the situation had not changed dramatically. As Table 6–3 reveals, states in the Snowbelt regions have been the most agressive in targeting aid to distressed communities. In 1982, Northeast states had taken action in just over half of the nineteen specific housing, economic development, community development, fiscal reform, and local self-help areas focused on by ACIR. North Central states had taken action in 45.6 percent; and the figures for the South and West were 31.6 percent and 35.9 percent, respectively. The Northeast states were especially active in the areas of housing, economic development, and community development; the North Central states took the lead in actions to enhance the capabilities of their local jurisdictions.

During the period from 1980 to 1982, while the federal government was taking steps designed to shift greater responsibility to states, the gap between the regions appears to have widened. While states in the Northeast and North Central areas were expanding the range of their targeted activities, states in the South and the West cut back slightly on theirs.

The fact that the states, taken as a group, did not significantly decrease their commitment to helping distressed communities may be encouraging. A number of states were suffering fiscal problems during that period, and, as ACIR concluded, "simply maintaining program levels in the current economic climate can be interpreted as a positive sign"

(Advisory Committee on Intergovernmental Relations, 1983b, p. 57). But there are some disturbing implications as well. As the national government cuts back on its targeted urban and regional development programs, we are entering a period when, if the states do not do it, it simply may not get done. The evidence suggests that, at least initially, the states are not jumping into the void. One reason for this may lie in the fact that some of the state programs in these areas were designed to take advantage of federal programs. State efforts to expand the supply of affordable housing relied, in part, on Section 8, for example; and some state economic development programs depended on CETA or federal Economic Development Agency funding that is no longer available. A second explanation may lie in the tendency for decentralization to accentuate existing differences among the states in political culture and the strength of various political coalitions. Left to their own impulses, some states will continue their recent tendency to respond to the need of their distressed communities. But states that have neglected declining areas in the past show no signs yet of turning over a new leaf.

SUMMARY AND CONCLUSIONS

Public policies to deal with urban and regional decline in this country have been a mixed bag. They involve the federal, state, and local governments as initiators and implementers of programs. They invariably depend upon a combination of decisions by public-sector and private-sector actors.

The federal government's role has been the more dramatic. This partly reflects the fact that actions taken in Washington, D.C., are generally more visible and necessarily carry a broader impact. It also reflects the fact that decline is largely a factor of decisions about investment. The federal government, through its monetary and fiscal policies, has more tools with which to influence private investment decisions than do either the localities or the states. But local governments are very active in the day-to-day battle against decline. It is the local government that inspects buildings, enforces housing codes, struggles to fill potholes, keeps the garbage off the street. Although states have been accused of turning their backs on the problem of decline in their major cities, both states and localities are coming to recognize that their fates are intertwined. When coupled with the Reagan administration's deliberate efforts to return major responsibilities to the states, this awareness suggests that we should expect an even greater state role in redevelopment efforts in the years to come. Even when federal programs are involved, the states and localities have not been watching idly on the sidelines. Programs such as public housing, urban renewal, and the Community

Development Block Grants were true examples of an intergovernmental approach. Those programs came to mean different things in different places as state and local officials implemented them with reference to their own values, their own skills, and their own assessments of the political environment.

Some politicians and policy experts discuss public-private partnerships as if this is a radically new innovation. As we have seen, however, programs such as the FHA mortgage guarantees, urban renewal, and the various housing subsidies, far from seeking to displace the private sector, were entirely dependent upon developers and financial institutions. The government, for the most part, sought the cooperation of those private actors with a juicy carrot rather than a stick. That these efforts have come to be remembered, by many, as governmental intrusions into the private realm reflects, as much as anything, the fact that Americans continue to measure their world against the standard of a totally free market. Few electable officials, at any level of American government, would consider policies that challenge the basic integrity of the market system. When officials, out of ignorance, or naiveté, or idealism, have proposed policies that threaten private interests in any consequential way, those officials have been rapidly and effectively reminded that the health of their community and the success of their administration depends upon those private interests being willing to play along.

It is this mongrelized nature of our past policies that makes the lessons of history so difficult to disentangle. Currently, we are moving toward a greater reliance on decentralization and privatization. The move toward decentralization is reflected in the shift from categorical to block grants that began in the early 1970s. The Regan administration has sought, in the 1980s, to accelerate this shift by encouraging the states to take over the Small Cities CDBG program, by relieving local governments of the requirement that they target their community development efforts to low-income areas, and by generally scaling back the extent of federal oversight and regulation. The move toward privatization is reflected in the deemphasis on those programs—such as public housing and urban renewal—in which government played a substantial role, and by a reorientation toward programs like enterprise zones and housing vouchers, which are presumed to further growth and efficiency by taking government out of the picture.

Privatization is reflected, too, in a growing readiness to accept the judgment of the market as to the viability of particular neighborhoods and regions. In a 1977 editorial, Irving Kristol, considered by some to be the father of neoconservatism, leveled a serious charge. "Any policy that anchors poor people in a declining city—whether it be by generous welfare payments, subsidized housing, or subsidized employment—is bound to be cruelly counterproductive," he wrote (Kristol, 1977). Kristol and others suggest that public policies should acknowledge that some areas are likely to continue to decline. Some of the older cities of the Northeast—burdened by an aging infrastructure, declining housing, and outmoded industries—may be irretrievably leaky vessels, made obsolete by ongoing changes in technology, energy usage, transportation, and popular tastes. Rather than use public resources to buy more cups with which to bail out a sinking ship, why not structure policies toward helping people to relocate to growing, economically vital areas? A 1980 presidential commission recommended just such a course. "Public policy should seek to loosen the tie between distressed people and distressed places just as a variety of technological developments has loosened the ties between industry and its traditional urban location," the commission reasoned in its report (Hicks, ed. 1982, p. 62). Unemployed steelworkers, for instance, might be given funds to help them find jobs and move their families to the Southwest.

The move toward decentralization and privatization reflects a mistrust of the federal government and a perception that its past efforts—no matter how well intentioned—have consistently failed. There certainly have been failures. But there have been successes as well. And the explanation for the failures is complicated. It would be a mistake to assume that decentralization and privatization are, in and of themselves, the answer to the intertwined dimensions of urban and regional decline.

The lessons of history, unfortunately, do not come well labeled or with explanatory footnotes. Although an inflexible, cookie-cutter approach in Washington may have suffocated local flexibility at times, it is also the case that local flexibility occasionally has meant catering to local biases, incompetencies, and corruption. Public officials sometimes may have failed to understand the market—building housing like Pruitt-Igoe in which nearly nobody wished to live—but history grants us no reason for confidence that, without public stimulus, the private market will show any interest in relieving the pain and disruption caused by urban and regional decline. Some of the failures—of programs like Section 236 and urban renewal—might be attributed to *over*indulgence of the profit incentive of private actors. In order to gain the cooperation of developers and financial institutions, public officials found themselves sweetening the package of incentives offered. But such a sweet carrot attracts those out for quick, windfall profits, and governmental reticence to "interfere" makes it more likely that abuses will occur.

History, then, grants no clear mandate for efforts to decentralize and privatize. Some states and localities are likely to use their discretion wisely and fairly. Others will not. In some places, private market forces may bring about spontaneous gentrification and commercial revitalization. In other places, an untethered market will mean a more rapid decline.

SUGGESTED READINGS

Bradbury, Katherine L., and Anthony Downs, eds. *Do Housing Allowances Work?* Washington, D.C.: Brookings, 1981.

Butler, Stuart M. *Enterprise Zones: Greenlining the Inner Cities.* New York: Universe Books, 1981.

Fainstein, Susan S., et al. *Restructuring the City.* New York: Longman, 1983.

Gelfand, Mark. *A Nation of Cities: The Federal Government and Urban America, 1933–1965.* New York: Oxford University, 1975.

Greer, Scott. *Urban Renewal and American Cities.* New York, Bobbs-Merrill, 1965.

Mayer, Martin. *The Builders.* New York: W.W. Norton, 1978.

Meeks, Carol B. *Housing.* Englewood Cliffs, N.J.: Prentice-Hall, 1980.

Mollenkopf, John. *The Contested City.* Princeton, N.J.: Princeton University, 1983.

Rosenthal, Donald B., ed. *Urban Revitalization.* Beverly Hills, Calif.: Sage, 1980.

Wolman, Harold. *The Politics of Federal Housing.* New York, Dodd Mead & Co., 1971.

7

Dealing With Growth

Most drivers were probably startled by the large billboard that stared down on the stretch of highway between Santa Fe and Albuquerque. Set against a beautiful mural of the local landscape was a one-word message: UNDEVELOP! (Cahn, 1975). To the citizens of a Newark or a Youngstown or a St. Louis, development and growth may be looked upon, longingly, as the antidote to debilitating population loss and economic decline. There is a certain irony in the discovery that elsewhere in the nation some regard growth as a source of problems rather than a cure.

Americans traditionally have taken pride in growth. Civic pride is swelled by claims to the tallest building, the largest shopping mall, the fastest-growing population, the busiest airport. According to Russell E. Train, former administrator of the U.S. Environmental Protection Agency: "Growth has been associated for over 100 years with prosperity, expanding opportunity, and social progress. It has produced so many benefits, both apparent and real, that for a long time it was as unquestioned as gravity itself" (Train, 1975).

But the love affair with growth has not been without its spats and quirks. Not all types of growth have been welcomed with open arms. Some communities have encouraged homeowners while discouraging renters, embraced middle- and upper-class whites while screening out minorities and the poor. Business headquarters, high technology firms, and other "clean" (nonpolluting) industries have been courted, while dirtier, noisier, unionized manufacturers have been rebuffed in various ways. Over the last fifteen years, moreover, an even stronger backlash against growth has emerged. It has taken the form, in some places, of a movement that seeks to freeze or strictly limit local growth of all kinds. Participants in this movement argue that past infatuation with growth has been a mistake. Growth, they warn, brings with it more costs and social traumas than expected but often fails to deliver on its promises of prosperity.

In this chapter, we will consider some of the forms that growth takes and the political and legal issues that are raised by state and local effort to limit or manipulate that growth. Although growth and decline would seem to be direct opposites, they both have their roots in the mobility of people and investment. Governmental efforts to regulate that mobility raise some of the very same issues that we encountered when we considered public policies toward urban and regional decline. If that leads you to expect those on the political left to be spearheading the call for a stronger governmental role, and those on the right to adopt a position of letting the market do its thing, however, you occasionally will be surprised.

VARIETIES OF GROWTH

Growth comes in different forms with differing implications for policy-makers in the states and localities that are affected. In this section, we discuss growth as it occurs in three locales: the suburbs, the Sunbelt, and rural areas.

Suburbanization: The View from the Suburbs

The Suburban Era. Throughout this century, most of the nation's growth has taken place in the suburbs. The decade between 1920 and 1930 marked the first time that the suburbs grew faster than the nation's cities, and they have done so every decade since. Shortly after 1969, the suburbs caught up to the cities in total population; in 1980, 59.9 percent of the country's metropolitan residents lived in the suburbs, compared to 40.1 percent inside the central cities.

Manufacturing and retail jobs were moving to the suburbs as well. Central cities lost over 1 million industrial jobs between 1954 and 1968, and an approximately equal number of new industrial jobs opened in the suburban rings of those same cities (Kain, 1968). Between 1950 and 1970, central cities tended to lose retail jobs to suburbs, which benefited from the growing popularity of large-scale shopping centers.

Suburbia as Myth. The rapid growth of the suburbs is intertwined with two related, but contrasting, myths. The first is the myth of suburbia as the American Dream. For many American families, especially during the post-World War II suburban boom, it was this mirage that drew them out of the central cities into a promised land that offered the best that our nation had to give. To those who retained an element of the pioneer spirit, the suburbs promised space and a little elbow room. To the concerned parent, they stood for good schools, a healthy environment, a place where kids could play baseball on grassy diamonds instead of stickball on hard city streets. The suburbs, too, seemed to offer a blend of privacy and communal spirit that was particularly compatible with the peculiar combination of individualism and grass-roots democracy that is America's heritage. In the suburbs, you could surround your home with tall fences, trees, and a dog to shield you from the nosey and overly garrulous on weekends when you preferred to be alone; then, on Wednesday evenings you could attent PTA meetings, on Fridays the JayCees, to nurture your links with your neighbors, to work to implement with others a view of the world that, happily, all of you shared. The American Dream also has always contained an element of materialism and status consciousness, and the suburbs offered social cachet and a ranch house full of opportunities to put "the Joneses" to shame.

During the 1960s, some of the values that nurtured this generally positive image of suburbia came under attack. The conformity that had attracted young families to communities filled with other young families just like themselves became a mark of "herd mentality" and lack of imagination. Folksingers poked fun at "little houses made of ticky-tacky," and satirists aimed barbs at "gray flannel" commuters who rode home to their wives, dog, and 2.3 children, sipped their two martinis, and then sallied forth to battle the crabgrass on their front lawns. *The myth of the idyllic suburb was replaced with the myth of the vanilla suburb: homogeneous, unsophisticated, bland.*

Although some suburbs might fit quite snugly within the bounds of these stereotypes, the truth is that suburbs vary tremendously in their composition and the nature of their growth. Table 7-1 shows the density, per capita income, and racial composition of the suburbs of twelve major cities. Anaheim's suburban residents, for example, are more than twenty-five times as densely packed as those in El Paso; they may gain some solace, however, from the fact that they earn nearly two-and-one-half times the income. In spite of the image of suburbia as lily white, the suburbs of Newark, Miami, Memphis, and Charleston each have a higher proportion of black residents than does the nation at large; Anaheim, San Jose, Miami, Jersey City, and El Paso all have proportionally larger Hispanic populations than does the United States. The suburbs of Binghamton, Boston, Buffalo, Jersey City, and Newark are losing population.

Citification of the Suburbs. The perception of suburbia as a homogeneous entity distinctly dissimilar from the central city around which it evolved probably was somewhat accurate at earlier stages in metropolitan development. It no longer is. Many suburbs are beginning to look like

Table 7-1 Diversity in the Suburbs

Suburban Area	Persons per sq. mile	Per Capita Income $	Percent Black	Percent Sp. Origin	Population Change 1970–80 (%)
Anaheim-Santa Ana- Garden Grove, Calif.	1,949	10,349	1.00	10.20	35.9
Allentown-Bethlehem- Easton, Pa./N.J.	305	7,709	0.05	0.08	7.1
Binghamton, N.Y./Pa.	120	6,709	0.07	0.06	-0.4
Boston, Mass.	1,214	8,362	1.40	1.30	-4.7
Buffalo, N.Y.	578	7,536	2.10	0.80	-7.9
Charleston, S.C.	116	6,137	28.60	1.40	28.0
El Paso, Texas	71	4,262	8.60	57.10	33.6
Jersey City, N.J.	10,031	6,921	2.40	31.00	-8.4
Memphis, Tenn. / Ark./ Miss.	131	6,616	21.20	1.00	9.4
Miami, Fla.	666	8,292	15.10	30.30	28.3
Newark, N.J.	1,668	9,530	13.80	4.30	-4.5
San Jose, Calif.	586	10,627	2.20	12.90	21.6

SOURCE: U.S. Bureau of the Census, State and Metropolitan Area Databook. Washington, D.C.: Government Printing Office, 1982.

cities in important ways. Racial change is one component of this citification, possibly the most visible and controversial. Between 1960 and 1980, the number of blacks living in the suburbs increased from 2.9 million to 6.2 million, an increase of almost 114 percent. During this period, the number of whites in the suburbs was increasing also, but only by about 61 percent. This appears, at least at first glance, to be a very positive sign. It may indicate that some of the racial barriers to freedom of choice in housing finally have been erased. But it would be precipitous to greet these signs too enthusiastically, as if they were firm evidence that the days of housing discrimination in the suburbs are at an end.

Evidence of black suburbanization ought to be weighed with the following qualifications in mind. (1) The sharp percentage rise, between 1960 and 1980, in the number of blacks in the suburbs is due, in part, to the fact that the number of suburban blacks in 1960 was so low. The suburbs are still predominantly white; in 1980, blacks made up 6.1 percent of the suburban population, although they constituted about 11.5 percent of the total United States population. (2) Not all of the increase in the number of blacks in the suburbs is due to blacks moving into the suburbs; some is due to the expansion of the suburbs to include previously rural areas in which a number of blacks have lived for many years. These new "suburbanites" hardly conform to the image of the upwardly mobile middle-class family. Indeed, many are small farmers, struggling along just above or just below the official poverty line. (3) Some black suburbanization is probably best understood as the extension of urban ghettoes across city lines (Clay, 1979, pp. 405–24; Farley, 1983, pp. 347–59).

In spite of these qualifications, it is the case that a movement toward suburbia by middle-class blacks is under way and, apparently, growing. This has brought some issues—busing, for example—out of the central cities, where, at least in the North, they were originally confined.

Race is only one dimension of the citification of the suburbs, however. As suburbs have grown and aged, many of the maladies long assumed to be peculiar to the large cities have reared their ugly heads in the suburbs as well. With jobs have come the density, congestion, and pollution that often accompany commercial and industrial development. With growing populations have come overloaded sewage and transportation systems. With time has come deteriorating and outmoded buildings and an aging population that requires special services. Crime, too, has slipped across the city lines.

Growing Cities: The Rise of the Sunbelt

Not all growth is in the suburbs and not all cities are in the throes of decline. The regional shift of population and business from the Snowbelt

Table 7-2 The Ten Fastest Growing Cities, 1970–1980 (of those with 100,000 or more residents in 1980)

	Population in thousands		
	1970	1980	Percent change
Anchorage, Alaska	48	173	259.8
Mesa, Arizona	63	152	141.8
Aurora, California	75	159	111.5
Lexington-Fayette, Ky.	108	204	88.8
Sterling Heights, Mich.	61	144	77.6
Arlington, Texas	90	160	77.5
Modesto, California	62	106	71.9
Garland, Texas	81	139	70.5
Tempe, Arizona	64	107	68.0
Colorado Springs, Colo.	136	215	58.8

SOURCE: U.S. Bureau of the Census, *Statistical Abstract of the United States, 1981.* Washington, D.C.: Government Printing Office, 1981. Table No. 24, pp. 21–3.

to the Sunbelt is, as noted in Chapter 5, the most dramatic demographic realignment of the past decade. Table 7-2 reveals that, of the ten fastest growing cities during the 1970s, eight are located in the South or West. Between 1970 and 1980, nonagricultural employment increased by 47 percent in the South, compared to an overall increase of 28.2 percent in the nation as a whole (Southern Growth Policies Board, 1981).

Why People Move South. A number of explanations have been offered for the recent rise of the southern, or Sunbelt, states. These include:

- *Increased availability of central air-conditioning:* overcoming the discomfort previously associated with some of the hotter areas.

- *A growing retirement population:* supported by pensions, Social Security, and savings, this "footloose" group is not tied by their jobs to any specific location and is drawn southward by the milder climate.

- *Mass access to cheaper transportation:* the national highway system and less expensive air travel costs mean that the family that moves to Texas or Florida need not sever its roots with family and friends up North.

- *Life-style changes:* particularly, growing emphasis on fitness, outdoor activity, and the beauty of unspoiled vistas.

- *Changing racial attitudes:* making the southern states more attractive to blacks, who have begun to shift back from northern cities, and to whites, many of whom were uncomfortable in the racially restrictive environment that prevailed in the South for many years.

- *Increased cosmopolitanism:* and the decline of the "redneck" image.

- *A relatively lower cost of living:* including lower taxes and cheaper land and housing costs.

- *Improvement in the quantity and quality of consumer services:* as incomes have risen, major retailers and prestigious shopping outlets have followed the market, greatly expanding shopping opportunities. (Kasarda, 1980, p. 376).

Why Businesses Move South. Deciding whether jobs follow people or people follow jobs may be as difficult (and ultimately as unrewarding) as puzzling over the traditional chicken versus egg debate. The availability of labor is an important consideration to businesses as they make locational decisions. Employers would be very reluctant to invest in the South if skilled managers and workers were not available and were unwilling to make the move. But today, it is the perception of the Sunbelt as a booming job market that serves as its major drawing card.

Why has business growth concentrated in the Sunbelt in recent years? The most common explanation focuses on economic advantages. The expansion of the national highway system and increased air travel mean that southern businesses can enjoy the appeal of the less congested South without losing access to important markets, financial institutions, and various support services that are more developed in the North. Increasing energy costs, the widespread conversion from coal to oil and gas, and federal deregulation of energy prices in the 1970s all served to further the economic advantages of doing business in the warmer, energy wealthy southern states.

A Rural Renaissance?

Earlier in this century, the song "How You Gonna Keep 'Em Down on the Farm?" struck a popular chord. The song reflected a genuine trend: except, possibly, for a brief period during the depression, the rural parts of the nation had consistently lost population relative to the rest of the United States throughout this century.

Early in the 1970s, however, a back-to-the-countryside movement was suddenly spotted. In March 1973, the Census Bureau asked a sample of respondents where they had lived three years before. The answers showed that more Americans had moved from metropolitan to nonmetropolitan areas than had made the journey the other way (Long, 1980).

A revival of growth in rural areas probably should not have been so surprising. *Many of the same factors that have been used to explain suburbanization and the growth of the Sunbelt might explain a back-to-the-countryside phenomenon as well.* Changes in transportation have made rural locations more accessible. The development of the streetcar and the automobile made suburbanization feasible; the further development of the highway system and private air transportation opened up the rural hinterlands in a similar fashion.

In spite of stories about long-distance commuters flying in to their central city offices on private planes every week, such "supercommuters" are only a small part of the story. Although it is easier for the rural resident to reach a job in the metropolitan area, jobs are decentralizing as well. Technological changes in the area of communications have been particularly important in this regard. As it has become easier and cheaper to communicate vast masses of data from computer to computer over telephone lines, some of the traditional advantages of a centralized location have been lost.

Those who no longer work also appear to be playing a role in the rural revival. Retirees have no need to locate near employment centers. Some are drawn to the recreational advantages of rural locations; some are attracted by the peace and quiet and unpolluted air. Others, living on pensions and limited fixed incomes, may be attracted by the lower cost of living (Baldassare, 1981, p. 106).

Along with these changes may have come a reorientation of Americans' values toward a greater appreciation of the rural life-style. The image of the hick and the redneck has been replaced, at least in part, by one of the ruddy-faced outdoorsman, used to clean air, hard work, and self-sufficiency. If this is the case, the early signs of a rural revival may presage a major reallocation of the population in decades to come. Recent opinion polls show that many more Americans *wish* they could live in rural areas than have moved there to date. According to one survey, 12 percent of those currently living in central cities, and 22 percent of those currently in the suburbs, indicate that a small town or rural area would be "the best place to live" (Abravanel and Mancini, 1980).

Challenges to the Market Model of Growth

The Market Model—Free Choice and Self-Limiting? Although the places in which growth is occurring may vary significantly in location, density, history, and culture, the underlying roots of the growth process seem to be pretty much the same in suburbs, Sunbelt, and rural hinterlands. As was the case with explanations of decline, growth is commonly explained with reference to a market-based model.

Population redistribution, according to this market-based model, is the *result of free and independent locational decisions by individual actors (households, firms)*. Each actor has its own goals and values. Some families may yearn for fresh air and breathing space; others cannot imagine living more than a half hour's commute from a major museum. Some businesses feel it is very important to locate in an area with a well-educated and sophisticated work force; others are more interested in cheap labor or in the structure of local tax policies. Whatever their particular priorities, each of these actors weighs the benefits of each possible location against its expected costs. As tastes change—or as changes in transportation, technology, and communication alter the costs of various locations—broad shifts are likely to occur.

This market perspective carries some potent policy implications. As interpreted by neoconservative analysts, the market model suggests that government intervention is undesirable and unnecessary. If growth results from free, independent decisions, *policies to alter its patterns will necessitate interfering with personal mobility and freedom of choice*. This is something that Americans are reluctant to do.

Government action may be unnecessary, in any event, since the market model seems to be *self-correcting*. Many of the advantages that initially are offered by the suburbs, the Sunbelt, and the rural areas can be expected to diminish as growth occurs. As people and businesses crowd in, they will increase the demand for land, labor, and energy. With increased demand comes a corresponding increase in price. Meanwhile, demand for those resources in other parts of the nation will be declining relatively, leading to a lowering of prices there. As factories and homes in the Snowbelt cities are left empty, their prices will fall until they become quite enticing to the next generation of home buyers and corporate planners. As unemployment rises in the Snowbelt, workers may become more desperate, more pliable, more willing to work longer hours for lower wages. As the population thins, energy demand in the North will slacken; utilities may have to offer bargain rates to new businesses in order to ensure that their generators are not left idle. The ultimate result? According to some neoconservative theorists, the outcome will be a stabilization of growth patterns, a new equilibrium. The Snowbelt cities and states will be a bit smaller and poorer than before, the Sunbelt cities and rural areas a bit larger and wealthier. But the rapid change of the past decade will run out of steam.

Government, Power, and Growth. Radical critics of the market model argue that the growth of suburbs, Sunbelt cities, and some rural areas has more to do with political power than it does with individual responses to market forces. Regional differences in wage, land, energy, and transportation costs, John Mollenkopf argues, are: (1) smaller than claimed; (2) declining; and (3) at least partially offset by some continued economic disadvantages of doing business in the South. To fully explain the extent and timing of the shift, it is necessary to consider political factors in addition to the more purely economic factors on which the market model heavily relies. Such political factors include lower taxes, less governmental regulation, weaker unions, and fewer disruptive demands by organized minorities and neighborhood-based citizens' groups (Mollenkopf, 1983).

According to radical analysts, the growth of the suburbs, the Sunbelt, and some rural areas has rested on the ability of business-oriented interests in those areas to capture the political apparatus and to use their power to create an environment that suits their interests better than those of the workers, minorities, or the unemployed. In Houston, for example, considered by some to be the "preeminent Sunbelt City": "In 1981 the mayor was a real estate developer; many earlier mayors have also had ties to real estate development. In 1981 one-third of the city council was in real estate or in fields closely related to it; most of the planning commission was composed of developers, builders, and other people tied in one way or another to the local real estate industry" (Feagin, 1984, p. 99). Through their control of the local government, these business-oriented interests have kept the public sector undernourished—taxes are low, services poor, regulation minimal.

Nor have business interests in the suburbs and the Sunbelt neglected opportunities to use the power of the federal government to promote their own growth when they have been able to do so. We have already mentioned that the FHA housing policies and the federal highway program helped to make suburban living more affordable and more convenient. Neoconservative analysts tend to portray this as another example of the tendency of governmental intervention to backfire. Liberals see it as a case of unintended, and correctable, spillover from generally productive policies. Radical analysts find it harder to ignore the fact that many private developers and other businesses reaped large profits as the value of suburban land increased. They suggest that these interests quite consciously used whatever influence they could muster to entice the federal government into taking actions from which they would gain.

The Snowbelt, according to this argument, has been forced to contribute to the expansion of the Sunbelt, through the federal taxes that its residents must pay. Federally subsidized water projects, along with the highway system, turned barren and inaccessible land into valuable properties. "During the early 1970s," Thomas L. Muller reports, "all but five of the twenty-nine southern and western states—Delaware, North Carolina, Idaho, Oregon, and Nevada—received more federal dollars than their tax contribution" (Muller, 1982, p. 444). At the same time, Illinois, Michigan, and Ohio received, as a group, only two dollars from federal agencies in return for each three dollars in federal taxes paid. Some of those federal taxes went to finance military bases and federal research contracts that tend to provide jobs and economic stimuli to the South. Others underwrote the cost of federal water projects that helped make nearly worthless land in the parched Southwest fertile and profitable.

How Far Will It Go? Are the various forms of growth self-limiting? For example, does the recent boom in the Sunbelt mark the beginning of a major redistribution of power, people, and wealth? Or is it simply a mark of a period of readjustment, a natural balancing-out period during which the South—long the loser in interregional competition—is simply showing the potential to catch up?

In rejecting the market model, many radical analysts also reject the notion that population shifts are destined to carry us, through the guidance of an invisible hand, to a more uniform development. Kirkpatrick Sale, for example, has argued that the realignment marks a major break with the past, one that will fundamentally reshape our national culture and political character. To Sale, the rise of the Sunbelt represents the imminent victory of a rabidly pro-growth faction that has not hesitated to raid the federal treasury, exploit nonunionized workers, abuse the environment, and engage in corruption and fraud. Sale warns that this faction is cementing its economic gains with newfound political muscle. Table 7-3 reveals the "winners" and "losers" in the reapportionment of congressional districts as a result of population shifts between 1970 and 1980; the Sunbelt states are clearly in the winner's column. The "cowboy conquest" will lead to a more conservative national politics, Sale predicts, and an even greater tendency of the national government to pour military and research dollars into the South (Sale, 1975).

GROWTH RECONSIDERED

The Pro-growth Coalition

Growth, like mom and apple pie, has proven to be a popular slogan for politicians because it "sells" in many places and to many different types of crowds. To unions and to the unemployed, growth signifies jobs. To the business community, growth means more people and other businesses to which to sell. Public officials like growth partly because it makes these other groups happy. But they like it also for its presumed impact on revenue: more people and more business mean that more money will be raised by the income, sales, and property taxes that are already in place. Middle-income groups that have no direct stake in growth may be convinced that they will benefit indirectly. Additional tax revenue, their

Table 7-3 Winners and Losers in Congressional Reapportionment

Winners	Change	Losers	Change
Florida	+4	New York	−5
Texas	+3	Illinois	−2
Arizona	+1	Ohio	−2
California	+1	Pennsylvania	−2
Colorado	+1	Indiana	−1
Nevada	+1	Michigan	−1
New Mexico	+1	Missouri	−1
Oregon	+1	New Jersey	−1
Tennessee	+1	S. Dakota	−1
Utah	+1		
Washington	+1		

SOURCE: *The World Almanac and Book of Facts, 1983.* N.Y.: Newspaper Enterprise Association, p. 210.

officials inform them, means that public services can be expanded while tax burdens are held in check. Finally, everyone within a growing jurisdiction may perceive a political advantage to growth. After each census, voting districts must be redrawn to reflect population change. Growing areas can anticipate, therefore, a net gain in legislative strength in state capitals and in Washington, D.C.

Harvey Molotch argues that the goal of growth—more than any other goal—serves to unify an otherwise fragmented elite. Elites in a local community may battle with each other over larger slices of the resources pie—each business seeking special tax benefits, wealthy landowners wanting more services for their neighborhoods, newspapers editorializing against leaders in both the private and public sphere—but nearly all recognize that they share an interest in increasing the size of the pie itself. This common interest in growth, Molotch argues "is the overriding commonality among important people in a given locale," and it shapes the local agenda in such a way that growth becomes the most central issue (Molotch, 1976, pp. 309–32).

Growth can mean more business, more demand for property, more jobs, more power. Realtors, lawyers, doctors, businessmen, landlords, property owners, unions, and politicians, have a potential stake in growth. The coalescence of these forces, if Molotch is correct, represents a forbidding political obstacle to efforts to put a limit or cap on growth.

Although growth has broad appeal in the abstract, the seams in the pro-growth coalition sometimes become more apparent when growth is confronted in more concrete terms. Unions and the poor seek growth for jobs they hope to compete for, but the high-tech and corporate offices that officials and other residents favor are often antiunion, hire few unskilled workers, and may fill many of their more desirable positions with employees who move with the firm. Developers seek growth on the periphery, where land is cheaper and available in large tracts, but downtown merchants may find that such construction is too far away to help their businesses. Residents who favor growth as a means to lower taxes may find themselves in conflict with those who seek growth to expand public services; both groups, moreover, may favor growth only on the condition that it be on the other side of town. And all groups may find that growth, when stared in the face, is an uglier and more troublesome neighbor than they expected.

Facing the Costs

Environmental Awareness Grows. The early 1970s saw the emergence of an environmental movement in the United States. Concerns about clean air and clean water were not, themselves, something new. Organizations such as the National Audubon Society and the Sierra Club had been raising consciousness about such issues for some time. What *was* somewhat new was the diffusion of these concerns to a broad segment of the American population. What was also new was the increased political sophistication and effectiveness with which the organizations of environmentalists began to pursue their concerns. It was under the broad banner of environmentalism that some of the early challenges to growth began to emerge. Growth—at least the kind of unregulated growth that seemed to be taking place on the metropolitan fringes and in a few rural boom towns—presented health threats, aesthetic costs, and a drain on limited local resources.

Pollution and Health. Scientists are increasingly looking to the environment as a factor in causing major diseases such as cancer and cardiovascular disease. Although the exact relationship between pollution and health remains controversial, the evidence does seem to suggest that dirty air and dirty water are genuine health dangers. These, in turn, are often most extreme in urban and industrial areas.

The young and the old are the most vulnerable to air pollution. Sulfur oxides, nitrogen oxides, acid particulates, and ozone are all forms of air pollution believed to contribute to illness and death. "It is generally agreed that there is an excess of lung cancer in urban as compared with rural areas and that carcinogenic and cancer inducing air pollutants are in higher (but not massive) concentrations in urban than rural settings" (National Academy of Sciences, 1979, p. 448). According to one estimate, general air pollutants may increase the risk of lung cancer in cigarette smokers by as much as 10 percent.

Automobile emissions are the major source of the air pollution we confront today. Transportation, in general, is the source of about 66 million tons of carbon monoxide that is released into the air each year. Industry, the second-leading source of carbon monoxide, is responsible for only about 2 million tons (Beyrer, et al., 1977, p. 117). Car and bus emissions are also a major source of hydrocarbons, nitrogen oxides, and lead. Although the precise health effects of high lead in the bloodstream are not known, many health experts fear that it may interfere with brain function, especially in young children. Lead levels in the blood of city dwellers are about 25 to 30 percent higher than those of rural residents (National Academy of Sciences, 1979, p. 452).

Aesthetic Degradation. There is a familiar saying that "you are what you eat." Some environmentalists would argue, just as forcefully, that you are what you *see*. What we see when we look around us may work on both a conscious and subconscious level to alter our moods, thoughts, and behavior. Open vistas relax us and seem to encourage us to think more broadly. Crowded and ugly scenes cramp our senses; chaotic surroundings seem to increase our feelings of being out of control. For such reasons as these, some environmentalists have drawn a battle line between rapid growth, on the one hand, and beauty and space, on the other. "[T]here can't be any more growth at the expense of our open space or prime scenic areas," a former president of the Sierra Club declared (*Forbes Magazine,* 1971).

This aesthetic argument traditionally has been associated with the protection of rural areas, but an appeal to aesthetic concerns has crept into debates about growth in more urban settings as well. During the 1950s, for example, business leaders and public officials in San Francisco combined to launch a large-scale construction effort intended to modernize a sagging downtown. Opponents warned of the dangers of "Manhattanization," conjuring up dark images of sunless sidewalks and overcrowded streets (Hartman, 1974; Mollenkopf, 1983). The growing call for "historic preservation" also had its roots in an appeal to aesthetic values. In many cities, laws passed to protect historic structures have proven to be a major weapon for no-growth activists seeking to stem the demolition of older, smaller buildings to make room for new office and commercial buildings of a much larger size.

The aesthetic argument against growth may sometimes seem naive and impractical. It especially seems so in times of economic hardship when growth, representing jobs, is curtailed in the name of a pleasant view. For many states and cities, however, aesthetic preservation carries an economic dividend. Tourism is the largest industry in Nevada and Florida, the third largest in Louisiana and California, and fourth largest in Arizona and New Mexico. The state of Florida alone receives about 25 million visitors per year, generating an estimated $5 to $6 billion for the economy (Sale, 1975, pp. 44–5). Growth control advocates warn that the pursuit of the short-term economic gains associated with growth may, if they mar the scenic landscape or obliterate the charming structures of an old downtown, prove to be a losing proposition once the long-term costs in lost tourism are taken into account.

Strain on Local Resources. We are a nation blessed with abundance. There is fuel, water, and land enough for all. But the distribution of those treasured resources is not matched neatly to the needs of shifting populations.

Water is a resource that most of us take for granted. But it is not inexhaustible. Some of the sharpest trends of population growth in this country are occurring in the very areas in which water supplies already are overtaxed. Officials and residents in some areas of the Southwest must look at further growth—with its implied demand for more water—as a mixed blessing, at best.

As much as 10 percent of the nation's land mass—about 225 million acres—has undergone severe or very severe *desertification,* a process marked by the lowering of water tables, shortages of surface water, salinization of existing water supplies, and wind and weather erosion (Council on Environmental Quality, 1980, pp. 347–8). Farms, with their need for irrigation, put the most immediate demands on the water supply. But rapid urban growth and industrialization are contributing factors. Arizona pumps water out of its underground aquifers at twice the speed at which those aquifers are refilled by nature (*World Press Review,* 1983, p. 30).

Strain on Public Services. Growth can also impose costs in terms of an increased demand for public services. More people and more businesses mean a greater need for schools, parks, police and fire stations, roads, and street repairs. It may mean that more teachers, police, fire, and sanitation workers must be hired. These things cost money.

In the long run, the wealth that is expected to accompany growth may prove this to be a wise investment. Many residents, however, live in the short run. They may be uncertain about whether they will be living in that community in the future, or they may feel themselves financially overburdened by existing taxes. Until new facilities are built, moreover, they may resent the overcrowding and poorer services they encounter. The same Houston that is widely championed as the living proof of the benefits of growth also offers 400 miles of unpaved streets, an average police response time to emergency calls of twenty-six minutes, commuting times on some routes nearly twice as long as five years before, and a public transportation system that is drastically inadequate (Bluestone and Harrison, 1982, p. 86). California residents opposed to further development in their community of expensive homes and vineyards rallied around the catchphrase "Grapes and cows need no schools" (Scott, 1975, p. 51).

Increased demands for service may exceed those that would be predicted by the number of new residents and businesses alone. The newcomers often come from areas in which the level and quality of public services is relatively high. They may carry higher expectations and be accustomed to a greater tradition of public-sector responsibility than is typical for the natives of the area.

Diseconomies of Scale. When it comes to efficiency in providing public services, bigger does not always equal better. Some political economists argue that there is a definite threshold of city size beyond which increases in population are associated with increases in the per capita cost of running a government.

Traditionally, it has been assumed that larger units of government tend to be more efficient. This seemed, after all, to be the case in the private sector, where larger businesses frequently proved they could operate more efficiently and, by selling comparable goods at lower prices, force smaller operations out of business. There are several factors that go into determining whether economies of scale exist. One of the most important has to do with technology and its capacity to increase worker productivity. Machines and productive techniques that increase the amount that a worker can produce are often too large, complex, and expensive for small businesses. Larger corporations *can* exploit them, and thereby reap the gains in efficiency that they provide.

But most of the services that local governments provide are labor intensive—that is, they rely primarily on people, not machines. It is possible to imagine sophisticated surveillance technology that would increase the area that one police officer could patrol, or modern computer facilities that would allow a single welfare caseworker to aid more families in a single day. Although these things are imaginable, however, they are not yet feasible by and large. Big city cops vary little from their small town counterparts in the manner in which they seek to limit crime. The same goes for teachers, fire fighters, sanitation workers. Although the locality must be large enough to support the purchase of police cars, fire trucks, and the like, beyond a low threshold, gains in size may open up very few cost-saving opportunities.

If the major public services provide few built-in efficiency advantages to larger cities, is there any reason to expect that growth may lead to *less* efficiency? Some political economists think so. One reason has to do with *the nature of bureaucracy.* As cities grow, they tend to expand the complexity of their bureaucracy. They do this vertically, by adding layers of managers to manage other managers, and horizontally, by creating new, more specialized positions: special divisions to handle investigative police work, offices in charge of handicapped students, staff responsible for handling toxic waste. With hierarchy and specialization may come a certain loss of coordination and control. In large bureaucracies, bosses cannot always know what those working at street level—the cop on the beat, the teacher in the classroom—are doing and accomplishing. The lower-level bureaucrats do not always understand accurately what it is that their supervisors want them to do. As in the childrens' game of "telephone," information is lost and distorted as it passes on down the line.

Another reason that increased size might result in a loss of efficiency has to do with the *match between what citizens want and what governments do.* In smaller cities, it may be more likely that citizens will be in agreement regarding the kind and amount of services they desire. With growth usually comes diversity in background and values. Residents of one neighborhood may desire well-equipped and well-maintained parks; those in another might prefer that their tax moneys be spent on more police patrols. Most cities have not yet found a way to target service packages precisely in line with each area's different needs. As a result, some residents and some areas must pay for services they do not really want, and others get less of that service than they need.

Threats to Community and Democratic Control. Small towns can be oppressive and constraining. Privacy may be limited, tradition and habit stifling, the sins of the parents more directly passed on to the daughters and sons. It is partly in response to the confining nature of small towns that, throughout most of this century, migration pulled the young and idealistic from the small cities to the large ones. Over the past decade and a half, however, the image of the small town has been pulled off the shelf and refurbished. Some analysts, including some on the political left as well as on the political right, now remember the small town as the nurturing place of communal spirit and democratic control. The loss of these values may be too high a price to pay for the other supposed advantages of growth.

Community, to conservatives, has come to stand for the values of voluntarism and self-help. The term conjures images of communal barn raisings, good-spirited charity, "taking care of our own." Thus, community stands as the counterpoint to big government. As population grows, as people become more crowded, as those born and raised in different areas, races, religions, and cultures are forced to work and socialize side by side, the norms and habits and expectations that hold a community together may frazzle and unweave. The erosion of community leaves a gap that bureaucrats, professional helpers, and politicians quickly try to fill; in the process, however, citizens may lose the instinct and capacity to take care of themselves. With the loss of community also comes the loss of a source of moral guidance. Some feel that the breakdown of community, under the assault of urbanization and growth, is associated with higher levels of vandalism, drug use, disrespect for authority, and crime.

To some on the political left, the term *community* sometimes conjures up images of New England town meetings, participatory democracy taken to its extreme. Milton Kotler, for instance, suggests that governance of neighborhood development corporations in low-income communities could be patterned after the face-to-face decision-making style of the town meeting (Kotler, 1969). Many who rallied behind the demand for community control of schools in the late 1960s and early 1970s seem to have envisioned a new, more intimate style of democracy, one that could be sustained only in a jurisdiction of limited size.

The actual relationship between growth and this elusive notion of community is less certain than either the liberal or conservative vision implies. Is it really growth that has undermined the sense of shared goals and the tradition of shared governance? It may be that community is falling under the force of some broader characteristics of modern Western culture—its emphasis on individualism, its celebration of creativity and change, its encouragement of spatial and interclass mobility. Or it may even be that we are dealing with a myth, a golden-hued memory of a time of peace and cooperation that never really existed. Still, the sense of "community lost" is a strong one, and the belief is widely shared that growth is one of the villains involved. As a force in the growth-control movement, this social cost may be as great a motivator as the more material and tangible costs discussed above.

THE STRUGGLE OVER GROWTH POLICY

Petaluma is known to some as the chicken and egg capital of northern California. It is known to many others as the birthplace of the no-growth movement. In the face of rapid growth—the city had grown from about 14,000 to about 30,000 between 1960 and 1971—residents of Petaluma decided that they had had enough, that they just could not take anymore. Officials decided to wrestle the bull of growth by the horns. For the first time in this country, a locality chose to legislate growth directly. Petaluma established, by law, a cap on how much the city could grow in any given year.

Indirect Growth Controls

Restrictive Zoning. The idea of local governments using their powers to shape and moderate growth was not hatched in Petaluma. During the 1930s and 1940s, most states passed legislation enabling their localities to regulate land use through zoning. Zoning can best be understood by envisioning a large map of a city, any city. Through its zoning power, the city can subdivide that map, specifying what uses are and are not permitted within each of the designated areas. Some areas may be zoned for residential uses, others commercial, still others industrial. Finer distinctions may be added as well. Some residential zones may allow apartment buildings, whereas others allow only single-family homes. Some commercial districts may allow commercial uses only on street level, with upper floors reserved for housing. Industrial zones may distinguish among potential uses according to the noise, pollution, or traffic that might be generated.

Zoning is one of the most central and most cherished of the powers that local governments can claim. Its popularity is largely due to its role in protecting the owners of private property. It is zoning that ensures that, two weeks after you move into your new home on a quiet road, construction does not begin on a fat-rendering factory next door.

Although its initial purpose was linked to the goal of ensuring compatible uses, zoning had implications for growth that did not remain hidden for very long. Some suburbs discovered quite early in the game that zoning power provides several mechanisms for indirectly limiting or otherwise influencing growth. Some of these include:

- *Large-lot-zoning:* Local jurisdictions can limit growth indirectly by establishing a minimum lot size upon which housing can be built. Because land is finite, setting a minimum lot size ultimately limits the number of dwellings that can be built. Because land is costly, moreover, large-lot zoning ensures that whatever housing is built will carry a hefty price tag. Jurisdictions may use large-lot zoning to ensure that any new growth in housing is affordable only by the wealthy. In some cases, large-lot zoning, combined with the cost of land, makes development so costly that developers are deterred from seeking to build in the area at all. Between 1960 and 1967, over 150 municipalities in New Jersey increased minimum lot sizes, whereas none reduced them (Danielson, 1976, p. 61). In the state of Connecticut, more than half of all the land on which residential construction is permitted is zoned for minimum lot sizes of one or two acres.

- *Restrictions on apartments:* Zoning can also limit growth by restricting the construction of multifamily homes. This can be done simply by failing to designate any area in which multifamily dwellings can be built, or by establishing a maximum proportion of the jurisdiction's dwellings that can be of the multifamily type. "In the New York metropolitan area, where exclusionary zoning is particularly widespread, over 99 percent of all undeveloped land zoned for residential uses is restricted to single family housing" (Danielson, p. 53). The use of zoning to limit the construction of multifamily housing can also take a more subtle form. Some suburbs intentionally zone land for multifamily construction that they know to be too expensive or otherwise unsuitable.

- *Banning mobile homes:* Mobile homes offer an inexpensive alternative for the many American families unable to afford to purchase their own homes. In 1980, the average sales price of a new mobile home was about $19,200; the median sales price of new, private one-family homes in the same year was $64,500 (U.S. Bureau of the Census, 1981). Yet popular impressions of mobile homes, and the people that live in them, are so negative that many suburbs have banned them entirely. By banning mobile homes, some of these jurisdictions are ruling out the one form of growth that is economically feasible today.

- *"Vasectomy" zoning:* It was W. C. Fields who said that "anyone who hates children and dogs can't be all bad." Most Americans probably still envision the ideal community as one inhabited by families, with children romping in large packs across freshly cut lawns, but Fields has some company today. We have already noted the fact that population growth, in general, can increase the need for expensive services. One kind of population growth is more expensive than most. Studies have found that families with children are especially costly for local governments; although they may contribute as much or more than other families to tax revenues, their need for schools and recreation facilities make them—from a narrow cost/benefit standpoint—a losing proposition. Localities do not have the authority to prohibit their residents from having children, but they can make it more difficult for families with children to find a place to live within their borders. One of the simplest ways to do this is for the locality to use its zoning power to restrict the number of multibedroom living units that can be built. Restrictions on three- and four-bedroom units can be made even more effective by combining them with a legal limit—of, for example, no more than three persons living in a one-bedroom dwelling—on how crowded existing units may become.

Zoning is not the only set of tools that localities can wield in order to limit growth indirectly. Through their power to issue building permits and enforce building codes, local governments may insist on high quality materials, expensive contruction techniques, and the provision of various amenities. This can discourage development by further boosting the price of housing, possibly beyond the reach of all but a select few. Prefabricated, mass-produced housing, which offers some of the affordability of mobile homes combined with the appearance of the traditional single-family structure, is severely limited due to the narrow and often conflicting building codes that many jurisdictions impose. Localities can also discourage growth through their control over the access to, and the delivery of, public services. By failing to extend water and sewer lines, or by charging excessive hook-up fees to those lines, for example, local officials can attempt to dissuade developers from building large tracts of housing in previously undeveloped areas. Finally, the local officials may indirectly limit growth simply by creating and projecting an anti-growth image. By acting slowly on permit requests and by aggressively enforcing building codes, such jurisdictions can create an atmosphere of inhospitality that is sufficient to deter developers, whose capacity to make a profit is often dependent upon their ability to move rapidly.

Weaknesses of Indirect Controls. By the early 1970s, residents in some communities, like Petaluma, had concluded that the indirect means of growth control needed to be supplemented by a more direct approach. Why were indirect controls not enough? Zoning and building permit authority allow local jurisdictions to dictate where growth cannot take place and to make the process of development more costly and time-consuming for the private interests (builders, savings and loans, potential in-movers, commercial investors) who bring about growth. When applied in a comprehensive, consistent, and determined manner, these tools have enabled some localities to keep fairly firm control over their own rate of growth. For a number of reasons, however, residents could not always count upon comprehensiveness, consistency, or determination on the part of their officials.

Part of the problem lies in the fact that most of the indirect restraints operate by making it more difficult or costly to build; they do not prohibit growth. As the postwar baby-boom generation has matured and begun to move into the housing market, the demand for owner-occupied housing has exceeded the supply. This demand has been augmented by certain federal government policies that further subsidized the purchase and construction of new homes. Where the *strength of demand* is strong, the deterrent effects of indirect growth controls may not be sufficient to deter developers, who foresee an opportunity to profit in spite of higher costs and delays.

Restraints on growth, moreover, nearly always stir counterattacks by developers and holders of undeveloped land who feel that their interests have been violated. These individuals and groups have the resources and, often, the organization to mount considerable pressure on city council members, zoning boards, and other local officials. In the face of this pressure, the *lack of expertise* possessed by public officials in some jurisdictions proves important. Planning and zoning officials in large cities are generally well-trained professionals with adequate staffs and legal support. This is often not the case in small or medium cities just beginning to confront the pressures of growth. Gaps or inconsistencies in a local zoning ordinance sometimes allow developers to work around the restrictions or to successfully challenge them in court.

More important than lack of expertise may be *lack of political will.* Public officials in many jurisdictions are more positively oriented toward growth than are their constituents. This is due, in part, to the personal backgrounds of these officials. Many have come from business backgrounds that have made them generally skeptical of all public-sector constraints on private investment. Some have a direct stake in growth: as lawyers who have developers and contractors as clients, as bankers who see growth as an opportunity for a more profitable return on local investment, as merchants who anticipate expanding markets. Presented with applications for zoning variances—applications often backed with the carrot of promised campaign contributions and the stick of threatened legal suits—such officials may be quick to make exceptions, sometimes to the extent that the exception becomes the rule. Unless citizens who favor the limiting of growth are constantly vigilant and able to sustain political pressure, they may find that the protections of indirect controls are more illusory than real.

Direct Limits on Growth

Petaluma Takes a Stand. It was against this background that cities such as Petaluma; Boulder, Colorado; Boca Raton, Florida; and Ramapo, New Jersey, took on pioneer roles in a movement intended to put direct limits on growth. Located almost forty miles north of San Francisco, the residents of Petaluma lived a stable existence, relatively isolated from the metropolis to the south, for many years. But the population of metropolitan San Francisco continued to spread outward, and highway improvements made in the 1960s brought Petaluma into commuting range. The rural outpost was fast becoming a commuter town (Frieden, 1979; Rosenbaum, 1978).

As population rose—from 14,035 in 1960 to 24,780 in 1970—dissatisfaction increased. In the fall of 1970, for the first time students in the Petaluma public school system were forced to attend double sessions. The following year, the Public Works Department reported to the city council that, if development continued at existing rates, the city's sewage treatment capacity would be exhausted within one year. "Considering the enormous cost of constructing new sewage treatment plants, this threat was enough to push the newly elected council strongly in the direction of growth limitation" (Rosenbaum, p. 50).

Surveys of Petaluma residents showed that most (56 percent) favored limiting the population to 40,000 or less, and that another 30 percent favored a size somewhere between 40,000 and 70,000. A citizens commission, appointed by the city council, concluded that a compromise figure of about 55,000 should be the target. To achieve this, the group recommended that an annual quota of no more than 500 building permits be allowed. The city council approved this cap on growth, and so did the public; in a referendum in June 1973, citizens voted for the 500-permit limit by 4,444 to 953. Although not literally a *no*-growth policy, this cap was well below the 880 units that had been built in 1971 and much below the rate of growth that had been predicted. More important than the specific rate of growth permitted, the Petaluma approach established the important precedent of setting a direct and explicit ceiling on growth.

The Movement Spreads. Other cities followed Petaluma's lead. As high-tech industries moved into Boulder, the population skyrocketed—from 37,718 in 1960 to 68,634 in 1970. The city responded, at first, with strategies to control growth indirectly. In 1958, for example, a line was drawn beyond which public water service would not be extended. When, in 1970, planners projected that the city would grow to 140,000 within twenty years, People United to Reclaim the Environment (P.U.R.E.) was formed. P.U.R.E. favored a limit of 100,000 people. In 1971, voters defeated an initiative that would have instituted such a ceiling, but the political message that residents favored stricter growth limits nonetheless was clear. The city council passed a resolution directing the city to take steps necessary to keep growth substantially below that experienced in the 1960s. In 1976, direct limits on growth were approved, in a public referendum, by a narrow 550-vote margin. Under the city's Slow Growth Ordinance, only 450 new units of housing would be constructed per year.

Boca Raton is located about forty miles north of Miami. Its population in 1960 was just under 7,000; by 1973, about 38,000 lived in the area. In November 1972, the city passed legislation that would establish an absolute cap of 40,000 dwelling units, enough to accommodate approximately l00,000 people. Ramapo, New Jersey, in 1969, passed legislation enacting an elaborate process for reviewing applications for building permits. In order to receive the city's permission to build, developers would have to meet an elaborate set of requirements having to do with the availability of facilities and services. The city set forth a schedule for its own extension of public services and public facilities, such as schools. Developers who wished to construct in areas that had not yet received such public facilities could build only if they agreed to provide those facilities themselves.

A GUISE FOR EXCLUSION?

Advocates of local growth restrictions argue that their position is an extension of basic American traditions of democracy and local control. To deny local governments this power would be to deny their residents the capacity to control their own fates. It would be to leave citizens throughout the country at the mercy of private-sector forces of growth and development. If a government is unable to channel these forces—forces that bear so directly on the quality of its citizens' lives—then government will be hard-pressed to sustain any legitimate claim to the loyalty of its citizens.

This is a powerful argument. Certainly it is the case that land-use controls have become a central preoccupation and responsibility of local governments. It is land-use regulation, along with public education, that provides local governments with their public identity. As federal and state involvement in education has grown (see Chapter Ten), the raison d'etre for local governments is increasingly linked, in the public's eyes, to their role in zoning and regulating construction and development. Kick this power out from underneath the local governments and, this line of reasoning suggests, their collapse as viable institutions will follow inevitably and soon.

There is, however, another view. This view looks skeptically at some of the lofty rhetoric of democracy and environmentalism in which the no-growth movement is wrapped. "Many growth opponents," writes Bernard Frieden, "use environmental arguments to mask other motives, such as fears of property tax increases or anxieties about keeping their community exclusive" (Frieden, 1979, p. 8). Is the no-growth movement simply a convenient and more socially acceptable excuse for the continuation of long-standing efforts to keep out minorities and the poor?

Discriminating Against Minorities and the Poor

There is no border guard at the city line or along the Mason-Dixon line to scrutinize the socioeconomic credentials of those who seek to move through. But the prohibitive cost of scarce housing may achieve the same result even more efficiently. The mechanism through which exclusion is achieved is an economic one—persons with sufficient wealth can, if they wish, find someplace to live, even in the most exclusive communities. But, although economic class is the weapon, some argue that the true motivating factor is race. The distinction is an important one, especially as far as the courts are concerned. No-growth policies that have the intent and effect of discriminating on the basis of race are unconstitutional and, if challenged, are likely to be invalidated by state or federal courts. Although it is illegal to discriminate against racial minorities, however, it is not necessarily illegal to discriminate against the poor, even though in many cases the poor and minorities are one and the same.

Do Potential Residents Have Rights? Why aren't the housing needs of low-income and minority populations taken into fuller account? One reason is that most of the costs of growth regulation fall on persons who are not yet citizens of the jurisdiction in which the growth decisions are made. Politicians and officials have little incentive to consider the desires of those who cannot vote in their elections. The courts, too, have looked skeptically upon the right of these nonresidents to file suit when they claim that discrimination has occurred.

William Alonso suggests that, when the interest of those outside the city are taken into account, the no-growth advocates' claim to democratic roots becomes less convincing. "What is the population of this city?" he asks.

> Is it only those living there now, or does it include those who would move in if they could? If we are speaking of a future community of which there are two alternative versions, it makes as much sense to consider the interests of *all* the people who would make up the expanded version, as to consider those of the original version. After all, even if growth is prevented, given the mobility of Americans, only a fraction of the future residents will consist of those living there now (Alonso, 1973, p. 193).

Alonso suggests that the decentralization of decision-making regarding land use contributes to an irrational and ultimately unproductive competition among jurisdictions seeking to lock in wealth while locking out the poor.

Impacts on the Poor Who Are Already Inside. Growth control policies are frequently assumed to pit those already inside against outsiders who are generally from a lower socioeconomic class. But not all those on the inside are wealthy, and not all those on the outside are poor. Partly because of this, not all those inside will be winners if limits on growth succeed.

Most jurisdictions that move aggressively in the direction of growth limitation do so because demand for property in their community is strong: because of convenience, climate, aesthetics, status, or an appealing style of life, there is a sizable pool of outsiders who want to get in. Although no-growth or slow-growth policies can frustrate those outsiders from their desire to acquire new housing in the area, growth limitations do not necessarily make the demand disappear. Instead, they may have the effect of channeling that demand into the existing housing stock. As outsiders bid aggressively for the housing and developable land that *is* available, market pressures will force the cost of that property to rise. To homeowners who wish to sell, this can represent a welcome windfall. But to renters, and to homeowners who do not wish to sell, the ramifications may be less pleasant. The dynamics in such localities may resemble those in the gentrifying inner city neighborhoods that we discussed Chapter 5. Landlords, sensing a strong demand for their buildings, will have an incentive to raise rents. Stable homeowners will find that their property tax assessments rise. For some of these stable homeowners—particularly the elderly and those on fixed incomes—higher taxes may mean less money for other necessities; others may even be forced into selling their homes. Again, the burden can be expected to fall most heavily on minorities and the poor.

Unfortunate Side Effect . . . or Shrewd Hustle?

Even if they do impose some costs on minorities and the poor, the long-term benefits of growth restrictions to the health of the broad community might outweigh those short-term hardships imposed on a limited subgroup. Some claim, however, that the costs imposed on minorities and the poor are more than an unfortunate side effect of a generally noble crusade. Bernard Frieden, for example, insists that it is the exclusion of such "undesirables" that is the underlying consistency behind the growth control movement. More noble goals—such as environmental protection—are modified, qualified, or simply dropped whenever it proves convenient.

Frieden's charge that suburban growth policies are simply fancy rationalizations for discriminating against the poor is difficult if not impossible to prove conclusively. We are not able to probe minds in order to discover the true intent of the no-growth advocates. Frieden builds his case indirectly. His argument rests, in part, on the *effect* of growth limitations where they have been implemented. The effect, he says, is to protect the environmental, social, and economic advantages of the wealthier suburban residents, without producing promised benefits for the public at large.

Marin County is a case in point. Situated in an almost idyllic natural setting, offering scenic vistas, ocean views, redwoods, and eucalyptus, Marin County is the wealthiest of San Francisco's suburban areas. The median per capita income for county residents in 1975 was $12,525, compared to $9,379 for residents living in San Francisco itself.

During the sixties and early seventies, Marin County residents sought to limit growth. One tactic for doing so was to persuade federal and state officials to purchase lands for public parks; this would remove the risk that those lands would be developed in the future, and would do so at little or no cost to the county itself. In trying to convince federal officials to establish a national seashore, proponents from the county argued that those lands represented a national treasure that ought to be preserved so that visitors from throughout the country could enjoy its beauty. Frieden charges that once the land had been purchased, however, county residents changed their tune. Residents fought the construction of roads and recreational facilities that would have made it possible for the broader public to take advantage of the park. The result? Marin County residents protected themselves from further development; won a beautiful park, maintained by national tax dollars, right in their own backyard; and made it unlikely that they would be confronted by low-income or other outsiders even as weekend visitors.

Growth control advocates, Frieden points out, nearly always insist that the limitation of housing construction is merely a means toward other ends: cleaner air, preservation of open space, reduction of congestion, and the like. At times, however, it seems as if that "tool" of preventing construction becomes the "tail that wags the dog." The result is a confusing array of no-growth arguments, each sensible when considered in isolation yet, when added up, appearing to suffer from internal inconsistencies. This is true, Frieden argues, even for respected organizations that cannot be accused of manipulating the environmental argument in a disingenuous effort to cloak other, more personal, interests.

> Sierra Club chapters, for example, have opposed some suburban housing on the grounds that it would generate unnecessary long-distance commuting; have opposed other housing near suburban job centers on the grounds that it should be located closer to the central cities; and have opposed new housing near the central cities on the grounds that it would use up scarce open space there. Another California environmental group . . . has objected to housing in the valleys near San Francisco because the valley soil is better suited to farming, and it has opposed new construction on the hillsides because it claims hill developments will increase the chances of landslides, floods, and fires (Frieden, 1979, p. 9).

The reasons differ, but the end result seems always to be the same. Housing construction is limited, the cost of housing rises, and minorities and the poor find that the wall around the central cities is harder than ever to penetrate.

LEGAL ASPECTS OF THE NO-GROWTH CONTROVERSY

Local governments' efforts to limit or put a cap on growth have not gone unchallenged. Petaluma, Boulder, Boca Raton, and Ramapo all found that passing legislation was simply the first step. More difficult and time-consuming was the attempt to defend their ordinances through the courts. Petaluma's plan, for example, was initially held to be invalid; the city was later vindicated by the California Court of Appeals. Boca Raton's proposed cap on growth was voided by the circuit court of Florida; the city appealed to the state supreme court and lost.

If growth control is to be a viable option, its mechanisms must be able to stand up to legal challenge. If federal or state courts consistently overrule anti-growth legislation, local governments might reasonably conclude that their power to control growth is an empty promise—a power in theory but not in fact. By the same token, low-income and minority groups are looking to the courts to protect *their* rights; because they are only "potential" residents, their ability to influence local growth policies through the electoral process is limited.

In this section, we will review some of the important legal issues and landmark cases. Federal courts, we shall see, have been generally supportive of local no-growth and land-use control efforts; they have hesitated to inject themselves into what has been perceived, traditionally, to be a local sphere. State courts, at least in *some* states, have been more aggressive, making them a potential obstacle to local discretion and a potential protector of the rights of the poor.

Who Can Sue?

Before the courts will rule on the merits of any particular growth control strategy, there must be a plaintiff, with standing to sue, one who can demonstrate to the court that he or she is directly affected by the policy in question. There is no shortage of individuals, corporations, and associations anxious to put local and state restrictions on development to a legal test, but not all of those who are willing are legally able to do so. Challenges traditionally have come from *developers,* who argue that their rights to do business have been infringed upon; existing *property owners,* who fear that the value of their property may decrease if certain forms of intense development are ruled out; *potential residents,* who would have liked to move into the neighborhood if affordable new housing were available; and *civil-rights organizations,* which claim to represent the broad interests of lower-income and minority groups. *By taking a narrow view of who has the right, or "standing," to sue, the Supreme Court has made it difficult for some of these groups to get their day in court.*

The Supreme Court addressed the question of standing in the case of *Warth* v. *Seldin* in 1975. Penfield, New York, a suburb of Rochester, boasted a strict zoning ordinance that some felt was being used, unconstitutionally, to exclude minorities and the poor. The plaintiffs included low- and moderate-income minorities, but the Court denied them standing on the grounds that the particular individuals involved had not demonstrated that, had Penfield's policies been different, there was a "substantial probability" that they would have been able to buy or rent housing there. *It was not enough, the Court ruled, for the plaintiffs to show that the zoning ordinance harmed the poor and minorities in general; those suing had to prove that it was* they *who were harmed.* An association of home builders was also denied standing in the same case. For the home builders to sue, the Court held, it was necessary that they prove that the association's members had actually suffered harm. But the home builders had not produced evidence that any of the association's members had applied recently for a building permit or variance that had been turned down.

Although the standing issue may seem technical and procedural, its impact can be considerable. It was on the basis of lack of standing that the California Court of Appeals, overturning a lower court, rejected the suit that two landowners and a builders' association brought against the Petaluma no-growth ordinance. The practical result of this narrow interpretation of standing may be what one lawyer has labeled the "Law of the Excluded Plaintiff": illegal instances of growth restraint may be permitted to operate simply because no one is considered eligible to bring a legal challenge (Sager, 1980, p. 160).

The "Taking" Issue

The Fourteenth Amendment of the U.S. Constitution requires that no state or its political subdivisions may deprive a person of property without due process of law. "Due process" means that states and localities must themselves act lawfully. The due process clause does not mean that states and localities can never take actions that have the effect of removing or reducing the value of privately held property. In order for them to do so, however, the courts have generally held that three criteria must be met: (1) the government must have a legitimate goal; (2) the means taken to pursue that goal must be reasonably necessary; and (3) the action taken cannot be unduly oppressive upon those who are affected. Property owners often cite the Fourteenth Amendment in challenging state and local growth regulations that, they argue, "take" away their property, or their ability to put their property to its fullest use, arbitrarily or without just compensation.

As with the standing issue, the Supreme Court has adopted a position that is generally favorable to state and local governments seeking to exercise control over growth. The "taking issue" reached the Supreme Court in the case of *Penn Central Transportation Co.* v. *New York City* (1978). New York City's Landmark Preservation Commission had declared the Grand Central terminal a historic landmark. The owner, Penn Central, wished to build a multistory office building above the terminal.

The landmark designation prohibited this, thus leading to the claim that the company's property had been "taken" without compensation.

The Supreme Court upheld a state court decision agreeing with the landmark designation. In doing so, the Court noted that Penn Central was free to use the terminal as it had in the past. The Court also considered it significant that although the landmark designation prohibited the construction of a new building at that site, it did permit the company to transfer development rights elsewhere. This meant that Penn Central could recover some of its loss by selling those rights to another builder who wished to be allowed to build, on another site, a larger building than the city's zoning laws would otherwise allow.

The Penn Central case will not be the last word on the taking issue. According to one knowledgeable observer, "a good deal of the reasoning on the taking issue is far from incisive; much of it is vague and fuzzy, and in fact some of it can be expected to cause a good deal of trouble in the future" (Williams, Jr., 1983, p. 219). The important precedent seems to be this: as long as the owner is left with a reasonable use (even if not a maximally profitable use), and as long as a substantial public interest is presumed to be served, the due process clause of the Fourteenth Amendment does not necessitate that the Supreme Court interfere with state or local regulations that limit development.

Discrimination and the Courts

Some civil-rights organizations have sought to challenge zoning and growth ordinances on the basis that they violate the "equal protection" clause of the Fourteenth Amendment. This clause, which is closely linked to the due process clause discussed above, has been "the cutting edge of the civil rights movement in the federal courts in recent decades, underlying the historic rulings of the Supreme Court on issues such as school desegregation and voting rights" (Danielson, 1976 p. 172).

The federal courts have generally taken the position that there is nothing inherently unconstitutional about a policy that falls more heavily on some groups than others. The village of Belle Terre, a small Long Island community of fewer than 1,000 persons, enacted an ordinance that restricted *all* land use to single-family dwellings occupied by families or unmarried couples. Totally excluded were boardinghouses, apartments, fraternities, and house-sharing by more than two unrelated individuals. The ordinance was challenged by three students from the nearby State University of New York at Stonybrook. They claimed that the ordinance was illegal on several grounds, including the claim that it violated the equal protection clause.

Although not directly involving minorities or the poor as plaintiffs, the *Belle Terre* case had clear relevance to those interests because they are more likely to depend upon housing arrangements such as those that were disqualified. The Supreme Court, in a 7–2 decision, emphatically supported the right of localities to enact such an ordinance, because it was not arbitrary and because it bore a rational relationship to permissible state goals. "The police power," the Court wrote, "is not confined to the elimination of filth, stench, and unhealthy places. It is ample to lay out zones where family values, and the blessings of quiet seclusion and clean air make the area a sanctuary for people." The fact that households consisting of more than two unmarried people were discriminated against did not disturb the Court: "every line drawn by a legislature leaves out some that might well have been included. That exercise of discretion, however, is a legislative not a judicial function" (Schidman and Silverman, 1980, p. 21).

The Supreme Court is not willing to abide exclusionary effects in all cases, however. It is least likely to when the exclusion can be shown to have a racial base. The *Hills* v. *Gautreaux* case, discussed in the previous chapter, established that, *under cetain conditions, federal courts could seek to force or encourage predominantly white suburbs to accept a greater amount of low-income housing.* In the following year, however, the Supreme Court indicated that discrimination based on wealth could be permissible even when discrimination based on race was not.

Arlington Heights is a predominantly white suburb of Chicago. When developers sought to build 190 townhouses for low- and moderate-income families in Arlington Heights, they found that *no* land in the village was zoned to allow such construction. The village officials refused to rezone and were, as a result, taken to court. The lower courts found that the *effect* of Arlington Heights' policies was to discriminate on the basis of race. The Supreme Court decided, however, that this was not enough. In order to overturn the ordinance, the Court ruled, it was necessary to demonstrate the *intent* to racially discriminate (*Village of Arlington Heights* v. *Metropolitan Housing Development Corp.*, 1977).

The Arlington Heights case set a tough standard for groups seeking to overturn zoning or growth policies based on racial discrimination. Civil-rights groups argued that unless careless officials admitted to racial motivations—an unlikely event—the Supreme Court had all but eliminated the due process clause as an effective tool for opening up the suburbs. But although it set a tough standard, the Supreme Court did indicate that it might be willing to overturn local ordinances under certain conditions. The Court made clear, first of all, that the plaintiffs need not prove that racial discrimination was the *sole* intent. The Court also indicated that it would be willing to *infer* intent if the plaintiff could show that a given policy was part of a historical pattern in which the local jurisdiction's policies had distinctly racial impacts not reasonably explainable by other than racial grounds.

"Hands Off" by the Federal Courts

The federal courts have treated local zoning and growth policies with kid gloves. In this area, perhaps more than any other, the courts have functioned as if the old concept of dual federalism was still in vogue. As zoning expert Richard F. Babcock has observed, "The United States Supreme Court considers land use policy a matter for the states to fashion, and the federal Constitution is not the vehicle to upset parochial municipal regulations" (Babcock, 1980, p. 84).

This tradition is long-standing. The first major zoning case considered by the Supreme Court was *Village of Euclid* v. *Amber Reality Co.* (1926). To some extent, it can be argued that all subsequent zoning tests have their roots in that landmark case (Linowes and Delaney, 1980, p. 46). *Euclid* established that, as far as zoning was concerned, state and local governments should be given the benefit of the doubt. A zoning ordinance was to be presumed valid unless it was "clearly arbitrary and unreasonable, having no substantial relation to the public health, safety, morals or general welfare." Since that time, the Court has preferred to leave the substance of land-use policy to state and local legislatures, with primary oversight by the state courts. In fact, the Supreme Court did not hear a single zoning case between 1928 and the 1974 decision in *Belle Terre*. During that same period, state courts were deciding over 10,000 such cases (Babcock, p. 84–5). When the federal courts *have* found existing land-use policies to be illegal, they have preferred to pass the ball back to the state legislatures, calling on them to make the necessary changes rather than seeking particular changes themselves.

Some State Courts Are More Assertive

If localities need not worry too much about federal judges looking over their shoulders as they draft zoning and no-growth laws, the same cannot necessarily be said about state judges. An inevitable consequence of federalism and the delegating of powers to lower levels of government is the potential for inconsistency (see Chapter 2). As Norman Williams, Jr., has noted, "The zoning case law of each state is, to a remarkable extent, a little world of its own, largely self-contained and with its own special set of primary assumptions and rules of law. . ." (Williams, Jr., 1974, p. 114). State courts in some states take a quite passive stance toward zoning and no-growth issues. The more traditional among them interpret the standing issue strictly and offer local governments a strong presumption of validity as far as the due process and non-taking criteria are concerned. Courts in a few states, however, have not been so shy.

The state court decision that probably has generated the most controversy and attention was *South Burlington County NAACP* v. *Township of Mount Laurel*. In March of 1975, the New Jersey Supreme Court unanimously ruled that the town of Mount Laurel could not use its zoning power in order to prevent the construction of new housing for low- and moderate-income families. The basis of the ruling gives it broad relevance. The court ruled that a locality, in devising its land-use policies, must give consideration to the *general welfare,* and the welfare of the region, and not simply to the narrower interests of the jurisdiction and its current residents. The ruling shifted the burden of proof to localities to show that they were actively pursuing policies to ensure that they offered "the reasonable opportunity for an appropriate variety and choice of housing, including, of course, low- and moderate-cost housing, to meet the needs, desires, and resources of all categories of people who may desire to live within its boundaries" (*South Burlington County NAACP* v. *Township of Mount Laurel,* 1975).

In spite of a few such decisions, there is no real evidence of any judicial assault on localities' discretion to legislate their own development and growth. Where state courts have overruled no-growth ordinances, as the Florida court did in Boca Raton, they have generally been careful to emphasize that their rulings were based on narrow grounds that do not reflect upon the legality of local growth regulation *per se*. "The court does not quarrel with the wisdom of citizens choosing various methods to control growth," the Florida court noted. "If a reduction in Boca Raton's overall residential densities to 40,000 units would rationally promote public welfare without unnecessary and unreasonable consequences to private property rights, the city could legally utilize a variety of techniques, including a form of a cap." The court overruled that particular cap because it seemed to have been developed haphazardly, "without the benefit of professional or scientific study." The city was free to try again.

Even where the state courts have spoken forcefully, as in *Mount Laurel,* court rulings are not easily translated into actual change. The town of Mount Laurel made only halfhearted efforts to open its doors to low-income housing. Two small tracts that were rezoned to allow residential development consisted of "swampy and undesirable land"; a substantial part of another tract, zoned for townhouses and garden apartments, "was actually in a flood plain" and was " 'carved out' of an industrial area" (Williams, Jr., 1974, p. 52). Frustrated, the New Jersey Supreme Court, in 1983, reaffirmed its initial decision in a case commonly referred to as *Mount Laurel II. Mount Laurel II* was intended to put some teeth in the court's effort to break down local obstacles to affordable new housing, and it may prove more effective than its predecessor. Even while setting this goal, however, the New Jersy court acknowledged the limitations of a judicial remedy. The court, it noted, enforces the Constitution: "We may not build houses. . .".

The reluctance of the courts to interject themselves into the local legislative arena in these issues, coupled with the high cost that legal challenges impose on the plaintiff and the difficulties in enforcing judicial remedies, seems to leave groups seeking to overturn no-growth ordinances with little in the way of viable strategies. In spite of the courts' light touch, however, no-growth efforts have remained an oddity, as yet never blossoming into the broad-scale movement that the rhetoric of proponents and opponents would have led one to expect. Even where legal challenges are not a factor, state and local governments frequently find that economic and political constraints make no-growth easier to say than to do.

SUMMARY AND CONCLUSIONS

More than most issues, growth policy stimulates a politics of strange bedfellows. In one corner, we find the liberal environmentalist fighting for growth controls as a means of preserving natural resources. At his side is the conservative suburban homeowner, determined to use local growth controls as a vehicle for maintaining tranquility, property values, and the status quo. In the opposite corner, calling for limitations on growth controls, stands a builder, who needs land on which to construct a housing development. At his side is the head of a local construction workers' union, eager for the jobs that such a development would produce. And backing them both is a representative from a civil-rights organization who hopes that large-scale housing projects will mean affordable housing opportunities for minorities and other less wealthy households that otherwise will be trapped in a central city that is in decline.

Part of the confusion is due to conflicts between ideology and self-interest. The conservative, striving for ideological consistency, might feel inclined to oppose growth controls as being an unnecessary and inefficient governmental intrusion on market forces. When that same conservative is a suburban homeowner, the unregulated market suddenly may seem threatening—a wild and untamed beast that can locate low-income highrise buildings next to pleasant tree-lined neighborhoods, replace lovely views with steaming factories, and line roadways with unrelieved strips of gas stations, car dealerships, and fast-food joints. Ideological consistency might normally lead the liberal to support growth regulation, because government is seen as the legitimate protector of the public interest against inequities and uncertainties that private, profit-maximizing activities leave in their wake. If that same liberal is a member of a low-income or minority group seeking access to an exclusive community, however, the legitimacy of such regulations may seem more dubious, the unregulated market may seem the more reliable ally.

Further complicating matters is the nature of our federal system. The most important land-use powers traditionally have been delegated to the local level in this country. But this poses a dilemma to analysts on both the right and the left. Neoconservatives have a commitment to New Federalism as well as to the market. On the growth control issue, these two commitments can come into conflict with each other. The neoconservative might want to see zoning and growth regulations weakened, but not at the cost of stripping local governments of one of the most significant powers still in their arsenal.

For those on the political left, the decentralization of decision-making about land use presents a different problem. Government regulation of land use and growth is favored as a means of furthering traditional liberal goals of rational planning and equity, but when that regulation takes place at too localized a level, the result may be a brand of chaos and inequity no more benign than that generated when market forces are allowed free play.

The idea that no growth is possible for the nation as a whole is, for the time being at least, a myth. Although it is true that birthrates in this country are falling, rates of new household formation continue to rise, pushed along by higher divorce rates, later marriages, a growing elderly population, and the desire of today's young people to set out from the parental nest at a younger age. "Short of making people move in with their mothers-in-laws, this household formation rate must be built for—with houses, stores, power plants, airports and all the other supporting systems of an urbanized society" (Reilly, 1975, p. 101). *Looked at from a national perspective, then, local efforts at no growth are really efforts to redistribute growth.*

Redistribution of growth may be rational for the nation as a whole. It is less likely to be so, however, when the shape of that redistribution is determined by localized politics rather than national goals. One man's rationality may be another man's knife in the back. It may be rational for a given city to erect a wall around itself, letting in only the wealthy and allowing new construction only when it is nonpolluting and noncongesting and able to guarantee that it will produce more in tax revenues than it will consume in public services. But the city's success may be unhealthy for the metropolitan area, the metropolitan area's success may be unhealthy for the states, and so on up the line.

A federal system aggravates this tendency of local jurisdictions to purchase their own good health at the cost of their neighbors. Local leaders are elected by local constituencies whose interests are likely to be parochial and self-concerned. And the decentralization of decision-making about land use that characterizes our federal system as it has evolved gives those local leaders power and discretion to pursue those parochial goals without consideration of their broader effects. "Only when these various growth considerations are viewed together can it be seen whether they add up, where joint action can be more effective than unilateral action for achieving complementary objectives, and where negotiation and compensation are needed to reconcile diverging purposes and intents" (Alonso, 1973, p. 205). Without coordination at a higher level, *some* jurisdictions will probably be able to profit from no-growth strategies. Those that win at the game will most likely be those that are already advantaged by economic and political strength (Logan and Schneider, 1981). The result, then, may simply be an exacerbation of existing inequities, which, from a national perspective, may not be rational at all.

As early as 1971, an influential report had noted signs that we were in the midst of a "quiet revolution," in which a broadened land-use role for the states was replacing the patchwork system of "thousands of individual local governments, each seeking to maximize its tax base and minimize its social problems, and caring less what happens to all the others" (Bosselman and Callies, 1972, p. 1). Hawaii, for example, passed a state land-use law as early as 1961, giving a state agency a substantial role in monitoring and regulating urban development on the islands and ensuring that the pressures for tourism-related growth do not overwhelm the state's farmlands or destroy its natural scenery. Concern over charges of local exclusionary zoning led Massachussetts, in 1969, to establish a statewide Zoning Appeals Law with some authority to overrule local decisions that are found to be unreasonable in view of "the regional need for low and moderate income housing." Other states, including California and Vermont, have established aggressive policies to balance growth against environmental concerns.

We have seen in this chapter that some states are exercising their strengthened role through judicial channels, instead of, or in addition to, legislative means. As the U.S. Supreme Court has become more conservative, especially since 1980, it has shown less willingness to impose its own conceptions on state or local officials about issues such as racial exclusion and the rights of private property owners. This leaves something of a judicial vacuum into which a few state courts—such as the New Jersey court in its *Mount Laurel* decisions—have been willing to step.

Although the trend toward a greater state role seems likely to continue for some time, history and prudence would suggest that we conclude by noting the unlikelihood of radical change in policy-making regarding land use and growth control. By the late 1970s, observers already were noting that the momentum behind the states' "quiet revolution" had begun to fade (Healy and Rosenberg, 1979). Traditions of local control are too strong to be easily overturned in most parts of this country. Reinforcing these traditions are those pro-growth interests, which often use their considerable political clout to counter attempts to move land-use decisions out of the localized arena in which they generally have found that they are able to get their own way.

Even where the states succeed in becoming more involved, the consequences may vary considerably, depending upon political culture and the particular balance of power among important interest groups. Some states have demonstrated a much greater sensitivity to the needs of minorities and low-income families than others. In such cases, a growing state challenge to parochial local policies may be coupled with statewide growth plans, offering provisions for sharing, among all jurisdictions, the costs and benefits of growth. All jurisdictions might be forced to accommodate some lower-cost housing, and taxing authority might be utilized to redistribute resources from wealthier to poorer jurisdictions. Other states have shown greater sensitivity to the needs of private development interests. Rather than substituting state regulations for local regulations, they might bring about a general lessening of the public-sector involvement and a greater reliance on market forces to bring about public goals. Benefits to minorities and the poor, in those states, presumably would be less direct, dependent upon the trickling down of advantages that may accompany growth.

SUGGESTED READINGS

Baldassare, Mark. *The Growth Dilemma.* Berkeley: University of California Press, 1981.

Bosselman, Fred and David Callies. *The Quiet Revolution in Land Use Control.* Washington, D.C.: Council on Environmental Quality, 1972.

Danielson, Michael. *The Politics of Exclusion.* New York: Columbia University Press, 1976.

Downs, Anthony. *Opening Up the Suburbs.* New Haven: Yale University Press, 1973.

Frieden, Bernard. *The Environmental Protection Hustle.* Cambridge, Mass.: MIT Press, 1979.

Healy, Robert G., and John S. Rosenberg. *Land Use and the States.* Baltimore: Johns Hopkins University Press, 1979.

Scott, Randall W., ed. *Management and Control of Growth,* vol. I. Washington, D.C.: Urban Land Institute, 1975.

Watkins, Alfred J., and David C. Perry, eds. *The Rise of the Sunbelt Cities.* Beverly Hills: Sage, 1977.

8

Understanding Crime

The woman, retired, sixty-two years old, lived alone. "She was an easy prey for them," the detective noted. Over the course of less than two months, the resident of Richmond, Virginia, was beaten and robbed several times by a group of local boys. Once, a bag containing over $2,000 was stolen. On another day, a television set was taken; so were a radio and wristwatch. She was kicked and punched and threatened with a knife. The boys apparently felt free to come and go at their ease. "They would raid the ice box," she told police (*Washington Post,* 1983).

Crimes like this are relatively unusual. Although official crime reports show violent crime rates to be increasing, there is a little less than one chance out of one hundred that the average American will become the victim of a serious assault in any given year. That is less than one-tenth of the risk of being injured in an accident at home and less than half the risk of being injured in a motor vehicle accident (Bureau of Justice Statistics, 1983, p. 18).

Yet dramatic crimes like this one have an impact that extends well beyond the immediate victim. Relatives, friends and neighbors become just as fearful as the victim (Ibid.). And some media studies suggest that more violent and sensational crimes are "extraordinarily overrepresented" in newspaper coverage of crime (Antunes and Hurley, 1977, pp. 756–61; Jacob and Lineberry, 1982, p. 79). Such incidents are often picked up by national news services, carrying the message of danger to distant communities.

The personal consequences can be tragic. Americans greatly value their freedom of movement; yet, due to fear of crime, the mobility of many Americans is seriously impaired. Asked what precautions they take after dark "most of the time," 48 percent of respondents in one study indicated that they drove instead of walked, 28 percent made sure that someone else went with them, 26 percent avoided certain places in the neighborhood, 19 percent took something with them "like a dog, whistle, knife, or gun," and 26 percent did not go out at all (Skogan and Maxfield, 1981, p. 191). Those most frightened are those who are physically the most vulnerable. One study found that as many as 89 percent of those over sixty-five years of age indicated that they never go out at night (Lawton, et al., 1976).

Occasionally, these personal concerns are translated into a demand for governmental action. When this happens, it is local officials whom the public looks to first. The responsibility for fighting crime traditionally is presumed to belong to the police. Two thirds of all judicial employees and three out of every four police personnel are employed at the local level (Bureau of Justice Statistics, 1983, p. 45). Herbert Jacob and Robert L. Lineberry looked at the extent to which crime issues were important in local election campaigns in ten cities. They found that crime was more likely to become a campaign issue in elections in the period from 1974 to 1978 than in the preceding quarter of a century (Jacob and Lineberry, 1982, p. 32). Asked "who should run law enforcement?" two-thirds of Americans answered local government alone; another 6 percent preferred local government in association with either state or federal officials. Although minorities are somewhat less trusting of local law enforcement officials, they, too, perceive law enforcement as more of a local than a state or federal responsibility (see Table 8–1).

Is it fair to expect local officials to bring the crime problem under control? Some argue that crime rises and falls in response to broad national forces that local officials can do nothing about. Can law enforcement officials even at the state and national level find a way to win the war against crime? It is possible that the roots of crime lie so deep in our social structure that government can do little more than contain the problem and soften some of its effects.

In dealing with crime, as in dealing with other policy issues, we will see that the underlying theories about the origin and perpetuation of a particular policy problem provide the soil from which policy initiatives spring forth. Not surprisingly, neoconservative analysts tend to be skeptical about the capacity of government to eliminate crime. Although they do not think government can cure criminals, they do think that government can limit the harm that criminals inflict. Liberals are more likely to hold to the hope that government can successfully eliminate the roots of crime. Where neoconservatives see crime fighting as a job for state and local law enforcement officials, liberals see the need for social reforms

TABLE 8–1 Americans' Views Regarding Who Should Run Law Enforcement

	White	Black	Hispanic	Total
Local Government	68.8	47.4	51.8	65.9
State	13.5	19.3	16.2	14.2
Federal	4.0	17.3	13.7	5.7
Local + State	2.9	1.0	1.1	2.6
Local + Federal	.2	.6	.3	.3
State + Federal	.4	0.0	0.0	.4
Local + Federal + State	3.0	.9	1.1	2.7
None	1.0	.5	1.9	1.0
Not Sure	6.2	13.0	13.9	7.2

SOURCE: Louis Harris & Associates, under contract to Office of Policy Development and Research, U.S. Department of Housing and Urban Development, *The HUD Survey on the Quality of Community Life: A Data Book.* Washington, D.C.: Government Printing Office, pp. 464, 469.

broader than can be handled by states and localities or by law enforcement institutions alone. Radicals, like liberals, believe that it is possible to reduce crime significantly, but, unlike liberals, they argue that political realities make it unlikely that the necessary steps will be taken by officials at any level of our government. This chapter will review the various theories of the cause of crime in order to better understand the nature of the problem that crime poses to policymakers at all levels of our federal system.

THEORIES ABOUT CRIME

Crime as Deviance: The Conventional Conservative View

The traditional conservative usually takes a hard line on crime. Criminals should be dealt with harshly and firmly in order that they be taught a lesson. If they do not change their ways, they should be isolated from others. Lock them up and throw away the key, some would say.

This hard line is based partly on moral outrage. But it also reflects a particular theory about the causes of crime and the types of policies that are likely to have an effect. Traditional conservatism has tended to assume that the roots of crime are in the individual criminal, rather than in the environment in which that criminal lives. Why are some people criminals and others are not? The answer offered is that criminals are different from you and me. Some of those who hold to such a deviance theory assume that the roots of the difference are biological. Others believe that culture, family, and early childhood experiences are at fault. Sometimes the assumption is that the sources of deviation are correctable. But usually it is argued that criminals cannot easily be made uncriminal. Because they are driven by nonrational impulses, even the threat of imprisonment may have little effect. The best that may be done with criminals such as these is to watch them carefully. Once they have committed a crime, the best hope is to keep them in prison, where they will be unable to do further harm.

Crime and Biology. Cesare Lombroso had a theory about crime. He did not believe that crime was the result of opportunity or chance. He did not believe that criminality was learned in a harsh, unloving home or through association with "the wrong crowd." Nor did he think crime was the result of an overly permissive upbringing, or the decline of organized religion, or widespread inequalities, or injustices based on race. Lombroso believed the roots of crime to be biological. Some people were born with a greater tendency to become criminals. Lombroso believed, moreover, that such people could be identified by examining the size and shape of their heads. And he set out, scientifically, to prove his point.

Lombroso, writing in the late 1800s, was influenced by Charles Darwin's new theory of evolution. Man had evolved, over thousands of years, from a primitive being to a sophisticated and civilized species. According to Lombroso, however, some members of the species had not yet completed the evolutionary trip. These individuals were biologically more primitive, characterized by physical characteristics that were vestiges of an earlier evolutionary stage. Among these "stigmata of degeneration" were: projecting eyebrows and jaw; low, retreating forehead, unusually large or unusually small head; asymmetrical facial features; large and protruding ears.

Lombroso and his students tested his theory by examining the heads and skulls of prisoners and comparing these to those of the noncriminal population. Their findings convinced them that Lombroso's basic thesis was correct: criminal behavior was related to biological inferiority.

Lombroso's approach was extreme and, if you will pardon the pun, wrongheaded. The physical characteristics of prison populations are as likely to reflect racial and ethnic biases in the legal process as differences in criminality per se. Some subsequent studies found quite different characteristics distinguishing prison populations; some even found prisoners more likely to exhibit physical characteristics that, according to Lombroso's own classification system, would indicate that criminals were drawn from a *more advanced* biological group.

Although the racial prejudices associated with Lombroso's work have been discredited, the basic premise—that criminals are different from the rest of us—continues to be the focus of serious study and policy debate. Recently there has been a resurgence of interest in biological explanations of crime. A new group of researchers, disparagingly and somewhat unfairly labeled "neo-Lombrosians" by their critics, are seeking to demonstrate that biological characteristics—some inherited, some acquired—do play a role in predisposing some individuals toward criminal behavior.

During the 1960s, considerable attention was focused on studies purporting to demonstrate that males possessing an extra Y chromosome were more aggressive and tended to be found in disproportionately high numbers among prison populations. Early discussions were overly simplistic and overly enthusiastic. Most males possessing this extra chromosome are *not* criminals, and most criminals do *not* possess this extra Y chromosome.

Criticisms of the early studies on scientific grounds were coupled with growing uneasiness about the political implications: Would those with an extra chromosome be subject to harassment and preventive detention? Did this mean there might also be evidence of racial and ethnic predispositions to crime? The result was a public backlash. What had been headline news became, virtually, an unmentionable.

Yet some researchers continue to believe that the relationship is a real one. Recognizing that many XYY males do not become criminals, they have focused their attention on determining the conditions under which this *predisposition* to aggression is likely to emerge. Some believe that they have established a link between the extra chromosome and levels of androgen, a male hormone; higher levels of androgen during the period of puberty, some argue, may lead to a relatively permanent effect on the neural system that makes this individual more likely than others to respond to situations aggressively (Ginsburg, 1974, pp. 59–61).

Studies of the brain have also provided some support for a biological explanation of crime. By placing electrodes in specific regions of the brain, for instance, scientists are able to stimulate an impulse that leads a domesticated cat to violently attack a human being. There is some evidence of a similar response in human beings (Moyer, 1974, pp. 19–46).

The brain is a physical organ. Is it possible that, just as we inherit a particular eye color or the shape of our ear lobe, some individuals may inherit a larger or more sensitive aggressive area within the brain? The link between the brain and behavior suggests nonhereditary explanations of criminality as well. The brain we are born with changes over time. Learning and experiences, especially in our childhood, alter the neurological structure of the brain in ways that may influence our behavior for the rest of our lives. Diseases that affect the brain—such as tumors, cerebral arteriosclerosis, senile dementia, Korsakoff's syndrome, Huntington's chorea, and epilepsy—conceivably could bring about an increase in aggressive tendencies and an increase, accordingly, in the resort to violence and violent crimes (Moyer, 1974, pp.24–5).

Other biologists are exploring the link between crime and certain allergies. Some are investigating an apparent relationship between criminal activity among women and hormonal levels associated with the menstrual cycle. One study of 249 female prisoners found that 62 percent of the crimes of violence were committed in the premenstrual week, whereas only 2 percent were committed in the postmenstrual week (Morton, et al., 1953, pp. 1182-91; Dalton, 1979, pp. 31-2).

The focus of the biological theories is on a particular type of crime—that stemming from a spontaneous, uncontrollable, emotional outburst. Biology may tell us something about murder and assault; it is much less likely to help us understand premeditated crimes or property crimes such as burglary and theft.

Deviant Cultures and Crime. "Theories about the causes and cures of crime," writes Edward Banfield, "tend to be variations of ones about the causes and cures of hard-core poverty" (Banfield, 1974, p. 179). This is certainly the case as far as Banfield's own theories about poverty and crime are concerned. Banfield is one of those who argue that many of the problems associated with poverty are traceable to the lower-class culture into which many of the poor are socialized as children (see Chapter 3). This lower-class culture is presumed to be characterized by a short time horizon, a taste for risk, acceptance of violence, little concern for others, and other indisputably unattractive traits. These are the traits that, according to the self-perpetuating culture-of-poverty perspective, keep the lower class mired in poverty even as affluence and opportunity are on the rise. They are also the traits, according to Banfield and others, that predispose certain persons toward crime.

It is not difficult to see how lower-class culture could be linked to a theory of crime. Individuals with a short time horizon would be unable to consider the full consequences of their actions: "Since the benefits of crime tend to be immediate and its costs (such as imprisonment or loss of reputation) in the future, the present-oriented individual is ipso facto more disposed toward crime than others" (Banfield, p. 183). Many of us may have been drawn to the possibility of committing a crime, but most of us censor those impulses before they are translated into action. Our heart starts pounding, our hands get sweaty, no matter how deserted the site we envision scenarios in which we are observed and apprehended. Those sharing a lower-class culture, it is argued, are not so constrained by this tendency toward risk-avoidance, nor are they put off by the possibility that their actions might force them into a position in which violence is the only recourse.

Culture is very much a product of the environment in which the individual is raised. In that sense, explanations of crime that are based on culture serve as a challenge to some of the biological theories discussed above. Culture is acquired, not inborn. Yet these two theoretical approaches share at least as much as they differ. Both explain crime by reference to attributes of the criminals themselves—attributes that mark them as different, in some important ways, from other citizens.

Policy Implications. What lessons for anticrime policy can be drawn from the deviance perspective? Whether the focus is on biological or cultural roots of criminality, the central issue as far as policy is concerned has to do with whether the presumed source of deviance is treatable. Some advocates of a biological approach to crime emphasize that their's is one of the more optimistic perspectives. *If crime can be traced to biological roots, it may be prevented by biological interventions,* such as those used successfully to combat other physically based problems. If aggression can be traced to hormonal imbalances, therapies based on hormones or drugs might be successful. Moyer reports claims by Japanese and American researchers to have had an 85 percent success rate in reducing violent behavior by means of operations to surgically remove a small part of the brain known as the amygdala (Moyer, 1974, pp. 33-4). Noting experiments to suppress aggression through the stimulation of electrodes in the brain, he notes that it would be possible to run a wire from an electrode planted in the brain to a battery pack located on the individual's belt. "You could then give him an 'anti-hostility' button and whenever he began to feel very mean he could press the button, calm himself down, and rejoin the civilized world" (Moyer, p. 36). Culturally induced predispositions toward crime might also be treatable; presumably this would entail severing or otherwise attenuating the link between the young child and the transmitters of lower-class culture—his or her family, neighbors, and friends.

If therapy is not possible—because the biological roots are untreatable, or because the biological or social responses called for are considered unconstitutional, unethical, or politically infeasible—deviance explanations tend to point toward a policy of incapacitation. Unless the criminal can be "cured," he or she is an ongoing threat to society. It may be possible to protect society only if such criminals are isolated in some way.

The Neoconservative Alternative: Rational Criminals, Dissolving Communities

The Criminal as Consumer. Superman and Batman, teachers and television, have conspired to carry one message loudly and forcefully to the American public: CRIME DOES NOT PAY. Belief in the accuracy of this message has helped to make the deviance theories of crime more convincing; after all, if criminals are more likely to suffer than gain, there must be *something* wrong with individuals who nonetheless opt for a life outside the law. Many analysts, however, reject the notion that criminals must be assumed to be immoral, unthinking, or in the grips of an uncontrollable physical urge. Some insist that we can gain more insight into crime if we assume that criminals are rational and calculating individuals, much like everyone else. Borrowing from the models of the decision-making behavior of consumers and businesses, they have developed a "rational choice" or "economic" theory of crime.

Picture a shopper standing uncertainly in the cereal aisle of a supermarket. Twenty, thirty, maybe even forty different brands of breakfast cereals are lined up on the shelf. Birds, elves, and athletes stare back at this shopper. How is he to decide what brand to buy? Economists, in devising models to predict consumer behavior, assume that such choices are made by means of a relatively explicit weighing of benefits and costs. This chocolate marshmallow cereal tastes great, but the sugar content may be bad for the teeth, and one morning's pleasure may be more than counterbalanced by the pain and expense of an afternoon in the dentist's chair. This other package offers a free prize, but the cereal inside costs two cents more per ounce. One cereal is high in fiber, another puts more vitamins in your breakfast than you will need in an entire day. One brand comes in a box that is difficult to open, another gets too soggy when covered by milk. Each consumer considers these advantages and disadvantages in light of his or her preferences, tallies up the pluses and minuses for each variety, and, presumably, is led to the choice that is most rational from the standpoint of providing the greatest "bang for the buck."

Individuals choosing between criminal and noncriminal behavior may make their decision in a similar fashion. Suppose a person, while walking down the street, spots an unguarded portable television perched on the back seat of a convertible with its top down. The rational-choice theorist supposes that this person, like the cereal shopper, will weigh the expected benefits of stealing that television against the possible costs that such an action would entail. On the benefit side of the ledger might be entered the following: the expected resale value of the television (is it new? is it color? is it there because its owner is about to bring it in for costly repairs?); one's own need for such a set; the chance to brag to friends and to impress them with one's courage and cleverness; any excitement and thrill provided by the act of the theft itself. On the cost side might be considered: the likelihood of being caught (is anyone watching? will a policeman turn the corner just as I reach inside?); the likelihood of being punished (could I talk my way out? would I just be given a warning?); the severity of punishment; feelings of guilt and embarrassment in facing family and friends.

Rational-choice theorists do not suppose that each of us goes through elaborate calculations every time we are confronted with the opportunity to engage in a crime. Most are tempted to consider the option only rarely. For many the guilt and moral sense of doing wrong are so great that even the chance for great financial payoff at minimal risk would not alter the conclusion. After ten years of eating "Jumbo Flakes" we may not give the other brands of cereal more than a passing glance. Nonetheless, the rational-choice approach may provide insights.

A rational-choice perspective might help to explain, for example, why the poor seem to be more likely to engage in crime than the middle or upper class. A street mugging might bring in only twenty-five to fifty dollars. To the poor person, this may seem like a substantial reward; it is enough, according to federal government estimates, to feed a poor person for about two weeks. To the wealthy it is insignificant: a steak dinner and a moderately priced bottle of wine. Even if both the rich and the poor person assessed the risks of performing a mugging identically, the poor person would be more likely to conclude that the benefits outweigh the probable costs.

Some recent evidence suggests that crime rates are higher in areas in which an above average proportion of women are in the labor force (Cohen, et al., 1980, pp. 90–118; Jacob, 1984, p. 57). Houses in which the women work are more vulnerable to burglaries, because they are left unguarded during the day. Such a finding fits neatly within the rational-choice perspective, which would predict that any factor that reduced the risks of getting caught would tip some individuals toward the conclusion that crime *does* pay.

The Decline of Community. When political scientist James Q. Wilson asked over 1,000 Bostonian homeowners about the biggest problems facing their city, he was somewhat surprised by the results. He expected that the traditional urban problems, such as housing, transportation, urban deterioration, and pollution, would head the list. What he found was that street crime was the issue troubling most respondents, and that a cluster of less predictable concerns were ranked closely behind. Wilson's respondents seemed to be distressed about rebellious youth, vagrancy, littering, public drunkenness, lewd behavior, juvenile delinquency, and a general breakdown in what they perceived to be the traditional standards of proper behavior. Although these Bostonians seemed to associate such activities with crime, most involve minor violations of the law and some are not illegal at all.

The common theme, Wilson decided, was a concern about the decline of community. "When I speak of concern for 'community,' I refer to the desire for the observance of standards of right and seemly conduct in the public places in which one lives and moves, those standards to be consistent with—and supportive of—the values and life styles of the particular individual" (Wilson, 1975, p. 24).

Human existence is, potentially, a very frightening thing indeed. We crave a sense of safety and security, but we live in an unpredictable and occasionally violent world. In small towns and villages, where people know and trust their neighbors, the sense of vulnerability is lessened. But this small-town sense of security is difficult to sustain in large cities. Neighbors are transient and the boundaries of the neighborhood are easily and frequently crossed by strangers. A sense of community—a sense that those around you share a commitment to certain standards of behavior—can ease the uncertainty that urban existence generates. But such a sense of community is a fragile thing, according to Wilson. It is communicated and nurtured through subtle signs and interactions. Informal rules about how to dress, when to make eye contact, and laundry room etiquette are rarely written down. But these seemingly trivial standards carry an important symbolic message: those who honor them announce to others that they are not a threat, that they are aware of the "rules" and are willing to observe them. Violations of those standards, whether born of ignorance or intent, send the message that no common rules are in effect.

What begin as violations of subtle social standards may quickly escalate into a more serious and threatening environment of crime. "Social psychologists and police officers tend to agree that if a window in a building is broken *and is left unrepaired,* all the rest of the windows will soon be broken" (Wilson and Kelling, 1982, p. 31). Small violations of social norms send a message that no one cares, and can, according to Wilson, send a neighborhood sliding down the pathway to disorder and crime. As the sense of community declines, residents deal with their insecurity through personal strategies—they "use the streets less often, and when on the streets will stay apart from their fellows, moving with averted eyes, silent lips, and hurried steps" (Wilson and Kelling, p. 32).

> [S]uch an area is vulnerable to criminal invasion. Though it is not inevitable, it is more likely that here, rather than in places where people are confident they can negotiate public behavior by informal controls, drugs will change hands, prostitutes will solicit, and cars will be stripped. That the drunks will be robbed by boys who do it as a lark, and the prostitutes' customers will be robbed by men who do it purposefully and perhaps violently. That muggings will occur (Ibid.).

Policy Implications. Although the neoconservative approach differs from the traditional conservative perception of the criminal-as-deviant, the policy recommendations that neoconservatives offer also emphasize punishment and incapacitation. The rational choice perspective suggests that crime could be reduced by public policies intended to increase the costs and decrease the benefits associated with criminal acts. Most proposals have focused on policies to alter the probability of being caught, the probability of being punished, or the severity of punishment. Proposals to increase the number of police are frequently based on the assumption that criminals are rational and calculating actors who, observing the frequency of police patrols, will decide that the risks of being apprehended have become too great. Proposals for stricter sentencing are frequently based on the assumption that criminals will be deterred if they calculate that their capture will lead to a lengthy period behind bars.

Stricter and more certain punishments are not the only policy strategy that is compatible with the rational-choice approach. "In theory," writes Wilson, "the rate of crime should also be sensitive to the benefits of noncrime—for example, the value and availability of jobs. . ." (Wilson, 1983, p. 81). But neoconservatives, like Wilson, are wary of the notion that reductions in crime depend upon the successful launching of a broad program of social reform. "The hope, widespread in the 1960s, that job-creation and job-training programs would solve many social problems, including crime, led to countless efforts to prevent crime by supplying jobs to crime-prone youths and to reduce crime among convicted offenders by supplying them with better job opportunities after their release from prison" (Ibid.). Such efforts have had a spotty record, at best.

If crime is encouraged by a breakdown in community, policy-remedies presumably must seek to reestablish, and help maintain, those informal social ties. Although this would seem to offer a clear orientation for policy-makers, its message may be less hopeful than it initially seems. The difficulty, as Wilson notes, "is that there is relatively little government can do directly to maintain a neighborhood community" (Wilson, 1975, p. 35). It is possible that the decline of community is an inevitable concomitant of modern life. Without dismissing the potential for broad social reforms to reduce crime, the neoconservative generally takes the position that we ought to do what we are most capable of doing—and that means fighting crime by increasing its costs rather than by increasing the benefits of noncriminal behavior.

Social Structure and Crime: The Liberal and Radical Perspectives

Blocked Opportunities. Beginning in the early 1960s, liberal criminologists sought to reshape the way policy-makers traditionally had thought about crime. "Crime reflects more than the character of the pitiful few who commit it," wrote Ramsey Clark, U.S. attorney general under President Johnson. "It reflects the character of an entire society" (R. Clark, 1970, p. 17). High levels of crime in urban ghettos could best be explained by the nature of the ghetto environment, *not* by the nature of those who lived there.

The conservative tends to focus attention on the criminal's impulses. The neoconservative tends to focus on the criminal's calculations. Both tend, in practice, to underplay the responsibility of society itself in creating the conditions under which crime is likely to thrive. By insisting that policymakers attack the "root causes" of crime, both liberals and radicals have sought to redirect attention away from the individual criminal and toward the character of the society in which the criminal lives.

Richard Cloward and Lloyd Ohlin were among the earliest and most influential advocates of the theory that crime was attributable to society's failure to provide opportunities for ghetto youth (Cloward and Ohlin, 1960). Young men and women growing up in poverty, they argued, share the same goals and aspirations as those fortunate enough to have been born into the middle or upper class. Like their more fortunate peers, they hope to achieve status, respect and material well-being. Like them, they have been led to expect that they *can* achieve more than their parents: to go further in school, to find a more prestigious job, to own a bigger home, a nicer car, an additional television set, more kitchen gadgets. Although their goals and values may be similar to those of white, wealthier, suburban youth, lower-income and minority youth quickly find that their opportunities are limited by who they are and where they live. Poorer schools, the expense of college, and the pressures to get a job in order to help support their families make it more difficult for these youths to obtain the education that is required if they are to push their way into better paying jobs. Discrimination in hiring practices keeps some minorities from competing on equal terms, even for those jobs for which they are adequately prepared. The young black boy who dreams of becoming a doctor will learn the harsh lesson that, for all but the exceptional, such ambitions are destined to go unfulfilled.

It is out of such blocked opportunities, according to this perspective, that the impulse to crime gains its initial momentum. The inner-city youth, in particular, is well aware of the opportunities that illicit action can hold. The role model in his or her neighborhood is more likely to be the successful criminal than the doctor, lawyer, or accountant. With awareness of the lack of legitimate opportunity, moreover, may come a bitterness and frustration that blossoms into a rejection of society and a desire for personal revenge.

Capitalism, Crime, and Social Control. Marxists see crime as more deeply embedded in the social structure than do liberals who subscribe to the blocked-opportunities theory of crime. What liberals portray as unfortunate but correctable flaws in the mechanisms by which our society seeks to integrate minorities and the poor, the Marxist sees as evidence of internal tensions so inherent in capitalism that they can never be addressed, other than superficially, as long as the basic economic structure remains intact. "In a society that values acquisition of property but is structured on economic inequality property crime is inevitable," writes Marxist criminologist Richard Quinney; "if a society cannot provide a humane, unalienating existence, it must contend with activities that are defined as criminal" (Quinney, 1979, pp. 241, 251).

The dynamics of capitalism, as interpreted by Marxist scholars, foster crime in several ways. First, *capitalism necessarily fosters inequality in income and wealth*. This is the case because of the system's need to minimize the cost of labor, the pressures on businesses to increase productivity by introducing technologies that displace existing workers and make their skills obsolete, and the need to provide the potential for windfall profits in order to entice private investors to back potentially productive but risky enterprises. Second, in order to ensure an expanding market for the products it generates, *capitalism must constantly urge the buying public to strive for higher levels of material accumulation*. It is not enough for businesses in a capitalist system to provide enough food, shelter, and clothing to meet the population's basic human needs; indeed, the power of capitalism as a productive source is such that the capacity to accomplish this task already has been achieved. Under capitalism, Marx argued, businesses must continue to grow, or die. Once the public's basic needs are met, there is an inevitable *drive to expand the market by creating new needs*. Thus the advertising phenomenon of Madison Avenue is born. At the same time that capitalism consigns some to poverty, it is forced to bombard them with advertisements carrying the message that happiness and status depend upon driving a new car, owning a personal computer, wearing designer jeans.

Marxist criminologists also offer a different perspective on the criminal justice system. The liberal focus on blocked opportunities tends to deemphasize the traditional crime-fighting institutions—police, courts, prisons. These institutions address only the symptoms of a social illness; without social reform, increases in manpower or budget authority are likely to have only an incremental effect, if any, on levels of crime. Where the liberal perspective pushes the criminal justice system to the periphery, the Marxists shove it back onto center stage. In doing so, however, they radically alter the terms on which it is considered. According to the Marxist perspective, police, courts, and prisons can be best understood not as mechanisms to fight crime but, rather, as *instruments of social control*.

The criminal justice system, from this perspective, primarily is a tool used by those who benefit from capitalism to manipulate and repress those who have a stake in bringing about radical reform. The tensions inherent in capitalism, Marxists believe, ultimately must erupt in the form of individual and collective challenges to the system. "Control over crime becomes the coercive means of checking threats to the social and economic order, threats that result from a system of oppression and exploitation" (Quinney, p. 79).

The criminal justice system serves this role through its authority to define what is and is not illegal and through the selective enforcement of laws. By defining as criminal certain behaviors that do not directly harm others—such as vagrancy, homosexuality, drug use, prostitution—officials gain a weapon that can be utilized effectively to isolate and harass low-income and minority communities that potentially represent a political threat.

Marxists charge that enforcement of such laws is politically determined; they are used most aggressively during times of tension and political unrest. Enforcement of most laws, moreover, is race- and class-conscious. If you steal fifty dollars you are a criminal, it is said; if you steal a million dollars you are a financier. Criminal codes enshrine such distinctions in the penalties they set forth for certain violations: the black teenager who shoplifts two steaks may spend several years in prison; the corporate president whose firm illegally disposes of toxic wastes that might cause disease and death is threatened, at most, by penalties of a fine and a public rebuke.

How could this have come to pass? To the Marxist, the answer is based, first, on the characteristics of the actor: given the concern with social control, any action by a member of those groups who are disadvantaged by the economic status quo must be taken more seriously than a transgression by a "respectable" individual with a stake in leaving the basic system undisturbed. The nature of the crime is relevant as well. Shoplifting—even of inexpensive items—is a direct challenge to the concept of private property, a concept that, in capitalism, is held to be sacrosanct. Dumping of toxic wastes or corporate price-fixing or consumer fraud or polluting of the environment—although potentially much more damaging—are extensions of the corporate drive for profit maximization and are treated, therefore, as the result of overexuberance rather than acts of criminal intent.

Policy Implications. Although they share a focus on aspects of the broader social structure, the blocked-opportunity and Marxist perspectives on crime lead in rather differing policy directions. The differences among them are determined, at least partially, by their perception of the likelihood that structural reform can be brought about. The liberal focus on blocked opportunities is the most optimistic. Although that perspective casts doubts on the likelihood that crime can be reduced by the traditional criminal justice mechanisms, it does hold out the prospect of significant gains to be made through other channels of social reform.

Programs to improve the schooling and job training available to the poor, and affirmative action plans to counteract historic practices of racial discrimination in hiring and promotion policies, are seen as ways to unblock opportunities and, thus, as tools for the eradication of crime.

The Marxist perspective is more pessimistic. Because Marxists trace crime to aspects of our economic system that are central rather than peripheral, they do not expect that anything short of a major and revolutionary overhaul can bring about a significant lessening of crime. Government in general, and the law enforcement apparatus in particular, historically have functioned to preserve and further the interests of those who own capital; they are not likely to engage wittingly in policies that challenge the system in any fundamental sense. Reforms of the criminal justice system—better educated police, better legal representation for the poor, less crowded prisons—and the kinds of mild social reforms associated with the blocked-opportunity thesis will soften and make less visible some of the harshest attributes of capitalism; they will not, however, substantially lessen the inequities or injustices that capitalism produces and that, in turn, are the producers of crime. "The only real solution to crime is to be found in the class struggle. It is a political struggle against capitalism" (Quinney, p. 97).

PATTERNS OF CRIME

Is Crime Exaggerated?

You may have heard these stories from your parents or your grandparents. Most of us have heard them sometime, often from someone we know quite well. The stories begin, "In my day. . . ," or "I remember when. . ." They go on to tell of simpler and safer times, when front doors were left unlocked, people walked the streets past midnight with no thought of danger, and bikes left overnight on the front stoop could be counted on to greet you in the morning.

One cannot help but wonder. Can these stories be believed? Have our streets truly become so much more dangerous? Or is this a case of double exaggeration: tales of crime-free days tinged with the same memory dust that magnified the snowdrifts our parents walked through to school, stories of today's mean streets inflated by lurid media accounts and personal insecurities?

Policymakers have both a short-term and a long-term interest in finding out the precise scope of the crime problem and the true nature of existing trends. The short-term interest is based on the immediate policy implications. Newspaper headlines give the impression that crime is rampant, growing rapidly and out of control. If this is true, we cannot afford a "business as usual" approach to crime policy. It may be necessary to reevaluate our fundamental philosophies of law enforcement, or to radically alter public spending priorities. If it is not true, the public must be made aware of this fact. Fear of crime has consequences nearly as destructive as crime itself. By acting as if crime is at crisis levels, policymakers may heighten fears, stimulate further flight from central cities, and encourage people to draw themselves into walled fortresses, further eroding any sense of community.

The longer term interest is tied to our need to gain a better theoretical understanding of crime itself. Some of the theories that we have just reviewed draw their force from the assumption that crime is on the rise. Neoconservatives, for example, suggest that rising crime is evidence of the correctness of their views. Court policies initiated in the 1960s have made it too easy for criminals to escape punishment, encouraging crime by decreasing its costs. In addition, the neoconservative focus on the decline in communities associates rising crime with nearly inevitable forces that accompany modernization and urbanization. The fact that crime is rising in spite of increasing incomes and social welfare programs, they argue, is added proof that the liberals' emphasis on blocked opportunities is misplaced. Marxist theories, too, would seem to predict an ever-increasing spiral of crime. Marx believed that the inequities and contradictions of capitalism inevitably would become more evident and destructive as the system continued to evolve. If crime is not as severe or as rapidly rising as commonly supposed, these theories may lose some of their appeal.

Reported Crime Is High and Rising. The most comprehensive and widely utilized information on crime is found in the *Uniform Crime Reports*. The FBI compiles these monthly and annual reports based on data provided by over 12,000 law enforcement agencies in about 8,500 cities throughout the United States. The most detailed information is provided on eight "index crimes." These crimes, and their definitions, are presented in Table 8-2.

These index crimes are also known as "Part I" crimes. Other, less detailed information is available in the uniform crime reports about various "Part II" crimes, including: simple assaults, fraud, embezzlement, vandalism, prostitution, drug abuse, gambling, drunken driving, vagrancy, and others generally regarded to be less serious or "victimless" crimes.

Official crime statistics show crime levels to be high and steadily rising. In 1980, every two seconds someone was the victim of an index crime. There was a violent crime every twenty-four seconds. The crime rate has nearly doubled since 1967, the increase being steady and substantial, with only a few dips along the way (see Figure 8-1). The increase, moreover, cuts across all types of crime (see Table 8-3).

TABLE 8–2 Definitions of the Index Crimes

Violent Crimes

Murder and nonnegligent manslaughter: This includes the willful killing of one human being by another. It does not include suicide, deaths caused by negligence, traffic fatalities, attempts to kill, or justifiable homicides. Justifiable homicides are those in which a felon is killed by a law enforcement officer or a private citizen.

Forcible rape: "The carnal knowledge of a female forcibly and against her will." The index includes attempts to rape; it does not include statutory rapes, in which no force is used and the victim is below the legal age of consent.

Robbery: The taking or attempting to take anything of value from someone by force or the threat of force or by putting the victim in fear. Robberies are classified as violent crimes even if actual violence does not occur.

Aggravated Assault: An unlawful attack for the purpose of inflicting severe injury. Aggravated assaults usually involve a weapon of some kind.

Property Crimes

Burglary: The unlawful entry, or attempted forcible entry, of a structure in order to commit a felony or theft.

Larceny-theft: The unlawful taking, or attempted taking, of property from another's possession. Examples include "thefts of bicycles or automobile accessories, shoplifting, pocket-picking, or the stealing of any property or article which is not taken by force and violence or by fraud." Not included are embezzlement, "con games," forgery, or the passing of worthless checks.

Motor Vehicle Theft: The theft or attempted theft of a motor vehicle. Boats, construction equipment, farm vehicles and airplanes are exluded.

Arson: This category was added by Congress in 1980. It includes any "willful or malicious burning or attempt to burn, with or without intent to defraud, a dwelling house, public building, motor vehicle or aircraft, personal property of another, etc."

SOURCE: U.S. Department of Justice, Federal Bureau of Investigation. *Uniform Crime Reports 1980.* Washington, D.C.: Government Printing Office, 1981, Appendix II.

There is an even more dismal side to the story. *Not only does it seem that the risk of victimization is increasing, but the mix of crimes being committed today seems to be more violent and frightening.* The two types of crime increasing most rapidly—rape and aggravated assault—are two

TABLE 8-3 Levels of Index Crime, 1980; and change, 1971–1980

	Total	Rate (per 100,000)	Change in rate (%) 1971–1980
Murder	23,040	10.2	+18.6
Rape	82,090	36.4	+77.7
Robbery	548,810	243.5	+29.5
Aggravated assault	654,960	290.6	+62.5
Burglary	3,759,200	1,668.2	+43.4
Larceny/theft	7,112,700	3,156.3	+47.1
Motor vehicle theft	1,114,700	494.6	+ 7.6
Total	13,295,900	5,899.9	+41.7

SOURCE: Department of Justice, Federal Bureau of Investigation. *1980 Crime in the United States, Uniform Crime Reports*. Washington, D.C.: Government Printing Office, September 1981, p. 41.

of the most violent. The evidence seems to suggest, moreover, that the proportion of violent crimes being committed by someone who is a stranger to the victim is increasing. Most murders still are committed by a relative, friend, or acquaintance, but murders by strangers are increasing nearly twice as fast as other murders. The same can be said about rapes. In 1967, about one-half of reported rapes were committed by someone known to the victim; by 1973, about two out of every three rapes were at the hand of strangers. Robbery is classified as a violent crime even if no actual physical injury is imposed, but the likelihood that robbery *will* involve actual violence is increasing. In 1967, one robbery in five resulted in physical injury to the victim; ten years later, the figure had grown to one in three. As one St. Louis cabdriver explained, "A stickup in St. Louis used to be 'your money or your life.' Now it's 'your money *and* your life" (Auletta, 1983, p. 44).

Official crime data, however, are subject to several distortions that can mislead us as to the extent of crime, fluctuations over time, and the characteristics of criminals. Therefore, before we review what we know about the who, what, and where of crime, we need to give some consideration to the methodology of crime measurement. The issues involved may appear technical, but their implications are broad. Our understanding about matters such as these can alter our evaluations of the causes of crime, the need for additional law enforcement expenditures, and the type of policy responses that are likely to work.

Many Crimes Go Unreported. Official tabulations of index crimes include only a subset of the "real" crime that takes place. The uniform crime reports include only those crimes reported to and recorded by police. Yet, *the victims of many crimes—even serious crimes—never report them.* We cannot be certain how many crimes go unreported, but some

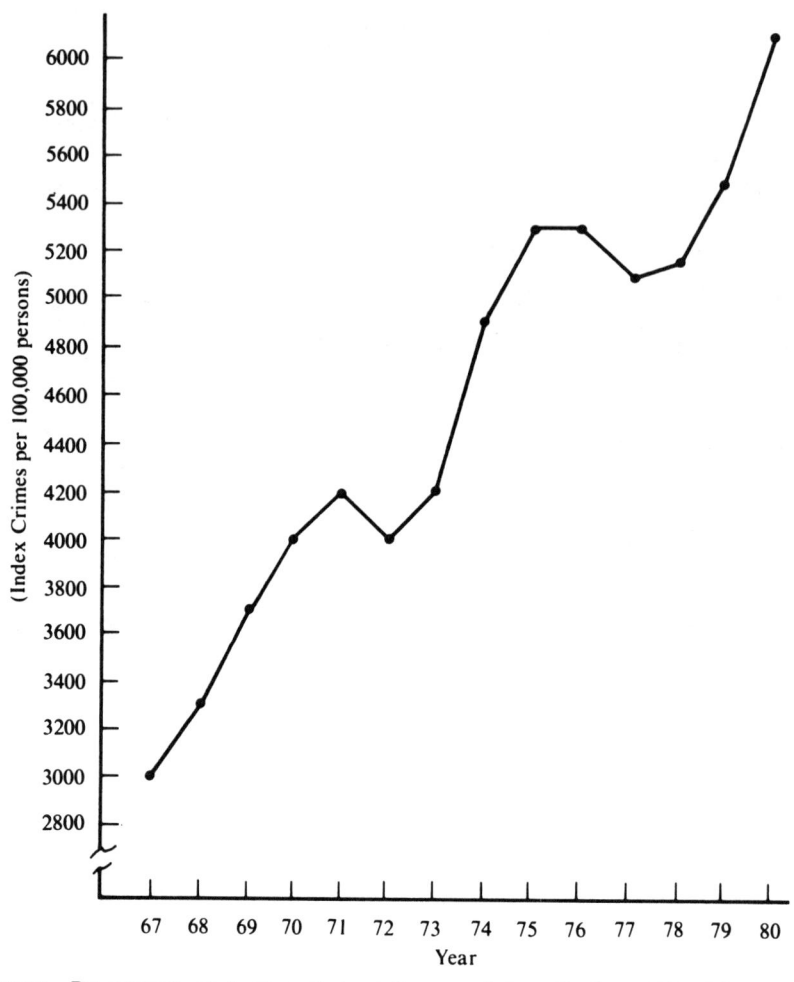

Figure 8-1 The Growing Crime Rate, 1967–1980

(Index Crimes per 100,000 persons)

SOURCE: Department of Justice, Federal Bureau of Investigation. *1980 Crime in the United States, Uniform Crime Reports.* Washington, D.C.: Government Printing Office, September 1981, p. 41.

evidence suggests that there may be two or three times as many crimes as the uniform crime reports reveal.

Beginning in 1973, the U.S. Bureau of Justice Statistics instituted a survey of about 60,000 households, each of which was to be interviewed twice a year. The respondents in the sample, selected so as to be representative of the general population, were asked whether they had been a victim of crime and, if so, whether they had reported the crime to the police. These "victimization surveys" tell us much about crime that official statistics cannot. They give us a sense of the tremendous number of unreported crimes and the reasons why crimes go unreported.

Overall, *only about one-third of all crimes are reported to the police.* Reporting rates vary for different crimes and for different groups. In 1981, the reporting rate for violent crime was 47 percent; the rate for personal crimes of theft was only 27 percent. Sixty-seven percent of motor vehicle thefts were reported, but only about half of all robberies without injury, simple assaults with injury, and attempting assaults with a weapon were called in to the police. Females, older victims, and those with higher incomes were more likely to report victimizations than were males, younger persons, and the poor (Bureau of Justice Statistics, 1983, pp. 24–5).

Why is it that so many crimes go unreported? The answer depends on the nature of the crime involved. Victims of petty larceny, attempted burglary, and simple assaults seem to feel that the crimes involved are simply not important enough to warrant contacting the police. For some other crimes—such as pickpocketing and larcenies involving more than fifty dollars—the victims are more likely to fail to call police because they feel that doing so is unlikely to help. About one out of every three victims who chose not to report an assault or a successful vehicle theft indicated that they did so because "it was a private matter," reflecting the fact that many of these crimes involve family, relatives, or close friends.

Some Crimes Go Unrecorded. The failure of victims to call the police is the major reason that official statistics understate the true extent of crime, but it is not the only reason. *Some crimes that are reported to the police never get recorded.* There are several reasons for this. Some involve deliberate manipulation by police. By failing to record crimes, a police department can make it appear to be more effective in combatting crime than is actually the case. Other nonrecordings are the result of sloppy administration or simple laziness on the part of officers who do not relish the paperwork or court appearance that might be involved. But most probably result from the fact that society often wants the police officer to act as a maintainer of order rather than as a strict enforcer of the law.

Consider the officer called to quell a disturbance at a bar. Students from rival high schools have been taunting each other, fist fights have broken out, and some glasses, bottles, and furniture have been destroyed. Or consider the officer called to respond to a domestic disturbance. A recently unemployed husband has struck his wife; neighbors called the police. In each instance, crimes have occurred. The police officer might choose to treat the situation as such, to make an arrest and file a report. To do so, however, might aggravate the situation, escalating what might have been a one-time episode into a more violent incident or a longer term estrangement. A few calming words or a stern lecture might be the

Table 8-4 Trends in Victimization Rates in the United States, 1973-1980

	Average yearly percent change
Rape	-0.16
Robbery	-0.43
Aggravated assault	-1.26
Personal theft	-1.35
Burglary	-1.21
Household larceny	2.43
Motor vehicle theft	-1.86

SOURCE: Jan M. Chaiken and Marcia R. Chaiken. "Crime Rates and the Active Criminal," in J. Q. Wilson, *Crime and Public Policy*. San Francisco: Institute for Contemporary Studies, 1983, p. 16.

more desirable course of action. Police, in such circumstances, often are free to exercise their discretion.

Researchers in one study accompanied police on their patrols in order to observe just how such discretion is actually applied. They took notes on each call that the police responded to, and recorded whether an official report of a crime was filed. Not surprisingly, the researchers found that police were more likely to file a report when a more serious crime was involved: reports were written in 72 percent of the felony cases and 53 percent of the misdemeanors. Nonetheless, the fact that reports were not filed in over one-quarter of the felony cases is significant.

What accounts for the failure to write reports in instances of serious crimes? One factor has to do with the complainant's preferences: in about 13 percent of the cases involving felonies, the complainant indicated that he or she did not wish the police to take formal action; in none of these cases did the police file official reports. Another factor involves the relationship between the complainant and the offender. Police filed reports in 91 percent of the felony cases in which the offender was a stranger to the victim, but in only 42 percent of the cases when the offender was a friend,

Table 8-5 Change in Violent Crime Rate, by City Size, 1970-1980 (Offenses known to the police per 100,000 population)

Cities with population:	1970	1980	% Change 1970-80
250,000 or more	1047	1414	+44.3%
100,000-249,999	503	812	+80.4%
50,000-99,999	300	602	+119.7%
25,000-49,999	243	455	+112.6%
10,000-24,999	188	352	+121.4%
Fewer than 10,000	171	296	+109.9%

SOURCE: U.S. Bureau of the Census. *Statistical Abstract of the United States, 1981.* Washington, D.C.: Government Printing Office, Table No. 296, p. 175.

neighbor, or acquaintance. Police also were more likely to file a report when the complainant was deferential toward the police than in cases in which he or she was antagonistic or merely civil. There was no evidence that police treated complaints by white citizens differently than those by blacks, but there was some indication that reports were more likely to be filed in felony cases with a white-collar complainant than in those in which the complainant was from a lower social class (Black, 1970, pp. 733–48).

Official Statistics May Exaggerate the Increase in Crime. Ironically, although victimization surveys suggest that *levels* of crime are greater than official statistics reveal, they also indicate that, at least over the past ten years, *increases* in crime may be much less substantial than commonly believed. If the rate at which citizens are reporting crimes to police, or the accuracy with which police are recording those crimes, is increasing, official statistics might show a crime wave, even where one does not actually exist. During the 1970s, police made well-publicized efforts to encourage citizens to more faithfully report all crimes. Efforts to convince victims of rape, battered wives, and those aware of child abusers to cooperate with authorities were particularly intense. Because they uncover crimes that may not have been called in to the police, surveys of victimizations provide a measure of crime that is less likely to be distorted by changes in Americans' tendency to report crimes. Table 8–4 reveals that victimizations, especially for serious crimes, have been fairly stable or even declining in frequency. "How different a picture they give from the 'crime epidemic' that some claim to see in the UCR statistics!" (Chaiken and Chaiken, 1983, p. 16).

The Distribution of Crime

Is Crime a Big City Problem? Most Americans think of crime as a big city problem. Residents of cities with populations of 250,000 or more are about four times more likely than suburbanites, and more than five times more likely than residents of towns or rural areas, to see crime as a "severe problem" (U.S. Department of Housing and Urban Development, 1978). Official crime statistics show that this association of crime with large cities is reasonable: residents of cities with a population of less than 10,000 are only about one-half as likely to be a victim of a reported index crime as those in cities with 250,000 or more, and only about one-fifth as likely to be victimized by violent crime. Rural residents are safer still.

The relationship between crime and city size, however, is weakening over time. Crime, as Table 8–5 indicates, is rising more rapidly in smaller places than in large cities. The "safety gap" has hardly disappeared: in

Table 8–6 Ideological Perspectives on Crime

	Traditional Conservative	Neoconservative	Liberal	Radical
Cause of Crime	Individual deviance	Rational choice/Low risks/Decline in informal community controls	Blocked opportunity	Inequities associated with capitalism
Policy Orientation	Therapy for curable/punishment and isolation for incurable	Deterrence and incapacitation	Rehabilitation/mild social reforms	Broad reform/public control over police/attack white-collar crime
Role of Law Enforcement	Capture and punish	Frighten potential criminals/reassure public/isolate criminals	Dispense justice	Maintain status quo

1980, one was still about 4.8 times as likely to be the victim of a violent crime in a city of more than 250,000 people as in one of fewer than 10,000. But the gap does seem to be fading.

SUMMARY AND CONCLUSIONS

Americans are concerned about crime. They expect their government to do something about it. They see crime as a local phenomenon and, by and large, their expectations are focused on local officials.

Local officials have responded in a variety of ways. After studying thirty-one years of anticrime efforts by ten local governments, however, one political scientist was forced to conclude that they "rarely resembled well-aimed shots at targeted problems; rather they were more like shotgun blasts in the general direction of trouble" (Jacob, 1984, p. 165).

If any of those local officials took the time and effort to look for a broad theoretical framework within which to orient a more focused attack, they would meet with further frustration. As we have now seen, the major ideological perspectives differ markedly in their perception of the nature of crime and the potential for successful action. Some of the differences are summarized in Table 8–6.

Attention to available data on crime patterns and crime trends leads us to be wary of explanations that presume crime to be rooted in contemporary policies or in uncontrollable forces of social change. Crime is high, but victimization data suggests that it has leveled off over the past decade. Although this information is helpful, it does not resolve for us the question of which crime theory is correct. Nor does it give policymakers much in the way of direction as to what they should do to meet the problems they face on a day-to-day basis. For additional insight into the possibilities for effective law enforcement we turn, in the next chapter, to the criminal justice institutions themselves.

SUGGESTED READINGS

Clark, Ramsey. *Crime in America*. New York: Simon and Schuster, 1970.

Cloward, Richard A., and Lloyd E. Ohlin. *Delinquency and Opportunity*. New York: Free Press, 1960.

Graham, High Davis, and Ted Robert Gurr, eds. *Violence in America*, 2d ed. Beverly Hills: Sage, 1979.

Merry, Sally Engle. *Urban Danger: Life in a Neighborhood of Strangers*. Philadelphia: Temple University Press, 1981.

Silberman, Charles E. *Criminal Violence, Criminal Justice*. New York: Random House, 1978.

U.S. Department of Justice, Bureau of Justice Statistics. *Report to the Nation on Crime and Justice,* Washington, D.C.: Government Printing Office, October 1983.

Wilson, James Q. *Thinking About Crime*. New York: Basic Books, 1975.

9

Fighting Crime: The Limits of Intervention

The complaint is familiar but wrongheaded. "Why don't they *do* something about crime?" ask irritated citizens after hearing the latest crime statistics or reading about some grisly incident in the newspaper. The complaint is wrongheaded because it assumes that the problem lies in lack of action by public officials. The true problem is not failure to act; it is failure to know what kind of action will work.

Evidence that state and local officials are doing *something* is found in the nation's prisons and jails. They are packed full. On any given day, more than half a million Americans are locked up behind bars. We are sending more people to jails and prisons now, in the 1980s, than at any other time in the nation's history.

Our prisons are so full that officials in some states are unable or unwilling to accept any more prisoners. Yet police still are busy trying to arrest more suspects, and the courts are busy finding more criminals guilty and sentencing them to prison. In about half the states, criminals sentenced to state prisons have had to be housed temporarily in local jails. This is not always appreciated by the local officials who are forced to deal with the overflow from the state system. One local sheriff in Arkansas became so frustrated that he tried to abandon some of his inmates by chaining them to the prison fence. "State officials armed with shotguns made him take them back" (Krajik and Gettinger, 1982, p. 5).

This chapter considers the traditional criminal justice institutions: the police, courts, and prisons. When crime rises, it is to these institutions that citizens and their elected officials look for relief. But history does not provide us with much guidance as to what these institutions can effectively do. During the first half of the century, reformers thought the answer could be found in the professionalization of the police force. Control of the police would be taken out of the hands of ward bosses and centralized under the direction of a nonpolitical chief. To minimize opportunities for corruption, police would no longer walk a neighborhood beat; they would patrol in police cars and rotate among beats on a regular basis. By the late 1970s, a new breed of reformers were demanding that these changes be undone. To improve community relations, they argued, we must reassign officers to foot patrol; to make the police responsive to the citizenry, we must take control away from a central authority and delegate it to the precinct or neighborhood level.

Some local officials have tried to outthink crime, waging a scientific and sophisticated war in which computers are a major weapon. In University City, Missouri, police used a federal grant to purchase a "police responsive early warning system" that, "at a cost of only 3,400 federal dollars, was said to have the capacity to anticipate requirements for police services and, in addition, to be able to 'predict and control crime by discovering its physical, social, and economic causes' " (Ginsberg, 1978, p. 344).

Others prefer to outmuscle crime. The New Orleans police department, "apparently not as convinced as its counterparts of the merits of complex crime-fighting technology," used some of its federal grant to buy a tank (Ibid.). Chief Ed Davis, of the Los Angeles Police Department, asked the city council to pay for two jet helicopters and hinted that he would be back to request money for a submarine (Fogelson, 1977, p. 220). The record does not show that either the "thinkers" or the "musclers" have enjoyed substantial or consistent success.

We begin this chapter with a closer consideration of four important goals—rehabilitation, deterrence, incapacitation, and punishment. Conservatives, neoconservatives, liberals, and radicals disagree about which of these goals law enforcement policy should pursue most vigorously, and these disagreements have concrete and specific implications for the way that police, courts, and prisons should go about doing their jobs. Tensions among these goals create some of the problems and uncertainties that plague efforts to devise a consistent and effective law enforcement policy. What is more, as we consider each of the major institutions in turn, we will find that there are limits on the capacity of police, courts, and prisons that make it difficult for them to pursue these goals in the manner that we expect.

COMPETING GOALS

Rehabilitation

The goal of rehabilitation is the first priority of many liberals, who believe that crime is bred by poverty, blocked opportunities, and the frustrations these cause. Rehabilitation is based on the premise that criminals share many of the same values and ideals as noncriminals. Although it is the broader social environment that deprived these individuals and led to their alienation, law enforcement institutions can play a role in showing criminals that there is a better way to live and giving them the support they need to turn their lives around.

Those who place a high value on rehabilitation usually have focused their attention on the role of prisons. They argue that if criminals are to be given the desire to rehabilitate themselves, they need a supportive environment; some will need psychological counseling. In addition, if they are to be given the chance to break out of the cycle that initially led them to crime, they must be given education and job training that will enable them to find and hold a job once they are released. Some advocates of rehabilitation argue that it is important for prisoners to retain some control over their lives and responsibility for their own actions while incarcerated. A rigid and militaristic environment, they argue, does little to prepare the prisoner for dealing with the difficult options and uncertainties that freedom will bring.

Police and courts can also play a role in furthering the rehabilitation of criminals. Advocates of rehabilitation argue that the law enforcement institution has a particular responsibility to act as a model of judicious and lawful behavior. Police who apply the law selectively based on considerations of race or class, who disregard or disparage legal protections deserved by criminal suspects, or who violate the law themselves will only reaffirm the suspicions of some criminals that laws are made to protect the privileged and that only the weak and the gullible need pay them any mind. Judges and prosecutors must show, by their actions, that the courts are dedicated to seeking justice, not enhancing their own convenience, building their own reputations, or responding to political pressures from those who demand only that they become more "tough."

Deterrence

Rehabilitation takes place after a criminal has been caught, and it depends on the notion that criminals can be convinced to go straight simply because they know that crime is wrong. Deterrence, in contrast, seeks to keep crime from occurring in the first place through an appeal to self-interest rather than morality. The primary goal of deterrence is to frighten potential criminals with the prospect of sure and severe consequences that outweigh any benefits that crime may promise. The assumption, of course, is that potential criminals are moderately rational and moderately well-informed. As such, the goal is at odds with the theory that criminals are deviants, driven by uncontrollable impulses or values antithetical to our own.

The idea that law enforcement should strive toward deterrence is appealing to neoconservatives for a couple of reasons. The goal of deterrence has roots in rational-choice models that borrow from conventional economic theory. Neoconservatives, who feel that the wisdom of market forces should be tapped whenever possible, are comfortable with that theoretical foundation and feel that it offers a more scientific and reliable base than the sociological and psychological approaches upon which criminologists traditionally relied. They are attracted also to the implication that reductions in crime do not depend upon eliminating the criminal impulse. Neoconservatives are skeptical of the notion that men by nature are good, and they are even more skeptical of the notion that government can somehow take bad men and make them better. It is safer, they reason, to base a law enforcement policy on the assumption that people will continue to take advantage of other people as long as they figure they can get away with it.

The role of police, courts, and prisons in pursuing a goal of deterrence is to ensure that the costs of crime are visible, certain, and severe. Police must make their presence obvious. They must solve crimes and capture criminals. Prosecutors and judges must increase the percentage of those convicted who spend time in prison or in jail.

Deterrence and rehabilitation are not necessarily incompatible. In practice, however, they sometimes point decision-makers in two different directions. Tough and aggressive cops may be scarier and therefore deter some potential criminals. But toughness and aggression can easily turn into brutality and unconstitutional behavior that advocates of rehabilitation warn against. Neoconservative advocates of deterrence argue that we must reduce plea bargaining and limit the discretion of judges and parole boards to alter sentences according to the characteristics of the defendant or the particulars of the crime. But advocates of rehabilitation counter that admitting guilt is an important first step toward rehabilitation, that the promise of getting out sooner is a critical incentive, that fairness and effectiveness depend upon the freedom of judges to assess the likelihood that this or that criminal is likely to be reformed, and that it makes little sense either to hold the rehabilitated criminal in prison longer than necessary or to let the unrepentant out simply because he or she has served for a predetermined length of time.

Incapacitation

The goal of incapacitation is to isolate criminals so that they will have no opportunities to engage in crime. Because incapacitation is usually achieved by keeping the criminal in prison, the strategy is complementary to deterrence in most instances. The logic, however, is simpler and more direct. Deterrence depends upon the potential criminal weighing costs and benefits before acting. Incapacitation, its advocates reason, has the advantage of reducing crime whether the criminal is rational or irrational, whether he or she is well or poorly informed. "Even if no criminal paid any heed to the risks he ran—an unlikely state of affairs—we could still reduce the crime rate by separating offenders (in prisons or on desert islands) from the rest of us," James Q. Wilson declares (Wilson, 1983, p. 84).

The simplicity and directness of incapacitation make it an appealing strategy to neoconservatives like Wilson. But Wilson and others have tried to give the approach a sounder intellectual basis than the simple "lock 'em up and throw away the key" notion. That notion is associated with the more conventional right wing and is based on the assumption that criminals are deviants who can never be trusted to reenter society. To the neoconservatives, the argument for incapacitation lies less in the proven flaws in the criminal than in the known shortcomings of government. While criminologists and politicians argue back and forth about the nature of crime, crime continues to cause personal tragedy and financial loss. If increasing the likelihood that criminals will spend time behind bars can achieve a sure and sudden drop in crime, let us do it, and do it now. But Wilson does not believe it is legally or practically possible to put criminals away forever. He favors surer sentences, if not necessarily longer ones.

If incapacitation is the goal, police, courts, and prisons could be expected to do much the same things as they would in pursuing deterrence. Whereas deterrence might call for a more visible and dramatic show of force, however, incapacitation is not dependent upon the impression it makes on the perceptions of potential criminals. It is more important that police catch criminals and obtain usable evidence, and this may sometimes depend upon keeping a *lower* profile and paying scrupulous attention to the rights of the accused. Similarly, it is possible to imagine tensions between deterrence and incapacitation as they serve as goals for courts and prisons. A dramatic announcement that all those convicted of drug possession must serve at least fifteen years in prison might put quite a scare into some potential drug users. But incapacitation depends upon the courts actually convicting those accused, and police, prosecutors, judges, and juries may be hesitant to put such a measure into effect.

Punishment

The idea that criminals should be punished is a longstanding one, usually associated with a conventional conservative point of view. Usually, punishment is defended as a means to other ends. Punishment, for example, serves as a deterrent if it convinces potential criminals that the costs of crime will be high. If it consists of imprisonment, punishment serves an incapacitation function at the same time. But punishment is a distinct goal, one that can be supported on its own terms.

Punishment refers to giving criminals their "just desserts" whether or not this has a direct and immediate impact on the likelihood of that criminal, or others, breaking the law again. Many associate punishment with simple vengeance—the desire of the victim to "get even." The image of those who were wronged taking the law into their own hands haunts modern societies, which see such impulses as sowing the seeds of anarchy and destruction. Some reason that it is better to institutionalize vengeance, to exact the deserved penalty through formal procedures, thereby ensuring that formal procedures will continue to stand.

But even this notion of institutionalized vengeance came to be rejected by many in recent years. Its roots seem barbaric to some, its practice too harsh. Those who favor rehabilitation believe that punishment per se tends to backfire, sparking resentment and a further desire for revenge. Child-care books and popular psychologists have gained a wide audience with their message that one should reason with one's child, entice the child into good behavior rather than attempt to force good behavior with the threat of a beating. The analogy, to some, seemed appropriate.

Partly for these reasons, calls for punishment came to be regarded in some circles as socially unacceptable. To vigorously call for punishment of criminals for the sake of punishment alone was to risk being branded as unsophisticated and crude. This is not to say that people did not continue to harbor a simple desire for criminals to be punished; it just meant that people found ways to express this desire in more genteel terms.

More recently, some analysts have suggested that the topic of punishment needs to be taken out of the closet and considered seriously and explicitly. Consider the case of the man who murders his wife in a sudden fit of jealousy or rage. Such a man is unlikely to murder again.

> Nonetheless, he cannot, as a routine matter, be put on probation or given a suspended sentence even if a showing were made that the incidence of wife slaying would not increase consequent upon a reduction in the frequency of imprisonment of wife slayers. The criminal law has general behavioral standard-setting functions; it acts as a moral teacher; and, consequently, re-

quires a retributive floor to punishment as well as a retributive ceiling (Morris, 1974, p. 78).

Punishment may be necessary, therefore, as a symbolic expression of society's rejection of certain types of behavior; failure to punish may blur the distinction between actions that are acceptable and those that are not. Such a symbolic expression is a reaffirmation of the ties that bind individuals to the society and a declaration that these ties are important and that they will be defended.

Table 9-1 summarizes the four goals and their implications for police, court, and prison policies. Although there can be tensions among the goals of deterrence, incapacitation, and punishment, the major conflict is between these goals and that of rehabilitation. It is this conflict that divides liberals and conservatives most sharply. Radicals are skeptical of all four goals. Even the goal of rehabilitation, to which they might be expected to be more sympathetic, implies that police, courts, and prisons really are driven by a simple desire to promote security and protect the rights of all citizens. Radicals believe the criminal justice system is used as a tool for controlling the poor rather than as a crime-fighting weapon. From this perspective, rehabilitation, deterrence, incapacitation, and punishment represent a range of strategies with which the political and economic elite can divide, manipulate, harass, and otherwise weaken those individuals and groups that represent a potential challenge to the existing distribution of wealth, property, and power.

THE LIMITS OF POLICING

The police, in theory, play a key role in pursuing several of the goals of law enforcement. One of the key functions of the police is *investigation*. This involves the interviewing of witnesses and sifting of clues in order to identify the perpetrators of crimes. We demand that the police sometimes act like Sherlock Holmes; a stray wisp of hair, a charred document in the fireplace, a footprint outside a window are roadmarks that we expect the police to follow accurately until the villain is revealed. Another important function is *apprehension,* the taking of suspects into custody. Whereas investigation calls for subtlety and painstakingly methodical attention to detail, apprehension calls for speed and force. Here we envision roaring sirens and screeching tires. Heavily armed officers surround the bank just as the robbers push through the revolving door; a police helicopter swoops down on a dark and isolated field to interrupt a major transaction involving illicit drugs.

Their role in investigating crimes and capturing criminals gives the police a critical "gateway" function; they are the necessary first step into

Table 9-1 Rehabilitation, Deterrence, Incapacitation, and Punishment As Policy Guides

	Rehabilitation	Deterrence	Incapacitation	Punishment
Ideological Underpinnings	Liberal	Neoconservative	Neoconservative	Conservative (revenge, teach lesson) Neoconservative (reaffirm social ties)
Implications for Police	A model of lawful behavior; suspects accord all legal rights	Visible presence increases potential criminal's perception of risks	Gateway into system. Solve crimes and capture criminals. Provide evidence that will hold in court	Solve crimes and capture criminals; may harass suspects as form of "street justice"
Courts and Sentencing	Punishment must fit criminal as well as crime	Must increase certainty of punishment to increase risk	Surer and longer prison terms. Reduce prosecutor and judge discretion	Provide "just desserts"; swift and fitting response
Prisons	Provide job training, education. Teach responsibility. Restrict freedom as little as possible; parole for those who turn over new leaf	Too many services may lower "costs" of crime. Time off for good behavior reduces certainty of "costs." Limit parole option	Main goal: keep off streets	Must be unpleasant. Nonprison alternatives may be appropriate, if tough
Underlying Premises	Criminal shares basic values; will prefer noncrime if option open	Potential criminal is rational; weighs costs and benefits	We do not know how to "cure" criminals; cannot commit crime while isolated	Only swift and forceful punishment has meaning to some. Social order is fragile; must send message: this is not tolerable

the rest of the criminal justice system. Unless police do their job moderately well, courts and prisons will stand empty, and neither deterrence nor incapacitation nor punishment will be feasible.

As the most visible arm of the criminal justice system, police are expected to play a particularly important role in crime *prevention.* A visible, forceful display of police presence, it is hoped, will deter potential criminals who, making a rational assessment of the costs and benefits of criminal activity, may be convinced that the risks of capture are simply too great.

The police devote much of their resources and orient much of their organizational structure around these goals of investigation, apprehension, and prevention. Most departments have separate detective divisions, which specialize in the investigative function. The detectives generally are better paid and granted higher status than the uniformed patrol officer.

In order to maximize the chances for apprehending criminals, police put great emphasis on *response time*—the time that passes between the first call to the police indicating that a crime has occurred and the arrival of the first police officer on the scene. Some police departments have gone so far as to invest in elaborate computer simulation techniques that digest information relating to speed limits, traffic patterns, stoplight timing, and the like in order to pinpoint where police cars ought to be assigned if response time is to be minimized and equalized throughout the city.

The desire of police to prevent crime, as well as capture criminals, is symbolized in their emphasis on a procedure known as *preventive patrol.* In most departments, whenever officers are not responding to a call for service, they are expected to cruise slowly throughout their beat. Although it is always hoped that officers engaged in preventive patrol might spot a crime in progress, the chances of this occurring are slim. But it is believed that by increasing the visibility of the police force, preventive patrol may discourage some prospective criminals. Police officials sometimes refer to preventive patrol as the "workhorse" or "backbone" of the department.

Because of their key role, public officials have tended to look first to the police when under pressure to do something about crime. "If elected, I will put more police on the streets," is a familiar campaign theme. Nevertheless, as social scientists have learned more about how crimes are solved and what police can and cannot do, they have come to have their doubts about the effectiveness of such an approach. Even if the manpower and dollars devoted to the policing were raised substantially, it is not likely that crime would decrease to a marked degree.

How Crimes Are Solved

In spite of the resources that police currently devote to investigation, it is unusual for police to solve a crime. In 1981, police made arrests in only

43.7 percent of violent crimes and only 17.1 percent of property crimes. (National Criminal Justice Information and Statistics Service, 1981).

When police *do* solve a crime, moreover, it is rarely due to the kind of careful and intricate detective work that appears to be so important on the television screen. The fingerprint on the coffee table, the foreign-made cigarette in the ashtray, the scrap of skin under the victim's fingernail—clues such as these rarely prove to be the key to the solution of a crime.

How *are* crimes solved? In most cases in which the police make an arrest, it is because the perpetrator gives himself up or remains at the scene of the crime until police arrive, or because the victim or witnesses are able to provide the name or relatively precise identification of a suspect when the police arrive. In a smaller, but significant proportion of the cases, bungling by the criminal is responsible for his or her eventual arrest.

> The list of blunders is almost endless: dropping merchandise while shoplifting; making noise during a burglary; driving over the speed limit during the getaway; leaving the keys to the getaway car on the counter of the store during a robbery; using one's own name to endorse and cash a stolen money order; holding up people who know one's identity without bothering to use a disguise. In one instance, a robber held up the front desk of a hotel where he had been employed as a desk clerk; in another, a robber held up the bank in which he had been depositing the proceeds from other bank robberies (Silberman, 1978, p. 80).

The incidence of such blunders is so great that Silberman was led to conclude that criminals must be manifesting a subconscious desire to be caught and punished (Silberman, p. 85). Those who are skeptical of such a psychoanalytic explanation may find another of Silberman's points more convincing. A high percentage of crimes are committed by individuals who are under the influence of alcohol or drugs; "whereas liquor and drugs fortify the nerves, they also muddy the judgement, leading to carelessness. . ." (Silberman, p. 81).

Nor is it likely that police can significantly increase their success in catching criminals before they leave the scene of the crime. Police efforts to shave reponse time generally have yielded results. In Kansas City, for example, a study found that, on average, police responded to assaults in about three minutes; to robberies in three and a half minutes; to burglaries in six minutes. But response time measures how long it takes for police to arrive *once they have been called*. On average, assaults were not reported to police until over an hour had passed after the assault took place. Robberies were not called in until twenty-three minutes had elapsed. Burglaries were reported to police a little over half an hour after being *discovered;* since many burglaries occur when residents are absent, many hours, or even days, often pass before the victims realize that the crime has taken place (Pate, et al., 1976). Putting more police and more cars on the streets might shave a few more seconds off the average time it takes for the police to respond, but unless the behavior of the victims changes, such improvements are unlikely to be reflected in an increase in arrests.

Do Police Deter Crime?

Will increases in the number of police deter criminals from engaging in crime? Probably not. The rational-choice theory of crime suggests that increases in the visibility of police should prevent some crimes by convincing potential criminals that the probability of capture is high. And some early studies seemed to lend this notion empirical support. For four months during 1954, the New York City Police Department flooded its Twenty-fifth Precinct with double its usual allotment of patrol officers. Crime, especially street crime, fell dramatically; the number of muggings declined from 69 to 7, auto thefts from 78 to 24, assaults from 185 to 132, when compared to the same months during the previous year (Wilson, 1975, p. 83; Banfield, 1974, p. 199). The Operation 25 experiment, however, was flawed in a number of respects, the most important of which was its failure to determine whether the saturation of the Twenty-fifth Precinct had simply pushed criminal activity elsewhere, into the surrounding neighborhoods.

The Kansas City Patrol Experiment. By far the most ambitious and methodologically sophisticated effort to study the deterrent effect of police presence is found in the Kansas City Preventive Patrol Experiment. The results of the Kansas City study are much less encouraging to those who hope that crime prevention can be attained simply by increasing the presence and visibility of police patrols.

Between October 1, 1972, and September 30, 1973, approximately 150,000 residents of a thirty-two-square-mile section of Kansas City, Missouri, were subjects in an experiment of which they were unaware. At that time, the Kansas City Police Department was headed by Clarence Kelley, a progressive law enforcement professional soon to be elevated to the post of the director of the Federal Bureau of Investigation. Police are generally considered to be quite traditional, unwilling to entertain new ideas or reconsider traditional methods for going about their jobs. Kelley, however, was willing to experiment on a grand scale, to subject some basic assumptions about policing to a rigorous empirical test. He was willing to do so in part because, as he put it, "Many of us in the department had the feeling we were training, equipping, and deploying men to do a job neither we, nor anyone else, knew much about" (Kelling, et al., 1974, p. iv). Along with The Police Foundation, a nonprofit research-oriented organization established by the Ford Foundation, the Kansas City Police Department set out to determine whether the conventional wisdom regarding the effectiveness of preventive patrolling was accurate.

The experiment took place within fifteen patrol beats. These beats were divided into three sets that were similar in terms of crime history, number of calls for service, income, population stability, and racial and ethnic composition. In the first set of beats—labeled "reactive" by the experimenters—preventive patrol was eliminated. Patrol cars normally assigned to these five beats were allowed to enter them only in direct response to calls for service. Some of these cars were reassigned to a second set of beats—labeled "proactive"—in which normal levels of preventive patrol were doubled or tripled. A third set of "control" beats was allocated its usual level of patrol.

Departmental records of reported crimes, traffic incidents, and arrests were monitored. In addition, a wide range of additional information was collected through victimization surveys and surveys to determine citizens' and business persons' attitudes toward, and perceptions of, crime and the police.

The results were striking. *The number of officers on preventive patrol seemed to have no measurable impact.* Levels of reported crime, victimization levels, citizen fear of crime, community attitudes toward the police, traffic accidents, and police response time were no different in the reactive beats than they were in the control and proactive beats.

The Kansas City results were shocking to many. Some police officials rejected them outright (Henig, et al., 1977). Yet, upon further reflection, we can see that the results should not have been so surprising. Many crimes, especially violent crimes, are crimes of passion. The jilted lover, the jealous husband, and the insulted coworker do not stop to calculate the likelihood that their behvior will be observed by cruising policemen before they strike out in anger. Many other crimes—most assaults, burglaries, murders—occur indoors or otherwise out of view of even the most alert patrolling officers. The rationale for patrol as a means to prevent crime is anchored in the image of the criminal as a rational calculating being. But even in the case of those crimes that are the product of forethought and calculation there are reasons to be skeptical about the capacity of normal levels of patrolling to deter criminals. One study relying on a complex model based on estimates of the number of patrol cars, average speed of patrolling vehicles, miles of streets to be patrolled, and the percent of the average officer's time spent on preventive patrol rather than other policing activities concluded that the average citizen, standing at a randomly chosen spot within one of Kansas City's control beats, might, if he kept his eyes constantly riveted on the street, see a police car every six hours or so (Larson, 1975). Such odds are unlikely to deter any but the most cautious of potential criminals.

Saturation Patrol. This is not to say that a strategy to blanket a city with a policeman on each corner would not have a deterrent effect on crime. When New York City transit officials tripled the level of patrol on the late-night shift in the subway system, crime *did* drop. But subway trains are small, contained areas. To produce a comparable police presence aboveground would call for a much greater increase in the number of police. Even in the subways, where the conditions are favorable, the decrease in crime did not come cheaply. Investigators calculated that each serious crime deterred cost the city over $35,000 in manpower and overtime expenses (Chaiken, et al., 1974). In the budgetary environment in which most state and local governments operate, such costs are difficult or impossible to justify. For this reason, if for no other, officials and citizens are forced to look for new approaches to the dilemma of preventing crime.

The Noncrime Functions of Police

If increasing police resources is not, in and of itself, likely to lead to the capture of many more criminals or the prevention of many crimes due to the fear of being caught, what should local officials—who have the major responsibility for shaping police policy—do? Some criminologists and leaders in the police community insist that police could be much more effective, *if* they were allowed to do their job. They argue that the police have been saddled with too many legal restrictions and too many noncrime responsibilities.

Ironically, crime fighting—the activity with which the police are most closely identified—is the activity which, in practice, they perform the least frequently. *Only about one out of every nine or ten calls for service that come to the police are crime related in nature. The average police officer makes only about one arrest each month for a Part I offense.* In addition to chasing criminals, police are expected to:

> rush accident victims to the hospital; bring alcoholics indoors on a winter's night, break into a locked house or apartment to see whether an elderly occupant is alive or well; persuade a mentally ill person who has barricaded himself in his apartment to return to the hospital; administer emergency first-aid to a heart attack victim, or someone who has taken a drug overdose, while waiting for the ambulance to come. Police also get cats out of trees, chauffeur dignitaries around town, rescue the drowning, talk suicidal people out of killing themselves . . . and provide advice and help to the sick and elderly, as well as to otherwise healthy people who simply cannot cope with some pressing problem (Silberman, 1978, p. 203).

Many departments have special traffic divisions, and these usually are provided with as much manpower as the patrol and investigative branches. "Where the regular beat patrol officers are also responsible for traffic, that task occupies more of their time than apprehending criminals" (Jacob, 1980, pp. 52–3).

Conservative politicians running on "law and order" platforms frequently charge that such responsibilities are distractions; they argue that by relieving the police of the need to handle such noncrime duties, we will free them to perform their "gateway" and deterrence roles more effectively. But some analysts argue just the opposite. They suggest that police need to put *greater* emphasis on their noncrime functions, because this is what they do best. Interestingly, both liberals and neoconservatives touch upon this theme.

Police As Helpers. According to some liberal analysts, police should shed their self-image of tough-guy crime fighters and begin to think of themselves as a "public service agency, devoted to close relationships with, and assistance to, the people and communities being policed" (Silberman, 1978, p. 243). This argument rests on at least three premises. First, although they do not directly relate to crime, *the many uses to which the police are put are important.* Some of them—ambulance service, first aid, suicide intervention—involve life-and-death situations. Many do not. But even the tasks that seem trivial to some—bringing home the third-graders who stopped at the park on the way home from school without telling their worried parents, helping a motorist who locked himself out of his own car—usually are marked by a sense of emergency and helplessness for some of the individuals directly involved.

Second, *treating the police primarily as crime fighters leads to unhappy and ill-trained police.* Police recruits are encouraged in the expectation that their's will be an exciting and dramatic career. They are taught to use their weapons, to spot suspicious persons, to engage in automobile chases, but they get little training in the activities in which they will spend most of their time: interacting with citizens, resolving minor disputes, providing a helping hand. The result is frustration on the part of the young officers, who find that they cannot do what they think they are "supposed" to do. Another result is incompetence: oriented toward dealing with criminals, many police officers end up treating *all* citizens as possible suspects, making them hostile and suspicious when they should be courteous and supportive.

Finally, some argue that the *police-as-helper will become better crime fighters as a byproduct* of the better community relations that occur. As we have seen, the ability of the police to solve crimes and capture criminals depends directly upon the cooperation of the public at large. If the public fails to report crimes rapidly, if the public refuses to serve as a witness in criminal trials, police are severely handicapped. A narrow approach to crime fighting led police to adopt some techniques that put barriers between them and the public. Keeping police inside their patrol cars increased the likelihood that response time would be rapid, but it kept police from mingling with residents and earning the trust and respect that would encourage cooperation on the part of the community. Aggressive questioning and militaristic demeanor may have "put the scare into" some neighborhood kids, but it did so at the cost of irritating racial antagonisms and convincing minorities and the poor that the police were not on their side.

Maintaining Order. The phrase "law and order" has become a code phrase for crime fighting; its two components—"law" and "order"—are so frequently linked that their meaning is blurred into a single impression. But enforcement of the law and maintenance of order are not identical functions. To the contrary. In order to enforce the law, police sometimes have to risk stirring unrest and disorder. Such might be the case, for example, if police were called to a local tavern because two recently laid-off autoworkers had begun a drunken scuffle. Laws against disorderly conduct and damage to private property might have been broken, but should the police haul the brawlers down to the station and charge them with a crime? If the goal is to calm things down, the best tactic might be to simply deliver a warning, then deliver the men to their homes. With a drunk and angry crowd on hand, to do otherwise might just stimulate further violence, even against the police themselves. The risk that enforcing the law may stir disorder is particularly high when police are dealing with a minority community in a time of interracial tension. Many of the urban riots of the 1960s were sparked by crowd resentment of police actions enforcing seemingly straightforward violations of traffic or disorderly conduct laws.

By the same token, in order to maintain peace and orderly conduct, it may be necessary for the police to act against individuals who are not violating any significant laws. Neoconservatives, who believe that the breakdown in community is responsible for much of the increase in crime and fear of crime, argue that the police must play a critical role in anchoring the many informal bulwarks against neighborhood decline. James Q. Wilson and George L. Kelling, for example, argue that police may have forgotten that order maintenance plays a role in *reinforcing community norms that prevent crime-prone environments from emerging* in the first place. Sometimes, they suggest, police can maintain order only by slipping outside the boundaries of legal behavior themselves. They write, somewhat nostalgically, of an earlier time. "Young toughs were roughed up, people were arrested 'on suspicion' or for vagrancy, and prostitutes and petty thieves were routed" (Wilson and Kelling, 1982, p. 33).

Although liberals and neoconservatives share the idea that the ultimate effectiveness of police actions depends upon the quality of their relationship with the community, they do not agree upon the means by which the police should nurture this relationship. The use of informal sanctions, such as Wilson and Kelling seem to favor, touches a sore spot for many liberals, who associate police discretion to rough up young toughs with the kind of brutality and racially motivated harassment that became hot issues during the late 1960s. At that time, liberals, finding a pattern in which police in many cities seemed to treat minorities differently from other citizens, fought hard for reforms that would limit the discretion of individual officers to determine whether and how to enforce the written law. Encouraging police to adopt local values, they worry, may give them license to enforce the biases of the majority and the strong even when those biases violate the rights of minorities and the weak.

SENTENCING AND THE COURTS

Sometimes it is referred to as the problem of "revolving door justice." It is the story of criminals—street muggers, prostitutes, drug dealers, rapists—arrested in the morning and back on the streets by noon. It is the story of accused and convicted criminals—out on bail while awaiting trial, out on parole after serving only part of a sentence—once again engaging in violent or threatening illegal acts.

Tales of revolving door justice are frustrating and debilitating. Police resent the fact that their efforts are undermined. The average citizen, too, is likely to throw up his or her hands and cry out, "What is the use?" Why bother to call the police to report suspicious activity? Why bother to take the time and effort to volunteer as a witness? Why take the risk of reporting vandalism, harassment, or even assault if the accused will be allowed to go free and, possibly, to seek revenge?

Although it is a source of distress, the phenomenon of revolving door justice may also be the focus of hope for effective reform. Police do not solve most crimes, and, as we have seen, there is not much hope that their record in this respect will be significantly improved. Although most crimes go unsolved, however, it is not the case that most criminals go uncaught. "Although a robber has less than a 20 percent chance of being arrested on any one offense . . . he has a 90 percent chance of being arrested if he commits ten robberies, and the odds go up to 99 percent by the twenty-first offense" (Silberman, 1978, p. 77; Silberman attributes this estimate to Glaser, 1975). One of the functions of the police is to serve as the gateway into the rest of the criminal justice system. Although the gate may be creaky, rusty, and difficult to open at times, the fact of the matter is that most criminals eventually pass through it. Perhaps reform efforts aimed at improving the effectiveness of courts and prisons—reforms designed to rehabilitate or incapacitate criminals once they are captured—hold greater promise than the traditional call for more or better police.

The Argument for Tougher Courts

"Judges Are Too Lenient." Complaints about revolving door justice usually are the springboard for calls to increase the certainty and/or severity of the punishments meted out by our system of courts. Courts, it is suggested, have "gone soft." Too many criminals are simply let free without any punishment at all. Critics of current court procedures present statistics indicating that only 1 to 2 percent of the crimes committed—and only 8 to 12 percent of arrests—result in someone being sent to prison (Van den Haag, 1975, pp. 158–66; Banfield, 1974, pp. 201–3). This, it is sometimes implied, represents a "fall from grace"—a regression from a time when tougher judges dished out "frontier-style justice" unhampered by public sympathies for the criminal-as-underdog or Supreme Court rulings specifying the rights of the accused.

The failure of the courts to send more criminals to prison for longer periods of time has fed the growing crime rate, it is argued, in several different ways. Lenient courts, first of all, *fail to deter*. Potential criminals who are rational, at least to the extent of weighing the likely costs and benefits of their actions, will not be dissuaded if the probability of punishment, even if they are captured, is very low or the severity of punishment, even if it is ordered, is mild. Lenient courts *fail to incapacitate*. Criminals who are in prison cannot commit further crimes against the law-abiding citizenry (though they may, and often do, commit crimes against their fellow inmates). Lenient courts *fail to punish*. They send a message, to the criminal and to the public at large, that the legal system is unsure of itself, that we as a society do not have enough confidence to stand firmly behind our judgments about what is right and what is wrong. Lenient courts, finally, may *fail to rehabilitate*. Some uncertain proportion of criminals is capable of becoming useful, productive, and law-abiding. Rehabilitation, in some cases, may require physical or psychological therapy; in some cases, it may depend upon exposure to moral guidance, education, or the acquisition of needed job skills. Such persons, and society at large, may be cheated if revolving door justice robs them of the chance to be exposed to the rehabilitation programs that most federal and state prisons now provide.

"We Have Protected the Rights of the Accused at the Cost of Sacrificing Victims' Rights." Among those who favor tougher and surer punishment of criminals, part of the blame for the current failures of the criminal justice system is directed at the U.S. Supreme Court, especially the Supreme Court as it operated under Chief Justice Earl Warren.

During the 1960s, the liberal Warren Court offered a number of rulings that broadened the rights of those accused of crime and, correspondingly, placed greater constraints on the activities of law enforcement personnel. In *Mapp* v. *Ohio* (1961), the Court ruled that evidence police gained by means of an illegal search and seizure could not be admissible in state or federal courts. In *Gideon* v. *Wainwright* (1963), the Court concluded that persons too poor to afford to hire their own lawyers had to be provided with counsel in cases in which they were charged with felonies. In *Escobedo* v. *Illinois* (1964), in order to protect suspects from being coerced or manipulated into incriminating statements, the Court established that individuals are entitled to consult with their lawyers as soon as police consider them to be suspects. In *Miranda* v. *Arizona* (1966), the Warren Court ruled that suspects must be informed of this right to counsel and their right to remain silent before undergoing questioning by the police.

Controversy regarding these standards focuses primarily on their application in the context of the "exclusionary rule." This rule holds that evidence obtained in violation of such standards—as, for instance, in cases in which stolen merchandise is discovered by police conducting what is later found to be an unwarranted search of an automobile—cannot be admitted as evidence in court. One study estimates that, in one year alone, from 45,000 to 55,000 felony and serious misdemeanor cases are dropped by prosecutors in the United States because of the exclusionary rule (Schlesinger, 1983, p. 194). Such decisions, some feel, have tilted the balance on the scales of justice too far in the direction of the defendant, with the rights of victims and society sacrificed.

"Plea Bargaining Allows Criminals to Go Free." Just as distressing to those who favor tougher courts is the widespread practice of plea bargaining. Plea bargaining refers to a process of negotiation between the prosecutor, defense attorney, and, sometimes, the judge. The goal of such negotiations, from the standpoint of the prosecutor, is to obtain a guilty plea. By convincing a defendant to plead guilty, the prosecutor saves his or her own time, as well as time and money for the court. A guilty plea also eliminates the possibility that a weak case, witnesses' fading memories, illegally obtained evidence, or a careless jury might let a guilty person go free. In return for a guilty plea, a prosecutor may offer to charge the defendant with a less serious crime, drop certain charges already filed, or recommend a light sentence to the judge.

Plea bargaining is not an exception; it is the rule. In spite of the fact that the accused in serious criminal cases are guaranteed the right to insist on a jury trial or a "bench trial" in front of a judge, trials to determine the guilt or innocence of the accused are a rarity. A review of court records in twenty-one states and the District of Columbia found that over half of the states obtained more than 90 percent of their convictions through guilty pleas; less than one-fourth obtained fewer than 80 percent of convictions that way (Jones, 1979, pp. 44–7).

Critics charge that plea bargaining lets some guilty persons go free and gives others much shorter sentences than they deserve. Plea bargaining, as practiced by some prosecutors, may even encourage crime. David A. Jones charges that prosecutors are usually satisfied if they can obtain a conviction on at least one charge; they are willing to overlook or bargain away possible charges against the defendant that involve other crimes he or she may have committed. "For this reason, it is to the advantage of the sophisticated and persistent offender (and he knows it) for him to perpetuate as many separate criminal transactions as possible between the moment he commits the first and the time he is imprisoned, as well as during virtually all periods of pretrial or postconviction release" (Jones, p. 201).

Severity Versus Certainty of Punishment. Surveys reveal that a large and growing segment of the American public subscribes to the notion that our courts are "not harsh enough." (See Table 9–2.) Popular sentiment for longer sentences, however, may overlook a distinction that criminologists have found to be significant. This is the distinction between severity of punishment and certainty of punishment. Severity of punishment refers to the *length* of prison sentences. Certainty of punishment refers to

Table 9–2 Changing Attitudes Toward the Courts

Year	% saying courts are "not harsh enough"
1965	48.9
1968	63.1
1969	74.4
1972	74.4
1973	73.1
1974	77.9
1975	79.2
1976	81.0
1977	83.0
1978	84.9
1980	83.0

SOURCES: Arthur L. Stinchcombe et al., *Crime and Punishment: Changing Attitudes in America.* San Francisco: Jossey-Bass, 1980; U.S. Department of Justice, Bureau of Justice Statistics, *Sourcebook of Criminal Justice Statistics, 1981.* Washington, D.C.: Government Printing Office, 1982. Data for years 1965–1969 are based on Gallup Poll surveys; for years 1972–1980, based on National Opinion Research Corporation surveys.

the *probability* that an individual convicted of a crime will go to prison at all.

Although there is not a complete consensus, most recent studies of this issue have concluded that increasing the probability of punishment is more likely to reduce crime than making the punishments more severe. States that still practice capital punishment—the extreme case of severity—do not seem to exhibit lower rates of murder, for instance; nor does it seem that homicide rates drop after a publicized execution (Schuessler, 1952; Savitz, 1958).

Other studies have devised measures of the certainty of punishment, based on the percentage of convicted criminals being sent to prison, and the severity of punishment, based on the average time spent in prison. Statistical analysis of such information has indicated that states with more certain punishment also show lower crime rates; the relationship between severity and crime is weak or nonexistent (Gibbs, 1968).

Mandatory Sentencing: One Popular Response. One outgrowth of such studies has been a growing demand for reforms of the processes by which sentencing decisions are made. Criminals convicted of the same crime currently may receive wildly different sentences, depending on the jurisdiction within which they are tried and even upon the particular judge who presides. Eisenstein and Jacob, for example, found that a person convicted of armed robbery in Baltimore could expect a sentence of about eighty-four months, whereas a person convicted of the same crime in Detroit would typically receive only thirty-five months (Eisenstein and Jacob, 1977, pp. 271-4).

Some neoconservatives, such as James Q. Wilson, have argued that such disparities indicate that judges are granted too much discretion in their sentencing power. They recommend that legislatures define much more narrowly and precisely the range of sentence appropriate for specific crimes. The institution of such "mandatory sentencing" legislation is intended to achieve two ends simultaneously: (1) to ensure that all persons convicted of serious crimes spend at least some time in prison no matter how clever their lawyer or how tenderhearted the judge; and (2) to ensure that all persons convicted of the same crime receive approximately equal sentences, no matter which court they are convicted in and no matter what their race, economic status, or personal idiosyncrasies.

Mandating sentences may deter rational criminals by convincing them that, if caught, the likelihood that they will spend time in prison is high. But some advocates of this approach argue that it will reduce crime even if potential criminals are ignorant or uncaring about the risks they undertake. Their reasoning is simple: a person sent to prison cannot victimize other persons who are outside of prison. "If much or most serious crime is committed by repeaters, separating repeaters from the rest of society, even for relatively brief periods of time, may produce major reductions in crime rates" (Wilson, 1975, p. 173). James Q. Wilson and Barbara Boland have estimated the impact that increased certainty of punishment will have due to the incapacitation functions of prisons alone. They calculate that if the average criminal commits two serious crimes per year, doubling the chance that he or she would serve a two-year sentence (from three chances in one hundred to six chances in one hundred) would reduce the rate of serious crime by about 9.7 percent. If the average criminal commits ten crimes per year, such an increase in the probability of imprisonment could reduce crime by 27 percent (Wilson and Boland, 1976, pp. 208–9).

The concept of mandatory sentencing has proven to be extremely popular. By the summer of 1983, forty-three states had instituted mandatory terms for at least some violent crimes (Meddis, 1983). It is not, however, without its problems. Some of these are practical problems. Mandatory sentencing means that more persons would be sent to prison. Prisons, as we shall see, are already overcrowded in most states. So far, there is not much evidence that the public is willing to pay the taxes to build and maintain the prisons that mandatory sentencing would require.

Another concern is that mandatory sentencing might backfire. Judges and juries are hesitant, in many instances, to sentence convicted criminals to prisons that they feel are so crowded, violent, and vicious that the punishment outweighs any but the most vicious of crimes. Will mandatory sentencing lead juries and judges to declare the accused innocent, rather than render a guilty verdict that automatically entails a prison term of several years? Today, most cases are resolved by guilty pleas, a fact that reduces the burden on our already overworked courts. Would mandatory sentencing, by limiting the court's discretion to engage in plea bargaining, lead more defendants to insist on a jury trial, pushing the workload of the courts to the breaking point?

Beyond these practical considerations, there are more fundamental challenges to mandatory sentencing. These challenges are rooted in the liberals' commitment to rehabilitation and their belief that decreasing crime depends upon demonstrating to all citizens that ours is a system that strives for fairness, justice, and equality for all. One such challenge involves the argument that plea bargaining and judicial discretion are both necessary *and* desirable. Another centers around the contention that prisons are "schools for crime," turning out people who are more vicious, skillful, and committed criminals than the ones they originally took in.

Judicial Discretion: A Different View

"Plea Bargaining as a 'Necessary Evil.' " Plea bargaining has had relatively few defenders and even fewer advocates. The notion that all accused are entitled to a jury trial is strongly imbued in American culture and in our national self-image. Plea bargaining short-circuits the judicial process and, it seems to many, poses potential risks: that guilty persons will be freed to commit more crimes, and that innocent persons will be intimidated into guilty pleas.

Most of those who have defended plea bargaining have not done so out of enthusiasm. Rather, they have argued that prosecutors and judges must be granted discretion to bargain if they are not to be overwhelmed by the workload that confronts them. They point, for instance, to the Manhattan Criminal Courts Building, sometimes referred to as "the world's busiest courthouse." There, 180 assistant district attorneys struggle to handle 100,000 arrests each year. Night court is kept open as late as 2:00 A.M., but still it is not always possible to handle all the scheduled cases in one day (Jaynes, 1978). Plea bargaining is a "necessary evil," this argument suggests. Without it, frenzied attorneys and harried judges would find it difficult to successfully put any criminals behind bars.

A Stronger Defense of Judicial and Prosecutorial Discretion. Some liberals argue that plea bargaining is more than simply an adaptation forced upon courts by recently mushrooming criminal loads. Plea bargaining, first of all, "is not a recent innovation; it was the subject of heated debate during the 1920s," and there is some evidence that it "had replaced jury trials as the principal means of settling criminal cases as early as the second third of the nineteenth century" (Silberman, 1978, pp. 278–9). Nor is plea bargaining found exclusively in big city courts, where caseloads are heaviest; to the contrary, a review of the experiences of eight states found that "counties with populations exceeding 1 million show the *lowest* guilty plea rates. . ." (Jones, 1979, p. 55).

The general notion that our courts have become "softer" is questionable as well. "For all the talk about the decline in punishment and the hobbling effect of the Warren Court," Charles Silberman argues, "what data are available indicate that contemporary criminal courts prosecute, convict, and incarcerate a larger proportion of those arrested for a felony today than did the courts of the 1920s" (Silberman, 1978, p. 261). Fewer than 20 percent of those arrested for a felony in Chicago in 1926 were convicted, and only about 15 percent spent time in prison or in jail.

Prosecutorial and judicial discretion may have evolved in so many jurisdictions, and have lasted so long, because they serve a positive role in making our judicial system more flexible, more sensitive, and more just. Many factors affect how "serious" society considers a crime to be, and many factors influence how severe a punishment society considers a particular criminal to "deserve." Was permanent damage inflicted? Is this a first offense, a second offense, a twentieth? Did the offender know the victim, and what was the relationship? Was a position of authority abused (a teacher sexually harasses a student, a psychiatrist seduces a patient)? Was the crime committed in a moment of rage, and was the incident provoked? Had the offender been drinking or was he or she under the influence of drugs? Did the offender have possession of a gun? Was the threat of violence explicit or simply implied? Was the accused acting alone, or as one member of a gang or crowd? Are there signs of contrition, of willingness to reform? Have apologies been made, and has restitution been offered? "Certainly it is simple to plot the name of a crime on a chart and arrive at a fixed sentence untouched by human hearts or minds," one judge has written. "It is much simpler than to go through the agonizing process of attempting to fit the punishment to the crime and the criminal. But does it provide justice?" (Forer, 1980, pp. 109–10).

The point is not that any of these factors should *excuse* a crime. But a criminal justice system that ignored the distinctions involved would violate many people's conceptions of what is right and what is fair. The call for mandatory sentencing is predicated on the need to send a symbolic message of rigor and toughness to the community of potential criminals. Some critics of mandatory sentencing, such as Charles Silberman, argue that this is *not* the message that needs to be communicated.

Of greater concern than the perception that the system is lax, Silberman argues, is the perception that the system is illegitimate. Such a perception undermines respect for the law and discourages cooperation with law enforcement officials. But Silberman suggests that the perception is based on public misunderstanding and the failure of the criminal justice system to communicate. The public *wants* sensitivity, flexibility, and wisdom. Silberman feels that, for the most part, that is what the system is delivering. But sensitivity and discretion are being interpreted as arbitrariness and favoritism, because the judicial system has failed to articulate clearly the manner in which it operates or the values for which it stands. The answer is not to do away with plea bargaining or to limit judicial discretion in the area of sentencing. "What is required," Silberman concludes, "is to make the appearance of justice conform to its substance. That, in turn, means making the invisible visible—spelling out the informal norms that guide the actions judges and prosecutors take, so that defendants, not to mention judges and prosecutors themselves, can see and understand what is happening" (Silberman, 1978, p. 298).

Advocates of continued judicial and prosecutorial discretion sometimes offer another, more practical, criticism of the trend toward mandatory sentencing. Mandatory sentencing is intended to ensure that more of those convicted of crimes go to prison. But there is not currently enough room in America's prisons even to hold those who have already been sentenced to serve time in them.

PRISON REFORM

Overcrowding

No Room at the Inn. As of June 30, 1983, there were 431,829 inmates in federal and state prisons, an all-time high (Bureau of Justice Statistics, 1983b, Table 2). By far, the bulk of these prisoners (more than nine out of every ten) were held in state institutions. This did not include over 200,000 persons held in local jails, or approximately 75,000 residents of public and private juvenile detention, treatment, or correctional facilities (Bureau of Justice Statistics, 1983; U.S. Bureau of the Census, 1981). These numbers have been increasing dramatically in recent years, particularly at the state level. Between 1960 and 1980, the population within federal prisons fell by about 2,600 (11.2 percent); during the same period, state prison populations increased by about 104,000, a whopping 54.8 percent. Although some of the increase in prisoners reflects an increase in the total U.S. population, the percentage of Americans who are incarcerated has reached an all-time high as well. (See Figure 9–1.)

Increases in the number of Americans who are incarcerated reflect, in part, the influence of conservative and neoconservative reformers. Legislative restrictions on plea bargaining and mandatory sentencing legislation seem to be having at least some effect in increasing the proportion of those convicted who go to prison. More important may be the informal pressures arising from the public's concern about crime. Prosecutors and judges are expected to be somewhat immune to political pressure, but they cannot be so entirely. Those who wish to remain in office must be sensitive to the danger of developing a reputation as one who is "soft" on crime. As the prisons fill beyond their capacity, the tensions between the goals of incapacitation, deterrence, and punishment, on the one hand, and rehabilitation, on the other, become more obvious and concrete.

Partly as a result of these increases in inmates, conditions in many American prisons are poor. Overcrowding is a major problem. Many authorities feel that correctional facilities should provide a minimum of sixty square feet of floor space per prisoner. By that measure, in 1978, federal prisons were at 150 percent of capacity, state prisons at 173 percent of capacity, and local facilities at 146 percent (U.S. Bureau of the Census, 1981, p. 190).

In our federal system, key decisions are decentralized to state officials. As in other policy areas we have considered, this results in considerable variation in conditions and policies from state to state. Although

Figure 9–1 Increases in Prison Population 1925–1983

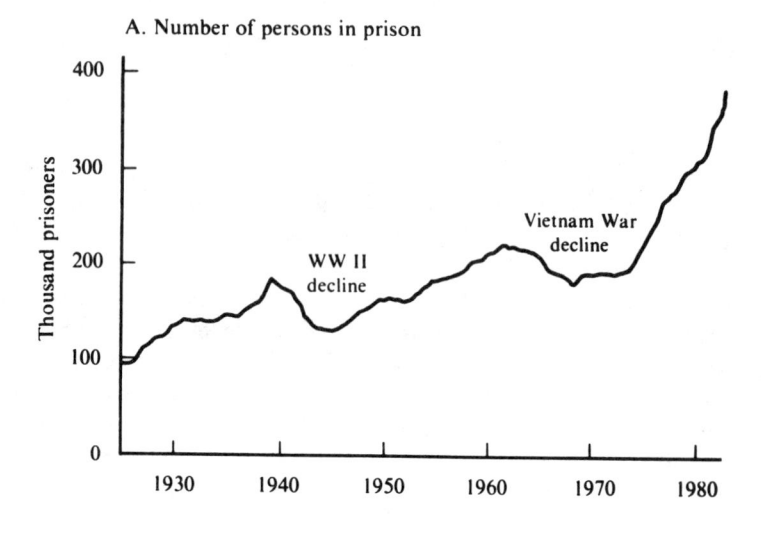

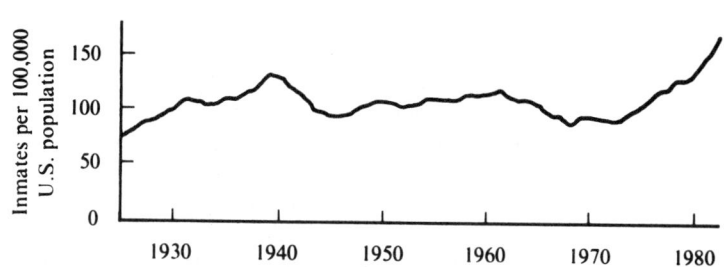

A. Number of persons in prison

[Graph showing thousand prisoners from 1930 to 1980, rising from about 100 to nearly 400, with labeled "WW II decline" around 1940s and "Vietnam War decline" around late 1960s]

B. Incarceration rate

[Graph showing inmates per 100,000 U.S. population from 1930 to 1980, ranging roughly between 75 and 150]

SOURCE: Bureau of Justice Statistics. *Report to the Nation on Crime and Justice.* Washington, D.C.: U.S. Department of Justice, October 1983, p. 81.

crowding is a problem throughout most of the nation, prisoners are much more densely packed in some states than in others. Nine out of every ten prisoners in Texas are in crowded dormitories or cells; fewer than one out of twenty prisoners in New Hampshire are so cramped.

Considered in the abstract, sixty square feet may not strike you as a strict enough standard for overcrowdedness. Remember, however, that this small amount of room typically must accommodate a bed, a sink, and toilet facilities of some kind. These typically take up about twenty-two square feet; a chair, table, and shelves frequently occupy another ten. The result is less than thirty square feet of space within which the cell's occupant can move. Most of this space, however, is constructively unusable: it is wedged between bed and wall, table and toilet. "A prisoner who is 5 feet 5 inches tall, standing in the center of his cell (facing the entrance) can extend his arms, and with no effort, touch both walls over the bed and desk" (National Institute of Justice, 1980, p. 59). Fewer than half of all state facilities meet the sixty square feet standard; 13 percent provide less than forty-five square feet per prisoner.

The Courts Step In. Crowding, poor facilities, unhealthful conditions, insufficient medical care, and nonexistent training and counseling have led prisoners to file a series of suits against state prison authorities. By far the majority of these suits are rejected by the courts. Over the past ten years or so, however, the courts have become more and more involved in overseeing prison conditions and administration.

When the population in Florida's state prisons rose from 7,000 to 16,000 between 1965 and 1975, for example, officials were forced to jam cells and house some inmates in tents and converted warehouses. In May 1975, a federal judge ordered the state to reduce its prison population to normal levels within a year. "A free democratic society cannot cage inmates like animals or stack them like chattels in a warehouse and expect them to emerge as decent, law-abiding, contributing members of the community," he ruled (Congressional Quarterly, 1978, p. 73).

By March of 1982, thirty-one states and the District of Columbia were under court orders or consent decrees requiring that they reduce overcrowding and improve prison conditions (Krajik and Gettinger, 1982, p. 19). In some cases, judicial orders have forced states to free some prisoners before their full sentences have been served. Michigan's Prison Overcrowding Emergency Act of 1981 represents an effort to systematize the state's response to periodic overcrowding. By law, the governor of Michigan is required to declare an emergency whenever the state's prison population exceeds capacity for thirty consecutive days. Enough prisoners must then be released to reduce the population to 95 percent of capacity. By September of 1983, the state had released nearly 2,000 prisoners as much as a year and a half early. At least ten other states have enacted statutes similar to Michigan's.

One undesirable effect of court-ordered limits on overcrowding may be to simply force the overflow of prisoners back into the local jail system. After a court ordered Alabama officials to reduce overcrowding in the state prisons, the jail population in Jefferson County (which includes Birmingham) jumped, suddenly, by over 100 percent (National Institute of Justice, 1980, p. 39). There, conditions can be even worse. The best of the jails, according to one Mississippi official, "is worse than the worst conditions at the state pen" (National Institute of Justice, p. 72).

Schools for Crime?

Prisons may do more than isolate hard-core criminals from the law-abiding citizenry. Some critics of mandatory sentencing argue that increasing the probability of punishment will actually increase crime by turning small-time, onetime, and part-time criminals into hardened, professional, and vicious criminals. "Jails and prisons in the United States today are more often than not manufacturers of crime," writes former U.S. Attorney General Ramsey Clark. "Of those who come to jail undecided, capable either of criminal conduct or lives free of crime, most are turned to crime" (R. Clark, 1970, p. 213).

The environment in such prisons does little to wean the new inmate away from crime. To the contrary, it is argued, prison exposes the young inmate to skilled and committed criminals who can provide tips about how to disarm a burglar alarm, where to fence stolen merchandise, how to gain access to major drug dealers or find employment in organized crime. More than criminal know-how, prison may imbue in the new inmate a particular culture, a set of attitudes and beliefs that make it more likely that he or she will make the jump to crime as a way of life.

This process of socialization may be fueled, in part, by the omnipresent threat and frequent reality of violence in prison. According to the federal judge who, in 1976, found conditions in Alabama's four state prisons unconstitutional, "robbery, rape, extortion, theft, and assault are everyday occurrences among the general inmate population" (quoted in Silberman, 1978, p. 380). Most of that violence is inflicted by one prisoner upon another, but sometimes the violence is imposed by the guards and prison authorities.

The state of Arkansas provides an extreme case. After three human skeletons were discovered buried in the grounds of the Cummins Prison in 1968, a federal grand jury was convened that ultimately indicted fifteen former prison employees. "Torture devices included such bizarre items as the 'Tucker telephone' [named after the Tucker prison farm, where it allegedly was employed], components of which were an old telephone, wiring and a heavy duty battery. After an inmate was stripped, one wire was fastened to his penis, the other to a wrist or ankle, and electric shocks were sent through his body until he was unconscious" (R. Clark, 1970, p. 213).

The drama of violence is juxtaposed with long stretches of deadly routine and boredom. Charles Silberman writes of the "extreme sensory deprivation of prison life"; the absence of color, the undifferentiated din, the lack of contact with nature itself. Most prisons offer some programs to provide job skills for prisoners, or offer treatment for those with underlying physical, mental, or emotional problems. But in reality, these programs provide little in the way of diversion or meaningful relief. "Imprisonment as treatment?" asks Lois Forer, a state trial judge in Pennsylvania. "It would be laughable if it were not so tragic. Every week I receive letters from prisoners complaining that they are not getting any treatment. They spend their days in the cell and in the prison yard. They watch television. They work at meaningless tasks for a few cents an hour"

(Forer, 1980, p. 86). Boredom and routine may not be too harsh a punishment for those who have been convicted of crime, but neither are they conditions likely to prepare the inmate for reentry into society.

Rehabilitation: Are We Kidding Ourselves?

The Rehabilitation Ideal. In order to understand our current arrangements for dealing with those convicted of crimes, it is important to keep in mind that prisons evolved, in this country, hand in hand with the rehabilitation idea. Prisons emerged in the late 1700s as an alternative to the brutality of corporal punishment and capital punishment. Their origin is credited to Pennsylvania Quakers, who believed that institutionalization could provide a suitable environment for repentance and rehabilitation (Morris, 1974, pp. 4–5; Congressional Quarterly, 1978, pp. 74–6). Indeed, the word *penitentiary* is derived from the word *penitent.*

Isolation, in this context, was conceived as a means of encouraging self-reflection, not simply as a method for keeping criminals away from potential victims. Regimentation was intended to inculcate personal order and discipline, not simply to keep the prisoners "in line." And it was out of a commitment to the notion of rehabilitation, rather than out of laxity or overconcern with prisoners' rights, that the elements of sentencing discretion that are today under attack originally evolved.

Indeterminate Sentencing. The goal of rehabilitation gave rise to the practice of indeterminate sentencing. Under indeterminate sentencing, prisoners are told the maximum amount of time they will be required to stay in prison, but the actual time they serve will depend upon authorities' estimates of the speed and extent of their rehabilitation. Prisoners who reform quickly may be released quickly; those who show few signs of personal reform will be forced to serve out their entire term.

Indeterminate sentencing greatly increases the discretion left to judges, parole boards, and prison officials. It contradicts, in logic and in practice, the current trend toward mandatory sentencing. According to some advocates of rehabilitation, however, indeterminate sentencing is the only policy that makes sense. Judges cannot predict, at the time of trial, which convicted individuals will become rehabilitated. Unless there is a chance for early release, they reason, there is little incentive for the prisoner to actively engage in therapy or training programs.

Can Prisons Rehabilitate? As those who favor mandatory sentencing indicate, however, evidence that prison programs *can* rehabilitate is very slim. Robert Martinson, after reviewing the results of 231 rehabilitation programs, concluded that: "With few and isolated exceptions, the rehabilitative efforts that have been reported so far have no appreciable effect on recidivism" (Martinson, 1974, pp. 22–54).

The point is not that convicted criminals are incapable of turning over a new leaf; many do. Rather, James Q. Wilson argues, the point is that law enforcement authorities do not know how to increase the likelihood that a given prisoner will do so. "In retrospect, little of this should have been surprising," he suggests, since "[i]t requires not merely optimistic but heroic assumptions about the nature of man to lead one to suppose that a person, finally sentenced after (in most cases) many brushes with the law, having devoted a good part of his youth and young adulthood to misbehavior of every sort, should, by either the solemnity of prison or the skillfulness of a counselor, come to see the error of his ways and to experience a transformation of character" (Wilson, 1975, p. 170).

We May Have No Choice But to Try. Still, the idea that prisons can and should rehabilitate dies hard. For some, rehabilitation is a moral commitment; no other goal, they argue, is consistent with a law enforcement system that professes to be just and humane. To others, the commitment is more pragmatically based; unless we can find a way to solve the problem of rehabilitation, they worry, we must accept the fate of living side by side with a growing core of criminals made tougher, more violent, and more desperate by their prison experience. Both these groups admit that rehabilitation is not easily brought about, but they reject the notion that it is an impossible dream.

There are, indeed, some apparent successes to which advocates of rehabilitation can point. The Vienna Correctional Center, in southern Illinois, is one example. That facility holds serious offenders in a low-security environment, with low levels of violence, few escape efforts, high staff morale, and good relations with the surrounding community (Silberman, 1978, pp. 417–23). There are other examples, but they are not plentiful. Nor is it clear that the techniques that seem to work at those institutions can be repeated elsewhere with the same success.

"Understandable disenchantment with the kind of rehabilitation now being offered," however, "does not necessitate abandonment of the goal of rehabilitation," Forer writes (Forer, 1980, p. 94). She argues that rehabilitation efforts should teach criminals to read and write and provide them with truly marketable skills. In this regard, some analysts have suggested that Martinson's pessimistic conclusion may be attributable to the fact that all of the programs he reviewed were conducted before 1967, prior to recent reform efforts that aim to make such programs more relevant and effective. One study found that prisoners who are provided with solid job training have a recidivism rate four to six times lower than those without such training (Rodgers, Jr., 1978, p. 214).

Deinstitutionalization and Alternative Sentencing

The idea that we can rehabilitate criminals is, some analysts argue, one of our older and more cherished—but less firmly based—myths. Prisons are necessarily rigid, authoritarian, and isolationist in nature. Reforms may make prisons more decent, sanitary, and humane, but they cannot turn prisons into what they are not; and they are not institutions well suited for instilling feelings of self-worth and personal responsibility, nor are they capable of replicating an environment analogous, in any important respects, to that in which the released prisoner must learn to reside. Rehabilitation may be possible, some argue, but it will depend upon finding alternatives to incarceration behind prison walls.

The search for alternatives to imprisonment has both a theoretical and a practical base. Theoretical considerations lead some to conclude that the best hope for reintegrating the criminal into society lies in the development of less restrictive environments that provide an opportunity for the gradual resumption of responsibility and productiveness. Court rulings that prisons *must* reduce overpopulation lend the weight of practicality to such notions. Unless thoughtful alternatives are available, hurried, ad hoc, and potentially dangerous short-term prison population reduction strategies are likely to be the result.

Probation and Parole. Probation and parole have provided the traditional means for limiting reliance on prisons. Judges, unwilling to impose a prison sentence on a convicted criminal, may order a probationary period instead; during this period, the individual is usually under some form of supervision, and failure to comply with the provisions set by the court can lead to being sent to prison.

Whereas probation comes instead of a prison sentence, parole is a mechanism for shortening a prison sentence. Parole boards, part of the executive rather than the judicial branch, are empowered to release prisoners prior to their serving their maximum sentenced time. In making such decisions, parole boards consider evidence regarding the likelihood that the individual has become rehabilitated. Parole, like probation, is conditional and may be revoked even for minor violations of the terms for release. There were, at the beginning of 1982, approximately 1.25 million persons on probation and 250,000 on parole in the United States (Glaser, 1983).

Highly visible cases in which persons released on probation or parole have been rearrested for vicious crimes have served to sharpen the public's mistrust of these procedures. The popularity of mandatory sentencing reforms is attributable as much to opposition to probation and parole as to resentment of plea bargaining. Nonetheless, follow-up studies, in which recidivism rates of those who receive probation or parole are compared to those of criminals who do not, suggest that these alternatives may contribute to rehabilitation—especially when applied to offenders not yet hardened by a long-term commitment to crime (Glaser, 1983).

Halfway Houses and Work Release. These programs are alternatives to probation and parole that offer an advantage of providing greater degrees of control and supervision. By releasing prisoners to live in a small, tightly run community-based facility, or by allowing prisoners to leave the prison during the day to engage in jobs on the outside, these programs seek to soften the transition between the rigid and authoritarian environment of the prison and the freer and more flexible environment in which most of us live.

Both halfway houses and work-release programs have produced some exciting success stories. Ramsey Clark relates, for example, the story of one young participant in a work-release program authorized by Congress in 1965; he commuted, by bus, to a job in a Texas state college thirty miles from the prison and earned straight As in the three courses that he took at the same time (R. Clark, 1970, p. 229). But such programs are often vigorously resisted by local residents, who fear that they will be exposed to a greater risk of crime. In a few instances, those fears have been borne out; supervision in one work-release program in Maryland was lax enough to allow several participants to use their time away from prison to engage in additional crimes. Although such experiences have led some to abandon their commitment to deinstitutionalization, others feel that tighter monitoring of participants is sufficient to eliminate the risks involved. Some even go so far as to recommend electronic monitoring: residents in halfway houses and participants in work-release programs would wear radio microtransmitters on nonremovable wristbands, allowing authorities to verify the pattern of their movement.

Alternative Sentencing. Some judges have imposed requirements for community service as an alternative to traditional sentencing options. A young mother from Virginia, convicted of shoplifting, was sentenced to spend fifty hours knitting sweaters for a pregnancy counseling agency. A college student, arrested for streaking at a bachelor party, was sentenced to forty-eight hours picking up trash from streets in Montgomery County, Maryland; another student, caught shoplifting, had to spend twenty-four hours doing fund-raising for the March of Dimes (Engel, 1983).

Such sentences can be imaginative and make a symbolic statement. One Illinois judge, for example, ordered a convicted pornographer to donate an expensive collection of books to the prison library. Sometimes, the service may be structured so as to reinforce a lesson that the court wishes to deliver to the convicted individual. A Baltimore youth who was found to have been drunk when he crashed his truck, killing ten teenagers, was sentenced to 3,600 hours of community service in the emergency room of a local hospital.

Community service sentences are most often utilized in cases involving first-time violators of white-collar crimes. Although this makes sense—these criminals are less likely to engage in other crimes, especially violent crimes—it introduces an element of unfairness that is troubling to some. White-collar criminals are more likely than street criminals to be white members of the middle or upper class. Why should a doctor convicted of engaging in thousands of dollars of Medicaid fraud or a stock manipulator who takes advantage of inside information to make an illegal "killing" be allowed personal freedom and meaningful activity while fulfilling the terms of their punishment, when poorer defendants—often convicted of crimes involving much less money and many fewer victims—are given no alternative but a prison cell?

Victim Compensation. Trial Judge Lois Forer recommends, instead, that creative sentencing be linked to the goal of victim compensation. White-collar criminals should be forced to pay fines equal to two or three times their illegal gains. These fines would be entered in a pool from which the courts, or other authorities, would be able to draw to provide help and assistance to the victims of crime. Poorer criminals, and even those convicted of violent street crimes, could be ordered to pay a set proportion of their earnings to their victim during their period of probation or after they are released from prison.

Forer's story about one of the cases she presided over shows how victim compensation might work, even in the case of violent crimes. Alfie shot his ex-girlfriend's new boyfriend in the face, blinding him for life. The prosecutor recommended ten to twenty years in prison; the serious nature of the crime demanded no less. Alfie's lawyer called for probation; he stressed that Alfie had no criminal record, that the gun had gone off unexpectedly, that putting Alfie in prison would not do anyone any good. "Both arguments were valid. Probation, which returns the defendant to society without punishment, would corrode the credibility of the law. Imprisonment for a long term would destroy the defendant and be costly to the taxpayers. Neither probation nor imprisonment would help the victim." Forer placed Alfie on probation for nineteen years, conditioning it on the requirement that he pay his victim twenty-five dollars per week. Although it was clear that this small sum would not fully compensate the victim, it was all that the defendant was likely to be able to afford (Forer, 1980, pp. 11–12). Forer favors such sentencing whenever possible, not only as a means of providing material and symbolic satisfaction to the victim—the "forgotten participant" in the criminal justice system—but as a step toward teaching the criminal to take responsibility for the outcomes of his or her actions, a critical lesson, she feels, if rehabilitation is to occur.

Alternative sentencing inevitably leads to granting even greater discretion to the judge. It asks that the judge make the penalty fit not only the crime but the criminal and the victim as well. Some judges will use this discretion less wisely than others. But, as Forer points out, poor judges *can* be held accountable for their actions. She recommends a greater use of appellate courts to review sentences, as well as the questions of guilt or innocence with which they currently occupy themselves. She and others are not yet willing to give up on the notion that the law enforcement system can do more to promote lawfulness than simply serve as an isolation ward. But, as was the case with police, it would seem that the road to more effective courts and prisons lies not with "more" but with "different."

SUMMARY AND CONCLUSIONS

Many a war has been declared against crime. Few and far between are the victories. In spite of a few temporary dips and valleys, crime, as we saw in Chapter 8, has continued to rise. It has continued to rise in spite of a wide array of law enforcement efforts and innovations at the local level. Just about every ten years, local reformers have fastened on a new theory of crime fighting and fought, with some success, to reshape local law enforcement institutions accordingly.

The professionalization of police departments during the early 1900s; the increase in sophisticated technologies of criminal investigation during the 1960s; the growing emphasis on community relations in the early 1970s; and ongoing experiments with foot patrol, "stop and frisk" policies, undercover operations, citizen crime watches, and mandatory sentencing in the courts have each, in turn, been hailed as a new pathway to victory. Yet each has seen early and sporadic successes overwhelmed by the force of crime trends that are seemingly impervious to local policy interventions.

Crime has continued to rise, too, in spite of the decision of the federal government, during the 1960s, to lend its considerable financial weight to the anticrime battle. Crime fighting has always been considered a local responsibility in this country, but in the face of racial tension and urban disorder, politicians at the national level were drawn into the act. The Law Enforcement Assistance Administration (LEAA) was established by Congress in 1968 to funnel grants to state and local governments so that they could bolster their law enforcement efforts.

LEAA enabled some state and local governments to improve training for police and corrections officers, to computerize and otherwise streamline court activities, and to purchase new and exotic crime-fighting equipment. All in all, LEAA allocated over $5 billion to states and local governments between 1968 and 1976. During that same period, the national rate of index crimes increased by over 50 percent. LEAA was abolished in 1982.

In the face of this history, policy analysts of all ideological stripes are driven toward a fatalistic attitude about crime. Both liberals and neoconservatives believe it is possible to do something about crime, yet each believes that political obstacles make it unlikely that public officials will be able to take the necessary steps. For liberals, the answer lies in broad economic and social reforms that will open legitimate opportunities for minorities and the poor. Coupled with that should be reforms of the criminal justice system to enable it to better pursue the rehabilitation goal. Both imply high costs and, possibly, a strong leadership role for the national government. Neither seems imminent in the face of strong pressures to shrink the public sector and reverse the impulse to centralize. For neoconservatives, the hope lies in deterrence and incapacitation. Although the political winds blow favorably in the direction of tougher courts and stricter penalties, this generally conservative sentiment runs afoul of another conservative goal that is at least as deeply held: the strong aversion to public spending and tax increases. As long as many federal and state courts continue to insist that convicted criminals do not forfeit their legal rights to a safe environment, failure to provide revenues to expand and improve the prison system may mean that efforts to funnel more criminals into prison will be counterbalanced by court rulings that force prison officials to let others go. Radicals, for their part, remain skeptical of any efforts to reduce crime. Unless such efforts are preceded by fundamental changes in the nature of the economic and political system, they will serve only to further weaken and discriminate against the poor.

This fatalism has produced a series of policy proposals that are characterized by an acceptance of the inevitability of crime. These policies are marked by a general acceptance of criminality and a readiness to scale down expectations: rather than eliminate crime, let us protect ourselves from unnecessary victimization; rather than striving for a world in which we feel secure, let us allow our insecurities to make ourselves less vulnerable; rather than save all citizens from victimization, let us compensate those who are victimized so that their trauma and loss are minimized.

One such proposal involves the call for greater emphasis on *target hardening*. Target hardening refers primarily to individuals' efforts to make it more difficult for criminals to break into their homes. The easiest and most frequently utilized method of target hardening involves locking one's doors. Other target-hardening strategies include purchasing high-quality locks, putting bars on windows, installing alarm systems, keeping a weapon, leaving lights on when leaving the house at night, stopping newspaper and mail delivery when on vacation, and obtaining a watchdog. A related strategy—Operation I.D.—has proven to be very popular with police and citizens in a number of communities. Under this program, citizens are encouraged to engrave their valuables with their names or identifying codes. Participants are given decals to post on their windows and doors. Operation I.D. decals, it is hoped, deter criminals by alerting them that the goods within the home will be easily identifiable—making it more difficult for them to sell the stolen merchandise and making it easier for police and the courts to link those goods to a specific crime.

Another example involves training persons in *avoidance* techniques. Herbert Jacob argues that, just as there are people who are career criminals, there may be others who are "career victims." These persons, who "lack street savvy" and who fail to protect their households, account for a disproportionate number of victimizations. By training these people to make them less vulnerable, Jacob reasons that some opportunistic crimes may be prevented (Jacob, 1984, p. 169).

Many current proposals for victim compensation also share this fatalistic orientation. As discussed by liberal judges such as Forer, victim compensation could be oriented around the goal of rehabilitating the criminal, by allowing a means of atonement and by replacing institutionalization with requirements to work. But most proposals are focused on the victim, not the offender. They propose that the public fund some form of insurance that would help victims replace stolen property and meet medical costs. Such compensation schemes are intended to reduce the psychological and economic burdens of crime and lessen the fear in which many Americans live. They are not intended to reduce crime, and they will not do so.

Somewhat ironically, there is a glimmer of hope to be found even among those who have concluded that the forces generating crime are outside the reach of governmental control. As noted in the previous chapter, most street crimes are committed by the young. Just as the movement of the postwar baby boom generation into their crime-prone teens coincided with the upsurge in crime during the 1960s, the anticipated decline in the proportion of the population that is young may signal that a "natural" decrease in crime is around the corner.

Unless it is accompanied by changes in social and criminal justice policies, it would be naive to expect such a demographic shift to have more than an incremental impact upon crime. Yet even an incremental reduction in crime rates, if it lasted over a number of years, could be significant. This is true, of course, in the sense that every crime averted represents an improvement in the quality of our lives. But the greater impact might be indirect. Proposals for meaningful and comprehensive reforms of the criminal justice system currently are stymied by the severe overload that the system confronts. Demographic changes might provide just the kind of "breathing space" that state and local officials need if they are to respond in anything other than the patchwork, crisis-oriented fashion that absorbs all their energies today. If this comes about, theoretical issues involving the relative importance of rehabilitation, deterrence, incapacitation, and punishment—issues that have been overshadowed by immediate financial and administrative concerns—are likely to rise to the surface in the form of ideological and political conflict.

SUGGESTED READINGS

Brown, Michael K. *Working the Street.* New York: Russell Sage, 1981.

Jacob, Herbert. *The Frustration of Policy: Responses to Crime by American Cities.* Boston: Little, Brown, 1984.

Forer, Lois G. *Criminals and Victims: A Trial Court Judge Reflects on Crime and Punishment.* New York: W.W. Norton, 1980.

Levin, Martin A. *Urban Politics and the Criminal Courts.* Chicago: University of Chicago Press, 1977.

Morris, Norval. *The Future of Imprisonment.* Chicago: University of Chicago Press, 1974.

Skogan, Wesley G., and Michael G. Maxfield. *Coping With Crime.* Beverly Hills, California: Sage, 1981.

Wilson, James Q. *Thinking About Crime.* N.Y.: Basic Books, 1984.

Wilson, James Q., ed. *Crime and Public Policy.* San Francisco: ICS Press, 1983.

10

Schooling Society

> "Now, what I want is Facts. Teach these boys and girls nothing but Facts. Facts alone are wanted in life. Plant nothing else, and root out everything else."
>
> The speaker, and the schoolmaster, and the third grown person present, all backed a little, and swept with their eyes the inclined plane of little vessels then and there arranged in order, ready to have imperial gallons of facts poured into them until they were full to the brim.
>
> —Charles Dickens, *Hard Times*

Dickens's Thomas Gradgrind is a "man of realities," a "man of facts and calculations." To him and others like him, the task of schools seems straightforward and unambiguous. Schools are the tool through which society passes its accumulated knowledge on to its young. Schools deal in the currency of "facts": solid little bits and pieces of universally recognized and uncontestable truth.

If this were the case, the task of schools would be much simpler than in fact it is. The curriculum—what is taught—could be the same in all schools throughout the nation. We would know, in the first week of October, that first-graders everywhere were learning to spell the words *run, dog,* and *play.* Ninth-graders, we could be confident, had memorized the names of presidents and soon would be introduced to the rudiments of algebra. Standardized tests could easily be administered yearly to determine which students had absorbed their quota of facts; only those who had would be passed on to the next grade. Local school boards would be spared the controversies over which subjects need be addressed, which books assigned.

Schools, however, are expected to do much more than shower their students with "imperial gallons of facts." They are expected to instruct students in values and proper behavior and to provide them with job-relevant skills. They are expected to teach children to obey authority at the same time they teach them to think for themselves. We expect our schools to help our children develop healthy bodies as well as healthy minds, to enforce order and stimulate creativity, to challenge the bright and to shepherd the dull.

These great and many expectations traditionally have helped to build a broad base of popular support for our public school system. Citizens have been willing to pay higher taxes in order to ensure that their community's school system match or surpass those in neighboring jurisdictions. Today, Americans spend over $115 billion each year simply to support their public elementary and secondary schools.

In recent years, however, public enthusiasm for the schools has begun to show signs of fading. The great expectations that once buoyed support now threaten to weigh the schools down with disillusionment and feelings of betrayal. This change in the popular attitude toward schools alters the political climate in which education decision-making occurs. We begin this chapter with an overview of some of the factors that may account for this public disenchantment. Although this disenchantment indicates that many Americans feel something is wrong with what schools currently are doing, it does not in itself provide a clear analysis of the problem, nor does it offer a consistent message about what can and should be done. A consideration of the perspective offered by conservative, liberal, radical, and neoconservative theorists can help in this regard. The chapter concludes with a consideration of two issues of broad importance: the relative advantages of public versus private education and the question of whether schools are capable of educating children at all.

THE ROOTS OF PUBLIC DISENCHANTMENT

Each year, the Gallup Poll asks a sample of Americans to give a letter grade to the public schools in their community. In 1975, 13 percent of those surveyed gave their schools a grade of A. By 1983, the proportion handing out the highest grade (6 percent) had been cut by more than half. During the same period, the proportion grading their community's school as C or lower increased from 44 percent to 52 percent (Gallup, 1983, p. 35).

This drop in confidence in the schools, which began even earlier than 1975, has a direct effect on the development of school policy at the state and local levels. Elected officials, who could once count on broad public support for proposals to expand educational expenditures, sense that cutting the cost of education is the road to political popularity these days. Resistance to educational spending reached a dramatic high point in the mid-1970s, when citizens, in public referenda, refused to approve additional school funding in several jurisdictions in spite of officials' insistence that the money was absolutely essential. Public schools in Toledo, Ohio, had to close down entirely when money ran out in 1976; they stayed closed from Thanksgiving until January, when the next year's budget could be drawn upon. In 1962, voters had approved 72.4 percent of the bond referenda for increased school spending; by 1975, this had declined to 46 percent.

The "Empty Nest" Syndrome

Broad demographic changes may account for some of the decline in popular support for the schools. The number of families with school-age children living at home is declining. This is partly due to a general aging of the U.S. population. Between 1950 and 1980, the percent of the population that was fifty-five years old and over increased from 16.9 to 20.9 percent (U.S. Bureau of the Census, 1981, p. 27). It is partly due to the growing tendency of the population to delay marriage and childbearing. In 1960, for example, only 28.4 percent of the women between the ages of twenty and twenty-four had never been married; by 1980, this figure had increased to 50.2 percent. Once married, moreover, there is a growing likelihood that families will not have children. In 1965, 14.2 percent of all married women aged fifteen to forty-four were childless; this figure had risen to 19.0 percent by 1979.

For those with no children in school, the personal payoff for school expenditures is limited. Economic self-interest may compel them to oppose school spending, and a desire for psychological consistency may lead them to rationalize this position with complaints about the inadequacy of schools. In a 1983 Gallup survey, 48 percent of parents of children attending public schools said they would vote to raise taxes if the local public schools needed more money. Only 36 percent of adults with no children in school said they would do the same. The middle-aged and elderly—those who are unlikely to have children in school now or in the future—are the most opposed to increased spending. Sixty-two percent of respondents over fifty years of age opposed raising taxes to raise additional school revenue, compared to forty-four percent of those eighteen to twenty-nine and 48 percent of those thirty to forty-nine (Gallup, 1983, p. 37).

Skepticism That Schools Equalize

If schools were helping to narrow differences among children—as proponents of many of the War on Poverty programs believed that they could—racial and class differences in standardized tests might be expected to fade the longer children remain in school. Yet some evidence suggests that quite the opposite occurs. Poorer and minority children, in many school districts, seem to fall further behind their counterparts as they move through the elementary and secondary school grades. In addition, although the children of minorities and the poor are tending to stay in school much longer than their parents, there is not much evidence that this increased schooling is translated into any greater equality in the distribution of our nation's wealth. William Ryan notes that:

> [T]he *amount* of schooling has increased tremendously and the range from top to bottom has decreased dramatically. Nevertheless, although the *absolute* standard of living has improved greatly for almost everyone, *relative* shares of wealth and income have changed only marginally in the direction of greater equality. . . . The first thing we have to get into our heads, then, is that, despite all the mythology and all the rhetoric, education does *not* provide leverage either to greater and broader social mobility or to absolute equality (Ryan, 1981, p. 122).

Skepticism That Schools Educate

Support for schools also is undermined by a growing concern that schools are failing to provide their graduates with the basic skills that they so badly need. This impression is based, in large part, on hearsay and anecdote. Readers of the *Washington Post* were distressed, a few years ago, to read about "Roger," who, in spite of twelve years in the city's schools and an amibition to be a lawyer, was unable to read even the destination signs on the buses he rode every day (Williams, 1978, p. 1). Employers complain about high-school graduates who are unable to read and correctly fill out job applications. But there also are more tangible indicators of declining performance. The average score on the Scholastic Aptitude Test (SAT), which is taken by about one-third of all high-school graduates, dropped from 476 to 426 between 1952 and 1982.

Many social scientists and professional educators had their confidence in schools weakened by the results of a major study performed in the late 1960s. Sociologist James Coleman conducted the study, which included over 570,000 students, 68,000 teachers, and 4,000 principals. The resulting *Equality of Educational Opportunity Report* (also known as the Coleman Report) seemed to discredit the notion that increases in school expenditures, improvements in school facilities, or upgrading of the teachers' qualifications had any significant impact on students' learning, as measured by standardized tests.

Threat to Traditional Values

Throughout most of American history, schools have been considered to be a reinforcer of traditional values. Parents count on schools to impress upon their children lessons such as respect for one's elders, the value of hard work and self-discipline, the sanctity of the property of others, and the importance of learning to live within the boundaries of a set of well-defined rules.

Over the past two decades, some parents have come to see the schools in a different light. They fear that rather than reinforcing traditional values, schools may have become a place in which the values taught in the family and church are questioned, challenged, and ultimately undermined. These parents complain that their children are exposed, in school, to other students whose dress, speech, and behavior are affronts to their own notions of what is acceptable. School is a place of hostile cultures and threatening ideas. Parents, who may have lived their lives in homogeneous and insulated communities, are disturbed to find that, in school, children are led to mingle with those whose religion and race are different from their own. School is a place where children of the religious are told they may not engage in formal prayer. It is a place where children are exposed to sex education, where Darwin's theory about the origin of man is given greater weight than that contained in the Bible. Teachers, once thought of as an extension of the parents' moral authority, may come to be viewed as sources of sedition and seduction. Patriotic parents hear about the teacher who spent four years in Canada as a draft dodger. Morally conservative parents read about the teacher who has twice been divorced, the unmarried teacher who has become pregnant, the teacher who is an admitted homosexual.

Loss of Local Control

Related to the sense that schools have become seedbeds of alien values is the belief, shared by many Americans, that educational policy is no longer being set by the local community. When it comes to the broad issues of privatization and decentralization, education provides an interesting case. More than almost any function other than waging war, education of its citizens has long been regarded in this country as a legitimate and necessary undertaking of the public sector. Although Americans have been quick to entrust government with the task of educating their children, however, they have been slow to pass that trust on to officials at the national level. Traditions of localism run strong in other policy areas, such as law enforcement and land-use controls. But the tradition of local control is felt most deeply and expressed most emphatically where decisions about schools are concerned.

The Tradition of Localism. The national government showed its allegiance to the goal of education with the Land Ordinance of 1785, which directed that one section of land in each township of the northwest territories should be set aside for the support of education. In the middle to late 1800s, the federal Morrill Acts provided land and money to the states to help them operate colleges for training in agriculture and the mechanical arts. Throughout our history, however, *the primary responsi-*

bility for expanding educational opportunities has rested with the localities and the states.

Massachussets was the trendsetter. The first public high school in the country—the English Classical School—was established in Boston, and in 1827, the state passed a law that called for every locality with 500 or more families to set up a school to teach American history, surveying geometry, bookkeeping, and the basic reading and writing skills (Boyer, 1983, pp. 44–5). "Towns of four thousand also were to offer courses in general history, rhetoric, logic, Latin, and Greek." Spearheading Massachussetts's efforts was Horace Mann, secretary of the state's Board of Education and the leading educational reformer of the nineteenth century. Pennsylvania, in 1834, was the first state to establish a system of free elementary education. By 1875, it had been joined by all the other states.

The lack of centralization of school decision-making allows each community to shape its schools according to the values it considers to be critical. Although constitutional authority for education belongs to the state, most of the power to operate the schools on a day-to-day basis has been delegated to the local school district. There are about 16,000 such districts, over four-fifths of them run by an elected school board. Vesting power in local boards has allowed some school districts to ban books like *Catcher in the Rye,* which some parents consider to be immoral, and Eldridge Cleaver's *Soul on Ice,* which some consider violent and politically subversive. It also makes it possible for some districts in politically more liberal communities to prohibit teachers from requiring books that parents consider to be racist (Mark Twain's *Huckleberry Finn,* for example) in language or tone. But localism can expand the curriculum as well as restrict it. Communities that were quick to recognize the potential importance of the computer, for example, were free to restructure their requirements to ensure that all students were exposed to simple programming, and some did so many years before the current fad (as we will see in Chapter 11).

In spite of the federal government's early involvement through the Land Ordinance, the tradition of localism is reflected clearly in the distribution of the financial responsibility for paying for schools. In the 1919–1920 school year, local governments raised 83.2 percent of the revenues for public elementary and secondary education. States kicked in another 16.5 percent, leaving less than .5 percent to the national government.

In recent years, the states have taken on a larger role, but responsibility for public education remains highly decentralized. About half of all governmental spending on public elementary and secondary schools is provided by the states. Another 42 percent of the total is provided by local governments. In 1983, only 7.4 percent of the money came directly from the federal government.

The tradition of localism remains very strong. Although perhaps overstated, the claims that "the 16,000 school districts have about 16,000 different approaches to education" is not all that far from the mark (Berkley and Fox, 1978, p. 257). Several trends, however, have combined to make educational decision-making seem more distant to the average citizen. These trends may contribute to disenchantment by turning what had been perceived as an extension of the community into something more alien and unresponsive.

Consolidation of School Districts. There has been a dramatic increase in the size of America's school districts. In 1932, there were about 127,500 school districts in the country. By 1977, there were fewer than 15,200. The movement toward combining, or consolidating, school districts was begun as part of an effort to obtain greater efficiency and to make it possible for each district to provide a fuller range of programs and a richer curriculum (Boyer, 1983, p. 233). The result, in some people's minds, has been a more impersonal and highly centralized decision-making process. The voice of the average parent is less likely to be heard when he or she is competing for attention with hundreds, or even thousands, of others.

Professionalization of Decision-making. Some of the power and control that parents feel they have lost has gravitated to the teachers and administrators who run the schools on a daily basis. This has resulted, in part, from changes that were made earlier in the century in an effort to insulate school policy from the influence of political machines.

At the turn of the century, school policies and machine politics, in many jurisdictions, were one and the same. Strong political parties dominated school board elections. Positions on the board, and positions as school administrators and teachers, were patronage plums, to be distributed to the politically loyal rather than the professionally qualified.

The Progressive Reform movement that emerged to challenge the machines was particularly successful in changing the structure by which education policy was set. School boards were made smaller, party labels were prohibited on school board ballots, and board members were made to run on a citywide, rather than ward by ward, basis. These changes were made in the name of removing education from some of the seamier political pressures. The effect, in many cases, was to make it more difficult for the average citizen to be elected to the school board. At the same time, professional educators used antimachine sentiment to increase their own autonomy. "It was argued that elected school board members represented political concerns whereas school people represented the children or students." (Spring, 1982, p. 91). The functions of boards were increasingly limited to setting broad policy goals. Most of the decisions about how those goals were to be translated into the day-to-day operation of the schools were defined as "administrative matters," to be handled by the professional staff.

The power of school professionals also grew, as teachers became increasingly organized in powerful unions that could present their demands and fight for them. During the 1960s, teachers in large-city school systems increasingly turned to unions and work stoppages as a means of pursuing their goals. The American Federation of Teachers (AFT) emerged as a more militant alternative to the NEA, prodding the NEA into a more active orientation at the same time. Teachers' demands, moreover, extended beyond the realm of salary and benefits. Contracts stipulating factors such as maximum class size, conditions under which teachers could be transferred, and disciplinary procedures for disruptive students inserted the unions into policy decisions previously considered the exclusive realm of the school board or administrators.

Involvement of the Courts. The decline of local control over education is usually mapped in fiscal terms. As already noted, local governments no longer dominate the picture as far as school finance is concerned. If power lies with control of the purse strings, the states are increasingly displacing localities as the arena in which education policy is shaped.

As important as this shift in fiscal responsibility, however, is the growing readiness of state and federal courts to inject themselves into controversies regarding how schools ought to be run. Most obvious has been the busing controversy, which we will discuss at greater length in Chapter 11. Federal Judge Arthur Garrity, faced with a resistant school board in Boston, went so far as to place the schools in the receivership of the courts, temporarily stripping the board of many of its important powers. During the 1960s and 1970s, courts and federal regulatory agencies offered rulings that limited the powers of local school authorities to set dress codes, forced local authorities to provide programs and services to the handicapped, and dictated that many school systems would have to spend a greater proportion of their recreational budgets on women's sports.

Localism as a Safety Valve. The varied and conflicting expectations that people hold for the schools have always been a potential source of tension and conflict. While policy-making was decentralized—while hundreds of thousands of local school districts were able to shape the schools to fit the values of their own communities—these tensions could remain latent. Decentralization, in this sense, was like a safety valve. As school districts became larger, and as state and federal officials, responding to broader constituencies, came to play a growing role, conflicting values and expectations could no longer be ignored. If schools are to perform the functions that some groups want them to, they will have to perform in ways that other groups find undesirable.

This suggests the possibility that the public disenchantment with schools detected in recent polls reflects long-standing disagreements that simply remained submerged in earlier years. Some of these disagreements are anchored in cultures and traditions that vary from place to place. Adding heat to the fire, however, are disagreements, anchored in political ideologies, about the nature of schools and the broad goals they can and should pursue.

EDUCATION FOR WHAT: IDEOLOGY AND THE GOALS OF SCHOOLING

Schools and Meritocracy: The Traditional Conservative View

Enlightenment for the Elite. In one sense, America's support for open education has been a means to substitute one kind of inequality for another. Americans generally have been quite tolerant of vast differences in wealth and social status, as long as they could believe that those inequalities reflected differences in productivity, intelligence, ambition, and skill. What Americans have resented is aristocracy—a system of class differentiation based on family and inherited position. In some other nations, which had a history that included feudalism and an inherited aristocracy, political conservatism included an intense resistance to open, public education, which was perceived as a threat to the traditional elites. In the United States, where the rising economic elite more often owed its wealth to success in business than to family ties, conservatives have shared, and sometimes championed, the goal of mandatory education for all children. Open, mass public education appealed to some as a tool for tearing down the privilege of aristocratic and replacing it with a system of differentiation based on intelligence and skill, a meritocracy.

The function of schools in a meritocracy is, first of all, to identify those children who have the aptitude and attitudes that will enable them to excel. These children are to be given intensive training in the fields that are considered important for those who are destined to fill social leadership roles. In many, and perhaps most, cases these children will turn out to be the children of parents who have already proven their ability through material or professional success. But meritocratic principles reject the assumption that only the children of the elite have talent. A key role for schools in maintaining a meritocracy is to identify those among the lower classes who have the native ability to rise above their peers. Jefferson referred to this goal as "raking a few geniuses from the rubbish" (Bowles and Gintis, 1976, p. 29).

Job Skills and Discipline for the Masses. The conservative philosophy accepts as natural that people are unequal in the skills and abilities with which they are born. For those with lesser abilities, education in a meritocracy takes on the role of preparing the student for a vocational career.

The "new belief that public schools could, and indeed should, prepare youth for work" had a major influence on the development of school policies around the turn of the century (Edson, 1982, p. 145). This was a period of rapid industrialization in the United States, and the new factories and assembly-line techniques demanded a new kind of work force, with different skills than were needed in the previous agricultural society.

Local governments responded by rapidly increasing the number of public high schools and by putting greater emphasis on manual training. "By multiplying manual training schools," an education reformer of that period argued, "we solve the problem of training all the mechanics our country needs" (Boyer, 1983, p. 48). Between 1870 and 1900, the number of public high schools in the nation increased by about 1,100 percent. The traditional curriculum, which included heavy doses of rhetoric, logic, Latin, and Greek, was denounced, by some, for being irrelevant to the children of the masses, who now, for the first time, were beginning to continue in school beyond the elementary grades. "Our school system is gravely defective," President Theodore Roosevelt told Congress in 1907, "insofar as it puts a premium upon mere literacy training and tends therefore to train the boy away from the farm and the workshop. Nothing more is needed than the best type of industrial school . . ." (Edson, 1982, p. 158).

This emphasis on schooling as a mechanism for training the nation's work force continues to influence education policy today. Complaints by local business owners about the poor quality of public school graduates frequently provide the first spark to efforts at school reform. Perhaps the most visible manifestation of this influence is seen in the explosive growth of community colleges and junior colleges, many of which specialize in providing technical skills. In 1960, there were 315 public two-year junior colleges enrolling about 390,000 students. By 1979, there were 926 such institutions, with over 4 million students (U.S. Bureau of the Census, 1981, p. 159).

Schools as the "Great Equalizer": The Liberal Ideal

Education and Upward Mobility. To many of the immigrants who came to this country around the turn of the century, America represented the land of opportunity. To some of them, schools were the key to upward mobility, the chance for their child to learn the language and gain the skills necessary to break out of the bonds of poverty.

Dreams can come true. And for some of the children of the lower and working classes, public education did, indeed, provide the ticket to personal advancement and material reward. Such Horatio Alger stories play a part in both conservative and liberal images of the role of education. But there is an important difference in the way that upward mobility is conceptualized. *The conservative, based on the principles of meritocracy, emphasizes equality of opportunity and the chance for exceptional individuals to advance to a higher socioeconomic class. Many liberals go further: they argue that schooling can bring about equality of results, significantly narrowing the gap that separates the rich from the poor.*

The belief that education plays a key role in bringing about a more equal society was elevated to new heights during the 1960s. The civil-rights movement and the War on Poverty brought greater political clout to individuals and groups committed to breaking down some of the walls separating the rich from the poor and black from white. This political pressure for equalization received support and legitimation from the federal courts, which identified schools as an area in which constitutional guarantees of equal treatment were particularly clear.

Education at this point came to be regarded as the "great equalizer." The notion was particularly popular among liberals, who retained confidence that, through aggressive and well-planned programs, the government could cure even the most serious of social ills. Reforms in schooling were to be the key. The basic argument was this: "if young people would stay in school, study hard, and develop skills, they would get better and better jobs, poverty would be eliminated, and the huge income gaps that are a major sign of inequality would grow narrower and narrower" (Ryan, 1981, p. 121).

Schools and Racial Equality. Although the idea of education as the great equalizer was not to reach its zenith until the 1960s, some would trace its launching to 1954. That is the year in which the U.S. Supreme Court issued its ground-breaking and earth-shattering rule in the case of *Brown* v. *The Board of Education of Topeka.*

At the time the Court issued its ruling, seventeen states and the District of Columbia required, by law, that public schools be segregated by race. In finding such segregation unconstitutional, the Court rejected the precedent set in the case of *Plessy* v. *Ferguson,* which an earlier Supreme Court had ruled on in 1896. The *Plessy* case had focused on a Louisiana law requiring all railroads to provide "equal but separate accommodations for the white and colored races." In finding that law constitutional, the Court had concluded that separate-but-equal was an acceptable standard: the Constitution protects the right of minorities to equal treatment under the law; it does not promise social equality or the right to commingle in public places.

Fifty-eight years later, the Supreme Court decisively rejected this argument. "Separate educational facilities are inherently unequal," Chief Justice Earl Warren wrote. To separate elementary and high-school students solely because of their race "generates a feeling of inferiority as to their status in the community that may affect their hearts and minds in a way unlikely ever to be undone."

The Court's position relied on a belief that schools are more than an arrangement for the inculcation of an agreed upon set of facts. Schools are the environment in which children do a good deal of their evolving into mature human beings. Most children spend more of their waking hours in schools than in any environment other than their own homes. Through their interactions with their teachers and other students, children come to develop a sense of their own selves—whether they are likable, whether they are funny, whether they are smart, and whether they are among those "most likely to succeed." Schools, too, play an especially central role in determining any individual's chances for personal fulfillment and success. For these reasons, the discovery of inequality in the educational system must be considered more serious, and more worthy of corrective action, than inequities that might be found in other social realms.

The Court put this recognition of the special place of schooling together with some evidence that poor self-image and feelings of racial inferiority were widespread among black children even at a very early age. Kenneth Clark, a black psychologist, had reported to the Court the results of studies he had made of a sample of black children from three to seven years of age. The children had been given dolls to play with. Some of the dolls had brown skin, some of the dolls were white and blonde. The black children, by a two to one margin, preferred to play with the white dolls. They were more likely to say that the black doll looked "bad," and the white doll was the one that looked "nice."

Segregated schools, the Court concluded, could be a powerful reinforcer of the message of racial inferiority. It would not do to take refuge in the notion that separate schools, if they were equal, need not carry the implication that one group was superior to another. Even three-year-olds were wise to the fact that society valued whites more than it did blacks. In that environment, separation inevitably would be interpreted as another signal that blacks were no good. This message would be particularly devastating when the separation resulted from an act of law. What could such a law mean, after all, except that the government itself had authoritatively acknowledged that blacks were inferior to whites?

The *Brown* decision indicated that the highest court in the nation had subscribed to the liberal tenet that education can play a special role in bringing about a more equal society. Formal segregation of schools was illegal. School systems throughout the South would have to be radically reorganized. Eventually, the shock waves from the *Brown* decision would spread to northern school districts as well.

Education and the Poverty Cycle. It was not until the early 1960s that Congress and the executive branches began to put the teeth of enforcement into the call for racial equality that the court had issued nearly ten years before. By then, schools also were being promoted as the logical point of attack for addressing another social problem. Education was a salve for many wounds. Education was to eliminate poverty, just as it was to heal divisions based on race.

The War on Poverty, we saw in Chapter 4, was not the massive, uniform, comprehensive, and consistent assault that its own rhetoric declared it to be. It consisted of a grab bag of programs, shaped by political trade-offs, agency turf battles, and local patterns of implementation as much as by any theoretically coherent strategy imposed from Washington, D.C. To acknowledge this, however, is not to say that theory and ideas played no significant role. Behind many of the proposals that were to grow into the War on Poverty programs was an evolving theory of the nature of poverty. This theory was shared by a core of academics and activist bureaucrats who came to Washington to serve in the Kennedy administration. It was a theory that drew heavily from elements of the culture-of-poverty perspective. Because it reasoned that the chains of culture grow heavier and more confining with age, it placed particular emphasis on the importance of education policies aimed at the young.

Poverty, these social reformers argued, is maintained by a vicious cycle. The children of the poor are robbed of the intellectual stimulation and stable emotional environment taken for granted by the middle- and upper-class child. Their first formal contact with the social institutions of the broader society does not come until they enter school at the age of five. By then, many of the poor children have already fallen behind their more fortunate peers in such areas as language development and social skills. School becomes a frustrating experience. Unable to meet teachers' expectations or compete with other students, the children of the poor experience school as an arena of failure. They avoid attending when able and quit as soon as they are allowed. Without the ability to read, write, or speak well, and without the certification of achievement that a school diploma provides, these kids have little or no chance to find a stable and well-paying job. Almost as surely as if it were carried on their genes, then, the poverty of the parents is passed on to their daughters and sons.

Although recognizing its tenacity, the reformers believed that the cycle could be broken. It would be necessary to reach the poor before they became so immersed in the culture of poverty that they were unable to shake off the defeatist attitude and bad habits that kept their parents, neighbors, and older relatives locked into the pattern of repeated failure. Logic dictated that schools would serve as a major weapon in this war, because schools had a chance to influence the poor child's development before he or she had fully matured.

Head Start and the Elementary and Secondary Education Act of 1965 (ESEA) are two of the programs that most clearly symbolized this particular theory about how the cycle of poverty could be breached. Head Start was designed to prepare disadvantaged children during the summer before they entered school. Besides providing certain "readiness" skills, which it was presumed most children of the middle and upper classes had already learned in their own homes, Head Start provided the preschool student with medical, dental, nutritional and social services and tried to involve the students' parents in the educational experience.

Title I of ESEA provided federal grants to the states, with the amount of the grant based on the number of children in low-income families. The money could be used for special programs intended to help the poor catch up to their peers, such as remedial math and reading programs, special guidance and counseling, or speech therapy. The funds also could be used to improve the educational facilities in schools serving the poor or to reduce class sizes. Although the amount of money available through Title I was far from sufficient to meet the national need, ESEA became an important resource for many school districts serving large numbers of the poor. It also marked a sharp break with the traditional pattern in which school funding was considered a role reserved to the localities and the states.

Preschool and elementary programs like Head Start, School Lunch, and many of the Title I activities focused on basic cognitive skills and reducing physical, nutritional, or emotional impediments to learning. Programs for secondary school students—like Upward Bound, which sought to identify underachieving low-income high-school students and prepare them for college work—sought to reduce dropout rates and encourage college attendance. Dropouts and potential dropouts were given programs designed to combine part-time jobs with educational and vocational training. Education Opportunity Grants, Guaranteed Student Loans, and Work Study would help lower- and middle income students pursue a college education they might not otherwise be able to afford (Levin, 1977, p. 147).

The education programs and training programs launched during this period shared the characteristic of seeking to use the education system to compensate the poor for the disadvantages in skills and basic competencies they had inherited. Equalization in the educational sphere would translate, seemingly automatically, into greater equality in income, occupation, and social status.

These were heady goals. They presumed that the poor would readily shed their alienation and mistrust once seated at nice desks in front of a teacher who was motivated and sincere. They presumed that job opportunities were plentiful once the poor were properly prepared. And they underestimated the political obstacles to any plans that would radically redistribute benefits and opportunities from advantaged to disadvantaged groups. It did not take long for it to become obvious that poverty and inequality would *not* vanish with a wave of the educational wand. Both radicals and neoconservatives believe that they can explain why.

Instrument of Social Control: The Radical View

To the radical analyst, the education system must be considered as a product of a political system that operates to preserve the advantages of the elite. Opening up the education system to a broader range of the public had less to do with the pursuit of equality and the aspirations of the poor, the radical argues, than with the realization, on the part of the upper classes, that schools can be an effective tool for protecting the status quo.

The major social function of education, according to more radical analysts like William Ryan, is "the nonviolent perpetuation of inequality" (Ryan, 1981, p. 122). Education fulfills this function, radical critics argue, through its power to shape the minds and expectations of the young. This power of socialization takes at least two forms. *Political socialization* molds children into passive citizens, unlikely to challenge the existing system or even to perceive its flaws. What might be referred to as *economic socialization* prepares the children of the middle and lower classes to expect and accept the low-paying and low-status jobs that are their destiny.

Creating a Passive Citizenry. The idea that schools play a legitimate role in producing good citizens has long been recognized. But what constitutes a "good citizen"? One might argue that a healthy and dynamic democracy depends upon citizens who are intellectually curious, creative, skeptical of conventional wisdom, resistant toward the exercise of brute domination, alert to ways that public and private institutions alter their lives, and driven to translate their ideas and beliefs into political activity. But some critics argue that this is exactly the type of person American schools are organized *not* to produce.

Schools work to shape political attitudes directly and indirectly. Curriculum, textbooks, and teachers provide students with their first formal exposure to concepts such as "democracy," "freedom," and "justice." What is taught may lead students into an unquestioned acceptance of the premise that our political and economic system is the ideal vehicle for pursuing these admirable ends. Students are taught, in many schools, to memorize a list of the flaws of communism, with no consideration of the aspects of socialist theory that continue to give it broad appeal to many peoples throughout the world. Lessons in the value of the free enterprise system are bolstered by readings and other teaching aids donated to the schools by business organizations. Radical analysts complain that these lessons carry the message—some subtly, some with a heavy hand—that an unregulated capitalist system is a benign system in which the opportunities for material well-being and personal advancement are equally available to all.

What is not taught may be as important as what is taught. Schools tend to provide a sanitized version of our institutions and their history. Controversy and conflict are treated as aberrations or are ignored. "The clamor over issues about which contemporary Americans sharply divide rarely enters the classroom; even those issues which divided our ancestors may still be handled gingerly. Characteristically, American history courses leave little time for the current scene; sometimes it is not even reached, as the course fuzzes away sometime between World Wars I and II" (Wirt and Kirst, 1972, p. 30). Racial discrimination is dealt with, if at all, as a part of a bygone era. Class strife—as represented in the history of the labor movement or efforts on the part of the poor to expand the rights of tenants and welfare recipients—is rarely discussed. Teachers who venture into the murky topic of economic justice—such as the Boston teacher who introduced his students to the black poet Langston Hughes's angry "Ballard of the Landlord"—may find themselves called to task by their superiors. Jonathan Kozol, the Boston teacher, was fired after the father of one of the white students in the class complained (Kozol, 1967).

Political socialization may take even more subtle forms. Samuel Bowles and Herbert Gintis, Marxist critics of the educational system, argue that schools systematically tend to reward those students who are docile, passive, and obedient and to punish those who are spontaneous, independent, and insistent upon thinking for themselves (Bowles and Gintis, 1976). Some education professionals have made no secret of their hope that the schools might produce a more pliant and less rebellious citizenry. Noah Webster, whose *Blue-Backed Speller* sold 75 million copies between 1783 and 1875, saw schools as a necessary part of the social machinery "which takes the child as soon as he can speak, checks his natural independence and passions, makes him subordinate to superior age, to the laws of the state, to town and parochial institutions" (Spring, 1982, p. 82).

Creating a Pliant Work Force. Those who see the schools as a mechanism for social control argue that open education serves the interest of the wealthy by preparing the poor for a passive economic role as well as a passive political life. Although the rich and the poor may attend the same schools, they are often quickly channeled onto different educational tracks. Standardized tests, administered at an early age, identify some students as "college material." These students, disproportionately drawn from the children of the upper class, are directed into an ambitious academic program designed to provide them with the skills and experiences needed by those who will become America's managers, leaders, and entrepreneurs. Others are set on a "vocational" track.

Conservatives consider such a tracking system to be a necessary instrument of any meritocracy—a benign means to help the young find and prepare for their proper niche. But the radical argues that this process does more than simply take note of, and respond to, distinctions that already exist among individuals. By labelling children at an early age, and treating them differentially, this tracking process creates class distinctions and perpetuates disadvantages that are based on factors other than the true potential of the individual child.

For many lower- and working-class children, the effect is simply to confirm the legitimacy of their lack of advancement. The schools, in the early part of the twentieth century, labelled many immigrants as "uneducable and incorrigible." Henry Goddard, one of the early exponents of "scientific" intelligence testing, gave I.Q. tests to immigrants arriving at Ellis Island. He concluded that 83 percent of Jews, 90 percent of Hungarians, 79 percent of Italians, and 87 percent of Russians were "feeble minded" (Riessman, 1978, p. 61).

Today, it is often black children who are found to score lower as a group. Poor performance on such standardized tests by entire groups, as opposed to individuals, could mean any of several things. It could mean that the tests themselves are biased in some fashion. It could mean that the socioeconomic status of those groups in society has a debilitating effect on their children even at an early age. It could indicate that the schools are failing to recognize and meet the special needs of these children. Or it could reflect some fundamental, perhaps even genetic, limitations of the groups as a whole. Radicals argue that it serves the purpose of the elite to ignore the first three possibilities while drawing attention to the last. This gives the schools the role of validating the favored position of the wealthy at the same time that it conveys the message that the poor are poor because of their own shortcomings.

Those who do poorly in their early years in school are not expected to rise to positions of leadership in either the public or private sphere. It is not necessary, therefore, that they be prepared to exercise authority or think creatively. Greater emphasis, in their classes, may be placed on instilling order and "good work habits." In high school, they will take auto mechanics instead of calculus, home economics instead of a foreign language.

Many of these students are destined to spend their lives in boring, routinized, low-paying jobs. They will be expected to follow orders unquestioningly, with little or no chance for professional advancement. The routinization and discipline of school prepare these students for the roles they will occupy later. This may make them better workers, but at the cost, perhaps, of keeping them from realizing their full potential as women and men.

The Limits of Schooling: The Neoconservative Perspective

As in other areas, the neoconservative position on education represents a delicate melding of elements drawn from other ideologies. Like the liberal, the neoconservative believes it is important for schools to provide the opportunity for advancement to persons of all races and classes. Like the traditional conservative—but unlike the liberal—the neoconservative is resigned to the likelihood that equalizing opportunities will not equalize results in any dramatic sense. Like the radical, the neoconservative believes that efforts to use the public schools to achieve racial and economic reform were doomed to failure. The radical attributes this failure to either insincerity or political naiveté on the part of those proclaiming the reforms; those with economic and political power effectively ensure that schools act as perpetrators of—not challengers to—the status quo. The neoconservative, however, argues that the failure is rooted in the limitations of the educational institution when stacked up against the task to which it was assigned. Inequality is perpetuated through community and family. The government, through public schools, simply is incapable of penetrating to these roots.

The Importance of Family. The neoconservative view of the limitations of schooling is linked to the self-perpetuating culture-of-poverty thesis that we discussed in Chapter 3. This thesis holds that the intellectual potential and personal motivation of the child may be fixed at a very early age. Parents who do not provide their children with a verbally rich environment make it unlikely that their children will develop the ability to think abstractly. Parents who do not provide an emotionally stimulating and supportive environment make it less likely that their children will develop a sense of self-worth and confidence that they can achieve their goals through experimentation and planning.

If the foundations of thinking and planning are laid so early, it is less likely that schools will be able to act as a force for equalization. They will not be able to undo the damage that already has been done. Without the necessary tools, the lower-class child experiences school as a series of frustrations, failures, and embarrassments.

The Destructiveness of Reform. Efforts to use the schools to achieve broad social reforms are not only fated to fail; according to the neoconservative perspective, such efforts can do considerable harm. Many neoconservatives can trace their movement away from conventional liberalism to disagreements about efforts to pursue racial equality through the schools. They argue that in attempting to apply the *Brown v. Board of Education* decision to nonsouthern schools, liberals on the courts and in elected office made a tragic mistake. Such efforts necessarily replaced equal opportunity with racial quotas and restrictions on personal freedom, they argue. Court-ordered busing for the sake of integration caused turmoil, heightened racial antagonism, stimulated flight from central cities, and unraveled the social ties and sense of community that are prerequisites to order and security. What is more, they argue, this destruction was done in the name of impossible goals: forced integration would not improve the self-image, academic accomplishment, or long-term economic advancement of American blacks. Chapter 11 will consider this argument—and counters to it—in greater depth.

Attempts to eradicate poverty through education similarly backfired. Because they failed to appreciate the central role of family, such efforts channeled millions of dollars into programs that raised expectations without having a chance to succeed. Enticing the poor to remain in school accomplishes little in and of itself. Besides being costly, the effort was disruptive to teachers and to those students who were ready and anxious to learn. Discipline and order are critical prerequisites to the learning environment. Even a few students who have no ability or desire to learn "can distract a whole class of serious students and wear almost any teacher down to the breaking point" (Banfield, p. 172).

Some neoconservatives believe that rather than encourage lower-class children to stay in school longer—as liberal reformers frequently urge—we should allow them to leave, perhaps as early as at age fourteen. Keeping nonlearners in school against their will just stimulates greater resentment on their part. "Four years of high school is too much for those who will do manual work," anyway, suggests Edward Banfield (Ibid.).

Unlike more traditional conservatives, many neoconservatives support the broad goals of social equality that motivated those who sought to use the schools as an instrument for social reform. But, like their conservative counterparts, their respect for the wisdom of the private market makes them wary of the manner in which educational reform sometimes seems to interfere with the freedom of parents and their children to make choices on their own. In looking for a way to broaden the range of choices available, some neoconservatives believe we must consider the likelihood that the best education, for at least some children, cannot be found in the public schools at all. They suggest that any policies intended to improve the education of the American public must consider alternatives available in the private sector as well.

PARALLEL SYSTEMS: PUBLIC VERSUS PRIVATE EDUCATION

Most of us take it pretty much for granted today that education is a right and that government has a responsibility to ensure access to education for both the rich and the poor. We do not guarantee that every family has the right to a nutritious diet or a warm place to sleep. But even the destitute can send their children to school; indeed, we insist that they do.

The tradition of open public education is deeply ingrained in American history. As early as 1779, Thomas Jefferson was fighting for a unified system of public schooling. "I hope the education of common people will be attended to . . .," a disappointed Jefferson wrote to James Madison, after his Bill for the More General Diffusion of Knowledge was defeated by the Virginia state legislature after years of efforts on his part (Wagoner, Jr., 1978, p. 17).

America's commitment to open schooling still stands out. Most European countries also provide education to almost all youth in the six-to-fifteen-year range. But beyond this point, the educational systems of those countries begin to focus more on an educational elite, and attendance falls off sharply. Approximately 77 percent of Americans between the ages of sixteen and eighteen continue going to school full time. This compares to 57 percent in Sweden, 63.1 percent in the Netherlands, and 35 percent in West Germany (Heidenheimer, et al., 1983, p. 27).

That the public sector continues to dominate the schooling process, particularly at the elementary and secondary levels, represents a problem to many conservative and neoconservative analysts. They feel that our overreliance on government-sponsored schools is a contributing factor in the loss of the public's faith in education. Some of them favor a deliberate policy of educational privatization. This section considers the advantages and disadvantages of private education in a theoretical sense. Later, in Chapter 11, specific proposals for privatizing schools—tuition tax credits and educational vouchers—will be reviewed in detail.

The Private Alternative

In one sense, of course, most education can be thought of as private education. That is because education is a process of learning—the accumulation of facts, experiences, and wisdom regarding the interpretation

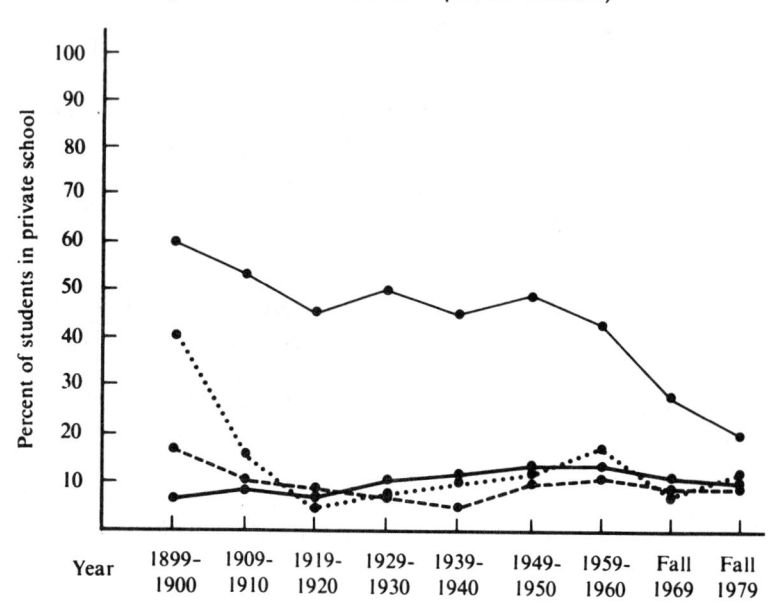

Figure 10–1 Private Enrollment, by Level of Institution, 1899–1900 to Fall 1979 (percent of all students in private schools)[a]

.... Kindergarten
———————— Grades 1-8
— — — — — Grades 9-12
———————— Higher Education

[a]Excluding subcollegiate departments of institutions of higher learning, residential schools for exceptional children, and federal schools.
[b]Data for 1911–1912.
SOURCE: National Center for Education Statistics. *Digest of Education Statistics.* Washington, D.C.: Government Printing Office, 1982, p. 8.

of facts and experience—that takes place in all aspects of our lives. Most education does not take place in schools.

When it comes to formal schooling, however, education today is dominated by the public sector. There are eight children attending public elementary and secondary schools for every one attending private institutions. Even at the level of higher education, where the private alternatives are much more extensive, about three-quarters of all students attend publicly controlled schools (National Center for Education Statistics, 1982, p. 7).

By the turn of the century, private schooling was clearly subordinate to public education at all levels except higher education. Since 1900, public schools have established an even firmer claim on the dominant position. Figure 10–1 traces the percentage of students in private schools from 1899 to 1979. The sharpest relative decline in private enrollments has come at the level of higher education. Private colleges and universities accounted for more than three out of five higher education students at the turn of the century; today, they account for only about one out of five. Trends at the other levels have been more gradual and erratic. Private elementary and secondary schools showed a relative drop during the first couple of decades, and then gradually rose. The last twenty years has seen another slight decline.

Even as they slipped relatively, however, private schools have continued to grow as far as absolute numbers are concerned. Four times as many kindergarten students attended private schools in 1979 as did so during the 1899–1900 school year. Nearly three times as many first- through eighth-graders, 12.5 times as many ninth- through twelfth-graders, and more than seventeen times as many college and university students attended private schools in 1979 as did so eighty years before.

Arguments for a Strong Private Alternative

Vincent E. Reed was a popular superintendent of public schools in the District of Columbia during the late 1970s. He recalls a time, some twenty years ago, when he was a principal at a public high school. About ten blocks away was a Catholic high school. The private school was much smaller, so small that there were not enough students to support a fifth-year language program like the one that Reed's school provided. But the Catholic school offered some courses that the public school did not have. "So we exchanged students. Their students came to the high school where I was and took the fifth year languages; and we went over and involved our youngsters in electronics and some other courses" (quoted in Gaffney, 1981, p. 4).

The story is a symbol, to Reed, of the way in which the presence of a private alternative can enrich the educational environment of the entire community. In spite of reservations about private education, some of which we will review below, some analysts feel that private schools play an important role that it would be foolhardy to underappreciate or to ignore.

Defenders of private education argue, first of all, that charges of elitism and racial separatism are outdated and overdrawn. According to one 1976 study, private schools, which account for about 10 percent of all elementary and secondary school students, contain about 17 percent of those whose family incomes are over $25,000 and about 6 percent of those incomes are below $6,000. Although this supports the popular impression that private schools draw disproportionately from among the wealthy, the figures do not show so extreme a class bias as some might have been led to expect. "Certainly private schools enroll a higher proportion of upper income than lower income students," Thomas Vitullo-

Martin admits. "But the differences are hardly enough to establish private schools as elitist" (Vitullo-Martin, 1982, p. 444).

In 1969, only 4 percent of private elementary school students were black; by 1979, the figure had doubled to 8 percent. Although this still compares unfavorably to a black school-age population of 15 percent, it again suggests that progress is being made (Vitullo-Martin, p. 445). The figures for Catholic schools are even more impressive. One survey of black students found that "a black young person attending a Catholic secondary school is just as likely as a young person attending a public secondary school to be in an all-black school—and is as likely also to be in a racially integrated one" (Greeley, 1981, p. 12). In San Francisco, Chicago, and New York City, over one-third of the Catholic school elementary and secondary students are either Hispanic or black (Vitullo-Martin, 1982, pp. 450–1).

Advocates of private education go further than challenging the image of private schools as lily-white enclaves of the well-to-do. They argue that the private alternative improves the educational system in a number of ways.

Diversity and Choice. The presence of private schools means that parents and children have a broader range of educational options than they otherwise could enjoy. In the supermarket of educational experiences, advocates of private education argue, public schools offer a choice among six or seven varieties of enriched white bread. There is a little variety within a given school district because the school board and central administrators impose a set of academic principles, moral tenets, and rules and regulations to which all principals and teachers learn to comply. There is little variation even across districts, some argue, because so many public school teachers and administrators have undergone a standard professional education in which they were exposed to a common set of preconceived notions and professional norms.

Private schools are a source of variety and spice. They offer alternatives, most obviously, in the different orientations toward values and morality that emanate from their religious backgrounds. But they offer variety in educational philosophies and tactics as well. Their administrators and teachers often are the product of a nontraditional training. About one-third of the teachers in inner-city Catholic schools, for example, are brothers or nuns. They presumably are less wedded to the convential wisdom and educational techniques that may be the fad in teachers' colleges at a particular time.

During the 1960s, when some parents began looking for schools that would emphasize creativity and deemphasize authority and rigidity, alternative schools were opened in many cities to meet that budding demand. Others feel that the public schools tend, on the whole, to be too liberal.

They prefer a back-to-basics orientation and stricter discipline, which some private schools proudly advertise. What such schools offer may not be right for every student, or even most students, but the fact that it is offered may mean that some students will have a better chance of finding an institution appropriate to their particular needs.

Innovation and Responsiveness. Because private schools are forced to compete in a marketplace for students, advocates of private education argue that they will tend to provide a more innovative and responsive style of education. The discipline of the marketplace forces private school administrators to keep their minds open to methods of instruction that effectively teach children while keeping costs low.

In Canada, some private schools receive grants from the government and others do not. One study compared Catholic schools receiving grants to those that did not by interviewing parents and teachers who had moved from one to the other. "The interviews led us to suspect that public money had reduced commitment and produced other negative effects in the publicly supported Catholic schools, partly by destroying the jeopardy that seemed to make people feel needed, appreciated, and important in private schools; partly by weakening the connections between the schools and the church; and partly through other mechanisms. . ." (Erickson, 1982, p. 395).

The same researchers also performed a "before-and-after" study of Canadian private schools that began to accept governmental support only in 1978. One survey, taken before the change had taken place, asked the parents to assess how responsive their child's private school was to their own suggestions and concerns. The same question was asked in 1980, two years after the governmental support had begun. The results showed a sharp decline—"a whopping change"—in this measure of responsiveness. Parents, it seems, felt the school administrator's door was much more open in the days when the parents were the sole source of revenues (Erickson, p. 405).

Check Against Concentrated Power. Education, some feel, is far too powerful a weapon to be left in the hands of government alone. Political freedom, we are quick to realize, depends on a system that allows freedom of expression of dissenting ideas. Stephen Arons and Charles Lawrence III argue that we need to expand our concern beyond the freedom to express ideas to the freedom to *form* independent and original ideas.

Because schools play such a key role in inculcating values and beliefs, governmental monopoly over education creates the conditions under which a particularly insidious form of tyranny could thrive. "If the government were to regulate the development of ideas and opinions through, for example, a single television monopoly or through religious rituals for children—freedom of expression would become a meaningless right" (Arons and Lawrence III, 1982. p. 228). We recognize this kind of threat easily enough, but schools may be just as potent a tool for the manipulation of consciousness. Citizens could be granted all the formal liberties we associate with democracy: freedom of assembly, freedom of speech, freedom to vote. By manipulating consciousness through control of the schools—by weeding out dissenting views and skeptical thinking in young and impressionable minds—tyrannical leaders could extend these other freedoms with little fear that they would develop into a challenge to their power. "To the degree that government regulation of belief formation interferes with personal consciousness, fewer people conceive dissenting ideas or perceive contradictions between self-interest and government sustained ideological orthodoxy." (Ibid.).

On this issue, theorists on the political right and the political left sometimes find themselves on common ground. Those on the right who favor a sharp return to reliance on a free market system sometimes argue that children are taught in public schools to look upon government as a wise and kind friend in need. Principles of self-help and personal responsibility are undermined. Those on the left who favor subordinating the needs of capital to a broader definition of the public interest argue that public schools tend to deify the market system. To both groups, then, private education is a necessary seedbed for intellectual dissension, a line of protection against a governmental monopoly that might have a stake in producing a citizenry that is politically acquiescent.

Criticisms of Private Education

There are others, however, who argue quite the opposite case. They fear that the presence of a private alternative works to undermine some of the social goals that we would like education to serve. Although very few go so far as to call for the elimination of private education, these analysts are deeply wary of policies that would shift the balance any further to the private sector.

Private Education as "Elitist". Private schools cost money. Sometimes they cost a lot of money. The average tuition at elite private schools averages over $3,500 per year. Tuitions as high as $6,000 are not unusual (Greeley, 1981, p. 13). The children of the poor, as a result, usually cannot attend private schools. Neither can many of the children of the middle class.

To those who cling to the idea that education should be a tool for increasing social equality, the exclusive nature of many private schools is a source of dismay. These schools skim some of the brightest and most able students from the population. Those who fail to meet the standards of the private schools—due to lack of money, lack of ability, emotional problems, or physical handicaps—are unceremoniously let go. The public schools, which have a legal obligation to attempt to educate *all* children, do not have the luxury of screening their students in this way. There is a danger that they will become the dumping ground, inheriting all those that the private schools find too costly or difficult to retain.

Private Schools and Segregation. The ruling in *Brown* v. *Board of Education* applied only to publicly funded schools. As public schools began to integrate, some southerners attempted to use private schools as the vehicle for their efforts to sidestep the order of the Court. This period, in which "segregation academies" popped up to accommodate white children unwilling to go to schools in which blacks were present, left a bitter taste in the mouths of those committed to the goal of civil rights. In their minds, private schools are simply a way for white students to build a haven outside the reach of the law.

The most dramatic example of the use of private schools to maintain segregation occurred in Prince Edward County, Virginia. Prince Edward County had been, along with Topeka, one of the original defendants in the *Brown* case. Rather than accept the implications of the Court's ruling, county officials chose, in 1959, to completely close down the public school system. Instead of funding public schools that would be required to integrate, state and county officials provided tuition grants to white students to allow them to attend segregated private schools. The public schools remained closed—and no black students recieved a public education in the county—between 1959 and 1963.

That Catholic schools, and some other private schools, may be increasing the number of poor and minority children in their ranks does not relieve these critics of their concern. They point out that most of the minority population in private schools is concentrated in a few large inner-city schools. These schools began to accept minorities as the neighborhoods around them began to change. Some churches, citing financial strains, have begun to close such schools—evidence, critics charge, that their commitment to educating minorities is too shallow to be relied upon.

Private Schools and Religious Indoctrination. Most private schools in the United States are parochial schools, funded and administered by an institution of organized religion. Over 60 percent of private elementary and secondary students go to Catholic schools. Smaller numbers go to schools associated with other faiths. In total, fewer than one-fourth of private schools are unassociated with a religion of any kind.

The association between private education and religious education is important in several senses. First, it ensures that many people will formulate their attitude toward private education on the basis of the fears, hopes, suspicions, and uncertainties they harbor toward organized religion, in general, or Catholicism, in particular. Second, it generates legitimate concerns regarding the substance of education. Religious beliefs and principles may clash with the beliefs and principles that most Americans expect to be introduced as part of a solid education. Can private religious schools be counted on, for example, to teach the evolutionary theories of Charles Darwin? Religion is anchored in faith and tradition; science is based on skepticism and experiment. Can religious institutions be expected to instill in young Americans the modes of rigorous and critical thought upon which scientific innovation and economic progress are believed to rest?

The overlap between private education and religious education, finally, gives education policy discussions a legal dimension that would otherwise not exist. The First Amendment of the U.S. Constitution states that "Congress shall make no law respecting an establishment of religion, or prohibiting the free exercise thereof." Precisely what the Founding Fathers meant to accomplish with this amendment is not easily determined. At the time it was drafted, six states had religions that were established by law. Maryland required Christianity; Pennsylvania and South Carolina supported belief in one eternal god; the law in Delaware required acceptance of the doctrine of the Holy Trinity (Woll, 1981). The courts, however, have determined that the amendment means more than that the state and federal governments are not to set up official religions or punish individuals for their personal religious beliefs. Any "excessive entanglements" between the government and religions must be avoided. Any public policy with "the purpose or primary effect of aiding or inhibiting private religious education" stands the risk of being found in violation of the law.

Are Private Schools Better Schools?

The belief that private schools are better schools is shared by many Americans. It is a belief held by moderate-income families that have sacrificed their vacations, their color televisions, or additions to their homes in order to be able to afford to send their children to private school. It is a belief held by other, perhaps poorer, families, who feel "trapped" in the public school system.

This belief has been built, primarily, on a foundation of anecdote, hearsay, and personal experience. "Aunt Maude says her Billy has done so much better since he transferred into that special private school." "Our neighbor tells us that, when he interviews job applicants, he can tell, without looking at their resumes, which ones have graduated from private schools.... They're always better dressed, better mannered, more articulate."

Newspapers, books, and the broadcast media occasionally feed the popular impression with stories about private schools whose students demonstrate special abilities or dramatic achievements. The Nairobi Day School, in East Palo Alto, California, is one example. The school charges its poor black students only $540 per year. Yet the "school's methods are so successful," one admirer notes, that it "offers a money-back guarantee for those who fail to learn to read within a year" (Poole, Jr., 1980, p. 185).

As long as the evidence remained unsystematic and anecdotal, tales about the greater effectiveness of private schools were easily dismissed by those who required a stronger kind of proof. After all, most of us recognize that the children going to private school are not a random sample. Their parents are wealthier and better educated, on the whole, than are those of public school children. The willingness of these parents to take on the financial burden of funding a private education may be a sign, too, of a greater commitment to education. These children are more likely to succeed no matter what kind of school they happen to attend. This makes the evidence of success on the part of private school graduates difficult to interpret confidently. "Put simply, when good students go to good schools, how are we to know which is responsible for the good performance that is likely to be observed?" (Alexander and Pallas, 1983, p. 170).

Early in the 1980s, a new study of the effectiveness of private schools was published. Its solid data base and well-known author ensured that it would be given attention and respect. Its finding that private education *did* result in greater cognitive acheivement—even when family background was taken into account—ensured that it would stir controversy as well.

High School Achievement in Private and Public Schools. Some people have a talent for stirring emotions and stimulating controversy. University of Chicago sociologist James S. Coleman is one of those people. In each of the last three decades, Coleman has conducted a study that challenged firmly held beliefs about schools and education policy.

In the 1960s, it was his study of *The Equality of Educational Opportunity*. That report's finding that facilities in predominantly black schools were not dramatically inferior to those in schools attended primarily by white students contradicted the claims of many civil-rights advocates and countered the expectations of Congress, which had commissioned the report. A second finding—that black students who attend schools with middle-class white students score better on standardized tests—seemed to add fuel to the arguments of those who favored busing for the purpose of integrating northern schools. And the conclusion—that students in well-financed schools perform little or no better than others, once family and class background are taken into account—put into question the common premise that social inequalities could be reduced simply by spending more money on educating the poor.

In the 1970s, Coleman struck a nerve with his analysis of "white flight" in urban school districts. Policies designed to force the integration of schools might be counterproductive, Coleman concluded, because there is "a sizable acceleration of the general loss of whites from the central city school districts when substantial desegregation occurs within that system" (Coleman and Kelly, 1976, pp. 252–3).

The latest Coleman brouhaha centers on a study he co-authored with Thomas Hoffer and Sally Kilgore. The study was based on a sample of over 58,000 sophomores and seniors from 1,015 public and private high schools. Private schools, particularly Catholic schools, produce better cognitive outcomes than do public schools, the study concluded. Even when family background factors, such as mother's and father's education, income, and race, are statistically controlled for, students in Catholic high schools perform better on tests of achievement in reading, vocabulary, mathematics, science, civics, and writing (Coleman, et al., 1982).

If the fact that they attract students from a higher socioeconomic class is not sufficient to explain the stronger performance of private schools, what, then, does account for the differences in student performance? One possibility that Coleman and his co-authors consider is the safer and more disciplined environment that is provided in private schools. Students in private schools report fewer absences, more homework, fewer fights, and greater teacher interest than do students in the public schools.

Elusive Answers. Coleman's prestige, and the impressive quality of the data, ensured that the study would receive attention. Shortly after the first reports of the study were made public, one observer notes, the "Coleman study was already being used as political ammunition" by those who favored policies that would reimburse parents for some of the cost of sending their children to private schools (Husen, 1981, p. 11).

But the great attention focused on the study, along with the political sensitivity of the topic, ensured that it would be subject to intensive critical analysis as well. No study of this scope can be expected to be perfect, so it is not surprising that critics have been able to find methodological soft spots into which they can effectively sink their claws. Some of the criticisms are substantial enough, however, to alert us to the fact that the question "Are private schools better schools?" is still far from having a definitive answer.

The most substantial challenge is based on the question of whether

Coleman, et al., have controlled for the most important background variables. Karl Alexander and Aaron Pallas argue that they have not. They note that the Catholic high school students in the Coleman sample are twice as likely as their public school counterparts (69 percent versus 34 percent) to report that they are on a college preparatory track (Alexander and Pallas, 1983, p. 171). This, they suggest, reflects differences in the capabilities, background, and motivation that predate high school, differences that make these students more likely to succeed no matter what kind of high school they attend. When students on a college-oriented academic track in public schools are compared to those on the academic track in private schools, differences in test scores are slight.

Advocates of public education, in spite of criticisms such as these, cannot easily shrug off or dismiss the Coleman, et al., study. The finding that students in private schools seem to perform better even when some family background variables are controlled for is especially impressive in light of the history of social scientists' efforts to measure the cognitive impacts of the schooling experience. Many of those other studies have found it difficult to find *any* measurable gains in student performance associated with differences among schools.

EDUCATION AND LIFE CHANCES: DO SCHOOLS MAKE A DIFFERENCE?

The belief that schools can function as a great equalizer rests on a two-part foundation. The first is the premise that "better schools mean better skills." By improving schools, particularly schools populated by children of the lower class, it would be possible to narrow the differences in cognitive and social skills that separate the rich from the poor. The second is the premise that "better skills mean better jobs." Once the children of the poor are given the skills to allow them to compete effectively in the job market, inequalities in income and occupational prestige will begin to narrow as well. Both premises have come under attack. The attacks on the first have come largely from the neoconservative camp; those on the second are often voiced by those on the political left.

Better Schools . . . Better Skills?

As has already been mentioned, James Coleman's massive report on *Equality of Educational Opportunity* struck the first major blow against the conventional wisdom that differences in students' performance owes much to differences among the schools themselves. The report was based on data collected, in 1965, from 4,000 public elementary and secondary schools. Superintendents, principals, teachers, and students in the sixth, ninth, and twelfth grades completed questionnaires.

The Coleman Report, as it is frequently referred to, analyzed information regarding both the inputs and the outputs of the educational process. Inputs included attributes of the schools and teachers themselves. Thus, the study collected detailed information on the presence or absence of chemistry labs, the number of books in the school library, the salaries and education of the teachers, and the like. Outputs referred to students' performance, as measured by standardized achievement tests.

The report found quite a bit of variation in students' performance both within and between schools. But variations in output seemed largely unrelated to variations in input. Some schools were often in wealthier communities with a stronger tax base from which education revenues could be drawn. Often, too, the students at these schools had higher test scores. But this, Coleman suggested, was attributable to the more favorable family backgrounds of the students rather than to the characteristics of the schools themselves. *When differences in family background were statistically controlled for, the relationship between school inputs and outputs was slight.*

Such a conclusion would seem to represent a direct challenge to the belief that schools can become a major vehicle for bringing about social equality. As Coleman notes:

> [O]ne implication stands out above all: That schools bring little influence to bear on a child's achievement that is independent of his background and general social context; and that this very lack of an independent effect means that the inequalities imposed on children by their home, neighborhood, and peer environment are carried along to become the inequalities with which they confront adult life at the end of school (Coleman, et al., 1966, p. 325).

The Coleman Report was to have a great intellectual impact. It was "pathbreaking, a watershed" (Mosteller and Moynihan, 1972, p. 27). To some, it seemed threatening as well. Those who favored aggressive public action aimed at improving educational opportunities for minorities and the poor worried that the report would be used as an excuse for inaction: if spending more money on schools does not ensure that students' learning will improve, why should we bother at all? William Ryan, one such critic, labelled the report "a triumph of sophisticated research design over common sense" (Ryan, 1971, p. 44). Some in the educational profession found the report disturbing as well. Their requests for more money to hire better teachers and build better facilities would lose some of their urgency and legitimacy if policymakers and taxpayers interpreted the Coleman Report to mean that education does not count.

The intense reaction to the report, however, grew partially out of misunderstanding. Both celebrants and critics presumed the study to make broader claims than its data and design allowed. The Coleman Report did *not* represent a test of the effect of school versus no school. As Frederick Mosteller and Daniel Moynihan later observed: "To the simple of mind or heart, such findings might be interpreted to mean that 'schools don't make any difference.' This is absurd. Schools make a very great difference to children. Children don't think up algebra on their own" (Mosteller and Moynihan, 1972, p. 21). To really test the effect of school versus no school, it would be necessary to compare students with similar backgrounds, some of whom had attended school, others of whom had not (Madaus, et al., 1980, p. 176). But an experiment like this cannot normally be conducted, because in the United States, and in most Western countries, *all* children are required to go to school. There are, however, a few "natural experiments," cases in which unusual events led to some children being unable to attend school. Reviewing some of these natural experiments, Christopher Jencks found evidence that a true test of the effect of school versus no school would find that schooling does make a difference. In Holland during World War II, in Prince Edward County, Virginia, during the period of "massive resistance" to school integration, and in New York City during its lengthy school strikes, some students were deprived of their normal exposure to school. In each case, those students' scores on standardized tests suffered in relation to those of students whose education continued on its normal schedule (Jencks, 1972, p. 87).

Instead of testing the effect of school versus no school, the Coleman Report assessed the effect of different levels of school resources among existing schools. This, for a couple of reasons, is a much weaker test. It is weaker, first of all, because there was not as much variation in some of the school characteristics as we might have expected. Almost every student, for example, attended a school with a chemistry lab. The likelihood of attending a school with a chemistry lab ranged from a low 94 percent for blacks and Puerto Ricans, to 99 percent for students with an Indian or Oriental background. The range for biology labs was not that much greater—84 percent for students of Puerto Rican ancestry to 96 percent for Indians and Orientals. "Given this limited variation, it is not too surprising that the absence or presence of a laboratory did not turn out to be significantly related to other variables" (Madaus, et al., 1980, p. 177).

The Coleman Report was not designed to consider differences in what schools do with the various resources at their disposal. As Jencks points out, "This tells us that if schools continue to use their resources as they now do, giving them more resources will not change children's test scores. If schools used their resources differently, however, additional resources might conceivably have larger payoffs" (Jencks, 1972, p. 97).

Better Skills . . . Better Jobs?

But what if schools were able to dramatically improve the skills and performance of children from lower-class backgrounds? Would this have the expected effect of narrowing the gap in income and status that separates the rich from the poor? Chances are that most of you have been told by your parents or teachers or guidance counselors that going to school "pays." You may have seen figures claiming to prove that a high-school diploma is worth an extra one or two thousand dollars a year in earnings; that each year in college adds to the yearly income that eventually will be earned. Maybe that promise of additional income is the only reason you are sitting in college right now.

It *is* true that those with more years of formal education tend to find more prestigious and highly paid jobs. It may not be true, however, that it is the skills and knowledge gained through that education that account for the better job. Children from wealthier families tend to get more schooling than do the children of the poor. These children enjoy a range of advantages over poorer children, even before the advantages associated with schooling are taken into account. They tend to do better in standardized tests. Their verbal skills are likely to be superior. Their dress and demeanor may make them more attractive to potential employers. Their family, friends, and relatives may have "connections" that help them to find a well-paying job. "All this means that only part of the observed economic differential between those with more schooling and those with less is due to school per se" (Jencks, et al., 1979, p. 160).

Some of the best evidence available suggests that additional years of schooling beyond high school do translate into greater economic gains. The effects of elementary and secondary education on income and occupational status are small, however, and due primarily to class background rather than the presence or absence of skills that schools provide. Men who complete high school tend to get better first jobs than men who do not, largely because they come from more advantaged homes and have a higher initial ability. This opens up the possibility that "discouraging male high school students from dropping out of school, would not greatly improve their occupational prospects" (Jencks, et al., 1979, p. 166). Apparently, for black children and the children of the poor, it is necessary to attend college in order to reap the large income and occupational benefits that are presumed to flow automatically from education (Jencks, et al., p. 175).

It is far from clear, moreover, whether added years of schooling, even at the college level, are "important for *doing* the job—or just for *getting* it" (Berg, 1974). Additional years of education may be more important as a source of credentials than as a source of job-related skills.

Employers, seeking to find their way through a sea of applications, may tend to fixate on a high-school or college diploma as a convenient symbol of achievement. Many have raised the minimum amount of education they require even though the jobs they are seeking to fill have become no more complicated or intellectually demanding than they were in the past. They can afford to do this because the pool of job-seekers in the United States is much better educated than it was ten or twenty years ago.

Although the employers may take it for granted that those who are better educated will make better employees, this may not always be the case. Ivar Berg, for example, has studied the performance of employees in a broad range of middle-level occupations. A comparison of 4,000 insurance agents found, for example, that the dollar value of policies sold by those with more schooling was no higher than that of other agents. Lesser educated laboratory technicians in a chemical company actually had higher job performance evaluations than those with more years of schooling. What is more, the better educated technicians tended to have a higher level of job turnover. When, similarly, Berg studied air-flight controllers working for the Federal Aviation Agency, he found that those without a college diploma were more likely to win honors and awards for job performance than were those who had earned their degree.

None of this is meant to suggest that education is unimportant or a waste of time. Changes in technology make additional education absolutely essential in the performance of certain jobs. Individuals seeking personal advancement are likely to gain in employability if they continue their education beyond the secondary years.

But simple assumptions about the relationship between education and equality have been bruised. Putting more money into schools is not likely to have a major effect upon poverty—certainly not unless the schools also change what they do. Giving the poor a better education may only give us a better educated pool of the unemployed, unless efforts to generate more jobs and greater economic growth are successful at the same time.

SUMMARY AND CONCLUSIONS

Tradition has it that, if you want to look knowledgeable when buying a car, you should kick the tires. Tradition also has it that, when buying a home, it is important to ask, "How are the schools?" I have often wondered, and occasionally asked, *why* one should kick the tires. No one I have spoken to really knows just what information is supposed to be gained through the act. People are a little clearer on the point of asking about schools. They know that their children will be required to attend school, they have heard that homes in neighborhoods with good schools enjoy better prospects for resale, and they are certain that they do not want their child to spend thirty or more hours each week in an environment that is demonstrably not good. But many are as unsure about how to tell a "bad" school from a "good" one as they are about how to spot a car that is a lemon.

Nonetheless, the fact that so many movers express deep interest in, and concern about, the quality of the school system is instructive. It is, first of all, one more sign of the high priority Americans put upon education. Secondly, and perhaps more interestingly, it suggests that many Americans sense that it is easier to find good schools then to create them.

Those who are dissatisfied with conditions or services where they live are faced with a choice between "exit" and "voice." Exit represents the option of leaving, of seeking better conditions through residential mobility. Voice refers to the use of political resources, seeking, through voting, lobbying, or protest activities, to change the environment rather than simply to escape it. Political economists reason that people make their choice betwen voice and exit largely on the basis of their assessment of which course, in the past, has proven the more likely to succeed. That the decision to move and the desire for good schools are closely linked for many American families might, then, reflect resignation to the ineffectiveness of politics and public policy as a means of changing schools for the better.

This chapter has suggested that one reason for this apparent failure of education policy may lie in ideological conflict over goals. Traditional conservatives see the schools as a mechanism for educating an elite to lead and training the masses to work. Liberals see the schools as a mechanism for narrowing the gap between the wealthy and the poor. Although radicals would *like* to see the schools play this role, they do not believe that they can be made to do so unless political changes first remove control over education policy from the hands of elites who benefit from retaining a docile and manipulable lower class. Neoconservatives are skeptical of the notion that schools can fulfill any broad social program— whether liberal or conservative in origin—with precision and effectiveness. This is the case no matter who is in control. The limits lie in governmental institutions, and their inability to replace, or overcome the influences of, private forces such as family and community. People who are so divided over the broad issues and goals are not likely to come to easy agreements over specific programs and narrower priorities.

Yet when one looks at state and local decision-making regarding education policy, one does not usually encounter explicit references to these broad ideological issues. The battles are fought on narrower grounds. Not, "Are schools capable of bringing about racial equality?" but, "Should local school districts be forced by the courts to bus their children to achieve racial balance?" Not, "Should schools be structured so as to narrow, rather than exacerbate, the differences between the rich and the poor?" but, "Should states reduce their reliance upon local property taxes as a means of funding education?" Not, "Is the primary purpose of schooling to meet a public interest in an educated citizenry or to serve private desires for individual advancement?" but, "Should the government provide tax credits and vouchers to better enable families to exploit the alternative of private schools?" Not, "Should schools provide a broad education oriented around the traditional liberal arts, or should they concentrate on narrower technical skills?" but, "How many computers and computer-oriented courses should a good school provide?"

The next chapter considers some of the current controversies being debated in front of local school boards, in state legislatures, and in the state and federal courts. They are considered on their own terms, because they present many interesting issues, not all of which are anchored in broader ideological conflicts. At the same time, the intimated technicalities and administrative concerns will be given only a brief nod of acknowledgment. Although significant to those entrusted with implementing public policy, these technicalities and adminstrative concerns should not be mistaken for policy itself. Policy has to do with setting broad goals and weighing competing interests. Discussions about the number of children/hours spent on buses before and after integration or assessments of the relative merits of tuition tax credits as opposed to education vouchers can easily distract attention from the deeper philosophical and political conflicts lurking in the background. This may have the desired effect of keeping the discussion dispassionate and under control. But it does so at the cost of missing the heart of the issue, and it allows policy to be set by default.

SUGGESTED READINGS

Bowles, Samuel, and Herbert Gintis. *Schooling in Capitalist America.* New York: Basic Books, 1976.

Coleman, James S. *Equality of Educational Opportunity.* Washington, D.C.: U.S. Government Printing Office, 1966.

Coleman, James S., Thomas Hoffer, and Sally Kilgore. *High School Achievement.* New York, Basic Books, 1982.

Everhart, Robert B. *The Public School Monopoly.* Cambridge, Massachusetts: Ballinger, 1982.

Jencks, Christopher. *Inequality: A Reassessment of the Effect of Family and Schooling in America.* New York: Basic Books, 1972.

Madaus, George F., Peter W. Airasian, and Thomas Kellaghan. *School Effectiveness: A Reassessment*. New York: McGraw-Hill, 1980.

Peterson, Paul E. *School Politics Chicago Style*. Chicago: University of Chicago Press, 1976.

Ravitch, Diane. *The Great School Wars*. New York: Basic Books, 1974.

Wirt, Frederick M., and Michael W. Kirst. *Conflict in the Schools*. Berkeley, California: McCutchan, 1982.

11

Controversies in the Classroom: Policy Issues of the Eighties

In one sense, education policy in the near future seems to promise less heat and controversy than it did through the 1960s and 1970s. The great equalizer thesis may not be dead, but it is wounded. The expectation that education can and should be the primary tool for healing long-standing social ills is no longer widely shared. As the burden of expectations lightens, the level of emotion generated also might be anticipated to ease.

Although schools have been relieved of some of their responsibilities for meeting social ambitions, they remain the focus of many personal ambitions and concerns. Families that love their children remain deeply concerned about the institution that becomes, for all intents and purposes, those children's second home. They want their children to have a healthy and productive experience in the schools. Although some may have scaled down their perceptions about the likelihood that a good education will be the key to upward mobility and material success, most recognize that the schools have the potential—even if they do not always live up to it—to give their children knowledge and experiences that will better prepare them for the challenges they will face as adults.

In this chapter, we will look in detail at several of the major controversies that education policymakers will be forced to confront in the coming years. Two of these—busing and school finance reform—are issues inherited from the previous two decades; they remain unresolved. The others—vouchers and high technology in the classroom—are of more recent vintage. The manner in which they are addressed may alter the shape of education for years to come.

BUSING: THE ISSUE THAT WILL NOT DIE

After *Brown:* Desegregating Southern Schools

In spite of the Supreme Court's ruling in *Brown* v. *Board of Education,* racial desegregation of southern schools did not begin in earnest until the 1960s. As late as 1964, fewer than 1 percent of black children were attending integrated schools in seven of the eleven southern states. In order to avoid compliance with the *Brown* decision, state and local officials in those states had engaged in a series of delaying tactics and legal maneuvers. Virginia officials called for a deliberate policy of "massive resistance."

The 1964 Civil Rights Act gave the executive branch of the federal government the responsibility and the power to enforce the decision the Court had made ten years earlier. The Department of Health, Education and Welfare (HEW) was given the role of monitoring the progress of integration. Any jurisdiction that continued to avoid compliance could have its federal aid cut off; this punishment was more severe and more immediate than any the courts had been able to hand out. The law also gave the Justice Department a role in bringing suit against jurisdictions that remained segregated. "The law multiplied enforcement resources, shifted the burden of initiating cases from private groups, and made local officials realize that they were eventually going to have to desegregate. . . . The results were phenomenal" (Orfield, 1978, p. 279).

Change came rapidly once the federal government made it clear that it intended to enforce the law. Desegregation began in nearly every southern rural school district within a year. About 70 percent of black students in the South were still going to all-black schools in 1968. By 1972, this figure had improved to fewer than 10 percent.

The experience proved that desegregation was possible. Once a serious effort was made, change came amazingly rapidly and with relatively little violence or disruption. Later, as the definition of equality expanded, the courts would find themselves addressing the issue of a different kind of racial segregation. The barriers to racial equality in northern school districts were more subtle and more complex. They also have proven to be more difficult to eliminate.

The Court Looks to the North

While great strides were being made, during the late 1960s and early 1970s, in desegregating the schools in the southern states, segregation in the North, particularly in large school districts, was getting worse. Blacks and other minorities in the Northeast and North Central states were, by 1978, more likely to be attending schools with minority enrollments of 90 to 100 percent than were minorities in the South (see Figure 11–1). It took a while, but by the mid-1970s the federal courts were ready to turn their attention to the North. They found a segregation that was different than they had encountered in the South. But in many nothern jurisdictions, they found a segregation that was illegal, nonetheless.

A Different Kind of Segregation. School districts in the North for the most part had never been segregated by law. They did not racially isolate blacks from whites in a dual school system, such as had been found unconstitutional in the *Brown* v. *Board of Education* case. Segregation in northern schools seemed to be a more or less natural outcome of residential segregation. Because whites tended to live with other whites, and blacks tended to live with other blacks, school attendance zones most often drew racially homogeneous groups into neighborhood schools.

The difference between segregation in the South and segregation in the North has commonly been referred to as the difference between *de jure* and *de facto* segregation. But this distinction, although potentially useful, has confused as much as it clarifies. The definition of *de jure* segregation is relatively straightforward. It refers to segregation "by law"; the formal separation of blacks from whites. The definition of *de facto* segregation is a bit more slippery. Traditionally, it is defined as segregation "in fact." This is intended to describe the situation in which segregation is wholly natural, resulting from individuals' free choices about where they would like to live. But traditionally, it also has been suggested that *de facto* segregation describes the situation in the northern schools, and this is where the water gets muddy. For *in most large northern school districts, free choice by individuals tells only a part of the story about how the schools became segregated.*

There is a large gray area between pure *de jure* segregation (dual school systems) and pure *de facto* segregation (resulting from freely made residential decisions). And it is in this gray area that the situation of most large northern school districts can be found. When the courts have explored the roots of segregation in these school systems, they have found that public officials deliberately devised policies to maintain and increase racial segregation. They did this in a number of ways: by gerrymandering attendance zones, so as to keep black students confined to predominantly black schools; by building new schools in locations that would further rather than decrease racial segregation; by overcrowding minority schools and building temporary additions to expand minority schools, rather than shifting black students to underutilized schools in white neighborhoods; by allowing white students to freely transfer to schools outside their normal attendance zone in order to allow them to move to a school with

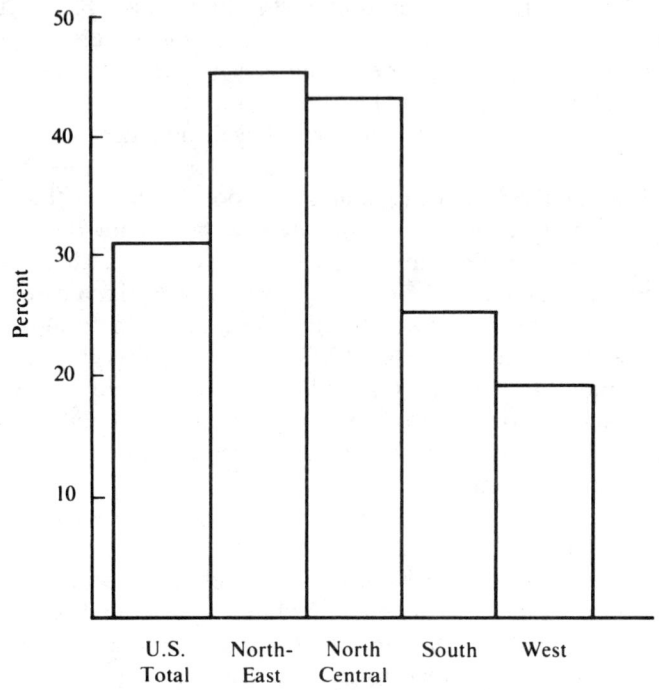

Figure 11–1 Percent of Minorities Attending Predominantly Minority Schools, by Region, 1978

Source: Bureau of the Census, U.S. Department of Commerce. *State and Metropolitan Area Databook.* Washington, D.C.: Government Printing Office, 1983, p. 475.

fewer minorities; by deliberately building low-income public and subsidized housing on sites that would not threaten existing patterns of segregation in the public schools.

Public officials in northern schools did *not* rely on "natural" processes in order to maintain effectively segregated school systems. Until one comes to grips with this fact, it is difficult to understand the manner in which the Supreme Court applied the logic and findings of the *Brown* case to the situation they encountered in northern schools. Some conservative and neoconservative accounts suggest that the Supreme Court radically expanded its definition of segregation when it began to order integration in the North. They give the impression that the Court had decided that purely *de facto* segregation is unconstitutional, a decision that many Americans find difficult to understand. This is not the case. The courts have not ordered busing for the purpose of integration unless the existing segregation has been found to be the result of decisions made by public officials—decisions with the foreseeable effect of increasing segregation *beyond* that which would result from the free locational decisions of individual families.

Swann v. *Charlotte-Mecklenburg Board of Education.* The Charlotte-Mecklenburg, North Carolina, school system is the thirty-first largest in the nation (Daniels, 1983; Orfield, 1978; Rodgers, 1975, pp. 125–59). The 540-square-mile system includes about 73,000 public elementary and secondary students. About 48,000 students depend on buses to get them to their assigned schools, and about one-quarter of these are riding buses because of a federal court order issued in 1969 and upheld by the U.S. Supreme Court in 1971. Ironically, the Court's interpretation of the situation in this southern district probably did more to open the door to busing in northern schools than any other single case.

The situation in the Charlotte-Mecklenburg school system in 1969 was this: the school system had once operated as a dual system based on race; it no longer did. Although officials had eliminated formal segregation, housing patterns and habits born of years of racial separation resulted in little integration taking place. Advocates of integration argued that it was not enough for school officials to remain racially neutral if racial neutrality meant that segregation would continue. They argued that aggressive action, including busing, was needed if desegregation in law was to become desegregation in fact. School officials, and others opposed to court intervention, countered that efforts to redraw attendance zones or alter transportation patterns in order to meet racial quotas would call for injecting color into a decision-making process that should be color-blind.

The Supreme Court, in upholding the order of the lower court, concluded that Charlotte-Mecklenburg officials had an affirmative *obligation to bring about desegregation.* They had an obligation, moreover, to do so immediately. The Court ruled that unless local officials moved rapidly to undo the segregation that their earlier unconstitutional practices had helped to bring about, the *federal courts had the discretion and authority to develop and implement their own integration plans.* Such plans could include racial ratios as targets, though rigid quotas might not be allowed. Desegregation plans also could involve busing, although the Court recognized that specific busing plans might not be acceptable if "the time or distance of travel is so great as to either risk the health of the children or significantly impinge on the educational process." Because busing might be the only way to integrate schools in fact, "Desegregation plans cannot be limited to the walk-in school."

Before the *Swann* ruling, northern school districts had considered themselves immune to court-ordered integration on the grounds that their current school assignment policies were racially color-blind. In ruling that officials under some circumstances have an affirmative obligation to bring about integration, *Swann* alerted northern officials that the defense of racial neutrality might not suffice. Still, *Swann* dealt with a jurisdiction that had a history of segregation through a dual system. As long as *de jure* segregation was defined so narrowly as to include only cases in which a formal mandate for segregation had existed, northern officials could retain their complacence.

Keyes, et al., v. School District No. 1, Denver, Colorado. It was not until 1973 that the Supreme Court finally got around to grappling face-to-face with a major case of segregation in a non-southern city. The *Keyes* case clarified a number of aspects of the *Brown* decision and made its relevance to northern school districts more readily apparent.

Denver had never had an explicit policy of keeping white students and black students in separate schools. Evidence indicated, however, that Denver school officials had made a series of decisions—about school location, boundary zones, and the like—that had the effect of increasing segregation in the schools. In *Keyes,* the Supreme Court made it clear that segregation is unconstitutional if a "pattern of intentional segregation has been established in the past," whether or not that segregation was formally and explicitly mandated by law.

Two other aspects of the *Keyes* decision are important for understanding the subsequent profusion of desegregation cases outside the South. First, *racially discriminatory policies may be cause for remedial action, even if those policies are limited to the past.* "If the actions of the school authorities were to any degree motivated by segregative intent and the segregation resulting from those actions continues to exist, the fact of remoteness in time certainly does not make these actions any less 'intentional.' "

Second, *it is not necessary to find racial discrimination in every school within a district* in order to find segregation within the whole district to be unconstitutional, or in order to order remedies on a district-wide scale. The Court based this on what has been called the "spread theory": if intentional segregation can be proven to have taken place in a substantial portion of the district, it can be assumed that the effects of this discrimination spread throughout the entire district. The spread theory made it much more feasible for civil-rights organizations to file suits calling for court-ordered busing, because it meant that they would not be forced to undertake the expensive and highly infeasible task of proving that the racial composition of *each* school in the district was traceable to specific intentional actions on the part of school authorities.

Is Busing Practical?

Americans' attitudes toward integration and busing display a curious pattern. Public opinion polls show growing support for the idea of racial integration. Yet as Gary Orfield has noted, "Even as acceptance of integration was growing, public support for further action against racial discrimination virtually disappeared" (Orfield, 1978, p. 109). By the mid-1970s, surveys revealed that nearly three out of every four Americans opposed busing students for the purpose of racially integrating public schools. Even black citizens, who in the Sixties looked to busing as a necessary tool for improving their educational opportunities, now are sharply divided on the issue.

Can one claim to favor integration and oppose busing without sacrificing logical consistency in the process? Most contemporary critics of busing insist that their position is not based on any opposition to the ideals expressed by the Supreme Court in *Brown* v. *Board of Education*. Their objections are based on practical concerns. "Integration may be desirable," they seem to be saying, "but experience shows that busing is too disruptive, too costly, and too risky a means for bringing it about."

Distance, Time, and Safety. Parents of children affected by court-ordered busing frequently express great concern over the distance their children will be bused, the time they must spend on the bus, and the threat to the safety of their children due to the possibility of accidents during the ride to and from their assigned schools. It is reasonable and understandable for parents to be concerned about their children. But vivid portrayals of busing as a threat to a system in which children walk safely to nearby neighborhood schools can be misleading. The following are among the points they obscure.

- *Most children already ride buses to school.* More than half of all public school pupils are transported to school at the public expense. Of those who do not rely on buses, more than half depend on cars, rather than walking, to get to their schools (U.S. Bureau of the Census, 1981, p. 150).

- *Some children actually spend less time on buses after court-ordered plans go into effect.* Existing school attendance zones are often outdated or inefficiently drawn. Sometimes they have been gerrymandered for purposes of maintaining segregation. As a result, some children spend more time on buses than necessary *before* court-ordered plans take effect. In a number of southern districts, busing was resisted in spite of the fact that desegregation resulted in a decline in the total amount of busing miles (Orfield, 1978, p. 140).

- *Parents who respond to court-ordered busing by fleeing to the suburbs or by sending their children to private schools usually end up subjecting their children to longer rides to school.* Suburban and rural areas are less densely populated, so schools are more likely to be long distances from most children's homes. In central cities, about 20.3 percent of all elementary school students rely on buses to get to school; this compares to 48.3 percent of children in the suburbs and 58.6 percent of children in nonmetropolitan areas (U. S. Bureau of the Census, 1981, p. 150). Children who are shifted to private schools to avoid desegregation have a 70 percent longer bus ride than those who remain in the public schools (Rossell and Hawley, 1982, p. 214).

- *Riding a bus to school is safer than walking, and busing to public schools is probably safer than busing to private schools.* Estimates indicate that children who walk to school are two or three times more likely to suffer accidents than are children who ride buses (Orfield, 1978, pp. 134–5). Parents who shift their children to private schools, moreover, are probably deluding themselves if they think that this will make the transportation safer. Private and parochial schools "are the primary purchasers of the nearly wornout buses disposed of by public schools after 8 or 9 years of use" (Orfield, p. 135; Rossell and Hawley, 1982, p. 214).

The Cost of Busing. Some argue that in these days of tight budgets and fiscal constraints, the costs of busing are enough to make desegregation impractical. But these costs have often been exaggerated. A review of the cities undergoing court-ordered busing in the late 1960s and early 1970s shows that, in most, the increased expense amounted to less than 2 percent of the school system's budget. Yet six out of seven people polled in 1972 estimated that costs were at least 25 percent. (Orfield, 1978, p. 114). Nationwide, busing for the purposes of integration is less costly than busing for extracurricular purposes such as field trips, athletic events, and nonacademic activities. In addition, a number of states spend more on providing free transportation to private school students than they do on busing for integration (Orfield, p. 130).

White Flight. Many American children and teenagers have been haunted by the worry, "What if I gave a party, and nobody came?" Similarly, some supporters of school integration find themselves faced with the nagging question, "What if we integrate inner-city schools, and no white children show up?"

James Coleman, as we noted in the last chapter, has suggested that court-ordered busing may accelerate the withdrawal of white children from inner-city school systems. If such white flight is substantial, it may indicate the ultimate hopelessness of attempting to bring about racial integration through forced busing in the schools. Full-scale desegregation efforts, unless they involve suburban along with central city school districts, may be self-defeating. Such efforts may succeed in spreading the available white children more evenly throughout the school district, but if the pool of white children shrinks drastically, this will do little to promote genuine integration among the races. In the large cities, in particular, it may hasten "the time when the city schools become nearly all black and the suburbs nearly all white" (Coleman and Kelly, 1976, p. 254).

Coleman's argument has been picked up by neoconservatives, who argue that court-ordered busing represents just one more example of the tendency of well-meaning public officials to do more harm than good. But liberal defenders of busing have questioned whether the specter of white flight is as threatening as Coleman makes it appear. Most of the decline in white students in central city school systems, they note, is due to factors other than school integration. Even without the threat of busing, for instance, many families would find suburbia a more attractive place to live. The most rapid surge of suburbanization preceded the begininng of court-ordered busing in northern schools. Nearly as important in explaining the decline in white public school students is the general drop in birthrate. There simply are fewer children, and especially fewer white children, than there were fifteen or twenty years ago, and this has resulted in fewer white students in private schools and in the suburbs as well as in the central cities (Rossell and Hawley, 1982, pp. 206–8).

Although white enrollment would be declining in the cities even without busing, the evidence does seem to indicate that court-ordered busing frequently accelerates the process, at least in the first year or two. Some research suggests, however, that this effect is short-lived. Busing plans may simply speed the out-migration of families that were likely to move to the suburbs anyway. After the initial shock and confusion, moreover, some white families apparently begin to drift back into the public schools (Farley, et al., 1980, pp. 123–39). Nonetheless, the threat of white flight remains potent. It has helped to convince Congress, in recent years, to put limits on the Department of Justice's role in promoting busing as an answer to school segregation. Also motivating Congress has been an even stronger challenge. Not only is busing impractical, some critics now argue, it does not even accomplish the academic goals by which it is justified.

Does Busing Work?

Impact on Black Students. The Supreme Court, in the *Brown* case, did not state that its ruling depended upon a belief that integration would lead to better academic performance on the part of black students. Many supporters of busing, however, have argued that integrated schooling can have such a positive effect. Many black parents, for instance, have argued that busing is the only way that their children can receive the better quality of instruction and facilities that they associate with schools predominantly attended by whites. Those who advocate education as a means of breaking the cycle of poverty for blacks, also saw busing as a tool for increasing the skills of black students, and thereby increasing their ability to compete for better paying and more stable jobs.

In light of the belief that busing will lead to better academic achievement on the part of black students, early studies of the effects of busing were disappointing. Neoconservative critics of busing found support for their concerns in David Armor's investigation of voluntary busing in the Boston metropolitan area (Armor, 1972, pp. 90–126). Armor's conclusion was that busing had failed. He found that bused black students scored no better on standardized tests than their brothers and sisters who were not bused. Their grades, in addition, were likely to fall. Discouraged by this, and by evidence that the black students' self-concepts and aspirations suffered and that relations between white and black students deteriorated as well, Armor argued that court-ordered busing would be a mistake.

Armor, however, studied a voluntary program, in which a relatively few number of black students were involved. It was, moreover, a one-way busing program. Black students were bused to suburban schools, but no white students were bused the other way. Critics of Armor's study argue that such a program is not a good test of the busing concept, because it tends to drop a few blacks into a strange and somewhat unresponsive school system in which little or no efforts may have been made to accommodate their special needs. Critics also note that Armor's expectation that academic gains would be obvious in the first year or two were unrealistic. They question his relative deemphasis of the finding that the bused black students were nearly four times as likely to go on to a full four-year university than the siblings to whom Armor compared them (Pettigrew et al. 1973).

Subsequent studies have been considerably more favorable. Robert L. Crain and Rita Mahard, for example, reanalyzed over ninety studies with 323 separate samples of black students who were reassigned from segregated to desegregated schools by government action. They found that 173 of the samples showed positive effects on test scores, 50 showed no difference between bused and nonbused black students, and 98 showed a negative effect. Just as importantly, they found that the studies with a stronger research design—those studies in which greater confidence could be placed in the findings—were the most likely to show a positive effect associated with busing (Crain and Mahard, 1983, pp. 839–59).

Impact on White Students. Opponents of busing sometimes argue that white students will be forced to suffer academically, as teachers are forced to water down the curriculum to accommodate black children with academically disadvantaged backgrounds. This fear seems to have been misplaced, as nearly all studies indicate that white students involved in busing plans do not suffer a decline in academic achievement (Orfield, 1978, pp. 121–6; Crain and Mahard, 1981). One reason white students may not be harmed is that, in most of the cases studied, white students have remained in the majority even after desegregation has occurred. Even when white students find themselves in predominantly black schools, "tracking" of students within those schools sometimes results in white students remaining in the majority in the classes for "better" students.

Making Busing Work Better

One reason the busing issue does not fade away is that it cannot. It cannot, at least, unless the Supreme Court substantially reconsiders its reasoning in past cases. In spite of the public's desire to treat integration and busing as separate issues, "Virtually all of the court decisions . . . are based on exactly the opposite conclusion—that busing is the *only* available way to end urban segregation" (Orfield, 1978, p. 114). Once the courts find that unconstitutional segregatory actions by public officials has taken place—as the courts have found in nearly every case that has come before them—the law holds that something must be done. Also, as long as residential patterns in our major cities remain as segregated as they are now, no plan to integrate schools can succeed unless busing plays a significant role.

In light of the fact that the Supreme Court—even the relatively conservative Supreme Court of recent years—seems unwilling to back away entirely from its past positions, and in light of the fact that busing is less disruptive and more effective than many opponents have charged, some educational professionals argue that it is time to start asking a new set of questions. Instead of asking questions designed to discover whether busing, as currently implemented, is doing all that we might hope, we should roll up our sleeves and begin to ascertain how busing can be made to work better.

Some answers have already begun to emerge. By studying the districts in which busing has been put in effect, analysts have identified a series of factors that help to determine whether busing is likely to be effective, orderly, nonviolent, and minimally disruptive.

Cooperation by Local Officials. The public's image of busing is heavily influenced by those relatively few cases in which resistance has been violent and turmoil prolonged. Most cities that have integrated have done so peacefully. The stance taken by local officials is a good predictor of whether or not this will occur.

Charles V. Willie and Susan L. Greenblatt reviewed integration efforts in ten cities. "When public officials speak out against court orders to desegregate the schools," they concluded, "they stimulate resistance by the public at large which may get out of hand and become violent" (Willie and Greenblatt, 1981, p. 324). This was the case, for example, in Boston, where antibusing efforts were spearheaded by Louisa Day Hicks, a member of the city council. In Milwaukee, on the other hand, where local officials took upon themselves the responsibility for bringing desegregation about peacefully, disruption was minimal.

Support from State Officials. Local officials frequently complain that state authorities are indifferent to the problems they face in trying to bring about integration. A Detroit administrator, for example, claims that "there is a vacuum at the state level for any school districts, administrators, and boards who might want to do something progressive" (Willie, 1982, pp. 86–7). Sometimes state efforts have slipped from unresponsiveness to outright hostility to the local desegregation efforts. Willie and Greenblatt found that "in several states legislative representatives were in the forefront of the movement to resist desegregation" (Willie and Greenblatt, 1981, p. 337).

When state officials choose to, they have the resources and authority to make busing plans move along more smoothly. The Massachusetts Board of Education, for example, threatened to cut off state funding to Boston if the local school board did not submit a desegregation plan. The Pennsylvania Human Relations Commission initiated antidiscrimination suits against more than fifteen local districts. Wisconsin supported local officials by providing special funding for minority students transferring to suburban school systems, and for white students transferring from the suburbs to predominantly minority city schools (Willie and Greenblatt, 1981; Willie, 1982).

Preparation and Planning. The disruption and chaos that accompany some busing efforts are due to the fact that local officials refused to accept, until the last minute, the likelihood that busing ultimately would take place. When busing could be avoided no longer, such jurisdictions were forced to move quickly, with only slapdash planning and no time at all to prepare. When officials *have* taken the time to plan, Orfield argues, they have been able to reduce disruption, even under the most challenging of situations. Clark County, Nevada, for example, is a huge school system, about 8,000 square miles. Yet officials there were able to achieve integration without raising the average time and distance of the bus ride taken by most students (Orfield, 1978, p. 132). Preparation can also ensure that teachers, pupils, and administrators are better prepared to handle the cultural, racial, and class-based tensions that may surface.

Mandatory and Metropolitan-wide Busing. Even supporters of busing have tended to regard it as a "necessary evil." It is inconvenient, at best; seriously disruptive, at worst. Without it, however, the critically important goals of upholding the law and pursuing racial equality cannot be reached. Because they view it as a necessary evil, supporters, like opponents, of busing often are led to adopt the position that less is better. Voluntary busing, therefore, is to be preferred over mandatory busing. Busing on a small scale is to be preferred over busing on a large scale.

But lesser may not be better. Although voluntary efforts are less likely to cause political turmoil, for example, it seems that they are also less likely to work than mandatory plans with legal force behind them. "Voluntary plans do reduce white flight," Rossell and Hawley indicate, "but for school districts with more than 30 percent minority, and sometimes those with less than 30 percent minority, they produce almost no desegregation" (Rossell and Hawley, 1982, p. 213). Voluntary plans, moreover, may draw the involvement of only the brightest and most ambitious minority students and the most liberal and open-minded of whites. The goal of helping the most disadvantaged minorities and the goal of breaking down the prejudices of the more racist whites, if this happens, simply would not be met.

Gary Orfield is one of the most insistent defenders of the notion that, when it comes to busing, bigger sometimes is better. He argues for metropolitan-wide busing plans, in which some city children are bused to suburban schools and suburban students are bused into the city system. Such plans may have the advantage of defusing the white-flight issue: it would no longer be possible for white families to escape integration simply by moving to a new home just across the city line. Metropolitan-wide busing might have another desirable effect. Because wealthier whites are often insulated by virtue of their suburban address, the burdens of desegregation efforts tend to be borne by working-class and lower-income whites. Metropolitan-wide busing would reduce this class inequity. By drawing into the process children from more advantaged socioeconomic backgrounds—students who will tend to bring with them stronger academic skills and more liberal racial attitudes—metropolitan-wide busing might increase the chances of success.

Incentives for Middle-Class and White Families to Remain. Even mandatory busing plans cannot force middle-class and white families to keep their children in the public school system. In order to convince these families that there is a reason to remain, officials need to explore ways to link desegregation with general improvements in the resources, facilities, reputation, and performance of the schools.

A popular method for accomplishing this is the *magnet school.* Magnet schools are schools that offer special programs, such as in the performing arts, computers, or science. Their role is to attract middle-class families that otherwise might be drawn to the private school or suburban alternative. It is hoped that by placing these schools in predominantly minority neighborhoods, integration can be encouraged through essentially voluntary means. The city of Buffalo is one that has experimented broadly with the use of magnet schools as a means to increase integration. Buffalo offers, among other things, a traditional school, featuring military-academy-like discipline and basic skills; an open school; a Montessori school; a bilingual school; a computer-based school; and a Native American school (*The New Republic,* 1983).

Although magnets often are presented as *alternatives* to forced busing, the evidence suggests that—like other voluntary plans—they do not promote much integration on their own. Pittsburgh's attempt to desegregate using only magnet schools did not bring enough desegregation to satisfy state authorities, who ordered that a mandatory assignment component be added as well. Even in Buffalo, the magnet schools account for less than one-third of the district's pupils—not enough to bring about genuine integration. "It's not practical to rely entirely on magnets for desegregation," a school official in Buffalo notes. "You need a variety of other approaches" (Maeroff, 1984, p. C6). Coupled with mandatory busing, however, the availability of magnets may reduce white flight and increase the political palatability of desegregation plans.

SCHOOL FINANCE REFORM

Serrano Sets the Stage

On August 30, 1971, the California state supreme court issued a decision with enormous implications. In California, as in nearly every state, the local property tax was the primary mechanism through which revenues were raised to support the public school system. Property taxes are based on the assessed value of residential and business holdings in a jurisdiction. Because some school districts contain property that is much more valuable than others, this makes it easy for some areas to raise substantial school revenues without imposing a high tax rate, whereas poorer areas can provide only skimpy funding even when more burdensome rates of taxation are imposed.

In the case of *Serrano* v. *Priest,* the California court ruled that the state's existing system of funding schools was illegal. The reliance on local property taxes, according to the court, "makes the quality of a child's education depend upon the resources of his school district and ultimately upon the pocketbook of his parents." An entirely new system of financing—one based on the wealth of the state as a whole rather than that of the individual districts—would have to be designed.

Serrano marked a new phase in the history of American educational reform. During the 1950s and 1960s, the issue of racial inequality had dominated. With *Serrano,* the focus broadened to include inequalities based on economic class. Many liberal educational professionals were "startled into virtual euphoria" (Shannon, 1973, p. 587). If the reasoning applied by the California court was applied throughout the nation, the distinction between "rich" districts and "poor" districts would begin to fade.

Rodriquez Cools the Momentum

Individuals and organizations rushed to introduce *Serrano*-like lawsuits over the rest of the country. At least fifty-two suits were filed in thirty-two states. (Cochran, et al. 1982, p. 295). One of those was in the state of Texas. Demetrio P. Rodriquez charged that the Texas school financing laws effectively prohibited his son, a student in the San Antonio school system, from receiving an equal opportunity to education. The poorest school districts in Texas taxed their residents at a rate more than twice as high as that imposed by the richest districts. In spite of this, these poorer districts could raise only about sixty dollars per pupil, whereas the districts blessed with a strong tax base raised nearly ten times as much. A U.S. district court agreed that the Texas system violated the equal protection clause of the Fourteenth Amendment to the U.S. Constitution. The state of Texas appealed.

The U.S. Supreme Court did not agree with Rodriquez or the lower court. On March 21, 1973, it handed down a 5–4 ruling in the case of *Rodriquez* v. *San Antonio Independent School Board.* Education, it ruled, was not a "fundamental right" afforded protection by the U.S. Constitution. What is more, although some districts clearly could afford to spend much more on the education of their children, there was no evidence that the education provided in the poorest districts was inadequate in an absolute, rather than relative, sense.

The Issue Goes Back to the States

The *Rodriquez* decision took the wind out of the sails of some reformers, but it did not put an end to the issue of school finance reform. The ruling left it open for state courts to decide whether existing finance mechanisms were in violation of *state* laws. It also made it clear that state legislatures were free to draw up new laws designed to make the system of funding schools a fairer one. *Rodriquez* by no means stated that the existing systems were desirable, admirable, or in any way immune to change. Rather, the case shifted the debate back to the state judicial and political arena.

Two weeks after the *Rodriquez* decision, the New Jersey supreme court ruled that that state's system of school finance violated a provision in the New Jersey Constitution holding that "the legislature shall provide for the maintenance and support of a thorough and efficient system of free public schools for the instruction of all the children in this state between the ages of five and eighteen years." Although the provision says nothing explicitly about equality, the court concluded that an equal opportunity for education was implied. Because the existing system, which relied heavily on property taxes, did not provide such equality, the state had a legal obligation to ensure that the constitutional requirement was met (Lehne, 1978).

The New Jersey case of *Robinson* v. *Cahill* demonstrates a number of useful points. First, it made it clear that *state courts can be more aggressive than the federal courts in addressing the issue of class-based inequalities in school funding.* Richard Lehne suggests that this confirms the growing tendency for state courts to take a more active and independent role in defining and protecting individuals' rights.

> As the United States Supreme Court has appeared to pull back from its earlier interpretations of the federal Bill of Rights, some state supreme courts have moved in to fill the gap. With increasing frequency, they have begun to rule that state constitutional provisions guarantee greater rights than do clauses of the federal Bill of Rights. Even when the wording of the counterpart constitutional provisions is identical, state supreme courts have refused to follow the interpretataions of the United States Supreme Court (Lehne, pp. 195–6).

Secondly, the case made it clear that *addressing inequalities in school finance reform would call for expanding substantially the role of states in providing educational revenues.* States that have sought to equalize funding across districts have tended to rely either on a "foundation program" or "power equalization." Under the foundation approach, the state figures out a minimum dollar amount that each district should spend on each of its pupils. The state also determines a minimum tax rate that it would like local districts to apply. If a district is so poor that it cannot raise enough to spend at the foundation level, even if it applies the recommended tax rate, the state will make up the difference. Wealthier districts get proportionally less aid; some, which raise more than the foundation level, get no aid at all.

The foundation plan sets a floor on school expenditures. Because some districts may still spend well above that floor, however, it does not guarantee that much equalization will occur. The power equalization approach is a little more aggressive. Under this plan, the state attempts to ensure that all districts using the same tax rate will raise equal amounts of money. The state sets a schedule of tax rates, along with a set of guaranteed revenues. Thus, every district that taxes at a rate of one dollar per hundred dollars of assessed property value might be guaranteed a revenue of $500 per pupil; those that taxed at a two dollar rate would be guaranteed $1,000; an so on. A poor district that chose to tax itself at the one dollar rate might raise only $150 per pupil; it would be entitled to state aid worth $350 for each student. If the same district had chosen to tax itself at the higher rate of two dollars per $100 of assessed value, it would raise $300 and be eligible for $700 of aid.

In New Jersey, the court ordered the state legislature to come up with a new finance scheme. It quickly became apparent that this would probably entail the institution of a state personal income tax. This was something that some legislators were unwilling to consider, which brings us to a third general point. *Plans to equalize expenditures across districts can be expected to encounter political resistance from wealthier jurisdictions and from other taxpayers who have a stake in vetoing a change in the tax structure.* The essence of all school finance reform plans is to redistribute wealth from richer areas to poorer areas. The residents and representatives of the wealthier areas, not surprisingly, are often inclined to battle against such plans. In New Jersey, state legislators dragged their feet for nearly three years. Finally, the state court lost patience. It ruled that unless the legislature passed an acceptable funding plan by June 30, 1976, no public official would be permitted to spend any money for the purpose of supporting the schools. The entire public school system of the state of New Jersey would be closed down tight. On June 30, the order went into effect. Realizing that they could delay no longer, legislators met in all-night sessions. By July 7, a new funding plan, based on a statewide income tax, had been approved (Lehne, 1978).

New Jersey and a series of other states have made some progress in the past ten years toward the goal of redressing the dramatic inequalities in school funding within their borders. But a final message is this one: *even where states have imposed new funding systems, the gap in spending between rich districts and poor districts remains.* State officials retain a basic allegiance to the notion that school funding should be a localized decision. They hesitate, for both political and philosophical reasons, to deny wealthy districts the right to tax themselves enough to give their children the finest of schools with the best paid and best trained teachers. As long as income and wealth are unevenly spread across the cities and towns of America, a decentralized eductional system will tend to reproduce those inequalities in the amount that is spent on schools. Although the growing role of the states has made ours a less decentralized system than previously, the system of local control is deeply ingrained. The battle for school finance reform, therefore, is likely to be with us for some time to come.

EDUCATION VOUCHERS AND TUITION TAX CREDITS

We might manage, with great effort, to force or cajole or otherwise encourage white children and black children to attend the same schools. We might manage, also with great effort, to equalize expenditures so that poor children may attend schools as well equipped and well staffed as those that wealthier children attend. But these will not guarantee that the schools themselves will do a better job.

The key to improving education, some critics of existing education policy suggest, does not lie in changing the color or the income of the children sitting in the classroom. Instead better education will depend upon changing the content of what is being offered to the students by their teachers and school administrators. But this is more easily said than done.

Many teachers and administrators are comfortable with the way schools are run today. Significant changes might threaten that comfort and challenge their professional beliefs about the proper way to structure the learning process. Teachers and administrators, accordingly, may believe that they have a stake in resisting changes. Also, because they currently play a major role in setting day-to-day policy for the schools, teachers and administrators have the power to use these beliefs to blunt external pressures for reform. In order to bring about significant change, therefore, it may be necessary, first, to alter the balance of power in the education policy decision-making process. Some conservative and neoconservative analysts argue that vouchers and tuition tax credits are a simple and effective mechanism for shifting power from education professionals—who have a stake in maintaining the status quo—to parents and their children—who have a stake in ensuring that they get the greatest education possible for the tax dollars that they pay.

Public Schools As Lazy Monopolies

Public schools—unlike bakeries, gas stations, and barber shops—do not have to compete for customers. Children are required by law to attend school. Although some have the alternative of attending private schools, most cannot afford to do so. Others, who can afford private school tuition, may not have a decent private school close enough to their home to make attendance feasible or convenient. The public schools, moreover, are guaranteed a relatively stable level of financial support regardless of the number of students they attract. This is because compulsory taxation forces area residents to support the public system, even if they elect to send their own children elsewhere.

In this sense, then public schools may be similar to other monopolies. Shielded from the pressures of competition, they have less incentive to ensure that the product they deliver satisfies their clients' needs. The bakery that offers soggy crusts, the barber who is impolite, the gas station that charges an extra dime per gallon risk losing customers and, ultimately, going out of business. Not so the public schools. They can afford to be a little complacent. If a few parents are so dissatisfied as to undertake the expense of sending their children to private school or moving to another school district, the short-term impacts on the school system are slight.

In light of this monopoly status, public schools may have less need to be innovative, less need to ensure the quality of their product, and less need to eliminate unnecessary costs. The protected status of the schools is furthered by the claim to professionalism that allows educators to insist that they, and only they, are competent to make judgments about the methods by which children should be taught, what they should be taught, and by what criteria the success or failure of their efforts should be evaluated. Many parents are intimidated by the aura of professionalism that surrounds teachers and administrators. As a result, they may be inhibited from raising objections or challenges. This inhibition may be shared by the local school board, whose members often are not themselves professionals. Although the school board may have the nominal responsibility for setting policy, members often defer to the school superintendent and staff members who seem more knowledgeable, or at least are more familiar with the jargon that is currently in vogue.

In Chapter 10, we saw that some conservatives and neoconservatives argue that private schools—for reasons such as these—may provide a better education than public schools. To some of these analysts, it is not enough that a private alternative be available. They argue that public policies should be designed to make that alternative available to a wider cross section of the American public. Some are even more ambitious. They argue that public policies, by exposing public schools to private market pressures, can force public schools to become as efficient and effective as their private counterparts.

Turning Students into Consumers

Education vouchers and tuition tax credits are intended to improve schools by exposing them to the pressures of the market and the discipline that competition brings to bear. This is to be done by empowering the student, along with the student's parents, to play the traditional role of the consumer who evaluates the quality of the goods, considers the price at which they are offered, and chooses the product that best meets his or her needs. Under voucher plans, parents would be given vouchers that could be used to gain admission to the public or private school of their choice. The school would be able to redeem the vouchers for cash.

Vouchers presumably would extend to all parents, including the poor, the opportunity to express their dissatisfaction with their current schools by taking their vouchers somewhere else. Public schools would no longer be able to take stable levels of funding for granted. Unless they performed well, they, too, could lose money to private schools or to more innovative or effective public schools.

Although the origin of the voucher concept is credited to conservative economist Milton Friedman, vouchers have drawn some support from liberals as well. During the early 1970s, the federal Office of Economic Opportunity (OEO) took the lead in urging local school systems to try out the idea. OEO had been formed, in the mid-1960s, to coordinate many of the Johnson administration's War on Poverty programs; by the turn of the decade, it had been substantially weakened, but it remained a liberal outpost within the much more conservative Nixon administration. To conservatives, the voucher plan offered the appeal of the unregulated market. To some liberals, it represented an opportunity to extend to poor and minority families the ability to exercise influence over an institution that had failed to adequately respond to their needs and demands.

Tuition tax credits are also intended to increase the competitive pressures on the educational system. By allowing parents of children going to private schools to deduct some proportion of their tuition from their income taxes, this program would make it financially more feasible for parents to choose the private sector alternative. U.S. Senators Packwood and Moynihan proposed such a plan in 1976. It would have allowed parents to deduct one-half the cost of private school tuition, up to a maximum of $500. Moynihan estimated that the cost to the federal government, in lost tax revenues, would have been about $5 billion a year. The Senate rejected the legislation by a vote of 56–41. In 1980, the Senate rejected a more modest tax credit proposal by an even more lopsided vote of 71–24.

Sources of Resistance

Milton Friedman first touted the idea of educational vouchers over twenty years ago (Friedman, 1962). For at least ten years, the idea has been championed as one whose time has come. In spite of this, and in spite of the apparent appeal to both liberals and conservatives, the idea remains on the drawing board. No jurisdiction seems willing to put it into practice. Why?

Some of the resistance is based on concerns about unanticipated and undesirable impacts that might result. Among these concerns are the following:

- *Segregation by race, class, religion, and ideology will increase:* The earliest attempts to implement a voucher program were linked to efforts by southern states to circumvent the Supreme Court's ruling in *Brown* v. *Board of Education* (Puckett, 1983, p. 470). For all the class and racial inequities in public schools, they remain much more diverse and heterogeneous than nearly every other institution in American society. It is in their public school that many children first come into regular contact with others from a cultural, religious, racial, or economic background different from their own. If families use the freedom given to them by vouchers to seek out schools populated by families similar to themselves, this facet of our pluralistic society may be undermined.

- *Public schools will be destroyed:* Voucher and tax credit plans, it is argued, would leave the public schools isolated and stripped of much of their political support. Private schools already skim off many of the best, brightest, and most highly motivated students; with the aid of vouchers and tax credits, good students who could not otherwise afford private tuition would be courted by private schools. Difficult students, students who remain too poor to afford tuition even with vouchers or tax benefits, and students whose parents do not have the time, energy, or expertise with which to shop around for the best school bargain, would be left to languish in a public school system that would gradually be limited to a smaller and smaller share of the nation's dollar investment in education.

- *The separation between church and state would be breached:* There is some uncertainty as to whether voucher and tax credit plans would even be considered constitutional by the Supreme Court. Voucher plans would entail direct governmental payments to private schools that redeem the vouchers given them in lieu of tuition. The Supreme Court ruled in the case of the *Committee for Public Education* v. *Nyquist* (1973), for example, that New York State could not provide grants to private elementary and secondary schools for the maintenance or repair of facilities, tuition reimbursement for low-income families in private schools, or income-tax relief for middle-income parents sending their children to private schools. Even though such aid had "a clearly secular purpose," the Court felt that such legislation still had the primary effect of advancing religion and the potential for causing excessive entanglement between the governement and religious institutions.

There are other criticisms of voucher and tax credit plans. By making it easier for parents to move their children among schools from year to year, for example, they might make it much more difficult for school administrators to project their income and enrollment, thereby undermining efforts to engage in rational planning for the future. Teachers' organizations worry that vouchers and tax credits may provide a convenient vehicle for "union-busting" efforts; teachers would find their salaries and benefits eroded by school administrators under pressure to cut costs in order to compete.

The market model, which makes voucher-type plans so appealing to conservatives and neoconservatives, takes it for granted that consumers have sufficient and accurate information about the products they are considering. When it comes to schools, this assumption may not apply. School officials typically are loathe to produce or release information that can readily be used to determine whether or not they are doing a good job. Wealthier parents are more likely to be able to bridge this information gap than poorer parents. Some liberal and radical critics argue that this may represent a "fatal flaw" in existing voucher and tax credit plans (Olivas, 1981, pp. 133–52).

Regulated Versus Unregulated Voucher Plans

Not all voucher plans are alike. Some voucher proposals have been carefully crafted in an effort to address some of the concerns expressed above.

Milton Friedman's early proposal was for a virtually unregulated voucher plan. "The role of government could be limited to insuring that the schools met certain minimum standards, such as the inclusion of a minimum common content in their programs, much as it now inspects restaurants to insure that they maintain minimum sanitary standards" (Friedman, 1962, p. 89). Beyond that, the market would determine how students and educational dollars should be distributed.

The federal officials in OEO had less faith than Friedman that the results of market dynamics would be equitable and benign. They favored a voucher plan developed by liberal sociologist Christopher Jencks. Jencks's plan sought to build in safeguards to ensure that vouchers would not exacerbate inequities between the rich and poor, or worsen segregation along racial and ethnic lines. Poor families would receive larger vouchers, making them more attractive to schools that might otherwise shy away from them for fear they would require expensive remedial programs. No school receiving vouchers would be allowed to discriminate. Schools with fewer applicants than places would be required to accept all applicants; schools with too many applicants would have to accept half of their students by a random lottery technique. In order to prevent schools from catering to an affluent elite that could afford to supplement their vouchers, no participating school would be allowed to charge tuition beyond the value of the basic voucher. Finally, costs of transportation would be covered, in addition to the voucher amount, in order to guarantee that inner-city and rural families would have access to a broad range of alternative schools (Puckett, 1983, p. 474).

A second highly regulated voucher plan has been offered by two California lawyers, John E. Coons and Stephen D. Sugarman. Coons and Sugarman are attempting to have their proposal approved by California voters as an amendment to the state's constitution. If approved, the Coons-Sugarman proposal would call for the state to make scholarships available to all children. The scholarships would be equal to approximately 90 percent of the average cost per pupil in public schools. Schools that accepted such scholarships—called "New Schools"—would be required to consider the scholarship amounts as full payment for children from low-income families, and charges to other families "shall be consistent with the family's ability to pay." Each New School, in addition, would have to reserve at least one-quarter of each year's admissions to students from families with incomes lower than 75 percent of California families (Coons, 1981).

By lacing their voucher proposals with such restrictions, Jencks and Coons and Sugarman have addressed some of the objections raised against Friedman's laissez-faire version. In doing so, however, they have turned a simple and antibureaucratic scheme into complex legislation that would undoubtedly be more expensive and difficult to put into effect. Whether the protections would work in practice, moreover, remains unclear. Those who would look to history for precedent will not find much guidance, as the experience in Alum Rock reveals.

The Track Record: Experimenting with Vouchers at Alum Rock

The Office of Economic Opportunity (OEO) and Jencks hoped to build support for their plan by sponsoring demonstration projects that would prove that vouchers work. Yet in one city after another—Minneapolis, Rochester, Kansas City, Milwaukee, Gary, San Francisco, Seattle, New Rochelle—the agency found local officials hesitant even to experiment with the voucher idea. Finally, in April 1972, after more than two years of searching for a local partner, OEO officials announced they had found a site for their demonstration project.

Alum Rock was a school district in east San Jose, California. The district housed about 14,500 students in the twenty-one elementary schools. About 12 percent were black, and somewhat over half were of Mexican-American descent. The district's superintendent, who was relatively new to the job, saw the demonstration project as a vehicle through which to further some of his own reform plans.

The Alum Rock experiment attracted national attention. In many people's minds, it was to provide the definitive test of the voucher idea. Abstract and theoretical discussions of the pros and cons of vouchers would be replaced by hard scientific evidence.

As it unfolded, however, the experiment was as interesting for what it did not test as for the specific findings it would produce. The admirable goal of testing a new reform in a systematic fashion suffered when it ran into political, legal, and bureaucratic realities. The California legislature refused to pass legislation that would make it possible for the project to include private schools. As a result, a critical facet of the voucher idea was lost from the very beginning. Alum Rock parents would be free to use their vouchers to move among schools and programs offered in the public system, but they would not be able to apply those vouchers toward tuition at private schools.

Principals, teachers, and school board officials—nervous about potential impacts of the plan—insisted on other alterations. Failure is an integral part of the private market dynamic; businesses that do not provide products and prices that satisfy consumers are replaced by those that do. In order to placate some officials and teachers, however, failure was eliminated as a possible outcome in the demonstration project. Limits were placed on the number of pupils each school could accept; any overflow from the successful and popular schools was to be reassigned to the undersubscribed schools. Teachers were given job guarantees. If enrollment dropped sharply in their schools, they would be reassigned elsewhere. "No one was to be put out on the street by consumer preference" (Cohen and Farrar, 1977, p. 83).

The results of this watered-down experiment are difficult to assess. Early reports suggested that the program was a success: "School Voucher Experiment Rates an 'A' in Coast Experiment," a *New York Times* article announced in May of 1973. But most parents did not actively exploit their new options for influence by switching among schools or by responding to opportunities to get involved in the decision-making process (Cohen and Farrar).

Both critics and advocates of vouchers can find support for their own expectations. The difficulty in finding a local host, and the alteration of the experiment at the local level, suggest to critics that vouchers are politically infeasible. The more officials and citizens find out about voucher and tax credit plans, these critics suggest, the less likely they are to be willing to put them into practice. When a tuition tax credit proposal was placed on the ballot in Washington, D.C., in 1981, voters in every part of the city rejected it overwhelmingly.

To advocates of vouchers and tax credits, however, the Alum Rock experience simply confirms the tendency of public monopolies to defend their prerogatives by blunting reform efforts. The true voucher concept has not yet been tested in the United States. When it is, these supporters argue, the result will be a leaner and more effective educational system, one that responds to the interests of students and parents rather than the comforts of administrators and teachers.

HIGH TECH IN THE CLASSROOM

Remember kindergarten? For many of us, it was a kind of glorified day care. Playing with blocks. Sitting around in a circle while Mrs. Cavendish read us a story. The most deeply imparted lessons, perhaps, were those having to do with order, discipline, and schedules. Milk and graham crackers at 10:00 A.M. Nap on the floor at 10:30. No talking while the teacher talked. Raise your hand if you need to go to the bathroom.

Now picture this. Two five-year-olds huddle enthusiastically in front of a computer terminal, earphones on their heads. A multicolor picture of a cat appears on the screen. "Say the word *cat*," a woman's voice instructs. The children do so. The letter *c* floats into the middle of the screen. "Say *cuh*," the voice suggests.

These children are learning to read and write, and the computer plays a critical role. Advocates of computer-assisted learning argue that the computer can introduce academic concepts earlier and with greater effect than can traditional teaching methods. The key is that the computer does more than simply prompt and guide. A teacher could do that, or a tape recording, or *Sesame Street*. "There is something that Ashley and Josh don't know. In the 16 learning actions that lead to the climax of typing 'cat' that little white computer is watching, counting, timing. If, when tested to show their computer skills, Josh and Ashley touch just two wrong keys, or take too long to respond just twice, the lesson backs up and leads the children through its learning steps again." (Asbell 1984, p. 69). The lessons are individualized, more so, perhaps, than these children are likely to get anywhere but in a one-to-one encounter with a parent or relative. And the computer has other advantages as well. It does not lose its patience. It does not get tired or cranky. It corrects the students silently, privately (Asbell, 1984, p. 69).

This is computer-aided instruction. Some believe it is the wave of the future. "Personal computers have brought education to the threshold of an order-of-magnitude change," one excited observer suggests. A "teacher who won't have a computer in his or her classroom is like a ditch digger who won't learn how to use a steam shovel. . . . In a competitive world, ditch diggers who refuse to adapt are going to go out of business" (Judd, 1983, p. 121).

The idea of restructuring our schools around computers and other forms of high technology has an appeal that cuts across the ideological spectrum. Liberals generally believe that increased knowledge and experience will make it possible for people—through their government—to solve social problems; they are attracted to the possibility of a technological quick fix. Some conservatives and neoconservatives are attracted to the role that computer instruction might play in providing job-related skills.

Lurking behind the flush of excitement are concerns that the promises of technology may offer more in potential than in practice. "Glossy full-page ads describe computers as the new electronic teachers and Congress has debated the value of giving an Apple to every teacher" (Boyer, 1983, p. 187). But *those offering a technological quick fix to the problems in our schools have a legacy of disappointments to explain.* "Educators with long memories will say 'here we go again.' They recall that virtually every new piece of hardware introduced into the schools in the past three decades has been oversold, misused, and eventually discarded. 'Technology breakthroughs' still fill school storerooms. They gather dust, unused after twenty years or more" (Ibid.).

Computers: High Hopes . . .

Computers can serve at least three broad functions in the classroom (Ullman, 1984). Their *most direct role is in teaching children how to use and program computers.* There is no doubt that we are entering an era in which the computer will be ubiquitous. Already the average citizen is likely to come into contact with computers in a range of activities in which the computer was never encountered before. We may deal directly with computers, for example, when we withdraw or deposit money at a bank. In many libraries, terminals are beginning to replace card catalogues. Terminals have even been located in shopping centers, programmed to answer patrons' questions about where to look for various products and inform them where sales are under way. The child of today, it is argued, cannot afford to be the computer-shy adult of tomorrow. Exposures to the basics of computer programming and interaction with computers at an early age may equip young students to be more competent citizens as well as open to them a range of potential employment opportunities.

Secondly, computers can *help students extend their normal capacities in research and writing.* By taking the drudgery out of solving mathematical equations and plotting graphs, for example, computers may encourage students to be more adventurous in the techniques they apply. Bibliographic and reference services are becoming increasingly available to those with access to a terminal. And the word-processing capabilities of computers mean that it will be easier for students to hand in an edited neat draft.

The application of computers in these areas are direct and of indisputable value. They do not, however, warrant the high hopes and dramatic rhetoric with which the advent of computer classrooms is being met. Most children will have no need to be computer technicians or computer programmers as adults. The computer is becoming more broadly used in large measure because it is becoming more simple to use. Computer firms spend millions of dollars seeking to make their products "user friendly." You do not need to be able to take apart a transmission (or even to recognize one when you see it!) in order to drive a car. Nor, for most Americans in the future, will it be necessary to understand the inner workings of the computer in order to put it to use. In addition, although research and writing applications are important, they remain, in many ways, second-order skills. Before the data analysis and bibliographic functions of the computer can be put to effective use, students must have learned how to determine what is an important research question. Word processors do not put together sentences or give the students an idea to express.

If computers are to make more than a marginal difference in the success of our schools, they will have to be able to do more than this—they will have to be able to *help people to learn*. The following are among the ways in which the computer may be able to enrich the process of education (Walker, 1983, pp. 103–5):

- *More active learning:* The traditional classroom is constrained by the teacher's need to maintain order and control over twenty or more children. The result is a passive experience for most students; they listen while the teacher instructs. Through computers, children may be able to learn by doing.

- *More varied stimuli:* Computers can present colored graphics, and move and rotate shapes through space. They can be linked, moreover, to a range of devices, including "videotape or videodisc players, electronic musical instruments, scientific instruments, physiological monitoring equipment, household appliances, and other computers" (Walker, p. 104).

- *Speedier learning:* Consider a normal high-school chemistry class. Teams of students cluster around the lab, each working on their experiment. One team's members are uncertain whether they have read the instructions correctly; another team is getting an unpredicted reaction; a third has completed the experiment and is wondering what to move on to next. The students must compete for the teacher's attention. Some will have to wait. In the meantime, valuable time that could be spent learning is lost. Some questions will be forgotten or left behind. The computer responds immediately and on demand.

- *Individuality:* Decker Walker cites an example of the capacity of computers to tailor a learning experience to each student's particular needs. The program is designed to diagnose problems with subtraction. When a student makes an error, the computer rapidly "tries every incorrect 'rule' for subtraction . . . to see if any of these mistaken ways of doing subtraction could produce this particular wrong answer." The student is then presented with further problems specifically designed to determine whether the child is indeed making a consistent, systematic error. With that information, the teacher and student are better able to iron out the problem (Ibid.).

- *Greater independence:* Students can better realize that they have the capacity to determine answers for themselves. Students who are willing and able to proceed at a faster pace are able to do so.

- *Aids to abstraction:* Scientific concepts—like a fourth dimension or black holes in space—and philosophical concepts—like justice and authority—can be extremely difficult to grasp intellectually. Computers may have the capacity to bring those concepts into greater focus. Decker discusses the experience of two writers who were unable to get any feeling for hypercubes (four-dimensional cubes) until they worked with a computer that allowed them to simulate what it would be like to move such a cube through our three-dimensional world. Computers might allow students to create their own societies, governed by a set of laws and relationships they define, and set those worlds into action to see what occurs.

. . . Or High Hype?

For all its promise, some observers warn that the computer may join some of its predecessors in the dustbin. Ernest Boyer, for example, notes the parallels between the computer and some of those earlier technological cure-alls that proved to be cure-nothings. In the early 1950s, there were the "teaching machines," which administrators were told could be "the most important invention since the printing press." Later, there was the talking typewriter, which called out the letter sounds as students struck its keys. This machine "presumably taught them how to read and write in a new and painless way. The few experimental models soon were discarded." And then there were the language laboratories of the 1960s.

Schools spent large sums of money to equip classrooms with individual carrels, each containing electronic recording and listening devices. Students, wearing headphones, would listen to foreign language tapes and recite into a microphone. The teacher, from a central location, could selectively eavesdrop on the lesson, correcting students with their pronunciation or reminding the daydreamers that they had better get back to work. "Frequently," the carrels "stood unused while students recited their lessons to their teachers" in the traditional face-to-face style (Boyer, 1983, pp. 187–8).

The problem, skeptics note, does not lie with the machine itself. Rather, the potential for disappointment lies in the inflated expectations and reckless enthusiasm with which each hot new technological innovation is pursued. "Educators seem confused about precisely what the new miracle machines will do," Boyer observes. "But the mood appears to be 'Buy now, plan later.' " The average grade school, by early 1984, owned 3.6 computers; the average high school had ten (*Time*, 1984, p. 62; Boyer, 1983, p. 189).

Such a rush to jump onto the computer bandwagon is understandable in political terms. Professional educators are battling for funding in a time of tight state and local budgets. Their position is weakened by the decline in public satisfaction with the schools. While home computers are selling like hotcakes and while parents are priming their five-year-olds with the message that their future employability depends upon gaining mastery of this powerful tool, educators see a chance for regaining public support by jumping on the bandwagon.

But "selling" the computer as a magical instrument may backfire. "Newspaper headlines may trumpet, 'Beacon Hill Lights Way, Computers in Every Classroom Next Fall,' " one critic writes. "If Beacon Hill hasn't done its homework," however, "less positive headlines might be just around the corner" (Railsback, 1983, pp. 118–19). Although the costs of microcomputers have declined dramatically, outfitting a school with a meaningful computer capacity requires a considerable investment. Rapid changes in technology, moreover, make the risks high. A system purchased today may seem outdated tomorrow. Unless all the options are carefully considered, by expert analysts, a school system may find itself investing in terminals and equipment that are not compatible with the best educational programs.

Some schools seem to be rushing in ahead of the capacities of their own teaching staffs. Unless existing teachers are given extensive training, they are likely to regard computer systems as alien and threatening. Most teachers do not want to be embarrassed in front of the students by the clearly superior knowledge of the class "computer whiz." Teachers, too, have invested time and personal sacrifice in their traditional teaching modes. They will not venture onto unfamiliar grounds unless they are coaxed *and* rewarded for doing so.

Ultimately, moreover, it must be remembered that there is much that computers cannot do. They cannot replace the personal touch of the teacher. They cannot converse with the students other than in patterns predrawn by their programmers. They cannot address the inequalities in income and the differences in family backgrounds that bring some students into class in the morning eager to learn yet drain others of the desire or self-confidence needed for success.

These concerns also touch themes consistent with a range of ideologies. Some conservatives prefer a more traditional "back-to-the-basics" approach, and some neoconservatives see the touting of computers as one more example of unflinching liberal optimism that schools can be an instrument of major social reform. Some liberals and radicals fear that a big fuss over computers might divert attention from deeper problems that should have a higher priority. A bright new computer terminal donated to a ghetto school might delude officials and citizens into believing that inequalities in educational opportunities are being solved. Yet wealthier school districts have access to superior equipment and training, and the skills provided to lower-class children might do little more than provide them access to low-paying jobs.

SUMMARY AND CONCLUSIONS

The Progressive movement, in the first half of the century, instituted reforms that, it was argued, would take control over schools out of the hands of politicians. The Progressives' notion was that education could be, and should be, a politically neutral enterprise, guided by professional educators who are motivated solely by considerations of what is best for the child and who have the expertise needed to evaluate and implement the best educational techniques. Their efforts produced some desirable results. Most notably, they helped to take teaching and school administrative jobs out of the patronage pot. Civil service and merit systems gave qualified people the chance to work in local school systems even if they did not vote for the party in power or belong to the most influential ethnic groups.

But the idea that education can be insulated from politics is questionable. It presumes that there is broad agreement as to the goals of the education system, and we have seen that there is not. Table 11–1 summarizes the ideological differences concerning broad goals, and shows how those differences translate into disagreements about the specific issues discussed in this chapter. In the face of such disagreements, politics cannot be escaped. That is because politics is the forum through which any society mediates its disagreements about what should be done.

States and localities are in the best position to address these issues. Even as the national government expanded its involvement in education,

Table 11–1 Ideology and School Policies

	Traditional Conservative	Neoconservative	Liberal	Radical
Goals of Schools	Select and nurture intellectual elite; train others for work with job skills and discipline	Educate those who want to learn; cannot undo inequalities due to family, community	Great equalizer; narrow gap between black and white, rich and poor	Serves elite through socialization and control
Integration and Busing	Threat to local control and, local values; disruptive to education	Integration is desirable, but forced busing does more harm than good	Necessary to undo past injustices; can improve minorities' opportunities, promote racial understanding	A potential distraction; minorities better served by seeking power to control schools
School Finance Reform	Threat to local control; wealthy have right to spend funds for own children	Like other attempts to use schools for social reform, will not work and may backfire	Reliance on property tax denies equal chance to children in poor districts	Current efforts leave inequities intact; window dressing; wealthy use power to prevent real change
Vouchers and Tuition Tax Credits	Allow market forces to impose efficiency, effectiveness, and responsiveness	Allow market forces to impose efficiency, effectiveness, and responsiveness; can give poor freedom to choose	Unless saddled with complicated protections, may promote segregation by race and class; may undermine valuable public schools	Benefits the rich at expense of middle class and poor; provisions to protect poor will be weak or unenforced
Computers in Classroom	Some prefer traditional subjects; may have role in vocational education	May provide job-relevant skills to those willing and able to learn	Exciting prospects, but must ensure access to poor	Poor will be trained for low-paying keypunch and repair jobs

the tradition of localism remained strong. The federal government, through the courts and through its financial clout, can influence what the states and localities do. But the experience with integration and busing shows that, even when the national government takes a strong stand, state and local officials hold the key to the ultimate result. The national government can force local school districts to bus students, but it has not yet found a way to force them to do so in a manner that makes the process more likely to succeed. At the same time, a more conservative Supreme Court makes it less likely that the national government will try to take a leadership role. The decision in the *Rodriquez* case is symbolic in this regard.

While the national government was confronting issues of racial and class equality, states and localities were free to deal with less controversial concerns. State and local officials, by and large, seemed to prefer it that way. Restricting discussion to technical questions of funding and administration meant that ideological divisions among the population and their representatives could be kept from erupting into overt conflict. By framing issues in the form of local control versus federal interference, these officials sometimes were able to unite local factions against a common outside foe.

If the trend toward decentralization of decision-making that was launched by the Nixon and Reagan administrations calls for New Federalism proves to be more than a short-term aberration, the atmosphere in which state and local officials operate is likely to change. Competing groups and competing philosophies will become more apparent. The illusion that education policy can be politically neutral will be more difficult to sustain.

SUGGESTED READINGS

Boyer, Ernest L. *High School: A Report on Secondary Education in America*. New York: Harper & Row, 1983.

Coons, John E., and Stephen D. Sugarman. *Education by Choice: The Case for Family Control*. Berkeley, California: University of California Press, 1978.

Gaffney, Edward McGlynn, Jr., ed. *Private Schools and the Public Good*. Notre Dame, Indiana: University of Notre Dame Press, 1981.

Glazer, Nathan. *Affirmative Discrimination*. New York: Basic Books, 1975.

Guthrie, James W., ed. *School Finance Policies and Practices*. Cambridge, Massachusetts: Ballinger, 1980.

Hawley, Willis D., ed. *Effective School Desegregation*. Beverly Hills, California: Sage, 1981.

Lehne, Richard. *The Quest for Justice: The Politics of School Finance Reform.* New York: Longman, 1978.

Orfield, Gary. *Must We Bus?* Washington, D.C.: Brookings Institution, 1978.

Willie, Charles V., and Susan L. Greenblatt. *Community Politics and Educational Change.* New York: Longman, 1981.

REFERENCES

Abravanel, Martin T. and Paul K. Mancini (1980) "Attitudinal and Demographic Constraints," in D. Rosenthal, ed.

Advisory Commission on Intergovernmental Relations (1976) *Improving Urban America: A Challenge to Federalism.* Washington, D.C.: Government Printing Office.

——— (1977) *Measuring the Fiscal Blood Pressure of the States.* Washington, D.C.: Government Printing Office.

——— (1980) *Public Assistance: The Growth of a Federal Function.* Washington, D.C.: Government Printing Office.

——— (1981) *The States and Distressed Communities.* Washington, D.C.: Government Printing Office (May).

——— (1982) *State and Local Roles in the Federal System.* Washington, D.C.: Government Printing Office.

——— (1983) *The States Transformed.* Prepublication draft.

——— (1983b) *The States and Distressed Communities: The 1982 Report.* Washington, D.C.: Government Printing Office.

——— (1984) *Significant Features of Fiscal Federalism.* Washington, D.C.: Government Printing Office.

Ahlbrandt, Roger S., Jr. (1973) *Municipal Fire Protection Services: Comparison of Alternative Organizational Forms.* Beverly Hills: Sage.

Alexander, John K. (1980) *Render Them Submissive: Responses to Poverty in Philadelphia, 1760–1800.* Amherst: University of Massachusetts.

Alexander, Karl L. and Aaron Pallas (1983) "Private Schools and Public Policy: New Evidence in Cognitive Achievement," *Sociology of Education* 56 (October).

Allman, T.D. (1978) "The Urban Crisis Leaves Town," *Harper's Magazine* (December).

Alonso, William (1973) "Urban Zero Population Growth," *Daedalus* 4 (Fall).

Anderson, Martin (1978) *Welfare.* Stanford, Calif.: Hoover Press.

Antunes, George F. and Patricia Hurley (1977) "The Representation of Criminal Events in Houston's Two Daily Newspapers, *Journalism Quarterly* (Winter).
Armor, David (1972) "The Evidence on Busing," *The Public Interest* (Summer).
Arons, Stephen and Charles Lawrence III (1982) "The Manipulation of Consciousness: A First Amendment Critique of Schooling," in R. Everhart, ed.
Asbell, Bernard (1984) "Writers' Workshop at Age 5," *New York Times Magazine* (February 26).
Auletta, Ken (1979) *The Streets Were Paved With Gold*. New York: Random House.
——— (1983) *The Underclass*. New York: Vintage.
Babcock, Richard F. (1980) "Eastlake v. Forest City Enterprises: Five Comments," in F. Schnidman and J. Silverman, eds.
Bahl, Roy (1984) *Financing State and Local Government in the 1980s*. New York: Oxford.
Balz, Dan (1982) "U.S. Money 'Exports' Ohio's Jobless," *Washington Post* (June 3).
Baldassare, Mark (1981) *The Growth Dilemma*. Berkeley, Calif.: University of California.
Banfield, Edward C. (1974) *The Unheavenly City Revisited*. Boston: Little Brown.
Bell, Daniel (1973) *The Coming of the Post-Industrial Society*. New York: Free Press.
Bellush, Jewel and Murray Hausknecht, eds. (1967) *Urban Renewal: People, Politics and Planning*. Garden City, New York: Anchor.
Berg, Ivar (1974) "The Great Training Robbery," in Lee Rainwater (ed.) *Inequality and Justice*. Chicago: Aldine.
Berkley, George E. and Douglas M. Fox (1978) *80,000 Governments: The Politics of Subnational America*. Boston: Allyn and Bacon.
Berman, Daniel S. (1969) *Urban Renewal: Bonzana of the Real Estate Business*. Englewood Cliffs, New Jersey: Prentice-Hall.
Beyrer, Mary K., et al. (1977) *Positive Health: Designs for Action*. Philadelphia: Lea & Febiger.
Bishop, John (1981) "The Impact of Unemployment and Welfare Assistance on Marital Stability," in John E. Tropman, Milan J. Dluhy, and Roger M. Lind (eds.) *New Strategic Perspectives on Social Policy*. New York: Pergamon.
Black, Donald J. (1970) "Production of Crime Rates," *American Sociological Review* 35 (August).
Bluestone, Barry and Bennett Harrison (1982) *The Deindustrialization of America*. New York: Basic Books.
Bluhm, William T. (1974) *Ideologies and Attitudes*. Englewood Cliffs, New Jersey: Prentice-Hall.
Bosselman, Fred and David Callies (1972) *The Quiet Revolution in Land Use Control*. Washington, D.C.: The Council on Environmental Quality.
Bowles, Samuel and Herbert Gintis (1976) *Schooling in Capitalist America*. New York: Basic Books.
Boyer, Brian D. (1973) *Cities Destroyed For Cash*. Chicago: Follett.
Boyer, Ernest L. (1983) *High School*. New York: Harper & Row.

Bradbury, Katharine L. and Anthony Downs, eds. (1981) *Do Housing Allowances Work?* Washington, D.C.: The Brookings Institution.

Bradbury, Katharine L., Anthony Downs, and Kenneth A. Small (1982) *Urban Decline and the Future of American Cities.* Washington, D.C.: The Brookings Institution.

Bratt, Rachel G., Janet M. Bird, and Robert M. Hollister (1983) "The Private Sector and Neighborhood Preservation," unpublished paper presented at the U.S. Department of Housing and Urban Development sponsored Conference on Neighborhood Action in an Era of Fiscal Austerity (March 31).

Bureau of Justice Statistics, (1983) *Report to the Nation on Crime and Justice.* Washington, D.C.: U.S. Department of Justice.

———— (1983b) "Bulletin: Prisoners at Midyear 1983," Washington, D.C.: U.S. Department of Justice (October).

Butler, Stuart (1981) *Enterprise Zones: Greenlining the Inner Cities.* New York: Universe Books.

Cahn, Robert (1975) "Where Do We Grow from Here?" in Randall W. Scott, ed.

Chaiken, Jan M., Michael W. Lawless, and Keith A. Stevenson (1974) *The Impact of Police Activity on Crime: Robberies in the New York City Subway System.* New York: Rand Corporation.

Chaiken, Jan M. and Marcia R. Chaiken (1983) "Crime Rates and the Active Criminal," in J.Q. Wilson, ed. 1983b.

Chernow, Ron (1978) "The Rabbit That Ate Pennsylvania," *Mother Jones* (January).

Choat, Pat and Susan Walter (1981) *America in Ruins.* Washington, D.C.: Council of State Planning Agencies.

Clark, Ramsey (1970) *Crime in America.* New York: Simon and Schuster.

Clark, Terry Nichols and Lorna Crowley Ferguson (1983) *City Money.* New York: Columbia University.

Clay, Philip L. (1979) "The Process of Black Suburbanization," *Urban Affairs Quarterly* 14 (June).

Cloward, Richard and Lloyd Ohlin (1960) *Delinquency and Opportunity.* New York: The Free Press.

Cochran, Clarke E., T.R. Carr, Lawrence C. Mayer, and N. Joseph Cayer (1982) *American Public Policy: An Introduction.* New York: St. Martin's.

Coe, Richard (1981) "A Preliminary Empirical Examination of the Dynamics of Welfare Use," in Hill et al. *Five Thousand American Families.*

Cohen, David K. and Eleanor Farrar (1977) "Power to the Parents?—The Story of Education Vouchers," *The Public Interest* 97 (Summer).

Cohen, Lawrence E., Marcus Felson, and Kenneth C. Land (1980) "Property Crime Rates in the United States," *American Journal of Sociology* 86.

Coleman, James S. et al. (1966) *Equality of Educational Opportunity.* Washington, D.C.: Government Printing Office.

Coleman, James S., and Sara D. Kelly (1976) "Education," in William Gorham and Nathan Glazer, eds. *The Urban Predicament.* Washington, D.C.: The Urban Institute.

Coleman, James, Thomas Hoffer, and Sally Kilgore (1982) *High School Achievement: Public, Catholic, and Private Schools Compared.* New York: Basic Books.
Congressional Quarterly (1978) *Crime and Justice.* Washington: D.C.: Congressional Quarterly, Inc.
Coons, John E. (1981) "Making Schools Public," in E. Gaffney, Jr., ed.
Council on Environmental Quality (1980) *The Eleventh Annual Report of the Council on Environmental Quality.* Washington, D.C.: Government Printing Office.
Cowan, Edward (1982) "Bill Gives I.R.S. More Pay Data," *New York Times* (March 23).
Crain, Robert L. and Rita Mahard (1981) "Some Policy Implications of the Desegregation-Minority Achievement Literature," in Willis D. Hawley, ed. *Assessment of Current Knowledge about the Effectiveness of School Desegregation Strategies.* Nashville: Center for Education and Human Development Policy, Vanderbilt University.
——— (1983) "The Effect of Research Methodology on Desegregation-Achievement Studies: A Meta-Analysis," *American Journal of Sociology* 88 (March).
Dahrendorf, Ralf (1959) *Class and Class Conflict in Industrial Society.* Stanford, Calif.: Stanford University.
Dalton, Katharine (1979) *Once a Month.* Pomona, Calif.: Hunter House.
Daniels, Lee A. (1983) "In Defense of Busing," *The New York Times Magazine.* (April 17).
Danielson, Michael (1976) *The Politics of Exclusion.* New York: Columbia University Press.
Davis, Karen and Cathy Schoen (1978) *Health and the War on Poverty.* Washington, D.C.: Brookings.
Dembart, Lee (1977) "Carter Takes 'Sobering' Trip to South Bronx," *New York Times* (October 6).
Dobelstein, Andrew W. (1980) *Politics, Economics and Public Welfare.* Englewood Cliffs, New Jersey: Prentice-Hall.
Dolbeare, Kenneth M. and Patricia Dolbeare (1978) *American Ideologies.* Chicago: Rand McNally.
Dommel, Paul R., et al. (1978) *Decentralizing Community Development.* Washington, D.C.: U.S. Department of Housing and Urban Development (June).
——— (1982) *Decentralizing Urban Policy.* Washington, D.C.: The Brookings Institution.
Downes, Bryan T. (1970) "A Critical Reexamination of the Social and Political Characteristics of Riot Cities," *Social Science Quarterly* 51 (September).
Drury, Margaret, Olson Lee, Michel Springer, and Lorene Yap (1978) *Lower Income Housing Assistance Program (Section 8).* Washington, D.C.: U.S. Department of Housing and Urban Development, Office of Policy Development and Research (November).
Dye, Thomas (1981) *Politics in States and Communities,* 4th edition. Englewood Cliffs, New Jersey: Prentice-Hall.
Ecker-Racz, L. L. (1970) *The Politics of State-Local Finance.* Englewood Cliffs, New Jersey: Prentice-Hall.

Edson, C.H. (1982) "Schooling for Work and Working at School," in R. Everhart, ed.
Eisenstein, James and Herbert Jacob (1977) *Felony Justice.* Boston: Little, Brown.
Elazar, Daniel J. (1974) "The New Federalism: Can the States Be Trusted?" *The Public Interest* 35 (Spring).
―――― (1984) *American Federalism: A View from the States,* 3rd edition. New York: Harper & Row.
Engle, Margaret (1983) "Community Service Growing as Alternative to Prison Time," *Washington Post* (November 6).
Erickson, Donald A. (1982) "Disturbing Evidence about the 'One Best System,'" in R. Everhart, ed.
Everhart, Robert B., ed. (1982) *The Public School Monopoly.* Cambridge, Mass.: Ballinger.
Ewen, Lynda Ann (1978) *Corporate Power and Urban Crisis in Detroit.* Princeton: Princeton University.
Farley, R., T. Richards, and G. Wurdock (1980) "School Desegregation and White Flight: An Investigation of Competing Models and Their Discrepant Findings," *Sociology of Education* 53.
Farley, John E. (1983) "Metropolitan Housing Segregation in 1980: The St. Louis Case," *Urban Affairs Quarterly* 18 (March).
Feagin, Joe R. (1975) *Subordinating the Poor: Welfare and American Beliefs.* Englewood Cliffs, New Jersey: Prentice-Hall.
―――― (1984) "Sunbelt Metropolis and Development Capital: Houston in the Era of Late Capitalism," in L. Sawyers and W. Tabb, eds.
Feaver, Douglas B. (1982) "Cities Court Disaster on Their Decaying Bridges," *Washington Post* (November 22).
Fishman, Charles (1983) "Food Stamp Diet Passes Block Family Test," *Washington Post* (August 5).
Fogelson, Robert M. (1977) *Big City Police.* Cambridge, Mass.: Harvard University.
Forer, Lois G. (1980) *Criminals and Victims: A Trial Court Judge Reflects on Crime and Punishment.* New York: W.W. Norton.
Forbes Magazine (1971) "Fellow Americans—Keep Out!" (October)
Frieden, Bernard J. and Marshall Kaplan (1975) *The Politics of Neglect.* Cambridge, Mass.: MIT Press.
Frieden, Bernard J. (1979) *The Environmental Protection Hustle.* Cambridge, Mass.: MIT Press.
Friedman, Milton (1962) *Capitalism and Freedom.* Chicago: University of Chicago.
Gaffney, Edward McGlynn, Jr., ed. (1981) *Private Schools and the Public Good.* Notre Dame, Indiana: University of Notre Dame.
Gale, Dennis E. (1984) *Neighborhood Revitalization and the Postindustrial City.* Lexington, Mass.: Lexington Books.
Gallup, George H. (1983) "The Fifteenth Annual Gallup Poll of the Public's Attitude Toward the Public Schools," *Phi Delta Kappan* (September).

Gans, Herbert J. (1962) *The Urban Villagers*. New York: The Free Press.
────── (1972) "The Positive Functions of Poverty," *American Journal of Sociology* 78.
Gibbs, Jack P. (1968) "Crime, Punishment, and Deterrence," *Southwestern Social Science Quarterly* 48 (March).
Ginsberg, Benjamin (1978) "Controlling Crime: The Limits of Deterrence," in Theodore J. Lowi and Alan Stone, eds., *Nationalizing Government*. Beverly Hills, Calif.: Sage Publications.
Ginsburg, Benson E. (1974) "The Violent Brain: Is It Everyone's Brain?" in C.R. Jefféry, ed.
Glaser, Daniel (1983) "Supervising Offenders Outside of Prison," in J.Q. Wilson, ed.
Glazer, Nathan (1967) "Housing Problems and Housing Policies," *The Public Interest* 7 (Spring).
Glendening, Parris N. and Mavis Mann Reeves (1977) *Pragmatic Federalism*. Pacific Palisades, Calif.: Palisades Publishers.
Goldberger, Paul (1982) "The Limits of Urban Growth," *New York Times Magazine* (November 14).
Goldwater, Barry (1960) *The Conscience of a Conservative*. New York: Hillman.
Goodman, Robert (1971) *After the Planners*. New York: Simon & Schuster.
Gorz, Andre (1964) *Strategy for Labor*. Boston: Beacon.
Greeley, Andrew M. (1981) "Catholic High Schools and Minority Students," in E. Gaffney, Jr. ed.
Greer, Edward (1979) *Big Steel*. New York: Monthly Review Press.
Grier, Eunice and George Grier (1968) "Equality and Beyond: Housing Segregation in the Great Society," in Bernard J. Frieden and Robert Morris, eds., *Urban Planning and Social Policy*. New York: Basic Books.
Grodzins, Morton (1966) *The American System*. Chicago: Rand McNally.
Gutman, Herbert (1976) *The Black Family in Slavery and Freedom, 1750–1925*. New York: Pantheon.
Haider, Donald (1974) *When Governments Come to Washington*. New York: Free Press.
Hale, George E. and Marian L. Palley (1981) *The Politics of Federal Grants*. Washington, D.C.: Congressional Quarterly Press.
Harrison, Bennett (1984) "Regional Restructuring and 'Good Business Climates': The Economic Transformation of New England Since World War II," in Sawyers and Tabb (eds.).
Hartman, Chester (1967) "The Housing of Relocated Families," in Bellush and Hausknecht, eds.
────── (1974) *Yerba Buena: Land Grab and Community Resistance in San Francisco*. San Francisco: Glide Publications.
Hays, Samuel P. (1964) "The Politics of Reform in Municipal Government in the Progressive Era," *Pacific Northwest Quarterly* 55 (October).
Healy, Robert and John S. Rosenberg (1979) *Land Use and the States*. Baltimore: Johns Hopkins University.
Harrington, Michael (1963) *The Other America*. New York: Macmillan.

Haveman, Robert H., ed. (1977) *A Decade of Federal Antipoverty Programs.* New York: Academic Press.

Heidenheimer, Arnold J., Hugh Heclo, and Carolyn Teich Adams (1983) *Comparative Public Policy* 2nd edition, New York: St. Martin's.

Henig, Jeffrey R., Robert L. Lineberry, and Neal A. Milner (1977) "The Policy Impact of Policy Evaluation: Some Implications of the Kansas City Patrol Experiment," in John Gardner, eds., *Public Law and Public Policy.* New York: Praeger.

Hess, Robert D. (1970) "The Transmission of Cognitive Strategies in Poor Families: The Socialization of Apathy and Underachievement," in Vernon L. Allen (ed.) *Psychological Factors in Poverty.* Chicago: Markham.

Hicks, Donald (1982) *Urban America in the Eighties.* New Brunswick: Transaction Books.

Hill, Martha S., Daniel H. Hill, and James N. Morgan (1981) *Five Thousand American Families: Patterns of Economic Progress.* Ann Arbor, Michigan: Institute for Social Research.

Hines, Theodore (1964) "Negro Boy Killed, 300 Harass Police," *New York Times* (July 17).

Hofstadter, Ricahrd (1959) *Social Darwinism in American Thought.* New York: George Braziller.

Hombs, Mary Ellen and Mitch Snyder (1982) *Homelessness in America.* Washington, D.C.: Center for Creative Nonviolence.

Hunter, Floyd (1953) *Community Power Structure.* Chapel Hill: University of North Carolina.

Husen, Torsten (1981) "Coleman II—Another Case of Politics and the Professors," *Change: The Magazine of Higher Learning* (September).

Jacob, Herbert (1980) *Crime and Justice in Urban America.* Englewood Cliffs, New Jersey: Prentice-Hall.

—— (1984) *The Frustration of Policy.* Boston: Little, Brown.

Jacob, Herbert and Robert L. Lineberry (1982) *Governmental Responses to Crime.* Washington, D.C.: U.S. Department of Justice (June).

Jacobs, Jane (1961) *The Death and Life of the Great American Cities.* New York: Vintage.

Jacobs, John (1979) *Bidding for Business: Corporate Auctions and the Fifty Disunited States.* Washington, D.C.: Public Interest Research Group.

Jaynes, Gregory (1978) "A Day in the World's Busiest Courthouse," *New York Times* (March 31).

Jeffery, C.R., ed. (1974) *Biology and Crime.* Beverly Hills, Calif.: Sage Publications.

Jencks, Christopher (1964) "Why Bail Out the States?" *New Republic* (December 12).

—— (1972) *Inequality.* New York: Harper Colophon.

—— (1979) *Who Gets Ahead?* New York: Basic Books.

Jensen, Arthur (1972) *Genetics and Education.* New York: Harper & Row.

Jones, Bryan D. (1983) *Governing Urban America.* Boston: Little Brown.

Jones, David A. (1979) *Crime Without Punishment.* Lexington, Mass.: Lexington Books.

Judd, Wallace (1983) "A Teacher's Place in the Computer Classroom," *Phi Delta Kappan* (October).
Kain, John F. (1968) "The Distribution and Movements of Jobs and Industry," in James Q. Wilson, ed., *The Metropolitan Enigma*. Cambridge, Mass.: Harvard University.
Kaplan, Harold (1963) *Urban Renewal Politics*. New York: Columbia University.
Kasarda, John D. (1980) "The Implications of Contemporary Distribution Trends for National Urban Policy," *Social Science Quarterly* 61 (December).
Kelling, George L., Tony Pate, Duane Dieckman, and Charles E. Brown (1974) *The Kansas City Preventive Patrol Experiment: A Summary Report*. Washington, D.C., The Police Foundation.
Kennet, David A. (1980) "Altruism and Economic Behavior: Private Charity and Public Policy," *Journal of Economics and Sociology* 39 (October).
Kettl, Donald (1979) "Can the Cities Be Trusted? The Community Development Experience," *Political Science Quarterly* 94 (Fall).
Klose, Kevin (1983) "Chicago Shenanigans," *Washington Post* (August 3).
Kotler, Milton (1969) *Neighborhood Government*. Indianapolis: Bobbs-Merrill.
Kozol, Jonathan (1967) *Death at an Early Age*. Boston: Houghton Mifflin.
Krajik, Kevin and Steve Gettinger (1982) *Overcrowded Time*. New York: The Edna McConnell Clark Foundation.
Kramer, Larry (1979) "Business Lures Useless, Nader Says," *Washington Post* (August 2).
Kristol, Irving (1972) *On the Democratic Idea in America*. New York: Harper & Row.
——— (1977) "Sense and Nonsense in Urban Policy," *Washington Post* (December 23).
Kurtz, Howard (1983) "Enterprise Zones Without Reagan," *Washington Post* (November 6).
Larson, Richard C. (1975) "What Happened to Patrol Operations in Kansas City? A Review of the Kansas City Preventive Patrol Experiment," *Journal of Criminal Justice* 3.
Laska, Shirley and Daphne Spain, eds. (1980) *Back to the City*. New York: Pergamon Press.
Lawton, M.P., L. Nahemow, S. Yaffe, and S. Feldman (1976) "Psychological Aspects of Crime and Fear of Crime," in J. Goldsmith and S. Goldsmith, eds. *Crime and the Elderly*. Lexington, Mass.: D.C. Heath.
Lehne, Richard (1978) *The Quest For Justice*. New York: Longman.
Lekachman, Robert (1976) *Economists at Bay*. New York: McGraw-Hill.
Lenberg Center for the Study of Violence (1968) "April Aftermath of the King Assasination," cited in Joe R. Feagin and Harlan Hahn (eds.) *Ghetto Revolts*. New York: Macmillan, 1973.
Levin, Henry M. (1977) "A Decade of Policy Developments in Improving Education and Training for Low-Income Populations," in Haveman, (ed.).
Levitan, Sar A. and Robert Taggart (1976) *The Promise of Greatness*. Cambridge: Harvard University.
Levy, John M. (1981) *Economic Development Programs for Cities, Counties, and Towns*. New York: Praeger.

Lewis, Arthur (1975) "The Worst American City," *Harper's Magazine* (January).
Lewis, Oscar (1966) *La Vida*. New York: Random House.
Lindblom, Charles (1977) *Politics and Markets*. New York: Basic Books.
Lineberry, Robert L. and Ira Sharkansky (1976) *Urban Politics and Public Policy*, 3rd edition, New York: Harper & Row.
Linowes, R. Robert and Julian Delaney (1980) "Downzoning—And How the Landowner May Fight It," in F. Schnidman and J. Silverman, eds.
Logan, John and Mark Schneider (1981) "The Stratification of Metropolitan Suburbs: 1960–1970," *American Sociological Review* 46.
Long, Larry (1980) "Back to the Countryside and Back to the City in the Same Decade," in S. Laska and D. Spain, eds.
Lowi, Theodore (1979) *The End of Liberalism*, 2nd edition. New York: Norton.
Lynn, Laurence E., Jr. (1977) "A Decade of Policy Developments in the Income-Maintenance System," in Haveman (ed.).
——— (1980) *The State and Human Services*. Cambridge, MIT.
McClelland, David (1961) *The Achieving Society*. New York: Van Nostrand.
McFarland, M. Carter (1978) *Federal Government and Urban Problems*. Boulder, Colo.: Westview.
Madaus, George F., Peter W. Airasian, and Thomas Kellaghan (1980) *School Effectiveness: A Reassessment of the Evidence*. New York: McGraw-Hill.
Maeroff, Gene I. (1984) "Magnet Schools Used as Tool for Equality," *New York Times* (January 31).
Martin, Roscoe (1965) *The Cities and the Federal System*. New York: Atherton.
Martinson, Robert (1974) "What Works? Questions and Answers about Prison Reform," *The Public Interest* (Spring).
Matthews, Jay (1982) "Federal Aid Reductions Spur Refugees to Flee Pacific Northwest," *Washington Post* (June 8).
Mayer, Martin (1978) *The Builders*. New York: W.W. Norton.
Meddis, Sam (1983) "Tough Laws Keep State Prisons Full," *USA Today* (August 22).
Meyerson, Martin and Edward C. Banfield (1955) *Politics, Planning and the Public Interest*. New York: The Free Press.
Miller, S.M., Frank Riessman, and Arthur Seagull (1966) "Poverty and Self-Indulgence: A Critique of the Non-Deferred Gratification Pattern," in Louis A. Fernamn, Joyce Y. Kornblum, and Alan Haber (eds.) *Poverty in America*. Ann Arbor: University of Michigan, pp. 285–302.
Miller, S.M. and Pamela Roby (1970) *The Future of Inequality*. New York: Basic Books.
Miller, William (1968) *A New History of the United States*. New York: Dell.
Mollenkopf, John H. (1983) *The Contested City*. Princeton, New Jersey: Princeton University Press.
Molotch, Harvey (1976) "The City As Growth Machine: Toward a Political Economy of Place," *American Journal of Sociology* 82 (September).
Montagu, M.F. Ashley (1941) "The Biologist Looks at Crime," *The Annals* 217 (September).
Morgan, James N. et al. (1974) *Five Thousand American Families*. Ann Arbor, Michigan: Institute for Social Research.

Morris, Charles R. (1980) *The Cost of Good Intentions.* New York: W. W. Norton.
Morris, David (1982) *Self-Reliant Cities.* San Francisco: Sierra Club Books.
Morris, Norval (1974) *The Future of Imprisonment.* Chicago: University of Chicago.
Morton, J.H. et al. (1953) "A Clinical Study of Premenstrual Tension," *American Journal of Obstetrics and Gynecology* 65.
Mosher, Edith K. and Jennings L. Wagoner, Jr., eds. (1978) *The Changing Politics of Education: Prospects for the 1980s.* Berkeley, Calif.: McCutchan.
Mosteller, Frederick and Daniel P. Moynihan (1972) "A Pathbreaking Report: Further Studies of the Coleman Report," in F. Mosteller and D.P. Moynihan, eds. *On Equality of Educational Opportunity.* New York: Random House.
Moyer, Kenneth (1974) "What is the Potential for Biological Violence Control?" in C.R. Jeffery, ed.
Muller, Thomas L. (1982) "Regional Impacts," in J.L. Palmer and I. Sawyer, eds.
Nathan, Richard P. and Charles F. Adams, Jr. (1977) *Revenue Sharing: The Second Round.* Washington, D.C.: Brookings.
National Academy of Sciences (1979) *Science and Technology: A Five Year Outlook.* San Francisco: W.H. Freeman.
National Advisory Commission on Civil Disorders (1968) *Report of the National Advisory Commission on Civil Disorders.* New York: Bantam.
National Center for Education Statistics (1982) *Digest of Education Statistics.* Washington, D.C.: Government Printing Office.
National Criminal Justice Information and Statistics Service (1981) *Sourcebook of Criminal Justice Statistics, 1981.* Washington, D.C.: Government Printing Office.
National Institute of Justice (1980) *American Prisons and Jails* Vol. I. Washington, D.C.: U.S. Department of Justice.
Neuberger, Richard (1941) "I Go to the Legislature," *Survey Graphic* 30, (July).
Newfield, Jack and Paul DuBruhl (1977) *The Abuse of Power.* New York: Viking.
Newman, Oscar (1972) *Defensible Space: Crime Prevention Through Urban Design.* New York: Macmillan.
Newsweek Magazine (1977) "The Plunderers," (July 26).
——— (1980) "Chaos in Taxachusetts," (December 8).
——— (1983) "A Racial Outburst in Miami," (January 10).
New York Urban Coalition (1983) *Neighborhood: The Journal for City Preservation* 6, no. 2.
Nixon, Richard M. (1973) *Weekly Compilation of Presidential Documents.* Washington, D.C.: Office of the Federal Register.
O'Brien, John O. (1981) "Chicago 'Welfare Queen' Accused in California Scam," *Washington Post* (March 15).
O'Connor, James (1973) *The Fiscal Crisis of the State.* New York: St. Martin's.
Olivas, Michael A. (1981) "Information Inequities: A Fatal Flaw in Parochial Plans," in E. Gafney, Jr., ed.
Orfield, Gary (1978) *Must We Bus?* Washington, D.C.: The Brookings Institution.
Orren, Karen (1974) *Corporate Power and Social Change.* Baltimore: Johns Hopkins.

Palmer, John L. and Isabel V. Sawyer, eds. (1982) *The Reagan Experiment.* Washington, D.C.: The Urban Institute.

Pascarella, Thomas A. and Richard D. Raymond (1982) "Buying Bonds for Business," *Urban Affairs Quarterly* 18 (September).

Pate, Tony, Amy Ferrara, Robert Bowers, and Jon Lowrence (1976) *Police Response Time: Its Determinants and Effects.* Washington, D.C.: The Police Foundation.

Patterson, James T. (1981) *America's Struggle Against Poverty 1900–1980.* Cambridge: Harvard University.

Peel, J.D.Y. (1971) *Herbert Spencer: The Evolution of a Sociologist.* New York: Basic Books.

Pierce, Neal R. (1977) "Middle Class Rushes Back to Cities," *Los Angeles Times* (June 10).

Peterson, Paul E. (1981) *City Limits.* Chicago: University of Chicago.

Pettigrew, Thomas F., Elizabeth L. Useem, Clarence Normand, and Marshall S. Smith (1973) "Busing: A Review of 'The Evidence,' " *The Public Interest* (Winter).

Piven, Frances Fox and Richard A. Cloward (1971) *Regulating the Poor.* New York: Vintage.

Poole, Robert W., Jr. (1980) *Cutting Back City Hall.* New York: Universe Books.

Pressman, Jeffrey and Aaron Wildavsky (1973) *Implementation.* Berkeley: University of California.

Puckett, John L. (1983) "Educational Vouchers: Rhetoric and Reality," *Educational Forum* 47 (Summer).

Quinney, Richard (1979) *Criminology.* Boston: Little, Brown.

Railsback, Charles E. (1983) "Microcomputers: Solutions in Search of Problems?" *Phi Delta Kappan* (October).

Reagan, Michael and John Sanzone (1981) *The New Federalism.* New York: Oxford University.

Reilly, William K. (1975) "Six Myths about Land Use in the United States," in R. Scott, ed.

Rich, Spencer (1982) "Welfare Benefits Form Crazy-Quilt Pattern across U.S.," *Washington Post* (January 30).

Riessman, Frank (1978) "The Service Society and the Crisis in Education," in E. Mosher and J. Wagoner, Jr., eds.

Robertson, Wyndham (1975) "Going Broke the New York City Way," *Fortune* (August).

Rodgers, Harrell R., Jr. (1975) "On Integrating the Public Schools: An Empirical and Legal Assessment," in Harrell Rodgers, Jr., ed., *Racism and Inequality.* San Francisco: W.H. Freeman.

—— (1978) *Crisis in Democracy: A Policy Analysis of American Government.* Reading, Mass.: Addison-Wesley.

—— (1979) *Poverty amid Plenty.* Reading, Mass.: Addison-Wesley.

Rodman, Hyman (1963) "The Lower Class Value Stretch," *Social Forces* 42, pp. 205–215.

Rosenbaum, Nelson (1978) "Growth and Its Discontents: Origins of Local Popu-

lation Growth Controls," in Judith V. May and Aaron B. Wildavsky, eds. *The Policy Cycle*. Beverly Hills, Calif.: Sage Publications.
Rosenfeld, Raymond A. (1980) "Who Benefits and Who Decides? The Uses of Community Development Block Grants," in Donald Rosenthal, ed.
Rosenthal, Donald B., ed. (1980) *Urban Revitalization*. Beverly Hills, California.
Rossell, Christine H. and Willis D. Hawley (1982) "Policy Alternatives for Minimizing White Flight," *Educational Evaluation and Policy Analysis* 4 (Summer).
Rubin, Robert J. (1983) Statement before the Subcommittee on Public Assistance and Unemployment Compensation, Committee on Ways and Means (November 3).
Ryan, William (1971) *Blaming the Victim*. New York: Vintage.
——— (1981) *Equality*. New York: Pantheon.
Sager, Lawrence G. (1980) "Burnt Bridges: Retreat of the Federal Judiciary from Land Use Litigation," in F. Schnidman and J. Silverman, eds.
Salamon, Lester T. and Alan J. Abramson (1982) "The Nonprofit Sector," in John L. Palmer and Isabel V. Sawhill (eds.) *The Reagan Experiment*. Washington, D.C.: Urban Institute.
Sale, Kirkpatrick (1975) *Power Shift: The Rise of the Southern Rim and Its Challenge to the Eastern Establishment*. New York: Random House.
Sanders, Heywood (1980) "Urban Renewal and the Revitalized City: A Reconsideration of Recent History," in D. Rosenthal, ed.
Savas, E.S. (1972) *Privatizing the Public Sector*. Chatham, New Jersey: Chatham House.
Savitch, H.V. (1979) *Urban Policy and the Exterior City*. New York: Pergamon.
——— (1983) "Demographic Trends in the New York Region: Devising a Policy Strategy for the Central City," unpublished paper presented at the 1983 Annual Meeting of the American Political Science Association, Chicago.
Savitz, Leonard (1958) "A Study on Capital Punishment," *Journal of Criminal Law, Criminology, and Police Science* 49 (Nov./Dec.).
Sawyer, Kathy (1983) "House Panel Votes to Raise Revolving Fund for Jobless," *Washington Post* (February 10).
Sawyers, Larry and William K. Tabb, eds. (1984) *Sunbelt/Snowbelt: Urban Redevelopment and Regional Restructuring*. New York: Oxford University.
Schill, Michael H. and Richard P. Nathan (1983) *Revitalizing America's Cities*. Albany: State University of New York Press.
Schiller, Bradley (1980) *The Economics of Poverty and Discrimination*, 3rd edition. Englewood Cliffs: New Jersey: Prentice-Hall.
Schlesinger, Steven R. (1983) "Criminal Procedures in the Courtroom," in James Q. Wilson, ed.
Schmenner, Roger (1980) "Industrial Location and Urban Public Management," in Arthur P. Solomon (ed.) *The Prospective City*. Cambridge: MIT.
Schnidman, Frank and Jane Silverman, eds. (1980) *Management and Control of Growth: Updating the Law* Vol. V. Washington, D.C.: Urban Land Institute.
Schorr, Philip (1975) *Planned Relocation*. Lexington, Mass.: Lexington Books.
Schuessler, Karl F. (1952) "The Deterrent Influence on the Death Penalty," *The Annals* 284 (November).

Scott, Randall W., ed. (1975) *Management and Control of Growth.* Vol. I, Washington, D.C.: Urban Land Institute.
Shannon, Thomas A. (1973) "Rodriquez: A Dream Shattered or a Call for Finance Reform?" *Phi Delta Kappan* 54 (May).
Sharkansky, Ira (1972) *The Maligned States.* New York: McGraw-Hill.
Sheehan, Susan (1976) *A Welfare Mother.* Boston: Houghton Mifflin.
Shefter, Martin (1977) "New York City's Fiscal Crisis: The Politics of Inflation and Retrenchment," *The Public Interest* 48 (Summer).
Silberman, Charles E. (1978) *Criminal Violence, Criminal Justice.* New York: Random House.
Simon, William (1978) *A Time for the Truth.* New York: Reader's Digest Press.
Skogan, Wesley and Michael Maxfield (1981) *Coping with Crime.* Beverly Hills: Sage.
Spring, Joel (1982) "The Evolving Political Structure of American Schooling," in R. Everhart, ed.
Steiner, Gilbert (1966) *Social Insecurity: The Politics of Welfare.* Chicago: Rand McNally.
Stedman, Murray S. Jr. (1979) *State and Local Politics,* 2nd edition. Cambridge, Mass.: Winthrop.
Sterba, James P. (1978) "Ad Slogans Tell Businessmen Grass Is (or Isn't)-Greener Elsewhere," *New York Times* (July 18).
Stockman, David A. (1983) Statement before the House Ways and Means Subcommittee on Oversight, and Public Assistance, and Unemployment.
Struyk, Raymond J. (1980) *A New System for Public Housing.* Washington, D.C.: The Urban Institute.
Struyk, Raymond J., Neil Mayer, and John A. Tuccillo (1983) *Federal Housing Policy at President Reagan's Midterm.* Washington, D.C.: The Urban Institute.
Sumner, William Graham (1963) *Social Darwinism.* Englewood Cliffs, New Jersey: Prentice-Hall.
Suttles, Gerald D. (1968) *The Social Order of a Slum.* Chicago: University of Chicago.
Tawney, Richard H. (1926) *Religion and the Rise of Capitalism.* New York: New American Library.
The New Republic (1983) "Magnet Schools: Busing Without Tears?" (November 7).
Thurow, Lester C. (1980) *The Zero-Sum Society.* New York: Penguin.
Time Magazine (1983) "Somber Prelude to the Fourth," (July 11).
Tittle, Charles R. and Allan R. Rowe (1974) "Certainty of Arrest and Crime Rates," *Social Forces* 52 (June).
Tivnan, Edward (1983) "Bittersweet Charity: The High Cost of Fund Raising," *New York Magazine* (August 15).
Toll, Seymour I. (1969) *Zoned America.* New York: Grossman.
Train, Russell E. (1975) "Growth With Environmental Quality," in Randall W. Scott, ed.
Ullman, Howard (1984) "False Notions About Computers," *New York Times* (January 13).
U.S. Bureau of the Census (1981) *Statistical Abstract of the United States: 1981.* Washington, D.C.: Government Printing Office.

—— (1983) Current Population Reports, Series P-60, No. 140, *Money Income and Poverty Status of Families and Persons in the United States, 1982*. Washington, D.C.: Government Printing Office.
U.S. Department of Health and Human Services (1980) *Social Security Bulletin, Annual Statistical Supplement*. Washington, D.C.: Government Printing Office.
—— (1982) *Characteristics of State Plans for Aid to Families with Dependent Children: 1982 Edition*. Washington, D.C.: Government Printing Office.
U.S. Department of Housing and Urban Development, (1978) *A Survey of Citizens' Views and Concerns about Urban Life*. Washington, D.C.: Government Printing Office.
—— (1979) *Evaluation of the Urban Homesteading Demonstration Program, Third Annual Report*. Washington, D.C.: Government Printing Office.
—— (1980) *HUD Statistical Yearbook 1979*. Washington D.C.: Government Printing Office.
—— (1981) *Evaluation of the Urban Homesteading Demonstration Program, Final Report*, Volume I, Washington, D.C.: Government Printing Office.
U.S. General Accounting Office (1982) *Revitalizing Distressed Areas Through Enterprise Zones: Many Uncertainties Exist*. Washington, D.C. (July 15).
U.S. Department of Justice, Federal Bureau of Investigation (1981) *Uniform Crime Reports*. Washington, D.C.: Government Printing Office.
U.S. News and World Report (1968) "Balance Sheet on the War in Vietnam," (April 8).
Valentine, Charles A. (1968) *Culture and Poverty*. Chicago: University of Chicago.
Van Den Haag (1975) *Punishing Criminals*. New York: Basic Books.
Veiller, Lawrence (1910) *Housing Reform*. New York: The Russell Sage Foundation.
Veiser, Milford (1964) "Urban Renewal: A Program for Private Enterprise," Statement before the Committee on Construction and Community Development of the U.S. Chamber of Commerce, September 18.
Verdier, James and Martha Smith (1982) *Tax Expenditures: Budget Control Options and Five Year Projections for Fiscal Years 1983-1987*. Washington, D.C.: Congressional Budget Office.
Vitullo-Martin, Thomas (1982) "The Impact of Taxation Policy on Public and Private Schools," in R. Everhart, ed.
Wagoner, Jennings L., Jr. (1978) "Thomas Jefferson and the Politics of Education," in E. Mosher and J. Wagoner, Jr., eds.
Walker, David (1981) *Toward a Functioning Federalism*. Cambridge, Mass.: Winthrop.
—— (1983) "American Federalism—Then and Now," in *The Book of the States, 1982-3*. Lexington, Kentucky: Council of State Governments.
Walker, Decker F. (1983) "Reflections on the Educational Potential and Limitations of Microcomputers," *Phi Delta Kappan* (October).
Washington Post (1983) "Richmond Woman, 62, Repeatedly Robbed by a Group of Boys," (September 29).
Watkins, Al and David Perry, eds. (1978) *The Rise of the Sunbelt Cities*. Beverly Hills, Calif.: Sage.

Weiss, Marc A. (1980) "The Origins and Legacy of Urban Renewal," in Pierre Clavel, et al., eds. *Urban Renewal and Planning in an Age of Austerity*. New York: Pergamon.

Wilcox, Clair (1969) *Toward Social Welfare*. Homewood, Ill.: Dorsey.

Williams, Juan (1978) "Secret of a Senior Classman: He Doesn't Know How to Read," *Washington Post* (April 30).

Williams, Norman Jr. (1974) *American Planning Law: Land Use and the Police Power*. Vol. 1. Wilmmette, Ill.: Callaghan & Co.

――― (1983) *American Planning Law: Land Use and the Police Power*. Vol. 3. Wilmette, Ill.: Callaghan & Co.

Williams, Walter E. (1983) "Taxes, Taxis and the Poor," *New York Times* (January 8).

Willie, Charles V. (1982) "Desegregation in Big City School Systems," *Educational Forum* 47 (Fall).

Willie, Charles V. and Susan L. Greenblatt (1981) *Community Politics and Educational Change*. New York: Longman.

Wilson, James Q. (1975) *Thinking About Crime*. New York: Basic Books.

――― (1983) "Thinking About Crime," *The Atlantic Monthly* (September).

―――, ed. (1983b) *Crime and Public Policy*. San Francisco: Institute for Contemporary Studies.

Wilson, James Q. and Barbara Boland (1976) "Crime," in William Gorham and Nathan Glazer, eds. *The Urban Predicament*. Washington, D.C.: The Urban Institute.

Wilson, James Q. and George Kelling (1982) "Broken Windows," *The Atlantic Monthly* (March).

Wiltshire, David (1978) *The Social and Political Thought of Herbert Spencer*. Oxford, England: Oxford University.

Wirt, Frederick M. and Michael W. Kirst (1972) *The Political Web of American Schools*. Boston: Little, Brown.

Wolman, Harold (1971) *The Politics of Federal Housing*. New York: Dodd, Mead & Co.

Woll, Peter (1981) *Constitutional Law: Cases and Comments*. Englewood Cliffs, New Jersey: Prentice-Hall.

World Press Review (1983) "The Southwest's Great Thirst," (August).

Yates, Douglas (1977) *The Ungovernable City*. Cambridge: MIT.

Index

Abramson, Alan J., 115, 120
Abravanel, Mark T., 214
Adams, Charles F., Jr., 18
Advisory Commission on Intergovernmental Relations, 2, 10, 27, 39–41, 89, 99–101, 117, 121, 132, 201–3
Aesthetic degradation, growth and, 220–21
Age, poverty and, 82
Ahlbrandt, Roger S., Jr., 27, 29
Aid to Families with Dependent Children (AFDC), 88, 91, 93–95, 98, 101, 105, 107–10
Air pollution, 219–20
Alabama, 294
Alexander, John K., 120
Alexander, Karl L., 331, 333
Alexandria, Virginia, 167
Allman, T. D., 141
Alonso, William, 231, 242
Alternative sentencing, 298–300
Alum Rock school district, 363–65
Anaheim, California, 209
Anderson, Martin, 75, 92, 95, 96, 107
Anti-Federalists, 13
Antunes, George F., 244
Arizona, 221
Arkansas, 100, 109, 294
Arlington Heights, Illinois, 237
Armor, David, 350

Arons, Stephen, 327, 328
Asbell, Bernard, 365
Atlanta, 37, 89, 162, 170, 174–75
Auburn, Maine, 186
Auletta, Ken, 62, 81, 135, 149, 261

Babcock, Richard F., 238
Bahl, Roy, 114
Baldassare, Mark, 214
Baltimore, 170, 197
Balz, Dan, 114
Banfield, Edward C., 46, 65, 67, 68, 81, 140–41, 146, 147, 165, 168 249, 278, 284, 322
Basic services, 5
Bell, Daniel, 45
Belle Terre case, 236–37
Berg, Ivar, 71, 336, 337
Berkley, George E., 9, 310
Berman, Daniel S., 173
Better Jobs and Income, 111
Beyrer, Mary K., 220
Bird, Janet M., 116
Bishop, John, 107
Black, Donald J., 265
Black families, 64–65, 67
Blacks, 212–13. *See also* Desegregation (or integration) of schools; Minorities; Racial discrimination
  poverty among, 80–82
  suburbanization of, 211
  urban renewal and, 170

389

Block, John R., 95
Block grants, 17. *See also* Community development block grants (CDBGs); Comprehensive Employment and Training Act (CETA)
Bluestone, Barry, 196, 221
Bluhm, William T., 46
Boca Raton, Florida, 229, 234, 239
Boland, Barbara, 288
Bosselman, Fred, 10, 242
Boston, 16, 116, 170, 171, 173, 311
Boulder, Colorado, 229
Bowles, Samuel, 313, 319
Boyer, Brian D., 182
Boyer, Ernest L., 309, 310, 313, 366, 368, 369
Bradbury, Katharine L., 132, 192
Bratt, Rachel G., 116
Brooke Amendment, 166
Brown v. The Board of Education of Topeka, 314–16, 322, 329, 342, 343, 361
Building code authority, 153, 154
Bureaucracy, 107, 222–23
Burke, Edmund, 43
Burke, Edward, 1
Businesses. *See* Private sector
Busing for school integration, 344–59
  cooperation by local officials and, 351–52
  cost of, 348
  impact on black students, 349–50
  impact on white students, 350–51
  Keyes decision and, 346
  practicality of, 346–49
  Swann ruling and, 345–46
  white flight and, 348–49
Butler, Stuart, 194

Cahn, Robert, 207
Califano, Joseph, 89
California, 36, 109, 132, 221
Callies, David, 10, 242
Calvin, John, 57
Calvinism, 57–60
Canada, 327
Carter, Jimmy, 111, 185
Cash grants, 89
Categorical grants, 15, 18, 20
Catholic schools. *See* Private education

Central government. *See* Federal system (federalism); National government
Centralization. *See also* Decentralization
  of welfare system, 97–104
Chaiken, Jan M., 265, 280
Chaiken, Marcia R., 265
Charity, 116–20
Charlotte-Mecklenburg school system, 345–46
Chattanooga, Tennessee, 30
Chernow, Ron, 156
Chicago, 1, 105, 131, 166, 167, 170, 179
Choate, Pat, 7, 134
Ciardiello, Florence, 163
Circuit breakers, 40
Cities. *See also* Model Cities program; Urban and regional development; Urban decline; Urban renewal
  aesthetic degradation of, 220–21
  crime in, 265–66
  growth of, 211–13, 222–23
  pollution of, 219–20
Citification of the suburbs, 209, 211
Civil Rights Act of 1964, 18–19, 343
Civil-rights organizations, growth control and, 234, 236, 237
Civil War, 100
Clark, Kenneth, 315
Clark, Ramsey, 254, 294, 298
Clark, Terry Nichols, 113–14
Classical economic theory, poverty and, 57–59
Clay, Philip L., 211
Cleveland, 131, 200
Cloward, Richard A., 73, 105, 109, 255
Cochran, Clarke E., 111
Coe, Richard, 94
Cohen, David K., 364
Cohen, Lawrence E., 252
Coleman, James S., 307, 331–33, 348, 349
Coleman Report, 331–32, 334–35
Colleges, community and junior, 313
Committee for Public Education v. Nyquist, 361
Community
  crime and decline of, 252–53

growth and threats to, 223–24
  sense of, 46
Community Action Agencies (CAAs), 103, 104
Community development, states and, 201
Community development block grants (CDBGs), 17–18, 37–38, 184–87
Comprehensive Employment and Training Act (CETA), 17–18, 122–23
Computer-aided instruction, 365–70
Connecticut, 99, 186, 196, 225
Conservatism, 43–44. *See also* Neoconservatism
  crime and, 246–50
  schools and, 312–13
Conservative elite, 37
Constitution, U.S., 12–14
Contracting out, 29–30
Coons, John E., 363
Cooperative federalism, 15
Corporations. *See* Private sector
Courts, 9–10. *See also* Criminal justice system
  rehabilitation of criminals and, 270
  schools and, 311–12
  sentencing and, 283–90
Cowan, Edward, 106
Crain, Robert L., 350, 351
Creative federalism, 15–16
Credentialism, 71
Creeping categorization, 18–19
Crime, 244–303
  biological theory of, 247–50
  blocked-opportunity theory of, 255–56
  conventional conservative view of, 246–50
  decline of community and, 252–53
  as deviance, 246–50
  deviant cultures and, 249–50
  distribution of, 265–66
  exaggeration of problem of, 258–59, 265
  index, 259–60
  liberal view of, 245–46, 254–55, 257–58, 281, 283, 301
  neoconservative view of, 245, 250–54, 271, 281–83, 301
  official reporting of, 259–60, 261, 265

radical view of, 246, 255–58, 274, 301
  rational-choice theory of, 251–52, 278
  social structure and, 254–58
  solving, 276–78
  unrecorded, 263–65
  unreported, 261–63
  violent, 260–61
Crime prevention, 276, 278–80
Criminal justice system, 268–303. *See also* Courts; Police; Prisons
  deterrence as goal of, 270–71
  incapacitation as goal of, 272
  punishment as goal of, 272–73
  rehabilitation as goal of, 270, 271
  social control and, 256–57
Criminals. *See also* Prisons
  as consumers, 250–52
  deinstitutionalization of, 297–98
  deterrence of, 270–71
  incapacitation of, 272, 284
  punishment of, 273–74, 284
  rehabilitation of, 270, 271, 284, 295–96
  sentencing of, 283–90
Cultural explanations of poverty, 61. *See also* Culture of poverty
Culture
  crime and, 249–50
  definition of, 62
  poverty as caused by, 62–64
Culture of poverty, 63–69
  liberal view of, 66–68
  neoconservative view of, 64–65
  welfare policy and, 68–69

Dahrendorf, Ralf, 49
Dalton, Katherine, 249
Daniels, Lee A., 345
Danielson, Michael, 180, 225, 226, 236
Darwin, Charles, 58–59, 247
Davis, Ed, 269
Davis, Karen, 109
Decentralization, 4, 27, 34–35, 41–42. *See also* Localism
  neoconservatism and, 46
  of welfare system, 112, 125
Deinstitutionalization of criminals, 297–98
Delaney, Julian, 238

Dembart, Lee, 135
Democratic control, growth and loss of, 223
Denver, 107
 busing for, 342–59. *See* Busing for school integration
 Keyes decision and, 346
 Swann ruling and, 345–46
Desertification, 221
Deterrence of crime, 270–71, 284
Detroit, 105, 143, 182
Deviance, crime as, 246–50
Dillon, Forrest, 13
Dillon's Rule, 13–14
Diseconomies of scale, growth of, 222–23
Distribution of income, 78–79
Dobelstein, Andrew W., 107, 121
Dolbeare, Kenneth M., 43
Dolbeare, Patricia, 43
Dommel, Paul R., 184, 186, 187
Downes, Bryan T., 130
Downs, Anthony, 192
Drake, Guy, 94
Drury, Margaret, 189
Dual federalism, 14–15
DuBruhl, Paul, 37, 150
Due process clause, 235
Dye, Thomas, 20–21

Ecker-Racz, L. L., 36
Economic development, 8, 201. *See also* Urban and regional development
Economic growth, welfare system and, 123–24
Edson, C. H., 313
Education, 5–6. *See also* Schools
 inequality and, 70–71
 life chances and, 333–37
 neoconservative view of, 321–23
 poverty and, 82, 316–18, 322
 private. *See* Private education
 public versus private, 323–33
 radical view of, 318–21
 upward mobility and, 313–14
Education vouchers, 359–65
Eisenhower, Dwight D., 23
Eisenstein, James, 287
Elazar, Daniel, 2, 23, 39
Elementary and Secondary Education Act of 1965 (ESEA), 317

Engel, Margaret, 298
Enterprise zones, 193–96
Environmental movement, 219
Erickson, Donald A., 327
Escobedo v. *Illinois*, 285
Ewen, Lynda Ann, 37
Exclusionary rule, 285
Existing Housing Program, 187–89
Expectations, lowering of, 45
Experimental Housing Allowance Program (EHAP), 192
Expertise, state and local governments' lack of, 35

Families
 black, 64–65, 67
 neoconservative view of schooling and, 321
 students' performance and, 334
 welfare system and, 107
Family Assistance Plan (FAP), 111
Farley, R., 211, 349
Farrar, Eleanor, 364
Feagin, Joe R., 56, 61, 99, 216
Feaver, Douglas B., 134
Federal Emergency Relief Act of 1933, 101
Federal government. *See* National government
Federal Housing Administration (FHA), 179–82
Federalists, 13, 14
Federal system (federalism), 10–20
 the Constitution and, 12–14
 cooperative, 15
 creative, 15–16
 creeping categorization and, 18–19
 dual, 14–15
 new, 16–20, 183
Ferguson, Lorna Crowly, 113–14
Fiscal crises, urban, 131–33, 149–50
Fishman, Charles, 95
Florida, 220, 293
Fogelson, Robert M., 269
Food stamps, 88–90, 91, 95
Ford, Gerald R., 111
Forer, Lois G., 290, 294–96, 299
Fortune (magazine), 149
Fourteenth Amendment, 235–36
Fox, Douglas M., 9, 310
Frieden, Bernard J., 176, 228, 230, 232, 233

Friedman, Milton, 43, 360, 362, 363
Full employment, 70

Gaffney, Edward McGlynn, Jr., 325
Gale, Dennis E., 142
Gallup, George H., 305, 306
Gans, Herbert J., 72, 170
Garcia, Robert, 193, 194
Garrity, Arthur, 311
General assistance, 88
Gettinger, Steve, 268, 293
Gibbs, Jack P., 287
Gideon v. *Wainwright*, 285
Ginsberg, Benjamin, 269
Ginsburg, Benson E., 248
Gintis, Herbert, 313, 319
Glaser, Daniel, 283, 297, 298
Glazer, Nathan, 161
Glendening, Parris N., 11
Goddard, Henry, 320
Goldberger, Paul, 142
Goldwater, Barry, 43
Goodman, Robert, 173
Grants-in-aid, 20. *See also* Block grants; Categorical grants; Matching grants
Great Depression, 100-1, 163, 179
Greeley, Andrew M., 326, 328
Green Bay, Wisconsin, 192
Greenblatt, Susan L., 351-52
Greer, Edward, 38
Grier, Eunice, 180
Grier, George, 180
Grodzins, Morton, 15, 23
Growth, 207-43
  aesthetic argument against, 220-21
  of cities, 211-213, 222-23
  coalition in favor of, 217-19
  community and democratic control as threatened by, 223-24
  costs of, 219-24
  direct limits on, 228-29
  discrimination against minorities and the poor in control of, 230-32, 236-40
  diseconomies of scale and, 222-23
  environmentalism and, 219
  indirect controls on, 224-28
  legal aspects of limits on, 233-40
  market model of, 214-17
  pollution and health issues and, 219-20

  public services and, 221-22
  radical analysis of, 215-17
  in rural areas, 213-14
  of suburbs, 208-11
  water supplies and, 221
Gutman, Herbert, 67

Haider, Donald, 21, 24
Hale, George E., 16
Halfway houses, 298
Hamilton, Alexander, 13
Harrington, Michael, 56, 75, 102
Harris County, Texas, 186
Harrison, Bennett, 138, 196, 221
Hartman, Chester, 171, 220
Haveman, Robert H., 103
Hawaii, 242
Hawley, Willis D., 348, 349
Hays, Samuel P., 152
Head Start, 103, 317
Health, growth and, 219-20
Health, Education and Welfare, Department of (HEW), 342
Health services, 6
Healy, Robert, 242
Heidenheimer, Arnold J., 323
Henig, Jeffrey R., 279
Hess, Robert D., 65
Hicks, Donald, 28, 148, 205
Hill, Martha S., 93
Hills v. *Gautreaux* case, 237
Hispanics. *See also* Minorities
  poverty among, 80-82
Hobbes, Thomas, 44
Hoffer, Thomas, 332
Hofstadter, Richard, 59
Hollister, Robert M., 116
Holmes, Oliver Wendell, 59
Hombs, Mary Ellen, 135
Homeowners, tax deductions for, 183
Home rule charters, 14
Homesteading, 196-99
Hoover, Herbert, 101
Housing
  mortgage guarantees and, 178-80
  public, *See* Public housing
  states and, 201
  subsidies for, 180-82
  urban decline and, 135-37
  vouchers (or allowances) for, 191-93
Housing Act of 1937, 163-64

Housing Act of 1949, 169, 172
Housing Act of 1968, 180–81
Housing Act of 1983, 193
Housing and Community Development Act of 1974, 183–90
  community development block grants (CDBGs) under, 184–87
  Section 8 of, 187–92
Housing and Urban Development, Department of (HUD), 175, 181, 182, 185, 187, 188, 192, 193, 198–99
Houston, 216, 221
Hunter, Floyd, 37
Hurley, Patricia, 244
Husen, Torsten, 332

Ideologies, 42–52. *See also specific ideologies*
  conservatism and neoconservatism, 43–46
  definition of, 42
  liberalism, 46–48
  Marxism and radical analysis, 48–52
Illinois, 1, 100
Incapacitation of criminals, 272, 284
Income, hidden (or illegal), 77–78, 106
Income Supplement Program, 111
Income tax deductions, for homeowners, 183
Income taxes, state, 36, 39
Incrementalism, 125
Indeterminate sentencing, 295
Individualism
  Calvinism and, 57–60
  classical economic theory and, 57–59
  poverty and, 56–61
  Social Darwinism and, 58–59
  welfare and, 59–61
Inequality, 54–56, 60. *See also Poverty*
Inflation, unemployment and, 70
Infrastructure, physical, 6–7
  deterioration of, 133–34
In-kind benefits, 77–79, 89–90
Intergovernmental system, 1–2

Jacob, Herbert, 244, 245, 252, 266, 281, 287, 302

Jacobs, Jane, 171
Jacobs, John, 8
Jails. *See* Prisons
Jaynes, Gregory, 289
Jefferson, Thomas, 13, 313, 323
Jencks, Christopher, 35, 62, 335, 336, 362, 363
Jensen, Arthur, 62
Jitneys, 30
Job Corps, 103, 122
Job Opportunities in the Business Sector (JOBS), 122
Jobs, schooling and, 336–37
Jobs provision, 120–24
Job training, 122–23
Johnson, Lyndon B., 15–16, 86, 102, 176
Jones, Bryan D., 129, 131
Jones, David A., 286, 289
Judd, Wallace, 365
Judicial discretion, 288–90
Judiciary. *See* Courts
Justice Statistics, U.S. Bureau of, 262–63

Kain, John F., 208
Kansas City, 277–80
Kaplan, Harold, 172
Kaplan, Marshall, 176
Kasarda, John D., 213
Kelley, Clarence, 278
Kelling, George L., 253, 279, 282
Kelly, Sara D., 332, 349
Kemp, Jack, 193–96
Kennet, David A., 116
Kettl, Donald, 18, 35, 186
Keyes, et al. v. School District No. 1. Denver, Colorado, 346
Kilgore, Sally, 332
Kirst, Michael W., 319
Klose, Keven, 1
Kotler, Milton, 224
Kozol, Jonathan, 319
Krajik, Kevin, 268, 293
Kramer, Larry, 156
Kristol, Irving, 45, 204–5
Kurtz, Howard, 196

Land use planning, 10
Law enforcement, 9–10
Law Enforcement Assistance Administration (LEAA), 300–1

Lawrence, Charles, III, 327, 328
Lawton, M. P., 245
Left, the. *See* Marxism; Radicalism; Structuralists
Legal Services program, 103, 104
Lekachman, Robert, 70
Levin, Henry M., 121, 317
Levitan, Sar A., 110, 119, 182
Levy, John M., 8
Lewis, Arthur, 127
Lewis, Oscar, 63, 64, 67
Liberalism, 46–48, 49–51
  crime and, 245–46, 254–55, 257–58, 281, 283, 301
  culture-of-poverty thesis and, 66–68
  schools and, 313–18
  urban decline and, 129, 145–46
  welfare system and, 107–9, 115
Lindblom, Charles, 73
Lindsay, John, 149–51, 165
Lineberry, Robert L., 13, 244, 245
Linowes, R. Robert, 238
Load-shedding, 30–31
Loans, Neighborhood Housing Services (NHS), 199–200
Local governments
  as dominated by a conservative elite, 37–38
  as lacking expertise, 35
  parochialism of officials of, 35–36
  penetrability of boundaries of, 38
  policy functions of, 4–10
  redistribution of income and, 38
  relative importance of, 1–3, 20–24
  revenue raising by, 36, 39–40
Localism
  schools and, 308–12
  welfare system and, 98–101, 112–15
Local self-help programs, 196–202
Local taxes, inelasticity of, 36
Locke, John, 47
Logan, John, 242
Lombroso, Cesare, 247–48
Long, Larry, 213
Los Angeles, 105, 269
Lowi, Theodore, 102
Lynn, Laurence E., Jr., 100, 116

McClelland, David, 65
McFarland, M. Carter, 182

Madaus, George F., 335
Mahard, Rita, 350, 351
Management
  urban decline and, 149–53
Mancini, Paul K., 214
Mandatory sentencing, 287
Manpower Development and Training Act (1962), 122
Mapp v. *Ohio*, 285
Marin County, California, 232–33
Market model of growth, 214–17
Marshall, John, 14
Martin, Roscoe, 36
Martinson, Robert, 295–96
Marx, Karl, 48, 69, 70, 109, 259
Marxism, 48–52. *See also* Radicalism
Massachusetts, 36, 132, 138, 242, 309
Matching grants, 15
Matthews, Jay, 54
Maxfield, Michael, 1, 245, 9
Mayer, Martin, 161, 164, 168, 170, 171, 180
Meddis, Sam, 288
Medicaid, 88, 89, 91, 109
Medicare, 88, 89, 91–92
Meritocracy, 70–72, 312–14
Mexican Americans, 81
Meyerson, Martin, 165, 168
Miami, 130
Michigan, 54, 293
Mill, John Stuart, 47, 48
Miller, S. M., 5, 66
Miller, William, 13
Minneapolis, 116, 186
Minnesota, 109
Minorities, 40, 170. *See also* Blacks; Hispanics; Race; Racial discrimination
Miranda v. *Arizona*, 285
Mismanagement, urban decline and, 149–53
Mississippi, 109
Missouri, 109
Mobile homes, 226
Model Cities program, 175–77
Mollenkopf, John H., 215–16, 220
Molotch, Harvey, 218
Morris, David, 134
Morris, Norval, 274, 295
Mortgage guarantees, 178–80
Mortgage payments, tax deductions for, 183

Morton, J. H., 249
Mosteller, Frederick, 334, 335
Mount Laurel, New Jersey, 239
Moyer, Kenneth, 248, 250
Moynihan, Daniel Patrick, 64–65, 334, 335
Muller, Thomas L., 216

Nader, Ralph, 156
Nathan, Richard P., 18, 142
National Advisory Commission on Civil Disorders, 130
National Association of Home Builders (NAHB), 165
National government. *See also* Federal system (federalism)
  growth of influence of, 20–21
  public housing and, 163–66
  relative importance of, 1–3
National Housing Act of 1934, 179
"Necessary and proper" clause, 13, 14
Neighborhood Housing Services (NHS), 196, 199–200
Neighborhood Youth Corps, 103
Neoconservatism, 43–46, 49–52
  crime and, 271, 281–83, 301
  culture of poverty and, 64–65
  education and, 321–23
  poverty and, 64–65, 77, 78, 86–87
  regional decline and, 147–48
  urban crisis and, 140–41
  urban decline and, 128–29, 146–47, 161–62
  welfare system and, 105–7
Neuberger, Richard, 2
New Construction and Substantial Rehabilitation Program, 187, 189, 190
New Federalism, 16–20, 131, 183
Newfield, Jack, 37, 150
New Jersey, 225, 239
Newman, Oscar, 167
New Orleans, 269
New York City, 6, 7, 30, 105, 129–31, 134, 135, 143, 162, 165, 167, 171, 225–26, 235–36
  mismanagement of, 149–51
  police in, 278, 280
New York State, 132, 151
New York Times, 131
Nixon, Richard M., 16–18, 111, 140, 166, 182, 183

Norris, 6
North Central states, 202. *See also* Snowbelt region
Northeast states, 202. *See also* Snowbelt region
Norwalk, Connecticut, 196

Oakland, California, 200
O'Brien, John O., 106
O'Connor, James, 143, 144
Office of Economic Opportunity (OEO), 360, 362, 363
Ohio, 114
Ohlin, Lloyd, 255
Olivas, Michael A., 362
Operation I.D., 302
Orfield, Gary, 342, 345, 346–48, 351
Orren, Karen, 38

P.U.R.E. (People United to Reclaim the Environment), 229
Pallas, Aaron, 331, 333
Palley, Marian L., 16
Palmer, Dorothy Mae, 105–6
Parochialism of state and local officials, 35–36
Parole, 297–98
Pascarella, Thomas A., 8
Pate, Tony, 278
Patterson, James T., 80, 100, 101
Peel, J. D. Y., 59
Peirce, Neal R., 142
Penfield, New York, 234–35
Penn Central Transportation Co. v. *New York city,* 235–36
Pennsylvania, 156, 309
People United to Reclaim the Environment (P.U.R.E.), 229
Perry, David, 149
Petaluma, California, 224, 228, 234
Peterson, Paul, 38, 115
Pettigrew, Thomas F., 350
Philadelphia, 105, 116, 170, 197
Phillips, A. W., 70
Phillips curve, 70
Phoenix, 192
Physical infrastructure, 6–7, 133–34
Pittsburgh, 30, 192
Piven, Frances Fox, 73, 105, 109
Plea bargaining, 285–89
Plessy v. *Ferguson,* 314

Police, 9, 278. *See also* Criminal justice system
  crimes solved by, 276-78
  functions of, 274, 276
  as helpers, 281-82
  maintenance of order and, 282-83
  noncrime functions of, 280-83
  prevention of crime and, 276, 278-80
  rehabilitation of criminals and, 270
  response time of, 276, 277
  sentencing and, 283-84
  unrecorded crimes and, 263-65
Political power, growth and, 215-17
Political socialization, schools, and, 318-21
Pollution, 219-20
Polsby, 37
Poole, Robert W., Jr., 30, 31, 331
Poverty (the poor), 54-85. *See also* War on Poverty; Welfare
  age and, 82
  cultural explanations of, 61-69. *See also* Culture of poverty
  cutoff point for, 76-77
  difficulty in defining, 75
  education and, 82, 316-18, 322
  feminization of, 80
  geographical distribution of, 79-80
  growth controls and discrimination against, 230-32, 236-40
  individualistic explanations of, 56-61
  measurement of, 75-79
  migration of, 113-14
  neoconservative view of, 64-65, 77, 78, 86-87
  race and, 80-82
  redistribution of income to, 38
  relative measures of, 76, 78-79
  states and localities as more responsive to, 40
  structural explanations of, 69-74
  voucher systems and, 31-32
  work experience of, 82-83
Pressman, Jeffrey, 23
Preventive patrol, 276, 278-80
Prisons, 9, 268. *See also* Criminal justice system
  overcrowding of, 291-93
  reform of, 291-92
  rehabilitation and, 270, 295
  as schools for crime, 293-95
Private education, 323-33
  arguments for, 325-28
  as better than public education, 330-33
  criticisms of, 328-30
Private sector. *See also* Privatization
  neoconservatism and, 45
  urban decline and, 155-57
  welfare programs and, 116-19
Privatization, 4, 27-34, 41-42
  as adoption of business techniques by public sector, 28
  by contracting out, 29-30
  as an economic concept, 33
  by load-shedding, 30-31
  as a moral and political concept, 33-34
  as public-private partnerships, 28-29
  voucher systems for, 31-32
  of welfare system, 112, 115-20
Probation, 297-98
Property taxes, 39, 183
Proposition 13, 36
Proposition 2 ½, 36
Prosecutorial discretion, 289-90
Pruitt-Igoe project, 161
Public assistance. *See* Welfare
Public employees, urban decline and, 149-50
Public housing, 88, 89, 161-68
  federal government and, 163-66
  resistance to, 164-66
Public Housing Administration, 167-68, 172
Public school system. *See* Schools
Public services
  growth and, 221-22
Puckett, John L., 361
Puerto Ricans, 81
Punishment of criminals, 273-74, 284. *See also* Sentencing criminals
Pyramiding, 96

Queensbridge project, 162
Quinney, Richard, 256-58

Race. *See also* Blacks; Minorities
  poverty and, 80-82

Racial discrimination (racism)
  growth controls and, 230–32, 236–40
  neoconservatism and, 46
  by state and local governments, 37
Racial equality, schools and, 314–16, 329
Racial integration. *See* Desegregation (or integration) of schools
Radicalism, 48–52. *See also* Structuralists
  crime and, 246, 255–58, 274, 301
  education system and, 318–21
  enterprise zones and, 196
  growth and, 215–17
  poverty and, 69–74, 78
  urban problems and, 129, 143–45, 154, 156
  welfare system and, 107–9, 115
Railsback, Charles E., 369
Raleigh, North Carolina, 184
Ramapo, New Jersey, 229
Rational-choice theory of crime, 251–52, 278
Raymond, Richard D., 8
Reagan, Ronald, 19–20, 70, 112, 115, 123, 185–87, 193–95
Reapportionment, 40
Redistribution of income and wealth, 38, 73
Reed, Vincent E., 325
Reeves, Mavis Mann, 11
Regional decline, 137–39
  neoconservative view of, 147–48
Regional development. *See* Urban and regional development
Regulation, state and local governments' role in, 7
Rehabilitation of criminals, 270, 271, 284, 295–96
Reilly, William K., 241
Religion, 329–30, 361
Revenue sharing, 17
Revolving door justice, 283–84
Rich, Spencer, 108
Riessman, Frank, 66, 320
Rioting, 130
Robertson, Wyndham, 149
Roby, Pamela, 5
Rochester, New York, 186
Rockefeller, Nelson, 21
Rodgers, Harrell R., Jr., 78, 296, 345

Rodman, Hyman, 67
Roosevelt, Franklin D., 15, 101
Roosevelt, Theodore, 313
Rosenbaum, Nelson, 228
Rosenberg, John S., 242
Rosenfeld, Raymond A., 38, 184, 185
Rossell, Christine H., 348, 349
Rubin, Robert J., 108
Rural areas, growth in, 213–14
Rural Homestead Act of 1862, 197
Rural-Metropolitan Fire Protection Company, 27, 29
Ryan, Williams, 73, 307, 314, 318, 334

Sager, Lawrence, 235
St. Louis, 161
St. Paul's Episcopal Church (Washington, D.C.), 117–18
Salamon, Lester T., 115, 120
Sale, Kirkpatrick, 137–38, 217, 220
Sales taxes, 36, 39–40
Samuelson, Paul, 70
Sanders, Heywood, 170, 174, 175
San Francisco, 170, 175, 220, 228
Savas, E. S., 30
Savitch, H. V., 143, 154
Savitz, Leonard, 287
Sawyer, Kathy, 54
Schidman, Frank, 237
Schill, Michael H., 142
Schiller, Bradley, 71
Schlesinger, Steven R., 285
Schmenner, Roger, 8
Schneider, Mark, 242
Schoen, Cathy, 109
School boards, 310–11
School districts, consolidation of, 310
Schools, 304–72. *See also* Education
  Coleman Report on, 331–32, 334–35
  computers in, 365–70
  conservative view of, 312–13
  egalitarian role of, 306–7, 313–18, 328–29, 333, 334
  liberal view of, 313–18
  local control of, 308–12
  meritocracy and, 312–14
  performance of students and differences among, 333–35
  professionalism of decision-making and, 310–11

public disenchantment with, 305–12
racial equality and, 314–16, 329
radical view of, 318–21
spending on, 306
traditional values and, 307–8
voucher and tax credit plans and, 359–65
Schorr, Philip, 171
Schuessler, Karl F., 287
Scott, Randall W., 221
Scottsdale, Arizona, 27, 29
Seagull, Arthur, 66
Seattle, 107, 127
Section 8 program, 187–92
Segregation of schools, 314–16, 329, 342–44. *See also* Desegregation (or integration) of schools
Self-help programs, local, 196–200
Sentencing criminals, 283–90
 alternative, 298–300
 indeterminate, 295
 mandatory, 287
Sharkansky, Ira, 13, 20
Sheehan, Susan, 75
Shefter, Martin, 151
Silberman, Charles E., 277, 280, 281, 283, 289, 290, 294, 296
Silverman, Jane, 237
Simon, William, 149
Skogan, Wesley, 9, 245
Small Cities program, 187
Smith, Adam, 57–58
Smith, Martha, 183
Snowbelt region, 128–29, 131–33, 137–39, 142, 147–49, 196
Snyder, Mitch, 135
Social control
 criminal justice system as instrument of, 256–57
 schools as instrument of, 318–21
Social Darwinism, 58–59
Social insurance programs, 90–92. *See also* Social Security
Socialization, education as, 318–21
Social Security, 88, 90–92
Social Security Act of 1935, 101
Social Security Administration, poverty measure developed by, 76–77
Social services, 6
South, the. *See* Sunbelt region

South Bend, Indiana, 192
South Burlington County NAACP v. Township of Mount Laurel, 239
Spencer, Herbert, 59
Spring, Joel, 310, 319
Stapleton houses, 163
State courts, growth control and, 238–40
State legislatures, 40
States (state governments)
 as dominated by a conservative elite, 37–38
 as lacking expertise, 35
 as more sensitive to urban needs, 39
 parochialism of officials of, 35–36
 penetrability of boundaries of, 38
 policy functions of, 4–10
 redistribution of income and, 38
 relative importance of, 1–3, 20–24
 revenue raising by, 36, 39–40
 taxes. *See* State taxes
 urban and regional decline and, 200–3
 welfare policy and, 98–101
State taxes, 39–40
 inelasticity of, 36
Stedman, Murray S., Jr., 36
Steiner, Gilbert, 102
Sterba, James P., 155
Sternlieb, George, 127
Stockman, David A., 77, 79, 92
Structural explanations of poverty, 69–74
Structuralists. *See also* Radicalism
 social-welfare policy and, 73–74
Struyk, Raymond J., 165, 167, 187, 200
Subsidies
 housing, 180–82
 tax, for homeowners, 183
Suburbs, 153–55, 168–69, 208–11
Sugarman, Stephen D., 363
Sumner, William Graham, 59, 60
Sunbelt region, 128, 138, 139, 147, 148
 cities in, 211–17
Sunset legislation, 40–41
Supplemental Security Income (SSI), 88
Supreme Court, U.S., 14–15. *See also specific decisions*

Suttles, Gerald D., 67–68
Swann v. *Charlotte-Mecklenburg Board of Education*, 345

Taggart, Robert, 110, 119, 182
Taney, Roger, 14
Target hardening, 301–2
Tawney, Richard H., 57, 60
Taxes
　elasticity of, 36
　enterprise zones and relief from, 193–96
Tax revolt, 36
Tenth Amendment, 12–14
Texas, 108, 114
Thurow, Lester, 71
Tivnan, Edward, 119
Toledo, Ohio, 305–6
Train, Russell E., 207
Transportation, 212
　load-shedding in, 30–31
　pollution and, 219–20
Tuition tax credits, 359–62

Ullman, Howard, 366
Unemployment, inflation and, 70
Unemployment compensation, 88, 90–91
Uniform Crime Reports, 259
University City, Missouri, 269
Unrest, urban decline and, 129–30
Upward Bound, 103
Upward mobility, schools and, 313–14
Urban and regional development, 178–203. *See also* Growth
　enterprise zones and, 193–96
　future of, 190–91
　homesteading and, 196–99
　Housing and Community Development Act of 1974 and, 183–90
　housing subsidies and, 180–82
　housing vouchers and, 191–93
　income tax deductions and, 183
　indirect policy approach to, 178–83
　local self-help programs and, 196–202
　Neighborhood Housing Services (NHS) and, 196, 199–200
　private sector and, 191–96

Urban decline, 127–37, 161–62
　crime and, 245, 250–54
　as crisis, 139–45
　fiscal crises and, 131–33, 149–50
　housing and, 135–37
　liberals and, 145–46
　as mismanagement, 149–53
　neoconservative view of, 128–29, 146–47, 161–62
　physical deterioration and, 133–34
　political aspects of, 153–57
　radical view of, 143–45, 154, 156
　violence and unrest and, 129–30
Urban development. *See* Urban and regional development
Urban Development Action Grant (UDAG), 29
Urban renewal, 168–75
　criticisms of, 170–73
　origin and design and, 168–70
　reevaluation of, 173–75
Urban revitalization, 141–43

Valentine, Charles A., 62
Van den Haag, 284
Veiller, Lawrence, 135
Verdier, James, 183
Veterans Administration (VA), 179, 180
Victim compensation, 299–300, 302
Vieser, Milford, 172
Village of Arlington Heights v. *Metropolitan Housing Development Corp.*, 237
Village of Euclid v. *Amber Reality Co.*, 238
Violence, urban decline and, 129–30
Virginia, 132
Vitullo-Martin, Thomas, 325–26
Volkswagen Corporation, 156
Vouchers, 31–32
　education, 359–65
　housing, 191–93

Wagner, Robert F., 164
Wagoner, Jennings L., Jr., 323
Walker, David, 18, 20
Walker, Decker F., 367, 368
Walter, Susan, 7, 134
War on Poverty, 67, 86–87, 102–4, 175, 316
Warren, Earl, 285, 315

Warth v. *Seldin,* 234–35
Washington, D.C., 116–18, 142, 167, 198
Washington, Harold, 1
Water supplies, 221
Watkins, Al, 149
Wayne County, Michigan, 131
Wealth of Nations, The (Smith), 57–58
Weaver, Robert B., 176
Webster, Noah, 319
Weiss, Marc A., 172
Welfare (social-welfare policies and programs), 86–126
  cash versus in-kind benefits, 89
  conservative and neoconservative view of, 105–7
  culture of poverty and, 68–69
  evolution of, 97–104
  fiscal limitations and, 114
  funding of, 90–91
  future of, 111–24
  individualism and, 59–61
  jobs provision and economic development and, 120–24
  liberal and radical view of, 107–9, 115
  living on, 94–97
  localism and, 98–101, 112–15
  most important programs available, 88–89
  permanent welfare class and, 93–94
  political and structural limitations and, 114–15
  privatization of, 115–20
  pyramiding and, 96
  recipients of, 92–93
  structuralists and, 73–74
  targeting of, 91–92
White, Kevin, 16
Wildavsky, Aaron, 23
Williams, Norman, Jr., 236, 238, 239
Williams, Walter E., 30
Willie, Charles V., 351–52
Wilmington, Delaware, 197
Wilson, James Q., 252–54, 272, 278, 282, 287–88, 296
Wiltshire, David, 59
Wirt, Frederick M., 319
Woll, Peter, 330
Wolman, Harold, 164, 165
Women
  crime and, 252
  poverty among, 80
Work force, schools and, 313, 319–21
Work incentives, 121
Work-release programs, 298
Work requirements, 121
Wyoming, 109

Yates, Douglas, 42
Youngstown, Ohio, 162

Zoning, 10, 54, 153, 224–28